Baseball Franchise Rankings

A Unique Book About Baseball History & Statistics

By Tim Goehlert

Dedication

*To my loving wife Rhiannon, who spent countless
hours, including several Saturday evenings,
staying home with me reading off an abundance
of statistics.*

Acknowledgements

This book would not have been possible without the generous assistance of many people. Thank you to all of my family and friends for your support over the years.

Special thanks to my wife Rhiannon for your love, encouragement, and tolerance. I truly could not have done this without you. Thanks for putting parts of your life on hold for me. Thanks to my cousin Amanda for the amazing job you did designing both the interior part of the book as well as the front and back covers. You turned this book into its final product. Thanks to my parents, my brother Matt and my Uncle Robert for continuously proofreading the manuscript and providing new ideas and advice. Your insight served me well when revisions were needed. Additional thanks to my parents Richard and Patricia for your support and advice, and for taking me to Red Sox games at an early age.

I would also like to thank several members from the Society For American Baseball Research (SABR) community. Thanks to everyone at the SABR Boston Chapter for your encouragement over the years. Thanks to Bill Nowlin for your advice and for proofreading the manuscript and thanks to Cecilia Tan for your assistance on the publication process. Thanks to the following SABR members for your clarification of specific details of playoff games: John Delahanty, David Warner, Jason Hinners, Steve Ferenchick, Mike Ross, William McClain, Bob Bogart, Howard Rosenthal, Ted Reed, Russ Lake, Barbara Sheinbein, Mal Allen, and Bob Mayer.

Also, thanks to the volunteers and employees who collected and published baseball data with the website Baseball-Reference.com.

Table of Contents

Introduction 1

Franchise Movement 7

Master Chart Legend 10

Team Year-to-Year Figures Legend 11

Master Chart – Total Points (full view) 12-13

Master Chart – Average Points (full view) 14-15

Master Chart – Total Points (half view) 16

Master Chart – Average Points (half view) 17

Franchise Sections 19

Arizona Diamondbacks 21

    Stats 21

    Streaks 22

    Extra Bases 22

    Scoring Opportunities 22

        1990's 22

        2000's 22

    Year-to Year Figures 23

Atlanta Braves 24

    Stats 24

    Streaks 25

    Extra Bases 25

    Scoring Opportunities 26

        1870's 26

        1880's 26

        1940's 26

        1950's 26

        1960's 27

        1980's 27

        1990's 28

        2000's 30

        2010's 31

    Year-to-Year Figures 31

Baltimore Orioles 35

    Stats 35

Streaks 36

Extra Bases 36

Scoring Opportunities 36

　1920's 36

　1940's 37

　1960's 37

　1970's 37

　1980's 38

　1990's 39

　Year-to-Year Figures 40

Boston Red Sox **43**

Stats 43

Streaks 44

Extra Bases 44

Scoring Opportunities 44

　1940's 44

　1960's 45

　1970's 45

　1980's 46

　1990's 47

　2000's 48

　Year-to-Year Figures 49

Chicago Cubs **52**

Stats 52

Streaks 53

Extra Bases 53

Scoring Opportunities 54

　1870's 54

　1890's 54

　1900's 54

　1910's 55

　1920's 55

　1930's 55

　1940's 56

　1960's 56

　1980's 57

　1990's 57

　2000's 57

　Year-to-Year Figures 58

Chicago White Sox..62

    Stats..62

    Streaks...63

    Extra Bases..63

    Scoring Opportunities 63

        1900's..63

        1910's..63

        1920's..64

        1950's..64

        1960's..64

        1980's..65

        1990's..65

        2000's..65

    Year-to-Year Figures 66

Cincinnati Reds..69

    Stats..69

    Streaks...70

    Extra Bases..70

    Scoring Opportunities 70

        1920's..70

        1930's..71

        1950's..71

        1960's..71

        1970's..72

        1980's..73

        1990's..73

        2010's..73

    Year-to-Year Figures 74

Cleveland Indians 78

    Stats..78

    Streaks...79

    Extra Bases..79

    Scoring Opportunities 79

        1900's..79

        1920's..80

        1940's..80

        1950's..80

        1990's..81

2000's 82

Year-to-Year Figures 83

Colorado Rockies **86**

Stats 86

Streaks 87

Extra Bases 87

Scoring Opportunities 87

1990's 87

2000's 87

Year-to-Year Figures 88

Detroit Tigers **89**

Stats 89

Streaks 90

Extra Bases 90

Scoring Opportunities 90

1900's 90

1910's 91

1930's 91

1940's 92

1950's 92

1960's 92

1970's 92

1980's 93

2000's 93

Year-to-Year Figures 94

Florida Marlins **97**

Stats 97

Streaks 98

Extra Bases 98

Scoring Opportunities 98

2000's 98

Year-to-Year Figures 99

Houston Astros **100**

Stats 100

Streaks 101

Extra Bases 101

Scoring Opportunities 101

    1970's 101

    1980's 101

    1990's 102

    2000's 103

Year-to-Year Figures 105

Kansas City Royals **107**

    Stats 107

    Streaks 108

    Extra Bases 108

    Scoring Opportunities 108

        1970's 108

        1980's 109

    Year-to-Year Figures 111

Los Angeles Angels of Anaheim **112**

    Stats 112

    Streaks 113

    Extra Bases 113

    Scoring Opportunities 113

        1970's 113

        1980's 113

        1990's 114

        2000's 115

    Year-to-Year Figures 117

Los Angeles Dodgers **119**

    Stats 119

    Streaks 120

    Extra Bases 120

    Scoring Opportunities 120

        1910's 120

        1920's 121

        1930's 121

        1940's 121

        1950's 123

        1960's 124

        1970's 125

        1980's 126

1990's 127

2000's 128

Year-to-Year Figures 129

Milwaukee Brewers **132**

Stats 132

Streaks 133

Extra Bases 133

Scoring Opportunities 133

1980's 133

1990's 134

2000's 134

Year-to-Year Figures 135

Minnesota Twins **136**

Stats 136

Streaks 137

Extra Bases 137

Scoring Opportunities 137

1920's 137

1930's 138

1940's 138

1960's 139

1970's 139

1980's 139

2000's 139

2010's 141

Year-to-Year Figures 142

New York Mets **145**

Stats 145

Streaks 146

Extra Bases 146

Scoring Opportunities 146

1970's 146

1980's 147

1990's 147

2000's 148

Year-to-Year Figures 149

70's..176
80's..177
90's..178
00's..178
10's..179
-to-Year Figures...180

gh Pirates..**183**
s...183
aks...184
a Bases..184
ing Opportunities 185
900's..185
920's..185
930's..186
960's..186
970's..186
990's..187
-to-Year Figures...189

is Cardinals..**192**
s...192
eaks...193
ra Bases...193
ring Opportunities 193
880's..193
920's..194
930's..194
940's..194
960's..195
970's..196
980's..196
990's..197
2000's..197
ar-to-Year Figures..200

ego Padres...**203**
ts..203
eaks...204
tra Bases..204

New York Yankees ....
   Stats...
   Streaks...
   Extra Bases...
   Scoring Opportunities ....
      1900's..
      1920's..
      1940's..
      1950's..
      1960's..
      1970's..
      1980's..
      1990's..
      2000's..
      2010's..
   Year-to-Year Figures ....

Oakland Athletics ....
   Stats...
   Streaks...
   Extra Bases...
   Scoring Opportunities ....
      1900's..
      1910's..
      1920's..
      1930's..
      1970's..
      1980's..
      1990's..
      2000's..
   Year-to-Year Figures ....

Philadelphia Phillies ....
   Stats...
   Streaks...
   Extra Bases...
   Scoring Opportunities ....
      1910's..
      1950's..
      1960's..

Pitts
  S
  S
  F
  S

St. L
  S
  S
  F
  S

San
  S
  S
  F

1970's 176

1980's 177

1990's 178

2000's 178

2010's 179

Year-to-Year Figures 180

Pittsburgh Pirates **183**

Stats 183

Streaks 184

Extra Bases 184

Scoring Opportunities 185

1900's 185

1920's 185

1930's 186

1960's 186

1970's 186

1990's 187

Year-to-Year Figures 189

St. Louis Cardinals **192**

Stats 192

Streaks 193

Extra Bases 193

Scoring Opportunities 193

1880's 193

1920's 194

1930's 194

1940's 194

1960's 195

1970's 196

1980's 196

1990's 197

2000's 197

Year-to-Year Figures 200

San Diego Padres **203**

Stats 203

Streaks 204

Extra Bases 204

New York Yankees **151**
    Stats 151
    Streaks 152
    Extra Bases 152
    Scoring Opportunities 153
        1900's 153
        1920's 153
        1940's 155
        1950's 155
        1960's 156
        1970's 157
        1980's 157
        1990's 158
        2000's 158
        2010's 160
    Year-to-Year Figures 161

Oakland Athletics **164**
    Stats 164
    Streaks 165
    Extra Bases 165
    Scoring Opportunities 166
        1900's 166
        1910's 166
        1920's 166
        1930's 167
        1970's 167
        1980's 167
        1990's 168
        2000's 169
    Year-to-Year Figures 171

Philadelphia Phillies **174**
    Stats 174
    Streaks 175
    Extra Bases 175
    Scoring Opportunities 175
        1910's 175
        1950's 176
        1960's 176

Scoring Opportunities 204
 1980's..204
 1990's..204
 2000's..205
 2010's..206
Year-to-Year Figures 207

San Francisco Giants **208**
 Stats 208
 Streaks 209
 Extra Bases 209
 Scoring Opportunities 209
  1880's..209
  1900's..210
  1910's..210
  1920's..211
  1930's..212
  1950's..213
  1960's..213
  1970's..214
  1980's..214
  1990's..215
  2000's..216
 Year-to-Year Figures 218

Seattle Mariners...**221**
 Stats 221
 Streaks 222
 Extra Bases 222
 Scoring Opportunities 222
  1990's..222
  2000's..223
 Year-to-Year Figures 224

Tampa Bay Rays **225**
 Stats 225
 Streaks 226
 Extra Bases 226
 Scoring Opportunities 226
  2000's..226

2010's..226
Year-to-Year Figures...227

Texas Rangers...**228**
Stats...228
Streaks...229
Extra Bases...229
Scoring Opportunities 229
1990's..229
2010's..230
Year-to-Year Figures...230

Toronto Blue Jays..**232**
Stats...232
Streaks...233
Extra Bases...233
Scoring Opportunities 233
1980's..233
1990's..234
Year-to-Year Figures...235

Washington Nationals...**236**
Stats...236
Streaks...237
Extra Bases...237
Scoring Opportunities 237
1970's..237
1980's..237
1990's..238
2000's..239
Year-to-Year Figures...240

Reference Tables..**243**

Regular Season Games Won 244

Regular Season Games Lost 245

Regular Season Winning Percentage 246

Postseason Games Winning Percentage 247

Year of Origin & Years Played 248

World Series Appearances 249

World Series Won..250

World Series Lost 251

League Titles..252

League Titles Before 1969 253

Division Titles 254

Wild Card Playoff Appearances..255

Postseason Games Won – All Rounds 256

Postseason Games Lost – All Rounds 257

Postseason Games Winning Percentage – All Rounds 258

Postseason Games Played 259

World Series Games Won 260

World Series Games Lost 261

World Series Games Winning Percentage..262

World Series Games Played 263

League Championship Series Games Won 264

League Championship Series Games Lost 265

League Championship Series Games Winning Percentage................266

League Championship Series Games Played 267

League Division Series Games Won 268

League Division Series Games Lost 269

League Division Series Games Winning Percentage.........................270

League Division Series Games Played..271

Postseason Series Won – All Rounds...272

Postseason Series Lost – All Rounds 273

Postseason Series Winning Percentage – All Rounds 274

Postseason Series Played – All Rounds..275

World Series – Series Winning Percentage 276

World Series – Series Played 277

League Championship Series – Series Won 278

League Championship Series – Series Lost.......................................279

League Championship Series – Series Winning Percentage 280

League Championship Series – Series Played...................................281

League Division Series – Series Won 282

League Division Series – Series Lost 283

League Division Series – Series Winning Percentage 284

League Division Series – Series Played 285

Most Wins In A Season for Each Franchise 286

Most Losses In A Season for Each Franchise 287

Highest Winning Percentage In A Season for Each Franchise 288

Lowest Winning Percentage In A Season for Each Franchise 289

Regular Season Winning Percentage of .500 or Higher
Streak for Each Franchise 290

Regular Season Winning Percentage Under .500
Streak for Each Franchise 291

Percentage of Seasons with a Regular Season
Won-Loss Record .500 or Higher 292

Percentage of Seasons In Postseason 293

Biggest Difference Between Regular Season and Postseason Winning Percentage 294

World Series Champion & Runner Up By Year 295-297

League Titles By Year – AL & NL 298-301

Division Titles By Year – AL 302-303

Division Titles By Year – NL 304-305

League Division Series Winners – By Year 306

Wild Card Playoff Teams By Year 307

League Titles By Year – Other Leagues 308

Score and Rank Comparison 309

References **311**

About the Author **313**

Introduction

As a Red Sox fan, it is difficult to acknowledge that the Yankees are the greatest baseball franchise of all time. However, their record of accomplishments proves how dominant they have been in comparison to others. The Yankees have won the World Series seventeen more times than the next closest franchise. They have played in the World Series twenty-two more times than the next closest franchise. The Yankees have made it to the postseason in 45% of their seasons. No other franchise has made it to the postseason in one-third of their seasons. It is obvious that the Yankees are the best franchise in baseball history. The interesting question is which franchise is next?

Is it the Cardinals, the franchise with the second most World Series Titles? Is it the Dodgers or the Giants, the franchises with the second most World Series Appearances? Or is it a different franchise? For instance, the A's have only won one fewer World Series Title than the Cardinals, and the Braves are tied with the Yankees for the most Division Titles. In order to determine the second greatest franchise of all time, several accomplishments have to be compared against each other.

Baseball Franchise Rankings is a reference book with a ranking system. It contains a unique scoring formula that ranks the thirty current baseball franchises in order of historical greatness. The system uses a variety of accomplishments as factors to determine each franchise's score. The more important the accomplishment, the more points a franchise receives for that achievement.

This system compares the franchises from the most successful to the least successful. You can see where your favorite franchise ranks and how many points they need to improve their score and surpass other franchises. It is the ultimate conversation starter.

Baseball Franchise Rankings is about more than just numbers and statistics. It provides detailed summaries about how teams were eliminated in seasons they contended for the Playoffs, League Title, or World Series. The scoring system awards more points to a team that advances further in the regular season and postseason. The summaries then explain the reasons why a team could not improve its score when it had the chance.

The other distinctive features of this book are:
• Unique compilations of statistics and facts
• A breakdown of dominant periods of success for each franchise
• Rare historical occurrences and events
• A chronological table for each franchise with data about their achievements and history
• A variety of statistical charts that list, compare, and rank different franchise accomplishments

Scoring System

The scoring system is straightforward and takes into account regular season and postseason accomplishments. Each level of achievement is worth twice the amount of points than the previous achievement. The point values for each type of accomplishment are:

For the postseason each franchise gets:

- 8 points for each World Series won
- 4 points for each League Championship Series won *(half a World Series win)*
- 2 points for each League Division Series won *(half a League Championship Series win)*

For the regular season each franchise gets:

- 4 points for each League Title before 1969 *(half a World Series win and the same as a League Championship Series win)*
- 2 points for each Division Title *(half a League Title)*
- 1 point for each Wild Card Appearance *(half a Division Title)*
- Plus or minus 0.1 points for every .001 their all-time regular season winning percentage is above or below .500.

Throughout baseball history, there have been different regular season and postseason formats. The table below outlines how many points a franchise gets in different regular and postseason structures. Franchises receive more points today than in eras with shorter postseason structures.

Period	1995-2010	1969-1993	1903-1968 (except 1904)	1871-1902 (and 1904)
Postseason	World Series (8)	World Series (8)	World Series (8)	
	League Championship Series (4)	League Championship Series (4)		
	League Division Series (2)			
Regular Season	Division Title (2) or Wild Card (1)	Division Title (2)	League Title (4)	League Title (4)
Points	15 or 16	14	12	4

1. There was no World Series in 1904 because the winner of the National League, the New York Giants, refused to play.
2. The 1981 postseason structure was different. Please see the notes at the end of the introduction for an explanation.

The other way a franchise gains points, and the only way it loses points, is with future changes to its all-time regular season winning percentage. A franchise's regular season won-loss record for every season affects its score. Each franchise gets plus or minus 0.1 points for every .001 their all-time regular season winning percentage is above or below .500. For example, a franchise with a .525 all-time regular season winning percentage gains 2.5 points.

A franchise with a .475 all-time regular season winning percentage loses 2.5 points. This is not 2.5 points for each season. It is for the franchise's total winning percentage of all their seasons played. On a yearly basis, a franchise's score will go up if its won-loss record is above .500. A franchise's score will go down on a yearly basis if its won-loss record is below .500.

It is important to factor in regular season winning percentage, even though the scoring system already rewards teams for regular season performance with Division Titles and Wild Cards. Sometimes a team is good in the regular season for years and never makes the playoffs. Sometimes a team misses the playoffs in a particular year, even though they were better than a team in a different league or division that made the playoffs. The World Series was not played before 1903; therefore, evaluation in those years can only be done using regular season performance.

A .500 record separates historically good regular season franchises from bad ones. For instance, the A's won the World Series nine times, but their all-time regular season winning percentage is .486. Therefore, they deserve a penalty for their poor regular season performance.

Using 0.1 points gives the right amount of points to this accomplishment category in comparison to the other categories. Using 1.0 or 0.5 awards or deducts too much. Using .01 makes the regular season category insignificant. For example, the New York Yankees have an all-time regular season winning percentage of .568, and the Tampa Bay Rays have one of .438. Using 0.1 points gives the Yankees 6.8 points for their winning percentage, and subtracts 6.2 points from the Rays.

Using the number 1.0 awards New York 68 points and deducts 62 from Tampa Bay. Using 0.5 awards the Yankees 34 and deducts 31 from the Rays. These options result in a very wide margin of points in relation to the other accomplishment categories. It places a greater emphasis on the regular season, and causes the regular season to influence the rankings too much. Regular season winning percentage is important, but less important than postseason categories.

Using 0.01 awards New York 0.68 and deducts 0.62 from Tampa Bay. This places too little of an emphasis on the regular season. The score for regular season would not affect the overall score enough to even matter.

Using 0.1 incorporates the right amount to the overall score in comparison to the other categories. It provides the right amount of reward and penalty for good and bad regular season records. With the inclusion of regular season winning percentage in the scoring system, every franchise's score can change every year. Using 0.1 keeps the ratio balanced with the number one (0.1 for every .001), which makes this portion of the system easier to follow. That is why 0.2 or 0.3 are not used.

The Master Charts

The Master Charts on pages 12-17 are data tables that contain the information used to calculate each franchise's score and rank. There is a Total Master Chart and an Average Master Chart.

The Total Master Chart ranks the franchises in order of total points using the scoring system. This chart shows the order of the historical greatness of the franchises from first to thirtieth. The Average Master Chart provides an alternative way of comparing franchises. This chart takes each franchise's total score and divides it by the number of years the franchise has played. The Average Chart standardizes the franchises by computing the average number of points each franchise earns per season. Several franchises have played for different number of seasons; therefore it is important to provide a method that compares their success per season.

The Franchise Sections

The Franchise Sections contains an in depth review of each franchise. For each franchise there are unique compilations of statistics, fun facts and trivia, postseason recaps, and rare information about each franchise.

The Franchise Sections consists of five parts: *Stats, Streaks, Extra Bases, Scoring Opportunities,* and *the Year-to-Year Figures.*

Stats

Are you interested in statistics? If so, this section is for you. It contains several types of statistical compilations relating to the success and failure of each franchise. For example:

- Won-loss records and winning percentages in each type of postseason series *(WS, LCS, LDS)*
- Most wins and most losses in a season with the year of each occurrence
- Highest winning percentage and lowest winning percentage in a season with the year of each occurrence
- Years and duration of longest streak of seasons with a won-loss record of .500 or higher (winning seasons), and longest streak of seasons with a won-loss record below .500 (losing seasons)
- Number of seasons in each decade with a won-loss record of .500 or higher
- Number of times in each decade the franchise made the postseason
- Percentage of seasons with a won-loss record of .500 or higher compared to number of years played
- Percentage of seasons in the postseason compared to number of years played

Streaks

This section details periods when franchises were very successful. These periods greatly contributed to the franchise's score and rank. Some example are:
- From 1912-1918 Boston won four World Series in seven years.
- From 1996-1999 Texas won three Division Titles in four years.

- From 1970-1979 the Cincinnati Reds won two World Series Championships, four League Championship Series, and six Division Titles in ten years.

Extra Bases

This section contains interesting milestones, unique facts, and rare historical events for each franchise. For example:

- The Braves three World Series championships occurred while the franchise was located in a different city, Boston in 1914, Milwaukee in 1957, and Atlanta in 1995.
- In 1927 and 1972 the Pirates were eliminated from the postseason on a wild pitch in both seasons.

Scoring Opportunities

This section provides captivating summaries detailing what happened to teams in specific years in which they contended for the Playoffs, League Title, or World Series, but fell short in some way. The summaries include exciting postseason recaps and thrilling descriptions of regular season pennant chases that came down to the final days of the season. The summaries give the reasons why the team could not earn more points and improve its score when it had the chance. Everyone knows how a team won the World Series; these recaps describe how a team lost or did not advance to the World Series. Types of summaries include:

- How a team lost a specific playoff series
- What caused a team to miss the postseason when they were so close at the end of the regular season
- What happened to a team when they were in first place all season long and then blew their lead and missed the postseason

An example is:

- San Francisco won 103 games in 1993 and led the National League West Division from May 11th to September 9th. The Giants led by 3.5 games over Atlanta on September 6th, then lost their next eight games and fell to 3.5 games behind the Braves on September 15th. The Giants won fourteen of their next sixteen games and were tied for first place with Atlanta with one game left in the season on October 3rd. On the last day of the year the Braves beat Colorado and the Giants lost to the Dodgers 12-1 and lost the division by one game.

Year-to-Year Figures

This section contains a chronological table of statistics for each franchise. These tables show the information that contributes to each franchise's score on a yearly basis and other information pertaining to year-to-year results. For instance:

- Their regular season won-loss record and winning percentage for that year
- Postseason result indications for each year
- The place they finished in the standings in their league or division that season
- The number of games finished behind first place or the number of games finished ahead of the second place team in the standings

The Reference Tables

The final section of the book consists of chronological charts of postseason results as well as listings that rank the franchises in various achievement-based categories. Each franchise's year of origin is included in some of the tables to serve as a way of comparing the franchise accomplishments over time. Some examples of what the charts show are:

- The amount of postseason series won by each franchise; which shows, for example, that Florida has won six postseason series since 1993, and the Cubs have only won three in their franchise history, and they have played a lot longer than the Marlins
- That the fourteen expansion franchises from 1961 to today all have an all-time regular season winning percentage below .500. The Astros and Angels are closest, both at .498
- How many more postseason games the Yankees have won compared to the next closest franchise

Notes

- There were postseason tournaments before the first World Series in 1903, however, baseball historians consider them exhibitions. Therefore, they do not count as professional championships or playoffs in this scoring system.

- A players strike in the middle of the 1981 season split the season into two halves. The winners of each half-season received division titles, so there were eight division winners instead of four. There was also a League Division Series round in the playoffs this season.

Therefore, eight teams received two points in the scoring system this year for winning a division, and teams that won the League Division Series got two points, like the structure since 1995.

- A players strike in August of 1994 cancelled the remainder of the regular season, the playoffs, and World Series. Since there was no postseason, teams did not receive points for the postseason for this year. Additionally, none of the teams that were in first place when the season ended receives any points for division titles for this year, because the teams did not play the remainder of the season.

- All of the information and data in this book is through the 2010 season.

Franchise Movement

It is important to know that when a franchise changed its name or location the history of that franchise went with the new team and to the new location. For example, when the Dodgers moved from Brooklyn to Los Angeles, all the franchise's history went too. All achievements and accomplishments by Brooklyn would become part of Los Angeles' franchise history. The treatment is the same for other franchises that changed their name or location. Below is a breakdown of the thirty current franchises, and the previous team names associated with their franchise history.

Arizona Diamondbacks
- Arizona Diamondbacks   1998 - 2010

Atlanta Braves
- Atlanta Braves   1966 - 2010
- Milwaukee Braves   1953 - 1965
- Boston Braves   1941 - 1952
- Boston Bees   1936 - 1940
- Boston Braves   1912 - 1935
- Boston Rustlers   1911
- Boston Doves   1907 - 1910
- Boston Beaneaters   1883 - 1906
- Boston Red Caps   1876 - 1882
- Boston Red Stockings   1871 - 1875

Baltimore Orioles
- Baltimore Orioles   1954 - 2010
- St. Louis Browns   1902 - 1953
- Milwaukee Brewers   1901

Boston Red Sox
- Boston Red Sox   1908 - 2010
- Boston Americans   1901 - 1907

Chicago Cubs
- Chicago Cubs   1903 - 2010
- Chicago Orphans   1898 - 1902
- Chicago Colts   1890 - 1897
- Chicago White Stockings   1871 - 1889

Chicago White Sox
- Chicago White Sox   1902 - 2010
- Chicago White Stockings   1901

Cincinnati Reds
- Cincinnati Reds   1960 - 2010
- Cincinnati Redlegs   1954 - 1959
- Cincinnati Reds   1890 - 1953
- Cincinnati Red Stockings   1882 - 1889

Cleveland Indians
- Cleveland Indians   1915 - 2010
- Cleveland Naps   1903 - 1914
- Cleveland Bronchos   1902
- Cleveland Blues   1901

Colorado Rockies
- Colorado Rockies   1993 - 2010

Detroit Tigers
- Detroit Tigers   1901 - 2010

Florida Marlins
- Florida Marlins   1993 - 2010

Houston Astros
- Houston Astros   1965 - 2010
- Houston Colt .45's   1962 - 1964

Kansas City Royals
- Kansas City Royals   1969 - 2010

Los Angeles Angels of Anaheim
- Los Angeles Angels of Anaheim   2005 - 2010
- Anaheim Angels   1997 - 2004
- California Angels   1965 - 1996
- Los Angeles Angels   1961 - 1964

Los Angeles Dodgers
- Los Angeles Dodgers   1958 - 2010
- Brooklyn Dodgers   1932 - 1957
- Brooklyn Robins   1914 - 1931
- Brooklyn Superbas   1913
- Brooklyn Dodgers   1911 - 1912
- Brooklyn Superbas   1899 - 1910
- Brooklyn Bridegrooms   1896 - 1898
- Brooklyn Grooms   1891 - 1895
- Brooklyn Bridegrooms   1888 - 1890
- Brooklyn Grays   1885 - 1887
- Brooklyn Atlantics   1884

Milwaukee Brewers
- Milwaukee Brewers   1970 - 2010
- Seattle Pilots   1969

Minnesota Twins
- Minnesota Twins   1961 - 2010
- Washington Senators   1901 - 1960

New York Mets
- New York Mets   1962 - 2010

New York Yankees
- New York Yankees — 1913 - 2010
- New York Highlanders — 1903 - 1912
- Baltimore Orioles — 1901 - 1902

Oakland Athletics
- Oakland Athletics — 1968 - 2010
- Kansas City Athletics — 1955 - 1967
- Philadelphia Athletics — 1901 - 1954

Philadelphia Phillies
- Philadelphia Phillies — 1945 - 2010
- Philadelphia Blue Jays — 1943 - 1944
- Philadelphia Phillies — 1890 - 1942
- Philadelphia Quakers — 1883 - 1889

Pittsburgh Pirates
- Pittsburgh Pirates — 1891 - 2010
- Pittsburgh Alleghenys — 1882 - 1890

St. Louis Cardinals
- St. Louis Cardinals — 1900 - 2010
- St. Louis Perfectos — 1899
- St. Louis Browns — 1883 - 1898
- St. Louis Brown Stockings — 1882

San Diego Padres
- San Diego Padres — 1969 - 2010

San Francisco Giants
- San Francisco Giants — 1958 - 2010
- New York Giants — 1885 - 1957
- New York Gothams — 1883 - 1884

Seattle Mariners
- Seattle Mariners — 1977 - 2010

Tampa Bay Rays
- Tampa Bay Rays — 2008 - 2010
- Tampa Bay Devil Rays — 1998 - 2007

Texas Rangers
- Texas Rangers — 1972 - 2010
- Washington Senators — 1961 - 1971

Toronto Blue Jays
- Toronto Blue Jays — 1977 - 2010

Washington Nationals
- Washington Nationals — 2005 - 2010
- Montreal Expos — 1969 - 2004

Master Chart Legend

Team .... The specific team that the row of information pertains to.

Year .... The team's year of origin.

Wins....................... The team's total amount of regular season wins.

Losses..................... The team's total amount of regular season losses.

Win % .... The team's overall regular season winning percentage.

WS.......................... The number of World Series Titles the team has won.

Lge.......................... The number of League Titles the team has won. This includes regular season League Titles before 1969 and League Titles earned by winning the League Championship Series.

LDS .... The number of League Division Series the team has won.

Div .... The number of Division Titles the team has won.

WC .... The number of Wild Card Playoff Appearances the team has had.

Points Awarded For:

Win % .... The amount of points awarded to or deducted from the score based on the team's all-time regular season winning percentage.

WS.................... The amount of points awarded for the number of World Series Titles the team has won. Each World Series Title is worth 8 points.

Lge.................... The amount of points awarded for the number of League Titles the team has won. Each League Title is worth 4 points.

LDS .... The amount of points awarded for the number of League Division Series the team has won. Each LDS won is worth 2 points.

Div .... The amount of points awarded for the number of Division Titles the team has won. Each Division Title is worth 2 points.

WC .... The amount of points awarded for the number of Wild Card Playoff Appearances the team has had. Each Wild Card Appearance is worth 1 point.

Score .... The sum of the points awarded for Winning Percentage, World Series Titles, League Titles, League Division Series Wins, Division Titles, and Wild Card Appearances.

Rank........................ The placement of the team's score from one to thirty in comparison to the other teams.

Additional Categories on the Average Master Chart:

Years played............ The number of years the team has played.

Points per Season... Also called the team's average score. This is the total score divided by the number of years the team has played. This indicates how many points each team earned on average for each season it played.

Rank........................ The placement of the team's score from one to thirty based on their average score in comparison to the other teams.

Team Year-to-Year Figures Legend

(The Year-to-Year Figures for each team are located at the end of each franchise's section in the Franchise Section of the book.)

Team Name.............Shows the team's city or state location and their team nickname for the specific year of the row of information.

League ....Shows the League and/or Division the team played in during that year. AL = American League and NL = National League. AA = American Association, a league from 1882-1891. NA = National Association, a league from 1871-1875. Cent stands for Central, as in AL or NL Central Division.

Year ....The specific year that the row of information in the table pertains to.

W............................The number of regular season wins the team had that year.

L ....The number of regular season losses the team had that year.

Win %.....................The team's regular season winning percentage for that year.

Fin..........................Indicates what place the team finished in their league or division in comparison to the amount of teams that were in that league or division for that year. If you see a number followed by a letter 't' (Ex: 4t) it means that the team was tied with another team in the standings that season.

GB/GA ....Shows how many games behind first place the team finished. Or if the team finished in first place it shows how many games ahead of the second place team they finished (Indicated with a + sign). For some teams there is an asterisk (*) that corresponds to a footnote at the bottom of the table for a further explanation regarding this number.

WS...........................Indicates if the team won the World Series that year.

Lge...........................Indicates if the team won a League Title that year. This could either be a Regular Season League Title from before 1969 or a League Title won by winning a League Championship Series.

LDS ....Indicates if the team won a League Division Series that year.

Div ....Indicates if the team won a Division Title that year.

WC ....Indicates if the team was a Wild Card playoff team that year.

Notes:

• The totals at the bottom of each team are the totals of the team's regular season wins and losses and the team's overall regular season winning percentage. There are also totals of the amounts of World Series, League Titles, League Division Series, Division Titles, and Wild Cards the team has won. This information matches what is on the Master Chart for each team.

• In 1892 and 1981 the regular season was split into two halves so for these years there are two listings for Fin and GB/GA, one for the first half of the season, and one for the second half of the season.

Master Chart – Total Points

Rank	Team	Year	Wins	Losses	Win %	WS	Lge
1	New York Yankees	1901	9670	7361	0.568	27	40
2	St. Louis Cardinals	1882	10107	9419	0.518	10	21
3	Los Angeles Dodgers	1884	10135	9199	0.524	6	22
4	Oakland Athletics	1901	8270	8752	0.486	9	15
5	San Francisco Giants	1883	10436	8958	0.538	6	21
6	Atlanta Braves	1871	10170	10014	0.504	3	21
7	Boston Red Sox	1901	8819	8233	0.517	7	12
8	Cincinnati Reds	1882	9915	9619	0.508	5	10
9	Chicago Cubs	1871	10318	9765	0.514	2	16
10	Pittsburgh Pirates	1882	9810	9684	0.503	5	9
11	Detroit Tigers	1901	8645	8437	0.506	4	10
12	Baltimore Orioles	1901	8079	8959	0.474	3	7
13	Philadelphia Phillies	1883	9135	10233	0.472	2	7
14	Minnesota Twins	1901	8232	8816	0.483	3	6
15	Chicago White Sox	1901	8628	8413	0.506	3	6
16	Cleveland Indians	1901	8691	8367	0.509	2	5
17	New York Mets	1962	3734	4064	0.479	2	4
18	Los Angeles Angels of Anaheim	1961	3967	4003	0.498	1	1
19	Toronto Blue Jays	1977	2674	2709	0.497	2	2
20	Kansas City Royals	1969	3210	3455	0.482	1	2
21	Florida Marlins	1993	1363	1485	0.479	2	2
22	Houston Astros	1962	3888	3921	0.498	0	1
23	Arizona Diamondbacks	1998	1035	1071	0.491	1	1
24	San Diego Padres	1969	3098	3580	0.464	0	2
25	Texas Rangers	1961	3747	4206	0.471	0	1
26	Seattle Mariners	1977	2522	2861	0.469	0	0
27	Colorado Rockies	1993	1364	1490	0.478	0	1
28	Milwaukee Brewers	1969	3166	3505	0.475	0	1
29	Tampa Bay Rays	1998	922	1181	0.438	0	1
30	Washington Nationals	1969	3167	3502	0.475	0	0

Master Chart – Total Points

			Points Awarded For:							
LDS	Div	WC	Win%	WS	Lge	LDS	Div	WC	Score	Rank
10	16	4	6.8	216	160	20	32	4	438.8	1
6	10	1	1.8	80	84	12	20	1	198.8	2
3	11	2	2.4	48	88	6	22	2	168.4	3
2	14	1	-1.4	72	60	4	28	1	163.6	4
2	7	1	3.8	48	84	4	14	1	154.8	5
6	16	1	0.4	24	84	12	32	1	153.4	6
5	6	7	1.7	56	48	10	12	7	134.7	7
1	9	0	0.8	40	40	2	18	0	100.8	8
1	5	1	1.4	16	64	2	10	1	94.4	9
0	9	0	0.3	40	36	0	18	0	94.3	10
1	3	1	0.6	32	40	2	6	1	81.6	11
2	8	1	-2.6	24	28	4	16	1	70.4	12
3	11	0	-2.8	16	28	6	22	0	69.2	13
1	10	0	-1.7	24	24	2	20	0	68.3	14
1	5	0	0.6	24	24	2	10	0	60.6	15
4	7	0	0.9	16	20	8	14	0	58.9	16
3	5	2	-2.1	16	16	6	10	2	47.9	17
3	8	1	-0.2	8	4	6	16	1	34.8	18
0	5	0	-0.3	16	8	0	10	0	33.7	19
0	7	0	-1.8	8	8	0	14	0	28.2	20
2	0	2	-2.1	16	8	4	0	2	27.9	21
2	7	2	-0.2	0	4	4	14	2	23.8	22
2	4	0	-0.9	8	4	4	8	0	23.1	23
1	5	0	-3.4	0	8	2	10	0	16.6	24
1	4	0	-2.9	0	4	2	8	0	11.1	25
3	3	1	-3.1	0	0	6	6	1	9.9	26
1	0	3	-2.2	0	4	2	0	3	6.8	27
0	2	1	-2.5	0	4	0	4	1	6.5	28
1	2	0	-6.2	0	4	2	4	0	3.8	29
1	1	0	-2.5	0	0	2	2	0	1.5	30

Master Chart – Average Points

Rank	Team	Year	Wins	Losses	Win %	WS	Lge	LDS
1	New York Yankees	1901	9670	7361	0.568	27	40	10
2	Arizona Diamondbacks	1998	1035	1071	0.491	1	1	2
3	Florida Marlins	1993	1363	1485	0.479	2	2	2
4	St. Louis Cardinals	1882	10107	9419	0.518	10	21	6
5	Oakland Athletics	1901	8270	8752	0.486	9	15	2
6	Los Angeles Dodgers	1884	10135	9199	0.524	6	22	3
7	Boston Red Sox	1901	8819	8233	0.517	7	12	5
8	San Francisco Giants	1883	10436	8958	0.538	6	21	2
9	Atlanta Braves	1871	10170	10014	0.504	3	21	6
10	Toronto Blue Jays	1977	2674	2709	0.497	2	2	0
11	New York Mets	1962	3734	4064	0.479	2	4	3
12	Cincinnati Reds	1882	9915	9619	0.508	5	10	1
13	Detroit Tigers	1901	8645	8437	0.506	4	10	1
14	Pittsburgh Pirates	1882	9810	9684	0.503	5	9	0
15	Los Angeles Angels of Anaheim	1961	3967	4003	0.498	1	1	3
16	Chicago Cubs	1871	10318	9765	0.514	2	16	1
17	Kansas City Royals	1969	3210	3455	0.482	1	2	0
18	Baltimore Orioles	1901	8079	8959	0.474	3	7	2
19	Minnesota Twins	1901	8232	8816	0.483	3	6	1
20	Chicago White Sox	1901	8628	8413	0.506	3	6	1
21	Cleveland Indians	1901	8691	8367	0.509	2	5	4
21	Philadelphia Phillies	1883	9135	10233	0.472	2	7	3
23	Houston Astros	1962	3888	3921	0.498	0	1	2
24	San Diego Padres	1969	3098	3580	0.464	0	2	1
25	Colorado Rockies	1993	1364	1490	0.478	0	1	1
26	Seattle Mariners	1977	2522	2861	0.469	0	0	3
26	Tampa Bay Rays	1998	922	1181	0.438	0	1	1
28	Texas Rangers	1961	3747	4206	0.471	0	1	1
29	Milwaukee Brewers	1969	3166	3505	0.475	0	1	0
30	Washington Nationals	1969	3167	3502	0.475	0	0	1

Master Chart – Average Points

Div	WC	Points Awarded For:						Score	Years Played	Points per Season	AVG Rank
		Win%	WS	Lge	LDS	Div	WC				
16	4	6.8	216	160	20	32	4	438.8	110	3.99	1
4	0	-0.9	8	4	4	8	0	23.1	13	1.78	2
0	2	-2.1	16	8	4	0	2	27.9	18	1.55	3
10	1	1.8	80	84	12	20	1	198.8	129	1.54	4
14	1	-1.4	72	60	4	28	1	163.6	110	1.49	5
11	2	2.4	48	88	6	22	2	168.4	127	1.33	6
6	7	1.7	56	48	10	12	7	134.7	110	1.22	7
7	1	3.8	48	84	4	14	1	154.8	128	1.21	8
16	1	0.4	24	84	12	32	1	153.4	140	1.10	9
5	0	-0.3	16	8	0	10	0	33.7	34	0.99	10
5	2	-2.1	16	16	6	10	2	47.9	49	0.98	11
9	0	0.8	40	40	2	18	0	100.8	129	0.78	12
3	1	0.6	32	40	2	6	1	81.6	110	0.74	13
9	0	0.3	40	36	0	18	0	94.3	129	0.73	14
8	1	-0.2	8	4	6	16	1	34.8	50	0.70	15
5	1	1.4	16	64	2	10	1	94.4	138	0.68	16
7	0	-1.8	8	8	0	14	0	28.2	42	0.67	17
8	1	-2.6	24	28	4	16	1	70.4	110	0.64	18
10	0	-1.7	24	24	2	20	0	68.3	110	0.62	19
5	0	0.6	24	24	2	10	0	60.6	110	0.55	20
7	0	0.9	16	20	8	14	0	58.9	110	0.54	21
11	0	-2.8	16	28	6	22	0	69.2	128	0.54	21
7	2	-0.2	0	4	4	14	2	23.8	49	0.49	23
5	0	-3.4	0	8	2	10	0	16.6	42	0.40	24
0	3	-2.2	0	4	2	0	3	6.8	18	0.38	25
3	1	-3.1	0	0	6	6	1	9.9	34	0.29	26
2	0	-6.2	0	4	2	4	0	3.8	13	0.29	26
4	0	-2.9	0	4	2	8	0	11.1	50	0.22	28
2	1	-2.5	0	4	0	4	1	6.5	42	0.15	29
1	0	-2.5	0	0	2	2	0	1.5	42	0.04	30

Master Chart – Total Points

Rank	Team	Year	Wins	Losses	Win %	WS	Lge	LDS	Div	WC	Win%	WS	Lge	LDS	Div	WC	Score	Rank
													Points Awarded For:					
1	New York Yankees	1901	9670	7361	0.568	27	40	10	16	4	6.8	216	160	20	32	4	438.8	1
2	St. Louis Cardinals	1882	10107	9419	0.518	10	21	6	10	1	1.8	80	84	12	20	1	198.8	2
3	Los Angeles Dodgers	1884	10135	9199	0.524	6	22	3	11	2	2.4	48	88	6	22	2	168.4	3
4	Oakland Athletics	1901	8270	8752	0.486	9	15	2	14	1	-1.4	72	60	4	28	1	163.6	4
5	San Francisco Giants	1883	10436	8958	0.538	6	21	2	7	1	3.8	48	84	4	14	1	154.8	5
6	Atlanta Braves	1871	10170	10014	0.504	3	21	6	16	1	0.4	24	84	12	32	1	153.4	6
7	Boston Red Sox	1901	8819	8233	0.517	7	12	5	6	7	1.7	56	48	10	12	7	134.7	7
8	Cincinnati Reds	1882	9915	9619	0.508	5	10	1	9	0	0.8	40	40	2	18	0	100.8	8
9	Chicago Cubs	1871	10318	9765	0.514	2	16	1	5	1	1.4	16	64	2	10	1	94.4	9
10	Pittsburgh Pirates	1882	9810	9684	0.503	5	9	0	9	0	0.3	40	36	0	18	0	94.3	10
11	Detroit Tigers	1901	8645	8437	0.506	4	10	1	3	1	0.6	32	40	2	6	1	81.6	11
12	Baltimore Orioles	1901	8079	8959	0.474	3	7	2	8	1	-2.6	24	28	4	16	1	70.4	12
13	Philadelphia Phillies	1883	9135	10233	0.472	2	7	3	11	0	-2.8	16	28	6	22	0	69.2	13
14	Minnesota Twins	1901	8232	8816	0.483	3	6	1	10	0	-1.7	24	24	2	20	0	68.3	14
15	Chicago White Sox	1901	8628	8413	0.506	3	6	1	5	0	0.6	24	24	2	10	0	60.6	15
16	Cleveland Indians	1901	8691	8367	0.509	2	5	4	7	0	0.9	16	20	8	14	0	58.9	16
17	New York Mets	1962	3734	4064	0.479	2	4	3	5	2	-2.1	16	16	6	10	2	47.9	17
18	Los Angeles Angels of Anaheim	1961	3967	4003	0.498	1	1	3	8	1	-0.2	8	4	6	16	1	34.8	18
19	Toronto Blue Jays	1977	2674	2709	0.497	2	2	0	5	0	-0.3	16	8	0	10	0	33.7	19
20	Kansas City Royals	1969	3210	3455	0.482	1	2	0	7	0	-1.8	8	8	0	14	0	28.2	20
21	Florida Marlins	1993	1363	1485	0.479	2	2	2	0	2	-2.1	16	8	4	0	2	27.9	21
22	Houston Astros	1962	3888	3921	0.498	0	1	2	7	2	-0.2	0	4	4	14	2	23.8	22
23	Arizona Diamondbacks	1998	1035	1071	0.491	1	1	2	4	0	-0.9	8	4	4	8	0	23.1	23
24	San Diego Padres	1969	3098	3580	0.464	0	2	1	5	3	-3.4	0	8	2	10	3	16.6	24
25	Texas Rangers	1961	3747	4206	0.471	0	1	1	4	1	-2.9	0	4	2	8	1	11.1	25
26	Seattle Mariners	1977	2522	2861	0.469	0	0	3	3	0	-3.1	0	0	6	6	0	9.9	26
27	Colorado Rockies	1993	1364	1490	0.478	0	1	1	0	3	-2.2	0	4	2	0	3	6.8	27
28	Milwaukee Brewers	1969	3166	3505	0.475	0	1	0	2	1	-2.5	0	4	0	4	1	6.5	28
29	Tampa Bay Rays	1998	922	1181	0.438	0	1	1	2	0	-6.2	0	4	2	4	0	3.8	29
30	Washington Nationals	1969	3167	3502	0.475	0	0	1	1	0	-2.5	0	0	2	2	0	1.5	30

Master Chart – Average Points

Rank	Team	Year	Wins	Losses	Win %	WS	Lge	LDS	Div	WC	Win%	WS	Lge	LDS	Div	WC	Score	Years Played	Points per Season	AVG Rank
															Points Awarded For:					
1	New York Yankees	1901	9670	7361	0.568	27	40	10	16	4	6.8	216	160	20	32	4	438.8	110	3.99	1
2	Arizona Diamondbacks	1998	1035	1071	0.491	1	1	2	4	0	-0.9	8	4	4	8	0	23.1	13	1.78	2
3	Florida Marlins	1993	1363	1485	0.479	2	2	2	0	2	-2.1	16	8	4	0	2	27.9	18	1.55	3
4	St. Louis Cardinals	1882	10107	9419	0.518	10	21	6	10	1	1.8	80	84	12	20	1	198.8	129	1.54	4
5	Oakland Athletics	1901	8270	8752	0.486	9	15	2	14	1	-1.4	72	60	4	28	1	163.6	110	1.49	5
6	Los Angeles Dodgers	1884	10135	9199	0.524	6	22	3	11	2	2.4	48	88	6	22	2	168.4	127	1.33	6
7	Boston Red Sox	1901	8819	8233	0.517	7	12	5	6	7	1.7	56	48	10	12	7	134.7	110	1.22	7
8	San Francisco Giants	1883	10436	8958	0.538	6	21	2	7	1	3.8	48	84	4	14	1	154.8	128	1.21	8
9	Atlanta Braves	1871	10170	10014	0.504	3	21	6	16	1	0.4	24	84	12	32	1	153.4	140	1.10	9
10	Toronto Blue Jays	1977	2674	2709	0.497	2	2	0	5	0	-0.3	16	8	0	10	0	33.7	34	0.99	10
11	New York Mets	1962	3734	4064	0.479	2	4	3	5	2	-2.1	16	16	6	10	2	47.9	49	0.98	11
12	Cincinnati Reds	1882	9915	9619	0.508	5	10	1	9	0	0.8	40	40	2	18	0	100.8	129	0.78	12
13	Detroit Tigers	1901	8645	8437	0.506	4	10	1	3	1	0.6	32	40	2	6	1	81.6	110	0.74	13
14	Pittsburgh Pirates	1882	9810	9684	0.503	5	9	0	9	0	0.3	40	36	0	18	0	94.3	129	0.73	14
15	Los Angeles Angels of Anaheim	1961	3967	4003	0.498	1	1	3	8	1	-0.2	8	4	6	16	1	34.8	50	0.70	15
16	Chicago Cubs	1871	10318	9765	0.514	2	16	1	5	1	1.4	16	64	2	10	1	94.4	138	0.68	16
17	Kansas City Royals	1969	3210	3455	0.482	1	2	0	7	0	-1.8	8	8	0	14	0	28.2	42	0.67	17
18	Baltimore Orioles	1901	8079	8959	0.474	3	7	2	8	1	-2.6	24	28	4	16	1	70.4	110	0.64	18
19	Minnesota Twins	1901	8232	8816	0.483	3	6	1	10	0	-1.7	24	24	2	20	0	68.3	110	0.62	19
20	Chicago White Sox	1901	8628	8413	0.506	3	6	1	5	0	0.6	24	24	2	10	0	60.6	110	0.55	20
21	Cleveland Indians	1901	8691	8367	0.509	2	5	4	7	1	0.9	16	20	8	14	1	58.9	110	0.54	21
21	Philadelphia Phillies	1883	9135	10233	0.472	2	7	3	11	0	-2.8	16	28	6	22	0	69.2	128	0.54	21
23	Houston Astros	1962	3888	3921	0.498	0	1	2	7	2	-0.2	0	4	4	14	2	23.8	49	0.49	23
24	San Diego Padres	1969	3098	3580	0.464	0	2	1	5	0	-3.4	0	8	2	10	0	16.6	42	0.40	24
25	Colorado Rockies	1993	1364	1490	0.478	0	1	1	0	3	-2.2	0	4	2	0	3	6.8	18	0.38	25
26	Seattle Mariners	1977	2522	2861	0.469	0	0	3	3	1	-3.1	0	0	6	6	1	9.9	34	0.29	26
26	Tampa Bay Rays	1998	922	1181	0.438	0	1	1	2	0	-6.2	0	4	2	4	0	3.8	13	0.29	26
28	Texas Rangers	1961	3747	4206	0.471	0	1	1	4	0	-2.9	0	4	2	8	0	11.1	50	0.22	28
29	Milwaukee Brewers	1969	3166	3505	0.475	0	1	0	2	1	-2.5	0	4	0	4	1	6.5	42	0.15	29
30	Washington Nationals	1969	3167	3502	0.475	0	0	1	1	0	-2.5	0	0	2	2	0	1.5	42	0.04	30

Franchise Sections

Arizona Diamondbacks

Stats

History
Year of Origin 1998

Years Played 13

Score & Rank
Total Points Score 23.1

Average Points Score 1.78

Total Points Rank 23

Average Points Rank 2

Postseason Results

	No.	Years
World Series Won	1	2001
League Championship Series Won	1	2001
League Division Series Won	2	2001, 2007
World Series Lost	0	
League Championship Series Lost	1	2007
League Division Series Lost	2	1999, 2002

Postseason Won-Loss Records and Winning Percentages

	Postseason Games		Postseason Series	
All Postseason Series	15-16	.484	4-3	.571
World Series	4-3	.571	1-0	1.000
League Championship Series	4-5	.444	1-1	.500
League Division Series	7-8	.467	2-2	.500

Regular Season Results
All-Time Won-Loss Record 1035-1071

All-Time Winning Percentage .... .491

	No.	Years
League Titles before 1969	0	
Division Titles	4	1999, 2001, 2002, 2007
Wild Cards	0	

Regular Season High & Low Points

		Year(s)
Most Wins in a Season	100	1999
Most Losses in a Season	111	2004
Highest Winning Percentage	.617	1999
Lowest Winning Percentage	.315	2004
Longest Streak with Won-Loss Record .500 or Higher	5 years	1999-2003
Longest Streak with Won-Loss Record Below .500	3 years	2004-2006

Years with .500 record or Better
1990's .... 1 (out of 2)

2000's 6

2010's 0

7 out of 13 seasons played = 54%

Years Making Postseason
1990's 1

2000's 3

2010's 0

4 out of 13 seasons played = 31%

Streaks

• 1999-2002: Won three Division Titles, one League Division Series, one League Championship Series, and one World Series in four years.

Extra Bases

• In 1999, Arizona became the earliest expansion team to make the playoffs, doing so in their second year of existence.
• In 2001 Arizona became the fastest expansion team to win the World Series, winning it in their fourth year of existence.

Scoring Opportunities

1990's
• In 1999 Arizona won the National League West Division and played the Mets in the LDS. Game 1 was tied at four after eight innings but the Diamondbacks gave up a Grand Slam in the top of the ninth inning with two outs and lost the game 8-4. Arizona tied the series up by winning Game 2, but lost Game 3 9-2. Game 4 was tied at three after nine innings. The Dbacks were retired in order in the top of the tenth and in the bottom of the inning they gave up a solo home run with one out and lost the game 4-3 to lose the series.

2000's
• The Diamondbacks won their third National League West Division title in 2002. In the LDS Arizona played St. Louis and lost Game 1 12-2. In Game 2 the Diamondbacks tied the score at one in the bottom of the eighth inning and had runners on first and second with two outs, but their next batter up flied out. In the top of the ninth Arizona gave up a single, a sacrifice bunt, and another single and let in the go-ahead run and lost the game 2-1. The Diamondbacks lost Game 3 6-3 and lost the series in a sweep, being outscored 20-6 in the three games.
• In 2007 Arizona won the National League West Division and swept the Cubs in the LDS. In the LCS against Colorado the Diamondbacks lost Game 1 5-1. Game 2 was tied at two after nine innings. In the top of the eleventh Arizona gave up a single and three walks, which included walking in the go ahead run with two outs. The Diamondbacks were retired in order in the bottom of the inning and lost 3-2. Arizona lost Game 3 4-1 and Game 4 6-4 and was swept in the series, being outscored 18-8 in the four games.
• The Diamondbacks were in first place in the National League West Division tied or by themselves from April 6th to September 5th in 2008. They were 4.5 games ahead of Los Angeles on August

29th but then went 3-11 and fell to 4.5 games behind the Dodgers on September 14th. Arizona went 10-4 the rest of the year, but LA went 7-6 over the same period and the Dbacks finished the season in second place two games out.

Year-to-Year Figures

Team Name	League	Year	W	L	Win%	Fin	GB/GA	WS	Lge	LDS	Div	WC
Arizona Diamondbacks	NL West	2010	65	97	0.401	5 of 5	27					
Arizona Diamondbacks	NL West	2009	70	92	0.432	5 of 5	25					
Arizona Diamondbacks	NL West	2008	82	80	0.506	2 of 5	2					
Arizona Diamondbacks	NL West	2007	90	72	0.556	1 of 5	+0.5*			1	1	
Arizona Diamondbacks	NL West	2006	76	86	0.469	4t of 5	12					
Arizona Diamondbacks	NL West	2005	77	85	0.475	2 of 5	5					
Arizona Diamondbacks	NL West	2004	51	111	0.315	5 of 5	42					
Arizona Diamondbacks	NL West	2003	84	78	0.519	3 of 5	16.5					
Arizona Diamondbacks	NL West	2002	98	64	0.605	1 of 5	+2.5				1	
Arizona Diamondbacks	NL West	2001	92	70	0.568	1 of 5	+2	1	1	1	1	
Arizona Diamondbacks	NL West	2000	85	77	0.525	3 of 5	12					
Arizona Diamondbacks	NL West	1999	100	62	0.617	1 of 5	+14				1	
Arizona Diamondbacks	NL West	1998	65	97	0.401	5 of 5	33					
			1035	1071	0.491			1	1	2	4	0

* In 2007 Arizona finished the season 0.5 games ahead of Colorado because the Rockies and Padres finished the season tied for second place one game behind the Diamondbacks and tied for the National League Wild Card. In the one game playoff, Colorado beat San Diego 9-8 to win the Wild Card and therefore only finish 0.5 games behind Arizona because they played one extra game.

Atlanta Braves

Stats

History

Year of Origin 1871   Years Played 140

Score & Rank

Total Points Score ....173.4   Average Points Score 1.24
Total Points Rank 6   Average Points Rank 9

Postseason Results	No.	Years
World Series Won	3	1914, 1957, 1995
League Championship Series Won	5	1991, 1992, 1995, 1996, 1999
League Division Series Won	6	1995, 1996, 1997, 1998, 1999, 2001
World Series Lost	6	1948, 1958, 1991, 1992, 1996, 1999
League Championship Series Lost	6	1969, 1982, 1973, 1997, 1998, 2001
League Division Series Lost	6	2000, 2002, 2003, 2004, 2005, 2010

Postseason Won-Loss Records and Winning Percentages

	Postseason Games		Postseason Series	
All Postseason Series	77-82	.484	14-18	.438
World Series	24-29	.453	3-6	.333
League Championship Series	27-33	.450	5-6	.454
League Division Series	26-20	.565	6-6	.500

Regular Season Results

All-Time Won-Loss Record 10170-10014
All-Time Winning Percentage 504

	No.	Years
League Titles before 1969	16	1872, 1873, 1874, 1875, 1877, 1878, 1883, 1891, 1892, 1893, 1897, 1898, 1914, 1948, 1957, 1958
Division Titles	16	1969, 1982, 1991, 1992, 1993, 1995, 1996, 1997, 1998, 1999, 2000, 2001, 2002, 2003, 2004, 2005
Wild Cards	1	2010

Regular Season High & Low Points

		Years(s)
Most Wins in a Season	106	1998
Most Losses in a Season	115	1935
Highest Winning Percentage	.899	1875
Lowest Winning Percentage	.248	1935
Longest Streak with Won-Loss Record .500 or Higher	15 years	1991-2005
Longest Streak with Won-Loss Record Below .500	11 years	1903-1913

Years with .500 record or Better

1870's	9 (out of 9)
1880's	6
1890's	10
1900's	2
1910's	3
1920's	1
1930's	5
1940's	3
1950's	8
1960's	9
1970's	2
1980's	3
1990's	9
2000's	8
2010's	1

79 out of 140 seasons played = 56%

Years Making Postseason

1870's	No Postseason
1880's	No Postseason
1890's	No Postseason
1900's	0
1910's	1
1920's	0
1930's	0
1940's	1
1950's	2
1960's	1
1970's	0
1980's	1
1990's	8
2000's	6
2010's	1

21 out of 140 seasons played = 15%

Streaks

- 1872-1878: Won six League Titles in seven years.
- 1891-1898: Won five League Titles in eight years.
- 1991-2001: Appeared in the League Championship Series nine times in ten years including eight straight years from 1991-1999.*
- 1991-2005: Won fourteen straight Division Titles, five League Championship Series, and one World Series in fourteen years.* They also won six League Division Series in seven years from 1995-2001.

*(Excludes 1994 as there was no postseason and no division titles were awarded that year due to the players strike)

Extra Bases

- The Braves franchise dates back longer than any other team as a continuous baseball franchise. The Braves and Cubs both date back to 1871, but Chicago did not play in 1872 and 1873 due to stadium damages caused by a fire in 1871.
- The Boston Red Stockings 1875 won-loss record of 71-8 gave them an .899 winning percentage, which is the highest in baseball history. It is technically .898734.
- From 1900-1945 the Braves franchise had only nine winning seasons in forty-six years. This came after the period of 1871-1899 in which they had twenty-five winning seasons in twenty-nine years.
- The Milwaukee Braves nearly made the World Series four years in a row in the late fifties with very close regular season finishes in 1956 and 1959 and World Series appearances in 1957 & 1958. In 1956 they finished one game behind the Dodgers and in 1959 they lost a

best of three games tiebreaker series against the Dodgers.

- After finishing with the worst record in the National League in 1990, the Braves became the first NL team to go from worst to first as they won the NL pennant in 1991.

- When Atlanta won the 2001 National League East Division title it marked their tenth division championship in a row. They became the first professional sports team to earn that accomplishment.

- The Braves three World Series Championships have all come while the team was located in different cities, Boston in 1914, Milwaukee in 1957, and Atlanta in 1995.

Scoring Opportunities

1870's

- In 1879 the Boston Red Caps trailed the Providence Grays in the National League by two games on September 23rd and had their five remaining games of the season against the Grays. Boston needed to win four out of the five games to win the league title, but the Red Caps lost four of the five games and finished the year in second place five games behind Providence.

1880's

- The Boston Beaneaters were in a close race with the New York Giants the entire year in 1889 and the two teams were tied with one game left on the season. The Giants beat the Cleveland Spiders in their final game and the Beaneaters lost to Pittsburgh 6-1 and lost the National League title by one game. Boston had the same amount of wins as New York but had two more games than the Giants and two more losses.

1940's

- The Boston Braves won the National League pennant in 1948 and played Cleveland in the World Series. Boston won Game 1 but lost Game 2 4-1. In Game 3 the Braves only trailed by two runs after four innings but they only got two hits and only one runner to second base the rest of the game and they lost 2-0. In Game 4 Boston trailed by one run in the top of the seventh when they had the tying run on first base with no outs, but their next three batters were all retired. In the top of the eighth the Braves had the tying run at second base with two outs, but their next batter popped out and they lost the game 2-1. Boston won Game 5 and trailed by one run in the bottom of the eighth inning of Game 6 when they had runners on second and third with two outs, but their next batter up grounded out and they lost the game 4-3 and lost the series.

1950's

- In 1956 the National League pennant race came down to the final day of the season as the Milwaukee Braves and Brooklyn Dodgers were in a close race. The Braves had a half-game lead over Brooklyn with two games left while the Dodgers had three games left in the season. Brooklyn won their three games against Pittsburgh and Milwaukee split their last two games against St. Louis and lost the pennant by one game.

- The Braves won the National League pennant in 1958. In the World Series Milwaukee played the Yankees and had series leads of two games to none and three games to one as they lost Game 3 4-0. The Braves lost Game 5 7-0 but still had a one game lead in the series with Games 6 & 7 at home. Game 6 went into extra innings tied at two and Milwaukee gave up two runs in the top of the tenth. In the bottom of the inning the Braves scored one run and had runners on first and third with two outs, but their next batter lined out and they lost 4-3. Game 7 was tied at two after seven innings but the Braves gave up four hits and four runs with two outs in the top of the eighth and lost the game 6-2 to lose the series.

- In 1959 the Braves tied the Dodgers for first place in the National League and a best-of-three game playoff was needed to determine the NL champion. The first game was played in Milwaukee and the Braves gave up a go-ahead solo home run in the top of the sixth inning. The rest of the game Milwaukee only got one batter on base and they lost the game 3-2. In the second game in LA, the Braves had a 5-2 lead heading into the bottom of the ninth inning, but gave up four singles to start the inning and let in three runs, which tied the score. In the top of the eleventh Milwaukee had the bases loaded with two outs but their next batter grounded out. In the bottom of the twelfth the Braves got the first two Dodgers out, but then gave up a walk and two singles and let in the winning run to lose the game 6-5 and lose the pennant.

1960's

- In the first year of divisional play in 1969, the Atlanta Braves won the National League West Division and played the Mets in the first NLCS. The Braves led Game 1 5-4 after seven innings, but in the top of the eighth they gave up four hits, two errors, and five runs and they lost the game 9-5. Then they lost Game 2 11-6 and Game 3 7-4 and were swept out of the playoffs, being outscored 27-15 in the three games.

1980's

- The Braves won the National League West Division in 1982 and faced St. Louis in the LCS. In Game 1 Atlanta led 1-0 in the fifth inning when the game was delayed by rain. The game was eventually cancelled due to the weather and had to be started over. If the Braves got three outs in the bottom of the fifth the game would have been official. In the second Game 1 Atlanta had only three hits and lost the game 7-0. In Game 2 the Braves had a 3-2 lead in the bottom of the eighth when St. Louis had runners on first and third with one out. The next Cardinals batter hit a high bouncer up the middle and the only play the Braves shortstop could make was a force out at second, which let the tying run from third score. In the bottom of the ninth Atlanta gave up a single, a sacrifice bunt, and another single that drove in the game winning run and lost 4-3. The Braves lost Game 3 6-2 and were swept in the series, being outscored 17-5 and outhit 34-15 in the three games.

1990's

• The Braves won eight of their last nine games in 1991 and won the National League West Division by one game over the Dodgers. In the LCS Atlanta beat Pittsburgh and in the World Series the Braves played Minnesota and lost Game 1 5-2. Game 2 was tied at two when Atlanta had runners on first and third in the top of the eighth inning with one out, but their next two batters popped up and flied out. In the bottom of the inning the Braves gave up a solo home run to the first batter of the inning and they lost the game 3-2. Atlanta won the next three games at home and took a three games to two series lead. Game 6 was tied at three after nine innings. The Braves got their first batter on base in the top of the tenth and eleventh innings but could not score either time. In the bottom of the eleventh Atlanta gave up a home run to the first Twins batter and lost 4-3. Game 7 was tied at zero in the top of the seventh when the Braves first batter up singled. Their next hitter doubled to deep left center field but the runner on first made a poor read on the ball and only advanced to third base when he could have scored. Atlanta loaded the bases with one out but then hit into a double play, which ended the inning. The game went into extra innings and the Braves gave up a double to the first Minnesota hitter in the bottom of the tenth inning. A sacrifice bunt advanced the runner to third and Atlanta intentionally walked the next two Twins batters to load the bases. The next Minnesota hitter singled over a drawn in outfield and the Braves lost the game 1-0 and lost the series. Five of the seven games in the series were decided by one run and the home team won every game.

• In 1992 Atlanta repeated as National League West Division champs and beat Pittsburgh again in the LCS. In the World Series against Toronto the Braves won Game 1. In Game 2 Atlanta had a 4-3 lead after eight innings but gave up a two run home run in the top of the ninth and lost the game 5-4. In Game 3 the Braves had a 2-1 lead after seven innings but gave up a solo home run in the bottom of the eighth inning that tied the score. In the bottom of the ninth they gave up a single, a stolen base, a sacrifice bunt, and two intentional walks, which loaded the bases. The next Toronto batter singled and drove in the game winning run and Atlanta lost 3-2. In Game 4 the Braves trailed by one run in the top of the eighth inning when they had runners on second and third with two outs, but their next batter up grounded out and they lost the game 2-1. Atlanta won Game 5 and Game 6 went into extra innings. The Braves gave up two runs in the top of the eleventh. In the bottom of the inning they scored one run and had the tying run on third base with two outs, but their next batter up grounded out and they lost 4-3 to lose the series. Atlanta outscored Toronto 20-17 in the series and all four of their losses were by one run.

• Atlanta won their third National League West Division in a row in 1993 and played Philadelphia in the LCS. Game 1 was tied at three after nine innings. In the top of the tenth the Braves had runners on second and third with two outs but their next batter struck out. In the bottom of the inning they got the first Phillies batter out but then gave up two doubles in a row and one run and lost 4-3. Atlanta won Games 2 & 3 to take a two game to one series lead but in Game 4 they trailed by one run after four innings. The Braves had chances to score the rest of the game but left two runners on base in the fifth, sixth, and eighth innings. In the bottom of the ninth they had runners on first and second with no outs. Their next batter attempted a sacrifice bunt but the runner on second was thrown out at third. Their next hitter grounded into a double play and they lost 2-1. Game 5 was tied at three in the bottom of the ninth when Atlanta had runners on first and third with one out, but their next two batters struck out and flied out and the game went into extra innings. In the top of the tenth Atlanta gave up a solo home run and they lost the game 4-3. The Braves lost Game 6 6-3 and lost the series. Three of their losses were by one run and two were in extra innings.

• The Braves won the National League East Division in 1996, swept the Dodgers in the LDS, and came back from a three games to one deficit in the LCS and beat St. Louis in seven games. In the World Series against the Yankees, Atlanta won the first two games, lost Game 3 5-2, and had a 6-0 lead in Game 4 after five innings. However, the Braves gave up three runs in the sixth inning and three more in the eighth, which tied the score. Atlanta had runners on first and second with one out in the bottom of the ninth but their next batter hit into a double play and the game went into extra innings. In the top of the tenth the Braves got the first two Yankees out but then gave up three walks, a single, and an error, and let in two runs and they lost the game 8-6. In Game 5 Atlanta trailed by one run in the bottom of the ninth inning and had runners on first and second with two outs but their next batter flied out and they lost 1-0. In Game 6 the Braves trailed by one run in the top of the ninth and had runners on first and second with two outs but their next batter popped out in foul territory and they lost 3-2 and lost the series.

• In 1997 Atlanta won the National League East Division and swept the Astros in the LDS. In the LCS against Florida the Braves lost Game 1 5-3, won Game 2, lost Game 3 5-2, and won Game 4. Game 5 was tied at one until Atlanta gave up the go ahead run in the bottom of the seventh. The Braves had a runner on first with two outs in the top of the eighth, but he was caught stealing second and they were retired in order in the ninth. Atlanta lost the game 2-1 and lost Game 6 7-4 to lose the series.

• The Braves won the National League East Division in 1998 and swept the Cubs in the LDS. In the LCS Atlanta faced the Padres. Game 1 was tied at two after nine innings but the Braves gave up a solo home run in the top of the tenth. In the bottom of the inning Atlanta had runners on first and second with two outs but their next batter flied out and they lost 3-2. The Braves only had three hits in Game 2 and lost 3-0. In Game 3 Atlanta trailed by one run in the top of the eighth when they had the bases loaded with one out, but their next two batters flied out and struck out. They gave up two runs in the bottom of the eighth and lost the game 4-1. The Braves won Games 4 and 5, but had only two hits in Game 6 and were shut out 5-0 and lost the series.

- In 1999 Atlanta won the National League East Division, beat the Astros in the LDS, and beat the Mets in the LCS. In the World Series the Braves met the Yankees. In Game 1 Atlanta had a 1-0 lead after seven innings but gave up three hits, two errors, three walks, and four runs in the top of the eighth and lost the game 4-1. The Braves lost Game 2 7-2 and had a 5-3 lead in the bottom of the eighth inning of Game 3 but gave up a two run home run that tied the score and the game went into extra innings. In the bottom of the tenth Atlanta gave up a home run to the first New York batter and lost 6-5. The Braves were held to five hits and one run in Game 4 and lost 4-1 being swept in the series.

2000's

- The Braves won the National League East Division in 2000 by one game over the Mets who were the wild card team. Atlanta's postseason stay was brief as they were outplayed by St. Louis and swept in the LDS. The Braves were outscored 24-10 in the series as they lost the three games by the scores of 7-5, 10-4, and 7-1.
- In 2001 Atlanta won the National League East Division, swept Houston in the LDS, and faced Arizona in the LCS. The Braves trailed by two runs in the top of the ninth inning of Game 1 when they had runners on first and third with two outs, but their next batter struck out and they lost 2-0. Atlanta won Game 2, but lost Game 3 5-1 and Game 4 11-4. In Game 5 the Braves trailed by one run in the bottom of the seventh inning when they had the bases loaded with two outs, but their next batter up struck out. Atlanta had the tying run on first base in the bottom of the ninth with one out, but their next two batters struck out and flied out and they lost 3-2 and lost the series. Atlanta was outscored 21-5 in their four losses.
- The Braves won the National League East Division in 2002 and played the Giants in the LDS. Atlanta lost Game 1 8-5 and won the next two games to take a two games to one lead in the series. In Game 4 the Braves gave up seven runs in the first three innings and lost the game 8-3. Game 5 was in Atlanta and the Braves trailed by two runs in the bottom of the seventh inning when they had runners on first and third with two outs, but their next batter up struck out. In the bottom of the ninth Atlanta got their first two batters on base but then their next two batters struck out and hit into a double play and they lost the game 3-1 to lose the series.
- In 2003 Atlanta won the National League East Division and met the Cubs in the LDS. In Game 1 the Braves trailed by two runs in the bottom of the eighth inning when they had the bases loaded with two outs, but their next batter grounded out and they lost the game 4-2. Atlanta won Game 2 but only had two hits in Game 3 and lost 3-1. The Braves won Game 4 and Game 5 was played in Atlanta, but they lost it 5-1 and lost the series.
- Atlanta won the National League East Division in 2004 and faced Houston in the LDS. The teams split the first four games with the Braves losing Game 1 9-3 and Game 3 8-5 and

winning Games 2 & 4. Game 5 was in Atlanta but the Braves lost 12-3 and lost the series. They were outscored 29-11 in their three losses.

- In 2005 the Braves won the National League East Division and met the Astros again in the LDS. Atlanta lost Game 1 10-5, won Game 2, and lost Game 3 7-3. In Game 4 the Braves had a 6-1 lead entering the bottom of the eighth but gave up four runs in the half inning and gave up a solo home run with two outs in the bottom of the ninth, which tied the score. In extra innings Atlanta had two runners on base in the eleventh and fourteenth innings but could not score either time. The game went into the eighteenth inning and with one out in the bottom of the inning the Braves gave up a solo home run and lost 7-6 to lose the series.

2010's

- Atlanta won the National League Wild Card spot in 2010 and played San Francisco in the LDS. In Game 1 the Braves trailed by one run in the top of the seventh inning when they had a runner on second base with one out, but their next two batters grounded out and flied out and they lost the game 1-0. Atlanta won Game 2 and in Game 3 they had a 2-1 lead after eight innings. But in the top of the ninth inning with two outs they gave up two singles, committed an error, and let two runs score and they lost the game 3-2. The Braves led Game 4 2-1 after six innings. In the top of the seventh Atlanta got the first Giants batter out, but then gave up two walks, two singles, committed an error on a play in which the San Francisco runner was really out, and let two runs score. In the bottom of the eighth inning Atlanta had a runner on second base with two outs but their next batter struck out. In the bottom of the ninth inning the Braves had runners on first and second with one out, but their next two batters struck out and grounded out and they lost the game 3-2 and lost the series. All three of Atlanta's losses in the series were by one run.

Year-to-Year Figures

Team Name	League	Year	W	L	Win%	Fin	GB/GA	WS	Lge	LDS	Div	WC
Atlanta Braves	NL East	2010	91	71	0.562	2 of 5	6					1
Atlanta Braves	NL East	2009	86	76	0.531	3 of 5	7					
Atlanta Braves	NL East	2008	72	90	0.444	4 of 5	20					
Atlanta Braves	NL East	2007	84	78	0.519	3 of 5	5					
Atlanta Braves	NL East	2006	79	83	0.488	3 of 5	18					
Atlanta Braves	NL East	2005	90	72	0.556	1 of 5	+2				1	
Atlanta Braves	NL East	2004	96	66	0.593	1 of 5	+10				1	
Atlanta Braves	NL East	2003	101	61	0.623	1 of 5	+10				1	
Atlanta Braves	NL East	2002	101	59	0.631	1 of 5	+19				1	
Atlanta Braves	NL East	2001	88	74	0.543	1 of 5	+2			1	1	
Atlanta Braves	NL East	2000	95	67	0.586	1 of 5	+1				1	

Team Name	League	Year	W	L	Win%	Fin	GB/GA	WS	Lge	LDS	Div	WC
Atlanta Braves	NL East	1999	103	59	0.636	1 of 5	+6.5		1	1	1	
Atlanta Braves	NL East	1998	106	56	0.654	1 of 5	+18			1	1	
Atlanta Braves	NL East	1997	101	61	0.623	1 of 5	+9			1	1	
Atlanta Braves	NL East	1996	96	66	0.593	1 of 5	+8		1	1	1	
Atlanta Braves	NL East	1995	90	54	0.625	1 of 5	+21	1	1	1	1	
Atlanta Braves	NL East	1994	68	46	0.596	2 of 5	6					
Atlanta Braves	NL West	1993	104	58	0.642	1 of 7	+1				1	
Atlanta Braves	NL West	1992	98	64	0.605	1 of 6	+8		1		1	
Atlanta Braves	NL West	1991	94	68	0.580	1 of 6	+1		1		1	
Atlanta Braves	NL West	1990	65	97	0.401	6 of 6	26					
Atlanta Braves	NL West	1989	63	97	0.394	6 of 6	28					
Atlanta Braves	NL West	1988	54	106	0.338	6 of 6	39.5					
Atlanta Braves	NL West	1987	69	92	0.429	5 of 6	20.5					
Atlanta Braves	NL West	1986	72	89	0.447	6 of 6	23.5					
Atlanta Braves	NL West	1985	66	96	0.407	5 of 6	29					
Atlanta Braves	NL West	1984	80	82	0.494	2t of 6	12					
Atlanta Braves	NL West	1983	88	74	0.543	2 of 6	3					
Atlanta Braves	NL West	1982	89	73	0.549	1 of 6	+1				1	
Atlanta Braves	NL West	1981	50	56	0.472	4, 5 of 6	9.5, 7.5					
Atlanta Braves	NL West	1980	81	80	0.503	4 of 6	11					
Atlanta Braves	NL West	1979	66	94	0.413	6 of 6	23.5					
Atlanta Braves	NL West	1978	69	93	0.426	6 of 6	26					
Atlanta Braves	NL West	1977	61	101	0.377	6 of 6	37					
Atlanta Braves	NL West	1976	70	92	0.432	6 of 6	32					
Atlanta Braves	NL West	1975	67	94	0.416	5 of 6	40.5					
Atlanta Braves	NL West	1974	88	74	0.543	3 of 6	14					
Atlanta Braves	NL West	1973	76	85	0.472	5 of 6	22.5					
Atlanta Braves	NL West	1972	70	84	0.455	4 of 6	25					
Atlanta Braves	NL West	1971	82	80	0.506	3 of 6	8					
Atlanta Braves	NL West	1970	76	86	0.469	5 of 6	26					
Atlanta Braves	NL West	1969	93	69	0.574	1 of 6	+3				1	
Atlanta Braves	NL	1968	81	81	0.500	5 of 10	16					
Atlanta Braves	NL	1967	77	85	0.475	7 of 10	24.5					
Atlanta Braves	NL	1966	85	77	0.525	5 of 10	10					
Milwaukee Braves	NL	1965	86	76	0.531	5 of 10	11					
Milwaukee Braves	NL	1964	88	74	0.543	5 of 10	5					
Milwaukee Braves	NL	1963	84	78	0.519	6 of 10	15					
Milwaukee Braves	NL	1962	86	76	0.531	5 of 10	15.5					
Milwaukee Braves	NL	1961	83	71	0.539	4 of 8	10					
Milwaukee Braves	NL	1960	88	66	0.571	2 of 8	7					
Milwaukee Braves	NL	1959	86	70	0.551	2 of 8	2					
Milwaukee Braves	NL	1958	92	62	0.597	1 of 8	+8		1			
Milwaukee Braves	NL	1957	95	59	0.617	1 of 8	+8	1	1			
Milwaukee Braves	NL	1956	92	62	0.597	2 of 8	1					
Milwaukee Braves	NL	1955	85	69	0.552	2 of 8	13.5					

Team Name	League	Year	W	L	Win%	Fin	GB/GA	WS	Lge	LDS	Div	WC
Milwaukee Braves	NL	1954	89	65	0.578	3 of 8	8					
Milwaukee Braves	NL	1953	92	62	0.597	2 of 8	13					
Boston Braves	NL	1952	64	89	0.418	7 of 8	32					
Boston Braves	NL	1951	76	78	0.494	4 of 8	20.5					
Boston Braves	NL	1950	83	71	0.539	4 of 8	8					
Boston Braves	NL	1949	75	79	0.487	4 of 8	22					
Boston Braves	NL	1948	91	62	0.595	1 of 8	+6		1			
Boston Braves	NL	1947	86	68	0.558	3 of 8	8					
Boston Braves	NL	1946	81	72	0.529	4 of 8	15.5					
Boston Braves	NL	1945	67	85	0.441	6 of 8	30					
Boston Braves	NL	1944	65	89	0.422	6 of 8	40					
Boston Braves	NL	1943	68	85	0.444	6 of 8	36.5					
Boston Braves	NL	1942	59	89	0.399	7 of 8	44					
Boston Braves	NL	1941	62	92	0.403	7 of 8	38					
Boston Bees	NL	1940	65	87	0.428	7 of 8	34.5					
Boston Bees	NL	1939	63	88	0.417	7 of 8	32.5					
Boston Bees	NL	1938	77	75	0.507	5 of 8	12					
Boston Bees	NL	1937	79	73	0.520	5 of 8	16					
Boston Bees	NL	1936	71	83	0.461	6 of 8	21					
Boston Braves	NL	1935	38	115	0.248	8 of 8	61.5					
Boston Braves	NL	1934	78	73	0.517	4 of 8	16					
Boston Braves	NL	1933	83	71	0.539	4 of 8	9					
Boston Braves	NL	1932	77	77	0.500	5 of 8	13					
Boston Braves	NL	1931	64	90	0.416	7 of 8	37					
Boston Braves	NL	1930	70	84	0.455	6 of 8	22					
Boston Braves	NL	1929	56	98	0.364	8 of 8	43					
Boston Braves	NL	1928	50	103	0.327	7 of 8	44.5					
Boston Braves	NL	1927	60	94	0.390	7 of 8	34					
Boston Braves	NL	1926	66	86	0.434	7 of 8	22					
Boston Braves	NL	1925	70	83	0.458	5 of 8	25					
Boston Braves	NL	1924	53	100	0.346	8 of 8	40					
Boston Braves	NL	1923	54	100	0.351	7 of 8	41.5					
Boston Braves	NL	1922	53	100	0.346	8 of 8	39.5					
Boston Braves	NL	1921	79	74	0.516	4 of 8	15					
Boston Braves	NL	1920	62	90	0.408	7 of 8	30					
Boston Braves	NL	1919	57	82	0.410	6 of 8	38.5					
Boston Braves	NL	1918	53	71	0.427	7 of 8	28.5					
Boston Braves	NL	1917	72	81	0.471	6 of 8	25.5					
Boston Braves	NL	1916	89	63	0.586	3 of 8	4					
Boston Braves	NL	1915	83	69	0.546	2 of 8	7					
Boston Braves	NL	1914	94	59	0.614	1 of 8	+10.5	1	1			
Boston Braves	NL	1913	69	82	0.457	5 of 8	31.5					
Boston Braves	NL	1912	52	101	0.340	8 of 8	52					
Boston Rustlers	NL	1911	44	107	0.291	8 of 8	54					
Boston Doves	NL	1910	53	100	0.346	8 of 8	50.5					

Atlanta Braves

Team Name	League	Year	W	L	Win%	Fin	GB/GA	WS	Lge	LDS	Div	WC
Boston Doves	NL	1909	45	108	0.294	8 of 8	65.5					
Boston Doves	NL	1908	63	91	0.409	6 of 8	36					
Boston Doves	NL	1907	58	90	0.392	7 of 8	47					
Boston Beaneaters	NL	1906	49	102	0.325	8 of 8	66.5					
Boston Beaneaters	NL	1905	51	103	0.331	7 of 8	54.5					
Boston Beaneaters	NL	1904	55	98	0.359	7 of 8	51					
Boston Beaneaters	NL	1903	58	80	0.420	6 of 8	32					
Boston Beaneaters	NL	1902	73	64	0.533	3 of 8	29					
Boston Beaneaters	NL	1901	69	69	0.500	5 of 8	20.5					
Boston Beaneaters	NL	1900	66	72	0.478	4 of 8	17					
Boston Beaneaters	NL	1899	95	57	0.625	2 of 12	8					
Boston Beaneaters	NL	1898	102	47	0.685	1 of 12	+6		1			
Boston Beaneaters	NL	1897	93	39	0.705	1 of 12	+2		1			
Boston Beaneaters	NL	1896	74	57	0.565	4 of 12	17					
Boston Beaneaters	NL	1895	71	60	0.542	5t of 12	16.5					
Boston Beaneaters	NL	1894	83	49	0.629	3 of 12	8					
Boston Beaneaters	NL	1893	86	43	0.667	1 of 12	+5		1			
Boston Beaneaters	NL	1892	102	48	0.680	1, 2 of 12	+2.5, 3		1			
Boston Beaneaters	NL	1891	87	51	0.630	1 of 8	+3.5		1			
Boston Beaneaters	NL	1890	76	57	0.571	5 of 8	12					
Boston Beaneaters	NL	1889	83	45	0.648	2 of 8	1					
Boston Beaneaters	NL	1888	70	64	0.522	4 of 8	15.5					
Boston Beaneaters	NL	1887	61	60	0.504	5 of 8	16.5					
Boston Beaneaters	NL	1886	56	61	0.479	5 of 8	30.5					
Boston Beaneaters	NL	1885	46	66	0.411	5 of 8	41					
Boston Beaneaters	NL	1884	73	38	0.658	2 of 8	10.5					
Boston Beaneaters	NL	1883	63	35	0.643	1 of 8	+4		1			
Boston Red Caps	NL	1882	45	39	0.536	3t of 8	10					
Boston Red Caps	NL	1881	38	45	0.458	6 of 8	17.5					
Boston Red Caps	NL	1880	40	44	0.476	6 of 8	27.5					
Boston Red Caps	NL	1879	54	30	0.643	2 of 8	5					
Boston Red Caps	NL	1878	41	19	0.683	1 of 6	+4		1			
Boston Red Caps	NL	1877	42	18	0.700	1 of 6	+7		1			
Boston Red Caps	NL	1876	39	31	0.557	1 of 8	15					
Boston Red Stockings	NA	1875	71	8	0.899	1 of 13	+15		1			
Boston Red Stockings	NA	1874	52	18	0.743	1 of 8	+7.5		1			
Boston Red Stockings	NA	1873	43	16	0.729	1 of 9	+4		1			
Boston Red Stockings	NA	1872	39	8	0.830	1 of 11	+7.5		1			
Boston Red Stockings	NA	1871	20	10	0.667	2t of 9	2					
			10170	10014	0.504			3	21	6	16	1

Baltimore Orioles

Stats

History
Year of Origin 1901

Years Played 110

Score & Rank
Total Points Score 70.4

Total Points Rank 12

Average Points Score 0.64

Average Points Rank 18

Postseason Results

Postseason Results	No.	Years
World Series Won	3	1966, 1970, 1983
League Championship Series Won	5	1969, 1970, 1971, 1979, 1983
League Division Series Won	2	1996, 1997
World Series Lost	4	1944, 1969, 1971, 1979
League Championship Series Lost	4	1973, 1974, 1996, 1997
League Division Series Lost	0	

Postseason Won-Loss Records and Winning Percentages

	Postseason Games		Postseason Series	
All Postseason Series	48-36	.571	10-8	.555
World Series	21-18	.538	3-4	.429
League Championship Series	21-16	.568	5-4	.555
League Division Series	6-2	.750	2-0	1.000

Regular Season Results
All-Time Won-Loss Record 8079-8959

All-Time Winning Percentage .... .474

	No.	Years
League Titles before 1969	2	1944, 1966
Division Titles	8	1969, 1970, 1971, 1973, 1974, 1979, 1983, 1997
Wild Cards	1	1996

Regular Season High & Low Points

		Year(s)
Most Wins in a Season	109	1969
Most Losses in a Season	111	1939
Highest Winning Percentage	.673	1969
Lowest Winning Percentage	.279	1939
Longest Streak with Won-Loss Record .500 or Higher	18 years	1968-1985
Longest Streak with Won-Loss Record Below .500	13 years	1998-2010

Years with .500 record or Better	
1900's	3 (out of 9)
1910's	1
1920's	5
1930's	0
1940's	3
1950's	1
1960's	8
1970's	10
1980's	7
1990's	5
2000's	0
2010's	0

43 out of 110 seasons played = 39%

Years Making Postseason	
1900's	0
1910's	0
1920's	0
1930's	0
1940's	1
1950's	0
1960's	2
1970's	5
1980's	1
1990's	2
2000's	0
2010's	0

11 out of 110 seasons played = 10%

Streaks

- 1966-1974: Won five Division Titles, one League Title, three League Championship Series, and two World Series in nine years.
- 1979-1983: Won one World Series, two League Championship Series, and two Division Titles in five years.

Extra Bases

- On the last day of the season in 1926 the St. Louis Browns won the shortest nine-inning baseball game of all time. The game was the second game in a doubleheader against the Yankees and it was eight and a half innings and played in fifty-five minutes. The two games in the doubleheader were played in a total of two hours and seven minutes and the Browns won them both, 6-1 and 6-2. The first game was one hour and twelve minutes long.
- In 1988 the Orioles lost their first twenty-one games of the year, which is an American League record.

Scoring Opportunities

1920's

- In 1922 the St. Louis Browns were in a close race with the Yankees for the American League pennant. The Browns led the league by a half game on September 6th but then went 8-6 while New York went 15-3 and St. Louis fell to 4.5 games back on September 23rd. The Browns won their last four games of the year while the Yankees lost four of their last five, but St. Louis came up short and finished the season one game behind New York in the standings.

1940's

• The Browns won their only American League pennant while the franchise was in St. Louis in 1944. In the World Series they faced the Cardinals and won Game 1. Game 2 was tied at two after nine innings and the Browns had a runner on base in the tenth and eleventh innings but could not score either time. In the bottom of the eleventh the Browns gave up a walk, two singles, and the game winning run and lost 3-2. The Browns won Game 3, but lost Game 4 5-1. In Game 5 the Browns trailed by one run in the bottom of the sixth when they had the bases loaded with one out, but their next two batters both struck out and they lost the game 2-0. In Game 6 the Browns trailed by two runs in the sixth inning when they had runners on second and third with one out, but on a ground ball hit to the third baseman their runner from third was thrown out at home plate. Their next batter flied out and their last nine batters were retired in order. The Browns were held to three hits in the game and lost 3-1 to lose the series.

1960's

• The Baltimore Orioles led the American League for the majority of the 1964 season in a very close race with the Yankees and White Sox. On September 18th the Orioles were tied with New York for first place. Baltimore went 8-4 the rest of the year, but ended up in third place as the Yankees were in the middle of an eleven game win streak, and the White Sox finished the season with nine straight wins. New York won the pennant by one game over Chicago, and two games over the Orioles.

• In 1969 the Orioles won the American League East Division and swept the Twins in three games in the first ALCS. In the World Series Baltimore faced the Mets and won Game 1. Game 2 was tied at one after eight innings. In the top of the ninth the Orioles got the first two New York batters out, but then gave up three straight singles and let in the go-ahead run. In the bottom of the inning Baltimore had runners on first and second with two outs, but their next batter grounded out and they lost 3-2. The Orioles lost Game 3 5-0 and Game 4 went into extra innings tied at one. In the top of the tenth Baltimore had runners on first and third with two outs but their next batter up struck out. In the bottom of the inning the Orioles gave up a double and a walk to the first two Mets batters. The next New York batter hit a sacrifice bunt and the Baltimore pitcher made a throwing error to first base that let in the game-winning run and the Orioles lost 2-1. Baltimore lost Game 5 5-3 and lost the series.

1970's

• The Orioles won their third straight American League East Division title in 1971 and won over 100 games for the third straight year. Baltimore beat Oakland in the LCS and in the World Series the Orioles won the first two games against Pittsburgh, but lost Game 3 5-1. In Game 4 Baltimore gave up the go ahead run in the bottom of the seventh and they was retired in order in the eighth and ninth innings and lost the game 4-3. The Orioles lost Game 5 4-0 but won

Game 6 in the bottom of the tenth to tie the series. In Game 7 Baltimore trailed by one in the bottom of the eighth inning when they had the tying run on third base, but their next batter up grounded out and they lost the game 2-1 to lose the series.

- Baltimore won the American League East Division in 1973 and won Game 1 in the LCS against Oakland. The Orioles lost Game 2 6-3 and had a 1-0 lead in the bottom of the eighth inning in Game 3 when they gave up the tying run with two outs. The game went into extra innings and Baltimore was retired in order in the top of the tenth and eleventh. In the bottom of the eleventh the Orioles gave up a home run to the A's first batter and lost the game 2-1. Baltimore won Game 4 to even the series, but in Game 5 they only had five hits and were shutout losing the game 3-0 and losing the series.

- In 1974 the Orioles repeated as American League East Division champs and faced Oakland again in the LCS. Baltimore won Game 1 but lost Game 2 5-0. In Game 3 the Orioles had only two hits and lost the game 1-0. In Game 4 the Orioles trailed by one run in the bottom of the ninth inning when they had runners on first and second with two outs, but their next batter up struck out to end the game and they lost 2-1 and lost the series.

- The Orioles won the American League East Division in 1979 and beat the Angels in the LCS. In the World Series Baltimore faced the team that beat them in the World Series in 1971, the Pirates. The Orioles won Game 1 and Game 2 was tied at two after eight innings. In the top of the ninth Baltimore got the first two Pirates batters out but then gave up a single, a walk, and another single, and let in the go-ahead run. The Orioles were retired in order in the bottom of the inning and lost 3-2. Baltimore won the next two games to take a three-games-to-one lead in the series and had Games 6 and 7 at home if needed. The Orioles lost Game 5 7-1 and lost Game 6 4-0. In Game 7 Baltimore trailed by one in the bottom of the eighth when they had the bases loaded with two outs, but their next batter flied out. Pittsburgh scored two more runs in the top of the ninth and the Orioles were retired in order in the bottom of the inning and lost 4-1 to lose the series. Baltimore was outscored 15-2 in the final three games.

1980's

- The 1982 American League East Division race came down to the final series of the year as the Orioles were three games behind Milwaukee with four games to play at home against the Brewers. Baltimore needed to win all four games to win the division and won the first three games by a combined score of 26-7. However, the Orioles lost the final game 10-2 and lost the division by one game.

- The 1989 American League East Division race also came down to the final series of the year as the Orioles were one game behind Toronto with three games left on the road against the Blue Jays. In the first game Baltimore had a 1-0 lead in the bottom of the eighth inning when they had two Blue Jays out with a runner on third, but the Orioles pitcher threw a wild pitch that let in the tying run. The game went into extra innings and Baltimore gave up the winning run in the bottom of the twelfth inning with two outs. The Orioles had to win the next two games to tie Toronto for the division title. In the second game Baltimore had a 3-1 lead entering the bottom of the eighth but gave up a two walks, a sacrifice bunt, two singles, and a sacrifice fly and let in three runs. The Orioles were retired in the top of the ninth and lost 4-3 being eliminated from the division title race. Baltimore won the last game of the season and finished two games behind the Blue Jays.

1990's

• In 1996 the Orioles won the American League Wild Card spot and beat Cleveland in the LDS. In the LCS Baltimore met New York and had a 4-3 lead in the bottom of the eighth inning in Game 1. There was one out and no runners on base when New York hit a fly ball to right field that would have been caught, but it was interfered with by a fan and ruled a home run, which tied the score. The game went into extra innings and the Orioles had runners on first and second with two outs in the top of the tenth inning, but their next batter up grounded out. In the bottom of the eleventh Baltimore gave up a home run to the first Yankees batter and lost 5-4. The Orioles won Game 2 and had a 2-1 lead in Game 3 entering the eighth inning, but gave up four runs in the top of the inning and lost the game 5-2. In Game 4 Baltimore only trailed by one run entering the eighth inning but gave up three runs in the top of the inning and lost the game 8-4. The Orioles gave up six runs in the third inning of Game 5 and lost the game 6-4 to lose the series.

• The Orioles returned to the postseason in 1997 by winning the American League East Division. They spent every day of the regular season in first place and beat Seattle in the LDS. In the LCS against the Indians Baltimore won Game 1. The Orioles had a 4-2 lead after seven innings of Game 2 but gave up a three run home run in the top of the eighth inning and lost the game 5-4. Game 3 was tied at one in the top of the ninth inning when Baltimore had runners on first and second with one out, but their next two batters fouled out and struck out. The game went into extra innings and the Orioles had the bases loaded in the top of the eleventh with two outs, but their next batter up struck out. In the bottom of the twelfth Baltimore got the first Cleveland hitter out, but then gave up a walk and a single, which advanced a base runner to third base. During the next at bat the Indians runner on third stole home and the Orioles lost 2-1. Game 4 was tied at seven in the top of the ninth when Baltimore had runners on first and second with one out, but their next two batters grounded out and fouled out. In the bottom of the inning the Orioles walked two batters and gave up a single with two outs, which drove in the game winning run, and they lost 8-7. Baltimore won Game 5 and Game 6 was tied at zero after nine innings. In the top of the eleventh the Orioles gave up a solo home run with two outs and they lost the game 1-0 to lose the series. All four of Baltimore's losses were by one run and two of the games in the series went to extra innings. Cleveland's wins in Games 3, 4, and 6 all came in their final inning at bat.

Year-to-Year Figures

Team Name	League	Year	W	L	Win%	Fin	GB/GA	WS	Lge	LDS	Div	WC
Baltimore Orioles	AL East	2010	66	96	0.407	5 of 5	30					
Baltimore Orioles	AL East	2009	64	98	0.395	5 of 5	39					
Baltimore Orioles	AL East	2008	68	93	0.422	5 of 5	28.5					
Baltimore Orioles	AL East	2007	69	93	0.426	4 of 5	27					
Baltimore Orioles	AL East	2006	70	92	0.432	4 of 5	27					
Baltimore Orioles	AL East	2005	74	88	0.457	4 of 5	21					
Baltimore Orioles	AL East	2004	78	84	0.481	3 of 5	23					
Baltimore Orioles	AL East	2003	71	91	0.438	4 of 5	30					
Baltimore Orioles	AL East	2002	67	95	0.414	4 of 5	36.5					
Baltimore Orioles	AL East	2001	63	98	0.391	4 of 5	32.5					
Baltimore Orioles	AL East	2000	74	88	0.457	4 of 5	13.5					
Baltimore Orioles	AL East	1999	78	84	0.481	4 of 5	20					
Baltimore Orioles	AL East	1998	79	83	0.488	4 of 5	35					
Baltimore Orioles	AL East	1997	98	64	0.605	1 of 5	+2			1	1	
Baltimore Orioles	AL East	1996	88	74	0.543	2 of 5	4			1		1
Baltimore Orioles	AL East	1995	71	73	0.493	3 of 5	15					
Baltimore Orioles	AL East	1994	63	49	0.563	2 of 5	6.5					
Baltimore Orioles	AL East	1993	85	77	0.525	3t of 7	10					
Baltimore Orioles	AL East	1992	89	73	0.549	3 of 7	7					
Baltimore Orioles	AL East	1991	67	95	0.414	6 of 7	24					
Baltimore Orioles	AL East	1990	76	85	0.472	5 of 7	11.5					
Baltimore Orioles	AL East	1989	87	75	0.537	2 of 7	2					
Baltimore Orioles	AL East	1988	54	107	0.335	7 of 7	34.5					
Baltimore Orioles	AL East	1987	67	95	0.414	6 of 7	31					
Baltimore Orioles	AL East	1986	73	89	0.451	7 of 7	22.5					
Baltimore Orioles	AL East	1985	83	78	0.516	4 of 7	16					
Baltimore Orioles	AL East	1984	85	77	0.525	5 of 7	19					
Baltimore Orioles	AL East	1983	98	64	0.605	1 of 7	+6	1	1		1	
Baltimore Orioles	AL East	1982	94	68	0.580	2 of 7	1					
Baltimore Orioles	AL East	1981	59	46	0.562	2, 4 of 7	2, 2					
Baltimore Orioles	AL East	1980	100	62	0.617	2 of 7	3					
Baltimore Orioles	AL East	1979	102	57	0.642	1 of 7	+8		1		1	
Baltimore Orioles	AL East	1978	90	71	0.559	4 of 7	9					
Baltimore Orioles	AL East	1977	97	64	0.602	2t of 7	2.5					
Baltimore Orioles	AL East	1976	88	74	0.543	2 of 6	10.5					
Baltimore Orioles	AL East	1975	90	69	0.566	2 of 6	4.5					
Baltimore Orioles	AL East	1974	91	71	0.562	1 of 6	+2				1	
Baltimore Orioles	AL East	1973	97	65	0.599	1 of 6	+8				1	
Baltimore Orioles	AL East	1972	80	74	0.519	3 of 6	5					
Baltimore Orioles	AL East	1971	101	57	0.639	1 of 6	+12		1		1	
Baltimore Orioles	AL East	1970	108	54	0.667	1 of 6	+15	1	1		1	
Baltimore Orioles	AL East	1969	109	53	0.673	1 of 6	+19		1		1	
Baltimore Orioles	AL	1968	91	71	0.562	2 of 10	12					

Team Name	League	Year	W	L	Win%	Fin	GB/GA	WS	Lge	LDS	Div	WC
Baltimore Orioles	AL	1967	76	85	0.472	6t of 10	15.5					
Baltimore Orioles	AL	1966	97	63	0.606	1 of 10	+9	1	1			
Baltimore Orioles	AL	1965	94	68	0.580	3 of 10	8					
Baltimore Orioles	AL	1964	97	65	0.599	3 of 10	2					
Baltimore Orioles	AL	1963	86	76	0.531	4 of 10	18.5					
Baltimore Orioles	AL	1962	77	85	0.475	7 of 10	19					
Baltimore Orioles	AL	1961	95	67	0.586	3 of 10	14					
Baltimore Orioles	AL	1960	89	65	0.578	2 of 8	8					
Baltimore Orioles	AL	1959	74	80	0.481	6 of 8	20					
Baltimore Orioles	AL	1958	74	79	0.484	6 of 8	17.5					
Baltimore Orioles	AL	1957	76	76	0.500	5 of 8	21					
Baltimore Orioles	AL	1956	69	85	0.448	6 of 8	28					
Baltimore Orioles	AL	1955	57	97	0.370	7 of 8	39					
Baltimore Orioles	AL	1954	54	100	0.351	7 of 8	57					
St. Louis Browns	AL	1953	54	100	0.351	8 of 8	46.5					
St. Louis Browns	AL	1952	64	90	0.416	7 of 8	31					
St. Louis Browns	AL	1951	52	102	0.338	8 of 8	46					
St. Louis Browns	AL	1950	58	96	0.377	7 of 8	40					
St. Louis Browns	AL	1949	53	101	0.344	7 of 8	44					
St. Louis Browns	AL	1948	59	94	0.386	6 of 8	37					
St. Louis Browns	AL	1947	59	95	0.383	8 of 8	38					
St. Louis Browns	AL	1946	66	88	0.429	7 of 8	38					
St. Louis Browns	AL	1945	81	70	0.536	3 of 8	6					
St. Louis Browns	AL	1944	89	65	0.578	1 of 8	+1		1			
St. Louis Browns	AL	1943	72	80	0.474	6 of 8	25					
St. Louis Browns	AL	1942	82	69	0.543	3 of 8	19.5					
St. Louis Browns	AL	1941	70	84	0.455	6t of 8	31					
St. Louis Browns	AL	1940	67	87	0.435	6 of 8	23					
St. Louis Browns	AL	1939	43	111	0.279	8 of 8	64.5					
St. Louis Browns	AL	1938	55	97	0.362	7 of 8	44					
St. Louis Browns	AL	1937	46	108	0.299	8 of 8	56					
St. Louis Browns	AL	1936	57	95	0.375	7 of 8	44.5					
St. Louis Browns	AL	1935	65	87	0.428	7 of 8	28.5					
St. Louis Browns	AL	1934	67	85	0.441	6 of 8	33					
St. Louis Browns	AL	1933	55	96	0.364	8 of 8	43.5					
St. Louis Browns	AL	1932	63	91	0.409	6 of 8	44					
St. Louis Browns	AL	1931	63	91	0.409	5 of 8	45					
St. Louis Browns	AL	1930	64	90	0.416	6 of 8	38					
St. Louis Browns	AL	1929	79	73	0.520	4 of 8	26					
St. Louis Browns	AL	1928	82	72	0.532	3 of 8	19					
St. Louis Browns	AL	1927	59	94	0.386	7 of 8	50.5					
St. Louis Browns	AL	1926	62	92	0.403	7 of 8	29					
St. Louis Browns	AL	1925	82	71	0.536	3 of 8	15					
St. Louis Browns	AL	1924	74	78	0.487	4 of 8	17					
St. Louis Browns	AL	1923	74	78	0.487	5 of 8	24					

Team Name	League	Year	W	L	Win%	Fin	GB/GA	WS	Lge	LDS	Div	WC
St. Louis Browns	AL	1922	93	61	0.604	2 of 8	1					
St. Louis Browns	AL	1921	81	73	0.526	3 of 8	17.5					
St. Louis Browns	AL	1920	76	77	0.497	4 of 8	21.5					
St. Louis Browns	AL	1919	67	72	0.482	5 of 8	20.5					
St. Louis Browns	AL	1918	58	64	0.475	5 of 8	15					
St. Louis Browns	AL	1917	57	97	0.370	7 of 8	43					
St. Louis Browns	AL	1916	79	75	0.513	5 of 8	12					
St. Louis Browns	AL	1915	63	91	0.409	6 of 8	39.5					
St. Louis Browns	AL	1914	71	82	0.464	5 of 8	28.5					
St. Louis Browns	AL	1913	57	96	0.373	8 of 8	39					
St. Louis Browns	AL	1912	53	101	0.344	7 of 8	53					
St. Louis Browns	AL	1911	45	107	0.296	8 of 8	56.5					
St. Louis Browns	AL	1910	47	107	0.305	8 of 8	57					
St. Louis Browns	AL	1909	61	89	0.407	7 of 8	36					
St. Louis Browns	AL	1908	83	69	0.546	4 of 8	6.5					
St. Louis Browns	AL	1907	69	83	0.454	6 of 8	24					
St. Louis Browns	AL	1906	76	73	0.510	5 of 8	16					
St. Louis Browns	AL	1905	54	99	0.353	8 of 8	40.5					
St. Louis Browns	AL	1904	65	87	0.428	6 of 8	29					
St. Louis Browns	AL	1903	65	74	0.468	6 of 8	26.5					
St. Louis Browns	AL	1902	78	58	0.574	2 of 8	5					
Milwaukee Brewers	AL	1901	48	89	0.350	8 of 8	35.53					
			8079	8959	0.474			3	7	2	8	1

Boston Red Sox

Stats

History
Year of Origin 1901   Years Played...110

Score & Rank
Total Points Score ....134.7   Average Points Score...................................1.22
Total Points Rank 7   Average Points Rank...7

Postseason Results

	No.	Years
World Series Won	7	1903, 1912, 1915, 1916,1918, 2004, 2007
League Championship Series Won	4	1975, 1986, 2004, 2007
League Division Series Won	5	1999, 2003, 2004, 2007, 2008
World Series Lost	4	1946, 1967, 1975, 1986
League Championship Series Lost	5	1988, 1990, 1999, 2003, 2008
League Division Series Lost	4	1995, 1998, 2005, 2009

Postseason Won-Loss Records and Winning Percentages

	Postseason Games		Postseason Series	
All Postseason Series	79-72	.523	16-13	.552
World Series	41-26	.612	7-4	.636
League Championship Series	22-29	.431	4-5	.444
League Division Series	16-17	.485	5-4	.556

Regular Season Results
All-Time Won-Loss Record 8819-8233
All-Time Winning Percentage .... .517

	No.	Years
League Titles before 1969	8	1903, 1904, 1912, 1915, 1916, 1918, 1946, 1967
Division Titles	6	1975, 1986, 1988, 1990, 1995, 2007
Wild Cards	7	1998, 1999, 2003, 2004,2005, 2008, 2009

Regular Season High & Low Points

		Year(s)
Most Wins in a Season	105	1912
Most Losses in a Season	111	1932
Highest Winning Percentage	.691	1912
Lowest Winning Percentage	.279	1932
Longest Streak with Won-Loss Record .500 or Higher	16 years	1967-1982
Longest Streak with Won-Loss Record Below .500	15 years	1919-1933

Years with .500 record or Better

1900's	6 (out of 9)
1910's	9
1920's	0
1930's	5
1940's	8
1950's	7
1960's	3
1970's	10
1980's	8
1990's	6
2000's	10
2010's	1

73 out of 110 seasons played = 66%

Years Making Postseason

1900's	1
1910's	4
1920's	0
1930's	0
1940's	1
1950's	0
1960's	1
1970's	1
1980's	2
1990's	4
2000's	5
2010's	0

20 out of 110 seasons played = 18%

Streaks

- 1912-1918: Won four World Series in seven years.
- 1986-1990: Won three Division Titles and one League Championship Series in five years.
- 2003-2009: Won two World Series, four League Division Series, two League Championship Series, one Division Title, and five Wild Cards in seven years. Went to the playoffs six times in the seven years and also appeared in the LCS four times in six years from 2003-2008.

Extra Bases

- After winning the World Series in 1915 and 1916 the Red Sox did not make it back to the postseason in consecutive years again until 1998 and 1999.
- The 1918 season ended early on September 2nd because of World War I and the World Series started on September 5th. On September 11th the Red Sox won the series and this marks the earliest date on the calendar that the World Series has been won.
- Each time the Red Sox lost a World Series they lost it in Game 7. This occurred in 1946, 1967, 1975, and 1986.
- Boston lost thirteen straight postseason games from 1986 to 1995, currently the longest postseason losing streak in history.
- In 2004 the Red Sox became the first team in baseball history to come back from a three game to zero deficit in a postseason series by winning the final four games of the ALCS against the Yankees. In Game 5 of that series the two teams played the longest postseason game ever at five hours and forty-nine minutes. In the 2004 World Series the Red Sox became the first team to have a lead in the first inning in Games 1-4 as they swept the Cardinals. Boston also never trailed in the series.
- From 1998-2005 Boston had eight straight second place finishes, all to the Yankees.
- The Red Sox only had six losing seasons from 1967-2010, occurring in 1983, 1987, 1992, 1993, 1994, and 1997. From 1959-1966 they had eight straight losing seasons.
- Boston had a 95-67 regular season won-loss record four times in the seven year span of 2003-2009, occurring in 2003, 2005, 2008, and 2009.

Scoring Opportunities

1940's

- In 1946 the Red Sox won the American League pennant and faced the Cardinals in the World Series. Boston won Game 1 but only had four hits in Game 2, and only one after the fifth inning, and lost the game 3-0. The Red Sox won Game 3, lost Game 4 12-3, and won Game 5 to take a three games to two lead in the series. Boston lost Game 6 4-1 and Game 7 was tied at three in the bottom of the eighth inning when St. Louis had a runner on first with two outs. The Red Sox gave up a double to center field and the Cardinals base runner scored all the way from first with the go ahead run. In the top of the ninth the Red Sox got their first two batters on base and had runners on first and third with one out, but their next two hitters fouled out and grounded out and they lost 4-3 to lose the series.

• The Red Sox won their last four games of the year in 1948 and tied Cleveland for first place in the American League on the last day of the season. A one game playoff was needed to determine the AL champion and it was the first one game playoff in AL history. Boston only had five hits in the game and gave up thirteen hits and eight runs and they lost the game 8-3 to lose the pennant.

• In 1949 the Red Sox had a one game lead in the American League over New York with two games left against the Yankees in New York. Boston only needed to win one of two games to win the pennant. In the first game the score was tied at four after seven innings, but in the bottom of the eighth the Red Sox gave up the go-ahead run and they lost the game 5-4. In the second game Boston only trailed by one run after seven innings, but in the bottom of the eighth they gave up four runs. In the top of the ninth the Red Sox scored three runs but lost the game 5-3 and lost the pennant by one game.

1960's

• Boston won the American League pennant in 1967 in a close four-team race that was decided on the last day of the season. In the World Series the Red Sox faced St. Louis and Game 1 was tied at one after six innings. Boston gave up a run in the top of the seventh and in their last three at bats the Red Sox got a runner on base in each inning but couldn't score and lost the game 2-1. Boston won Game 2, lost Game 3 5-2 and Game 4 6-0, and won Games 5 & 6. In Game 7 the Red Sox were held to three hits and lost the game 7-2 to lose the series.

1970's

• In 1972 the Red Sox led the American League East Division by a half game over the Tigers on October 1st with three games left to play at second place Detroit. Boston needed to win two out of the three games to win the division. But they lost the first two games of the series 4-1 and 3-1 and were eliminated from the division race before the last game, which they won. The Red Sox finished a half game behind the Tigers in the division because the two teams had an unbalanced schedule. At the beginning of the season there was a thirteen day players strike and when the season started the schedule had the Red Sox playing one less game than Detroit. The two teams had the same number of losses but Detroit had one more win.

• Boston won the American League East Division in 1975 and swept the three time defending World Series champion Oakland A's in the LCS. In the World Series against Cincinnati, the Red Sox won Game 1 and had a 2-1 lead after eight innings in Game 2. But they gave up three hits and two runs in the top of the ninth inning and lost the game 3-2. Game 3 was tied at five after nine innings. In the bottom of the tenth the Reds had a runner on first with no outs when their next batter hit a slow ground ball in front of home plate. The Boston catcher tried to get to the ball and throw to second base but the batter interfered with him and his throw to second was wild. The batter was not called for interference and this put runners on second and third. The Red Sox intentionally walked the next batter to load the bases and then got the first out of the inning. But the next Cincinnati batter hit a single and drove in the game winning run and Boston lost 6-5. The Red Sox won Game 4, lost Game 5 6-2, and won Game 6 in the bottom of the twelfth inning. In Game 7 the Red Sox had a 3-0 lead but Cincinnati tied it in the seventh, and Boston gave up the go-ahead run in the top of the ninth with two outs and lost the game 4-3 to lose the series. There were five one-run games in the series, and the Red Sox lost three of them.

- In 1978 Boston led the American League East Division from May 22nd to September 9th. The Red Sox were ahead of New York by seven games on August 30th but then went 3-14 and fell out of first place and trailed the Yankees by 3.5 games on September 16th. Boston won its last eight games of the season and tied New York for first place, forcing one game playoff, which would be played at home. The Red Sox led the playoff game 2-0 after six innings but gave up four runs in the top of the seventh, three of them on a home run. In the bottom of the ninth Boston trailed by one run and had runners on first and second with one out but their next two batters flied out and fouled out and they lost 5-4 and finished one game behind New York.

1980's

- The Red Sox won the American League Eastern Division in 1986 and beat the Angels in the LCS. In the World Series Boston played the Mets and won Games 1 & 2 on the road. But the Red Sox lost Games 3 & 4 at home, 7-1 and 6-2, which tied the series. Boston won Game 5 and scored two runs in the top of the tenth inning of Game 6 to take a 5-3 lead. In the bottom of the inning the Red Sox got the first two Mets out and were on the verge of winning the World Series. But then they gave up three straight singles and let in one run. During the next at bat the Boston pitcher threw a wild pitch that let in the tying run. The Mets batter then hit a ground ball to the first baseman who made an error that let in the game winning run and the Red Sox lost 6-5. In Game 7 Boston scored three runs in the top of the second but gave up three runs in the sixth and three in the seventh and trailed 6-3 after seven innings. The Red Sox scored two runs in the top of the eighth and had the tying run on second base with no outs, but their next three batters all got out. Boston let in two more runs in the bottom of the inning and were retired in order in the top of the ninth and lost the game 8-5 to lose the series they were so close to winning.
- In 1988 the Red Sox won the American League East Division by one game over Detroit and played Oakland in the LCS. Game 1 was tied at one after seven innings. In the top of the eighth Boston gave up a double and a single to the first two batters and let in the go-ahead run. In the

bottom of the ninth the Red Sox had runners on first and second with two outs but their next batter struck out and they lost 2-1. Game 2 was tied at three after eight innings. In the top of the ninth Boston had two A's out with runners on first and third. The next Oakland batter singled which drove in the go-ahead run and the Red Sox lost the game 4-3. Boston lost Game 3 10-6 and Game 4 4-1 and lost the series in a sweep.

1990's

- The Red Sox won the American League East Division in 1990 on the last day of the season over Toronto and faced the A's again in the LCS. Boston lost Game 1 9-1 and trailed by one run in the bottom of the eighth inning of Game 2. They had runners on first and second with one out but their next two batters grounded out and struck out. The Red Sox gave up two more runs in the top of the ninth and they lost the game 4-1. Boston lost Game 3 4-1 and in Game 4 they only had four hits and lost the game 3-1 to lose the series in a sweep, getting only four runs in the four games.

- In 1991 the Red Sox trailed Toronto in the American League East Division by a half game on September 21st but then lost eleven of their last fourteen games. The Blue Jays went 9-4 over the same period and Boston finished the season tied for second place with Detroit, seven games behind Toronto.

- Boston won the 1995 American League East Division and played Cleveland in the LDS. Game 1 was tied at three after nine innings and both teams scored a run in the eleventh. In the top of the twelfth the Red Sox had runners on first and second with one out but their next two batters both struck out. In the bottom of the thirteenth Boston had two Indians out but then gave up a solo home run and lost 5-4. The Red Sox got only three hits in Game 2 and lost 4-0 and lost Game 3 8-2 to lose the series in a sweep. A poorly constructed playoff format certainly didn't help Boston in the postseason. The Red Sox had the second best record in the American League but had to play the Indians who had the best record.

- The Red Sox won the American League Wild Card spot in 1998 and played Cleveland in the LDS. Boston won Game 1 but lost Game 2 9-5. In Game 3 the Red Sox trailed by three runs in the bottom of the ninth inning when they hit a two-run home run with one out. But their next two batters both grounded out and they lost 4-3. In Game 4 Boston led 1-0 after seven innings but gave up two runs in the top of the eighth. They had runners on first and third with two outs in the bottom of the inning but their next batter flied out and they lost the game 2-1 and lost the series. Two of their three losses were by one run.

- In 1999 Boston won the American League Wild Card spot again and beat the Indians in the LDS by coming back from a zero to two game deficit and winning the final three games. In the LCS against the Yankees Game 1 was tied at three after nine innings. In the bottom of the tenth the Red Sox gave up a home run to the first New York batter and lost 4-3. In Game 2 Boston led 2-1 after six innings but gave up two runs in the bottom of the seventh inning. In the top of the eighth the Red Sox had the bases loaded with one out but then their next two batters struck out and flied out. In the top of the ninth Boston had runners on first and third with two outs but their next hitter struck out and they lost 3-2. The Red Sox won Game 3 and only trailed by one run in Game 4 after eight innings. But in the top of the ninth Boston gave up six runs and they lost the game 9-2. The Red Sox lost Game 5 6-1 and lost the series.

2000's

• Boston won the American League Wild Card spot in 2003 and beat Oakland in the LDS by coming back and winning the last three games of the series after losing the first two. In the LCS against the Yankees, the Red Sox won Game 1 but lost Game 2 6-2. In Game 3 Boston only trailed by one run after seven innings, but they were retired in order in the eighth and ninth innings and lost the game 4-3. Boston won Game 4, lost Game 5 4-2, and won Game 6. In Game 7 the Red Sox had a 5-2 lead with one out in the bottom of the eighth inning, but the next four Yankees batters all got hits and Boston let in three runs that tied the score. In the middle of the rally, the Red Sox manager decided to leave his starting pitcher in the game and not use the pitchers out of the bullpen who had thrown well throughout the series. The game went into extra innings and in the bottom of the eleventh Boston gave up a home run to the first New York batter and lost the game 6-5 to lose the series.

• The Red Sox had the same regular season record as the Yankees in 2005 in the American League East Division. The Yankees were given the Division Title and Boston the Wild Card spot as New York won the regular season series and both teams were going to the postseason. In the LDS the Red Sox played the White Sox and lost Game 1 14-2. In Game 2 Boston trailed by one run in the top of the ninth when they had a runner on second base with one out, but their next two batters fouled out and grounded out and they lost 5-4. The Red Sox lost Game 3 5-3 and lost the series in a sweep.

• Boston won the American League Wild Card spot in 2008, finishing second in the AL East Division to Tampa Bay. The Red Sox beat the Angels in the LDS and played the Rays in the LCS. Boston won Game 1 and Game 2 went into extra innings tied at eight. The Red Sox had runners on first and second with one out in the top of the eleventh but their next two batters struck out and grounded out. In the bottom of the inning Boston walked the first two Rays batters, gave up sacrifice bunt, and then intentionally walked the next batter to load the bases with one out. Tampa's next batter hit a sacrifice fly that drove in the game winning run and the Red Sox lost 9-8. Boston lost Games 3 9-1 and Game 4 13-4 but won Games 5 & 6. In Game 7 the Red Sox got only three hits but were only down by two runs in the top of the eighth when they had the bases loaded with two outs. But their next batter struck out and they lost the game 3-1 and lost the series.

• In 2009 the Red Sox won the American League Wild Card spot for the seventh time. In the LDS they faced the Angels and lost Game 1 5-0 and Game 2 4-1 and only had eight hits total in the first two games. In Game 3 Boston had a 5-2 lead after seven innings but gave up two runs in the top of the eighth. The Red Sox scored one run in the bottom of the inning and got the first two Angels batters out in the top of the ninth. But then Boston gave up a single, a walk, and a double which drove in one run. The Red Sox intentionally walked the next batter to load the bases, but the Angels next hitter singled and drove in two runs that gave Los Angeles the lead. Boston was retired in order in the bottom of the ninth and lost 7-6 to lose the series in a sweep.

Year-to-Year Figures

Team Name	League	Year	W	L	Win%	Fin	GB/GA	WS	Lge	LDS	Div	WC
Boston Red Sox	AL East	2010	89	73	0.549	3 of 5	7					
Boston Red Sox	AL East	2009	95	67	0.586	2 of 5	8					1
Boston Red Sox	AL East	2008	95	67	0.586	2 of 5	2			1		1
Boston Red Sox	AL East	2007	96	66	0.593	1 of 5	+2	1	1	1	1	
Boston Red Sox	AL East	2006	86	76	0.531	3 of 5	11					
Boston Red Sox	AL East	2005	95	67	0.586	2 of 5	0*					1
Boston Red Sox	AL East	2004	98	64	0.605	2 of 5	3	1	1	1		1
Boston Red Sox	AL East	2003	95	67	0.586	2 of 5	6			1		1
Boston Red Sox	AL East	2002	93	69	0.574	2 of 5	10.5					
Boston Red Sox	AL East	2001	82	79	0.509	2 of 5	13.5					
Boston Red Sox	AL East	2000	85	77	0.525	2 of 5	2.5					
Boston Red Sox	AL East	1999	94	68	0.580	2 of 5	4			1		1
Boston Red Sox	AL East	1998	92	70	0.568	2 of 5	22					1
Boston Red Sox	AL East	1997	78	84	0.481	4 of 5	20					
Boston Red Sox	AL East	1996	85	77	0.525	3 of 5	7					
Boston Red Sox	AL East	1995	86	58	0.597	1 of 5	+7				1	
Boston Red Sox	AL East	1994	54	61	0.470	4 of 5	17					
Boston Red Sox	AL East	1993	80	82	0.494	5 of 7	15					
Boston Red Sox	AL East	1992	73	89	0.451	7 of 7	23					
Boston Red Sox	AL East	1991	84	78	0.519	2t of 7	7					
Boston Red Sox	AL East	1990	88	74	0.543	1 of 7	+2				1	
Boston Red Sox	AL East	1989	83	79	0.512	3 of 7	6					
Boston Red Sox	AL East	1988	89	73	0.549	1 of 7	+1				1	
Boston Red Sox	AL East	1987	78	84	0.481	5 of 7	20					
Boston Red Sox	AL East	1986	95	66	0.590	1 of 7	+5.5		1		1	
Boston Red Sox	AL East	1985	81	81	0.500	5 of 7	18.5					
Boston Red Sox	AL East	1984	86	76	0.531	4 of 7	18					
Boston Red Sox	AL East	1983	78	84	0.481	6 of 7	20					
Boston Red Sox	AL East	1982	89	73	0.549	3 of 7	6					
Boston Red Sox	AL East	1981	59	49	0.546	5, 2t of 7	4, 1.5					
Boston Red Sox	AL East	1980	83	77	0.519	4 of 7	19					
Boston Red Sox	AL East	1979	91	69	0.569	3 of 7	11.5					
Boston Red Sox	AL East	1978	99	64	0.607	2 of 7	1					

Team Name	League	Year	W	L	Win%	Fin	GB/GA	WS	Lge	LDS	Div	WC
Boston Red Sox	AL East	1977	97	64	0.602	2t of 7	2.5					
Boston Red Sox	AL East	1976	83	79	0.512	3 of 6	15.5					
Boston Red Sox	AL East	1975	95	65	0.594	1 of 6	+4.5		1		1	
Boston Red Sox	AL East	1974	84	78	0.519	3 of 6	7					
Boston Red Sox	AL East	1973	89	73	0.549	2 of 6	8					
Boston Red Sox	AL East	1972	85	70	0.548	2 of 6	0.5**					
Boston Red Sox	AL East	1971	85	77	0.525	3 of 6	18					
Boston Red Sox	AL East	1970	87	75	0.537	3 of 6	21					
Boston Red Sox	AL East	1969	87	75	0.537	3 of 6	22					
Boston Red Sox	AL	1968	86	76	0.531	4 of 10	17					
Boston Red Sox	AL	1967	92	70	0.568	1 of 10	+1		1			
Boston Red Sox	AL	1966	72	90	0.444	9 of 10	26					
Boston Red Sox	AL	1965	62	100	0.383	9 of 10	40					
Boston Red Sox	AL	1964	72	90	0.444	8 of 10	27					
Boston Red Sox	AL	1963	76	85	0.472	7 of 10	28					
Boston Red Sox	AL	1962	76	84	0.475	8 of 10	19					
Boston Red Sox	AL	1961	76	86	0.469	6 of 10	33					
Boston Red Sox	AL	1960	65	89	0.422	7 of 8	32					
Boston Red Sox	AL	1959	75	79	0.487	5 of 8	19					
Boston Red Sox	AL	1958	79	75	0.513	3 of 8	13					
Boston Red Sox	AL	1957	82	72	0.532	3 of 8	16					
Boston Red Sox	AL	1956	84	70	0.545	4 of 8	13					
Boston Red Sox	AL	1955	84	70	0.545	4 of 8	12					
Boston Red Sox	AL	1954	69	85	0.448	4 of 8	42					
Boston Red Sox	AL	1953	84	69	0.549	4 of 8	16					
Boston Red Sox	AL	1952	76	78	0.494	6 of 8	19					
Boston Red Sox	AL	1951	87	67	0.565	3 of 8	11					
Boston Red Sox	AL	1950	94	60	0.610	3 of 8	4					
Boston Red Sox	AL	1949	96	58	0.623	2 of 8	1					
Boston Red Sox	AL	1948	96	59	0.619	2 of 8	1					
Boston Red Sox	AL	1947	83	71	0.539	3 of 8	14					
Boston Red Sox	AL	1946	104	50	0.675	1 of 8	+12		1			
Boston Red Sox	AL	1945	71	83	0.461	7 of 8	17.5					
Boston Red Sox	AL	1944	77	77	0.500	4 of 8	12					
Boston Red Sox	AL	1943	68	84	0.447	7 of 8	29					
Boston Red Sox	AL	1942	93	59	0.612	2 of 8	9					
Boston Red Sox	AL	1941	84	70	0.545	2 of 8	17					
Boston Red Sox	AL	1940	82	72	0.532	4t of 8	8					
Boston Red Sox	AL	1939	89	62	0.589	2 of 8	17					
Boston Red Sox	AL	1938	88	61	0.591	2 of 8	9.5					
Boston Red Sox	AL	1937	80	72	0.526	5 of 8	21					
Boston Red Sox	AL	1936	74	80	0.481	6 of 8	28.5					
Boston Red Sox	AL	1935	78	75	0.510	4 of 8	16					
Boston Red Sox	AL	1934	76	76	0.500	4 of 8	24					
Boston Red Sox	AL	1933	63	86	0.423	7 of 8	34.5					

Team Name	League	Year	W	L	Win%	Fin	GB/GA	WS	Lge	LDS	Div	WC
Boston Red Sox	AL	1932	43	111	0.279	8 of 8	64					
Boston Red Sox	AL	1931	62	90	0.408	6 of 8	45					
Boston Red Sox	AL	1930	52	102	0.338	8 of 8	50					
Boston Red Sox	AL	1929	58	96	0.377	8 of 8	48					
Boston Red Sox	AL	1928	57	96	0.373	8 of 8	43.5					
Boston Red Sox	AL	1927	51	103	0.331	8 of 8	59					
Boston Red Sox	AL	1926	46	107	0.301	8 of 8	44.5					
Boston Red Sox	AL	1925	47	105	0.309	8 of 8	49.5					
Boston Red Sox	AL	1924	67	87	0.435	7 of 8	25					
Boston Red Sox	AL	1923	61	91	0.401	8 of 8	37					
Boston Red Sox	AL	1922	61	93	0.396	8 of 8	33					
Boston Red Sox	AL	1921	75	79	0.487	5 of 8	23.5					
Boston Red Sox	AL	1920	72	81	0.471	5 of 8	25.5					
Boston Red Sox	AL	1919	66	71	0.482	6 of 8	20.5					
Boston Red Sox	AL	1918	75	51	0.595	1 of 8	+2.5	1	1			
Boston Red Sox	AL	1917	90	62	0.592	2 of 8	9					
Boston Red Sox	AL	1916	91	63	0.591	1 of 8	+2	1	1			
Boston Red Sox	AL	1915	101	50	0.669	1 of 8	+2.5	1	1			
Boston Red Sox	AL	1914	91	62	0.595	2 of 8	8.5					
Boston Red Sox	AL	1913	79	71	0.527	4 of 8	15.5					
Boston Red Sox	AL	1912	105	47	0.691	1 of 8	+14	1	1			
Boston Red Sox	AL	1911	78	75	0.510	5 of 8	24					
Boston Red Sox	AL	1910	81	72	0.529	4 of 8	22.5					
Boston Red Sox	AL	1909	88	63	0.583	3 of 8	9.5					
Boston Red Sox	AL	1908	75	79	0.487	5 of 8	15.5					
Boston Americans	AL	1907	59	90	0.396	7 of 8	32.5					
Boston Americans	AL	1906	49	105	0.318	5 of 8	45.5					
Boston Americans	AL	1905	78	74	0.513	4 of 8	16					
Boston Americans	AL	1904	95	59	0.617	1 of 8	+1.5		1			
Boston Americans	AL	1903	91	47	0.659	1 of 8	+14.5	1	1			
Boston Americans	AL	1902	77	60	0.562	3 of 8	6.5					
Boston Americans	AL	1901	79	57	0.581	2 of 8	4					
			8819	8233	0.517			7	12	5	6	7

* In 2005 Boston and New York finished the regular season tied with the same won-loss record. Since both teams made the playoffs and the Yankees won the regular season series between the two teams, they won the AL East Division Title and Boston won the AL Wild Card.
** In 1972 the Red Sox finished 0.5 games behind Detroit. There was a 13-day player strike at the beginning of that season cancelling an uneven amount of games. The owners refused to make up the games because they did not want to pay the players for the time they were on strike. Therefore, Boston played one less game than the Tigers and finished the season with one less win and the same amount of losses.

Chicago Cubs

Stats

History

Year of Origin 1871   Years Played 138

Score & Rank

Total Points Score .... 94.4   Average Points Score 0.68
Total Points Rank 9   Average Points Rank 16

Postseason Results	**No.**	**Years**
World Series Won	2	1907, 1908
League Championship Series Won	0	
League Division Series Won	1	2003
World Series Lost	8	1906, 1910, 1918, 1929, 1932, 1935, 1938, 1945
League Championship Series Lost	3	1984, 1989, 2003
League Division Series Lost	3	1998, 2007, 2008

Postseason Won-Loss Records and Winning Percentages

	Postseason Games		**Postseason Series**	
All Postseason Series	28-55	.337	3-14	.176
World Series	19-33	.365	2-8	.200
League Championship Series	6-11	.353	0-3	.000
League Division Series	3-11	.214	1-3	.250

Regular Season Results

All-Time Won-Loss Record 10318-9765
All-Time Winning Percentage .... .514

	No.	**Years**
League Titles before 1969	16	1876, 1880, 1881, 1882, 1885, 1886, 1906, 1907, 1908, 1910, 1918, 1929, 1932, 1935, 1938, 1945
Division Titles	5	1984, 1989, 2003, 2007, 2008
Wild Cards	1	1998

Regular Season High & Low Points

Most Wins in a Season 116 1906
Most Losses in a Season .... 103 .... 1962, 1966
Highest Winning Percentage .... .798 1880
Lowest Winning Percentage .... .364 .... 1962, 1966
Longest Streak with Won-Loss Record .500 or Higher .... 14 years 1926-1939
Longest Streak with Won-Loss Record Below .500 .... 10 years 1953-1962

Years with .500 record or Better

1870's	4 (out of 7)
1880's	10
1890's	6
1900's	7
1910's	7
1920's	7
1930's	10
1940's	2
1950's	1
1960's	4
1970's	4
1980's	2
1990's	3
2000's	6
2010's	0

73 out of 138 seasons played = 53%

Years Making Postseason

1870's	No Postseason
1880's	No Postseason
1890's	No Postseason
1900's	3
1910's	2
1920's	1
1930's	3
1940's	1
1950's	0
1960's	0
1970's	0
1980's	2
1990's	1
2000's	3
2010's	0

16 out of 138 seasons played = 12%

Streaks

- 1880-1886: Won five League Titles in seven years.
- 1906-1910: Won two World Series and four League Titles in five years.
- 1929-1938: Won four League Titles in ten years.
- 2003-2008: Won three Division Titles and one League Division Series in six years.

Extra Bases

- The Chicago White Stockings record of 67-17 in 1880 gives them the second best regular season winning percentage in baseball history at .798. The 1875 Boston Red Stockings (Braves franchise) had a 71-8 regular season won-loss record and an .899 winning percentage.
- In 1906 the Cubs won 116 regular season games and this stood as the record for ninety-five years until the Seattle Mariners won 116 games in 2001 and tied Chicago for the record.
- From 1929-1938 Chicago appeared in the World Series every third year, 1929, 1932, 1935, and 1938, and lost in all four appearances.
- The Cubs had a twenty-one game consecutive winning streak in 1935 that is technically the all time record. The New York Giants had a twenty-six game winning streak in 1916, but that span included a tie with Pittsburgh after win number twelve. The 1880 Chicago White Stockings team had a twenty-one game winning streak as well, but theirs also had a tie in it, which was after the first win in the streak.
- Over the thirty year span of 1973-2002 they Cubs had a .500 or higher regular season won-loss record only seven times, occurring in 1977, 1984, 1989, 1993, 1995, 1998, and 2001. From

2003-2009 they had five seasons out of seven with a regular season won-loss record over .500.

• Chicago's last World Series championship in 1908 only occurred because they won a regular season game that they technically lost. The Cubs technically lost the famous 'Merkle's Boner' game on September 23rd, 1908. They let in the game winning run in bottom of the ninth inning, but because of a Giants base running mistake from first to second base the game was ruled a tie. At the end of the regular season the two teams were tied for first place so the game was replayed on October 8th. The Cubs won the game, won the National League pennant, and won the World Series. So Chicago's World Series drought could have easily been extended back one more year to 1907.

Scoring Opportunities

1870's

• In the inaugural professional baseball season of the 1871 National Association the Chicago White Stockings trailed the Philadelphia Athletics by one game on the final day of the season on October 30th when the two teams met in Chicago. The White Stockings record was 19-8 and the Athletics record was 20-7. If the White Stockings won the game the two teams would have the same record and be tied for first place. But Chicago lost the game 4-1 and finished two games back in the standings behind Philadelphia.

1890's

• In 1891 the Chicago Colts were in first place in the National League from July 21st to September 29th. They had a seven game lead over the Boston Beaneaters on September 4th, but Boston went 25-4 the rest of the season and had an eighteen game winning streak. On September 29th the two teams were tied for first place. Boston won four of their last five games of the year and Chicago lost their last four games and finished in second place 3.5 games behind the Beaneaters. The Colts went 12-12 after September 4th.

1900's

• The Cubs won the National League pennant in 1906 with a historic regular season. From July 26th to September 27th they went 50-7, they went 26-3 in August, and they won fifty-five of there last sixty-five games. They had a better record on the road than they did at home, 60-15 to 56-21. In the World Series the Cubs played the White Sox and trailed by one run after six innings in Game 1. The Cubs had one runner on base in the bottom of the eighth and ninth innings but couldn't score either time and lost 2-1. The Cubs won two of the next three games, Games 2 & 4, but they only had two hits in Game 3 and lost it 3-0. In Game 5 the Cubs trailed by two runs after six innings. They had one runner on base in the bottom of the seventh, eighth, and ninth innings but couldn't score in any inning and lost the game 8-6. The Cubs lost Game 6 8-3 and lost the series.

1910's

- Chicago won 104 games in 1910 and won their fourth National League pennant in five years. In the World Series they faced the Philadelphia A's and were outplayed. The Cubs lost the first three games 4-1, 9-3, and 12-5. Chicago won Game 4, but lost Game 5 7-2 and lost the series. The Cubs were outscored 32-11 in their four losses.

- In 1918 the Cubs won the National League pennant and played Boston in the World Series. In Game 1 Chicago trailed by one run in the bottom of the ninth when they had a runner on first with two outs, but their next batter flied out and they lost 1-0. The Cubs won Game 2 and in Game 3 they trailed by one run in the bottom of the ninth inning with two outs and a runner on second. On a passed ball their runner tried to score from second base and was thrown out at home plate and they lost 2-1. Game 4 was tied heading into the bottom of the eighth but Chicago gave up a single, a passed ball, and an error and let in the go-ahead run and lost the game 3-2. The Cubs won Game 5 but only had three hits in Game 6 and their last nine batters were retired in order and they lost 2-1 to lose the series. All four of the Cubs losses were by one run.

1920's

- The Cubs won the National League pennant in 1929 and met the Philadelphia A's in the World Series. In Game 1 Chicago trailed by one run going into the ninth inning, but gave up two errors and two runs in the top of the inning. In the bottom of the inning they scored one run and had runners on first and second with one out, but their next two batters grounded out and struck out and they lost 3-1. The Cubs lost Game 2 9-3 and won Game 3. In Game 4 Chicago had an 8-0 lead after the top of the seventh but gave up ten runs in the bottom of the inning and lost the game 10-8. In Game 5 the Cubs had a 2-0 lead entering the bottom of the ninth but gave up four hits and three runs and lost 3-2 to lose the series.

1930's

- In 1930 Chicago had a 5.5 game lead in the National League over the Giants on August 30th with the Cardinals 7.5 games back. The Cubs went 4-9 in their next thirteen games and fell out of first place on September 13th. Chicago went 9-4 the rest of the year and won their last six games of the season but finished in second place two games behind the Cardinals. St. Louis went 22-4 after August 30th and 11-3 after September 13th.

- The Cubs won the National League pennant in 1932 and played the Yankees in the World Series. Chicago lost Game 1 12-6 and Game 2 5-2. In Game 3 the Cubs trailed by two runs in the bottom of the ninth inning and had a runner on first with no outs, but their next three batters all got out and they lost 7-5. Chicago lost Game 4 13-6 to lose the series in a sweep. They were outscored 37-19 in the four games.

- Chicago won the National League pennant in 1935 and faced Detroit in the World Series. The Cubs won Game 1, lost Game 2 8-3, and Game 3 was tied at five after nine innings. In the bottom of the tenth Chicago's first batter up hit a double but their next three batters all got out. In the top of the eleventh the Cubs gave up a single and an error, and with two outs another single that drove in the go-ahead run. Chicago was retired in order in the bottom of the inning and lost 6-5. In Game 4 the Cubs trailed by one run in the bottom of the ninth and had runners on first and second with one out, but their next batter up hit into a double play to end the game and they lost 2-1. Chicago won Game 5 and Game 6 was tied at three after eight innings. In the top of the ninth the Cubs first batter up tripled but their next three batters all got out. In the bottom of the inning they gave up the game winning run on a single with two outs and lost 4-3 to lose the series. Three of Chicago's losses in the series were by one run.

- In 1938 the Cubs won the National League pennant and faced the Yankees in the World Series. In Game 1 Chicago trailed by two runs after six innings. The Cubs had one runner on base in the sixth, seventh, eighth, and ninth innings but couldn't score in any inning and lost the game 3-1. In Game 2 the Cubs led 3-2 after seven innings but gave up a two-run home run in the top of the eighth with two outs and gave up a two run home run in the ninth and lost the game 6-3. Chicago lost Game 3 5-2 and Game 4 8-3 and was swept in the series. They were outscored 22-9 in the four games.

1940's

- The Cubs won the National League pennant in 1945 and met the Tigers in the World Series. Chicago had a series lead of two games to one as they won Games 1 & 3 and lost Game 2 4-1. Before Game 4 a bizarre scenario happened involving a Cubs fan. A man who purchased two tickets wanted to bring his pet goat to the game with him. The ushers wouldn't let the fan or his goat in and as he walked away he yelled out that a World Series would never again be played at Wrigley field. Chicago lost the next two games at home, Game 4 4-1 and Game 5 8-4. The Cubs won Game 6 in twelve innings, but they gave up five runs in the first inning of Game 7 and lost the game 9-3 to lose the series.

1960's

- In 1969 the Cubs were in first place in the National League East Division from opening day on April 8th until September 10th, and had a nine game lead on August 15th. They had a five game lead over the Mets on September 2nd, but then lost eight games in a row and eleven out of twelve. During the same time, the Mets went 12-3 and on September 15th Chicago trailed New York by 4.5 games. The rest of the year the Cubs went 7-7 and the Mets went 11-4. Chicago had a 9-18 record after September 1st while New York went 24-8 over the same period and the Cubs lost the division by eight games.

1980's

- The Cubs won the National League East Division in 1984 and had the best overall record in the NL. In the LCS Chicago faced San Diego but because their home stadium did not have lights, the Cubs were not able to host night games. So in order to improve TV ratings the NLCS location schedule was reversed so the Padres got three home games and Chicago only got two. The Cubs won the first two games at home, but lost Game 3 7-1. Game 4 was tied at five in the top of the ninth inning when Chicago had the bases loaded with two outs, but their next batter up grounded out. In the bottom half of the inning the Cubs got the first Padres batter out, but then gave up a single and a two-run home run and lost 7-5. In Game 5 Chicago had a 3-2 lead after six innings, but committed two errors and gave up three hits and four runs in the bottom of the seventh and lost the game 6-3 to lose the series. The Cubs had leads in all three road games but lost all three.
- In 1989 the Cubs won the National League East Division and faced San Francisco in the LCS. Chicago lost Game 1 11-3 and won Game 2. The Cubs led Game 3 4-3 in the bottom of the seventh inning, but gave up a two run home run with one out that gave the Giants the lead. In the top of the eighth Chicago had runners on first and second with two outs but their next batter flied out and they lost the game 5-4. In Game 4 the Cubs trailed by two runs in the top of the ninth when they had the bases loaded with two outs, but their next batter up struck out and they lost 6-4. In Game 5 Chicago trailed by one run in top of the ninth when they had runners on first and second with two outs, but their next batter grounded out and they lost 3-2 to lose the series.

1990's

- The Cubs beat San Francisco in a one game playoff for the National League Wild Card spot in 1998 and played the Braves in the LDS. Chicago lost Game 1 7-1 and had a 1-0 lead in the bottom of the ninth inning of Game 2. They got the first Braves batter out, but then gave up a home run that tied the game. In the top of the tenth the Cubs had runners on first and third with one out but then hit into a double play. In the bottom of the inning they got the first Braves batter out but then gave up a walk, an error, and a single and let in the game winning run and lost 2-1. The Cubs lost Game 3 6-2 and were swept in the series being outscored 15-4 in the three games.

2000's

- In 2003 the Cubs won the National League Central Division and beat the Braves in the LDS. In the LCS against Florida Game 1 went into extra innings and Chicago gave up a solo home run to the first Marlins batter in the top of the eleventh and they lost the game 9-8. The Cubs won the next three games to take a three game to one series lead with Games 6 & 7 at home if needed. Chicago lost Game 5 4-0 and led 3-0 after seven innings in Game 6. There was one out and a Florida runner on second base in the top of the eighth when the Marlins batter hit a foul pop fly down the left field foul line. As the Cubs left fielder approached it appeared he would have a chance at making the catch. But as he jumped up the Chicago fans interfered with the ball and prevented him from catching it. If they had not interfered there was a good chance he would have caught the ball and this would have been the second out of the inning. After the foul ball the Florida batter walked and their next batter singled, which drove in one run. With runners on first and second the next Marlins batter hit a ground ball to the Cubs shortstop which could have been an inning ending double play, but the shortstop made an error on the play and the batter reached base, which loaded the bases. The next Florida batter doubled and two runs scored which tied the game at three. Chicago then gave up two walks, two hits, and a sacrifice fly and let in five more runs in the inning and lost the game 8-3. The Cubs had a 5-3 lead after four innings in Game 7. But they gave up six runs in the next three innings and lost the game 9-6 to lose the series they were only five outs away from winning.

- The Cubs were well behind the Cardinals for the National League Central Division title in 2004 but they were in the National League Wild Card race. With nine games left to play Chicago had the wild card lead by 1.5 games on September 24th. But after that the Cubs lost seven of their final nine games of the year and finished the season three games behind Houston for the fourth playoff spot. The Astros went 7-1 after the 24th.

- In 2007 the Cubs won the National League Central Division by two games over Milwaukee. In the LDS Chicago faced Arizona and Game 1 was tied at one after six innings. The Cubs gave up a solo home run to the first Diamondbacks batter in the bottom of the seventh and Arizona scored another run in the inning and Chicago lost the game 3-1. Games 2 & 3 were not as close as the Cubs lost both by the scores of 8-4 and 5-1. Chicago was outscored 16-6 in the three game sweep.

- Chicago repeated as National League Central Division champs in 2008 and had the best record in the National League. In the LDS they faced the Dodgers and were outplayed. The Cubs lost the first two games at home 7-2 and 10-3 and even though the score was closer, they weren't really close in Game 3 and lost 3-1 to lose the series in a sweep. Chicago was outscored 20-6 in the three game sweep.

Year-to-Year Figures

Team Name	League	Year	W	L	Win%	Fin	GB/GA	WS	Lge	LDS	Div	WC
Chicago Cubs	NL Cent	2010	75	87	0.463	5 of 6	16					
Chicago Cubs	NL Cent	2009	83	78	0.516	2 of 6	7.5					
Chicago Cubs	NL Cent	2008	97	64	0.602	1 of 6	+7.5				1	
Chicago Cubs	NL Cent	2007	85	77	0.525	1 of 6	+2				1	
Chicago Cubs	NL Cent	2006	66	96	0.407	6 of 6	17.5					
Chicago Cubs	NL Cent	2005	79	83	0.488	4 of 6	21					
Chicago Cubs	NL Cent	2004	89	73	0.549	3 of 6	16					
Chicago Cubs	NL Cent	2003	88	74	0.543	1 of 6	+1			1	1	
Chicago Cubs	NL Cent	2002	67	95	0.414	5 of 6	30					

Team Name	League	Year	W	L	Win%	Fin	GB/GA	WS	Lge	LDS	Div	WC
Chicago Cubs	NL Cent	2001	88	74	0.543	3 of 6	5					
Chicago Cubs	NL Cent	2000	65	97	0.401	6 of 6	30					
Chicago Cubs	NL Cent	1999	67	95	0.414	6 of 6	30					
Chicago Cubs	NL Cent	1998	90	73	0.552	2 of 6	12.5					1
Chicago Cubs	NL Cent	1997	68	94	0.420	5 of 5	16					
Chicago Cubs	NL Cent	1996	76	86	0.469	4 of 5	12					
Chicago Cubs	NL Cent	1995	73	71	0.507	3 of 5	12					
Chicago Cubs	NL Cent	1994	49	64	0.434	5 of 5	16.5					
Chicago Cubs	NL East	1993	84	78	0.519	4 of 7	13					
Chicago Cubs	NL East	1992	78	84	0.481	4 of 6	18					
Chicago Cubs	NL East	1991	77	83	0.481	4 of 6	20					
Chicago Cubs	NL East	1990	77	85	0.475	4t of 6	18					
Chicago Cubs	NL East	1989	93	69	0.574	1 of 6	+6				1	
Chicago Cubs	NL East	1988	77	85	0.475	4 of 6	24					
Chicago Cubs	NL East	1987	76	85	0.472	6 of 6	18.5					
Chicago Cubs	NL East	1986	70	90	0.438	5 of 6	37					
Chicago Cubs	NL East	1985	77	84	0.478	4 of 6	23.5					
Chicago Cubs	NL East	1984	96	65	0.596	1 of 6	+6.5				1	
Chicago Cubs	NL East	1983	71	91	0.438	5 of 6	19					
Chicago Cubs	NL East	1982	73	89	0.451	5 of 6	19					
Chicago Cubs	NL East	1981	38	65	0.369	6, 5 of 6	17.5,6					
Chicago Cubs	NL East	1980	64	98	0.395	6 of 6	27					
Chicago Cubs	NL East	1979	80	82	0.494	5 of 6	18					
Chicago Cubs	NL East	1978	79	83	0.488	3 of 6	11					
Chicago Cubs	NL East	1977	81	81	0.500	4 of 6	20					
Chicago Cubs	NL East	1976	75	87	0.463	4 of 6	26					
Chicago Cubs	NL East	1975	75	87	0.463	5t of 6	17.5					
Chicago Cubs	NL East	1974	66	96	0.407	6 of 6	22					
Chicago Cubs	NL East	1973	77	84	0.478	5 of 6	5					
Chicago Cubs	NL East	1972	85	70	0.548	2 of 6	11					
Chicago Cubs	NL East	1971	83	79	0.512	3t of 6	14					
Chicago Cubs	NL East	1970	84	78	0.519	2 of 6	5					
Chicago Cubs	NL East	1969	92	70	0.568	2 of 6	8					
Chicago Cubs	NL	1968	84	78	0.519	3 of 10	13					
Chicago Cubs	NL	1967	87	74	0.540	3 of 10	14					
Chicago Cubs	NL	1966	59	103	0.364	10 of 10	36					
Chicago Cubs	NL	1965	72	90	0.444	8 of 10	25					
Chicago Cubs	NL	1964	76	86	0.469	8 of 10	17					
Chicago Cubs	NL	1963	82	80	0.506	7 of 10	17					
Chicago Cubs	NL	1962	59	103	0.364	9 of 10	42.5					
Chicago Cubs	NL	1961	64	90	0.416	7 of 8	29					
Chicago Cubs	NL	1960	60	94	0.390	7 of 8	35					
Chicago Cubs	NL	1959	74	80	0.481	5t of 8	13					
Chicago Cubs	NL	1958	72	82	0.468	5t of 8	20					
Chicago Cubs	NL	1957	62	92	0.403	7t of 8	33					

Team Name	League	Year	W	L	Win%	Fin	GB/GA	WS	Lge	LDS	Div	WC
Chicago Cubs	NL	1956	60	94	0.390	8 of 8	33					
Chicago Cubs	NL	1955	72	81	0.471	6 of 8	26					
Chicago Cubs	NL	1954	64	90	0.416	7 of 8	33					
Chicago Cubs	NL	1953	65	89	0.422	7 of 8	40					
Chicago Cubs	NL	1952	77	77	0.500	5 of 8	19.5					
Chicago Cubs	NL	1951	62	92	0.403	8 of 8	34.5					
Chicago Cubs	NL	1950	64	89	0.418	7 of 8	26.5					
Chicago Cubs	NL	1949	61	93	0.396	8 of 8	36					
Chicago Cubs	NL	1948	64	90	0.416	8 of 8	27.5					
Chicago Cubs	NL	1947	69	85	0.448	6 of 8	25					
Chicago Cubs	NL	1946	82	71	0.536	3 of 8	14.5					
Chicago Cubs	NL	1945	98	56	0.636	1 of 8	+3		1			
Chicago Cubs	NL	1944	75	79	0.487	4 of 8	30					
Chicago Cubs	NL	1943	74	79	0.484	5 of 8	30.5					
Chicago Cubs	NL	1942	68	86	0.442	6 of 8	38					
Chicago Cubs	NL	1941	70	84	0.455	6 of 8	30					
Chicago Cubs	NL	1940	75	79	0.487	5 of 8	25.5					
Chicago Cubs	NL	1939	84	70	0.545	4 of 8	13					
Chicago Cubs	NL	1938	89	63	0.586	1 of 8	+2		1			
Chicago Cubs	NL	1937	93	61	0.604	2 of 8	3					
Chicago Cubs	NL	1936	87	67	0.565	2t of 8	5					
Chicago Cubs	NL	1935	100	54	0.649	1 of 8	+4		1			
Chicago Cubs	NL	1934	86	65	0.570	3 of 8	8					
Chicago Cubs	NL	1933	86	68	0.558	3 of 8	6					
Chicago Cubs	NL	1932	90	64	0.584	1 of 8	+4		1			
Chicago Cubs	NL	1931	84	70	0.545	3 of 8	17					
Chicago Cubs	NL	1930	90	64	0.584	2 of 8	2					
Chicago Cubs	NL	1929	98	54	0.645	1 of 8	+10.5		1			
Chicago Cubs	NL	1928	91	63	0.591	3 of 8	4					
Chicago Cubs	NL	1927	85	68	0.556	4 of 8	8.5					
Chicago Cubs	NL	1926	82	72	0.532	4 of 8	7					
Chicago Cubs	NL	1925	68	86	0.442	8 of 8	27.5					
Chicago Cubs	NL	1924	81	72	0.529	5 of 8	12					
Chicago Cubs	NL	1923	83	71	0.539	4 of 8	12.5					
Chicago Cubs	NL	1922	80	74	0.519	5 of 8	13					
Chicago Cubs	NL	1921	64	89	0.418	7 of 8	30					
Chicago Cubs	NL	1920	75	79	0.487	5t of 8	18					
Chicago Cubs	NL	1919	75	65	0.536	3 of 8	21					
Chicago Cubs	NL	1918	84	45	0.651	1 of 8	+10.5		1			
Chicago Cubs	NL	1917	74	80	0.481	5 of 8	24					
Chicago Cubs	NL	1916	67	86	0.438	5 of 8	26.5					
Chicago Cubs	NL	1915	73	80	0.477	4 of 8	17.5					
Chicago Cubs	NL	1914	78	76	0.506	4 of 8	16.5					
Chicago Cubs	NL	1913	88	65	0.575	3 of 8	13.5					
Chicago Cubs	NL	1912	91	59	0.607	3 of 8	11.5					

Team Name	League	Year	W	L	Win%	Fin	GB/GA	WS	Lge	LDS	Div	WC
Chicago Cubs	NL	1911	92	62	0.597	2 of 8	7.5					
Chicago Cubs	NL	1910	104	50	0.675	1 of 8	+13		1			
Chicago Cubs	NL	1909	104	49	0.680	2 of 8	6.5					
Chicago Cubs	NL	1908	99	55	0.643	1 of 8	+1	1	1			
Chicago Cubs	NL	1907	107	45	0.704	1 of 8	+17	1	1			
Chicago Cubs	NL	1906	116	36	0.763	1 of 8	+20		1			
Chicago Cubs	NL	1905	92	61	0.601	3 of 8	13					
Chicago Cubs	NL	1904	93	60	0.608	2 of 8	13					
Chicago Cubs	NL	1903	82	56	0.594	3 of 8	8					
Chicago Orphans	NL	1902	68	69	0.496	5 of 8	34					
Chicago Orphans	NL	1901	53	86	0.381	6 of 8	37					
Chicago Orphans	NL	1900	65	75	0.464	5t of 8	19					
Chicago Orphans	NL	1899	75	73	0.507	8 of 12	26					
Chicago Orphans	NL	1898	85	65	0.567	4 of 12	17.5					
Chicago Colts	NL	1897	59	73	0.447	9 of 12	34					
Chicago Colts	NL	1896	71	57	0.555	5 of 12	18.5					
Chicago Colts	NL	1895	72	58	0.554	4 of 12	15					
Chicago Colts	NL	1894	57	75	0.432	8 of 12	34					
Chicago Colts	NL	1893	56	71	0.441	9 of 12	29					
Chicago Colts	NL	1892	70	76	0.479	8, 7 of 12	19, 14					
Chicago Colts	NL	1891	82	53	0.607	2 of 8	3.5					
Chicago Colts	NL	1890	84	53	0.613	2 of 8	6					
Chicago White Stockings	NL	1889	67	65	0.508	3 of 8	19					
Chicago White Stockings	NL	1888	77	58	0.570	2 of 8	9					
Chicago White Stockings	NL	1887	71	50	0.587	3 of 8	6.5					
Chicago White Stockings	NL	1886	90	34	0.726	1 of 8	+2.5		1			
Chicago White Stockings	NL	1885	87	25	0.777	1 of 8	+2		1			
Chicago White Stockings	NL	1884	62	50	0.554	4t of 8	22					
Chicago White Stockings	NL	1883	59	39	0.602	2 of 8	4					
Chicago White Stockings	NL	1882	55	29	0.655	1 of 8	+3		1			
Chicago White Stockings	NL	1881	56	28	0.667	1 of 8	+9		1			
Chicago White Stockings	NL	1880	67	17	0.798	1 of 8	+15		1			
Chicago White Stockings	NL	1879	46	33	0.582	4 of 8	10.5					
Chicago White Stockings	NL	1878	30	30	0.500	4 of 6	11					
Chicago White Stockings	NL	1877	26	33	0.441	5 of 6	15.5					
Chicago White Stockings	NL	1876	52	14	0.788	1 of 8	+6		1			
Chicago White Stockings	NA	1875	30	37	0.448	6 of 13	35					
Chicago White Stockings	NA	1874	28	31	0.475	5 of 8	18.5					
Chicago White Stockings	NA	1871	19	9	0.679	2t of 9	2					
			10318	**9765**	**0.514**			**2**	**16**	**1**	**5**	**1**

Chicago White Sox

Stats

History
Year of Origin 1901

Years Played 110

Score & Rank
Total Points Score 60.6

Total Points Rank 15

Average Points Score 0.55

Average Points Rank 20

Postseason Results

Postseason Results	No.	Years
World Series Won	3	1906, 1917, 2005
League Championship Series Won	1	2005
League Division Series Won	1	2005
World Series Lost:	2	1919, 1959
League Championship Series Lost:	2	1983, 1993
League Division Series Lost:	2	2000, 2008

Postseason Won-Loss Records and Winning Percentages

	Postseason Games		Postseason Series	
All Postseason Series	28-27	.509	5-6	.455
World Series	17-13	.567	3-2	.600
League Championship Series	7-8	.467	1-2	.333
League Division Series	4-6	.400	1-2	.333

Regular Season Results
All-Time Won-Loss Record 8628-8413
All-Time Winning Percentage .... .506

	No.	Years
League Titles before 1969	5	1901, 1906, 1917, 1919, 1959
Division Titles	5	1983, 1993, 2000, 2005, 2008
Wild Cards	0	

Regular Season High & Low Points

		Year(s)
Most Wins in a Season	100	1917
Most Losses in a Season	106	1970
Highest Winning Percentage	.649	1917
Lowest Winning Percentage	.325	1932
Longest Streak with Won-Loss Record .500 or Higher	17 years	1951-1967
Longest Streak with Won-Loss Record Below .500	9 years	1927-1935

Years with .500 record or Better
1900's	8 (out of 9)
1910's	7
1920's	4
1930's	3
1940's	3
1950's	9
1960's	8
1970's	3
1980's	4
1990's	6
2000's	8
2010's	1

64 out of 110 seasons played = 58%

Years Making Postseason
1900's	1
1910's	2
1920's	0
1930's	0
1940's	0
1950's	1
1960's	0
1970's	0
1980's	1
1990's	1
2000's	3
2010's	0

9 out of 110 seasons played = 8%

Streaks

- 1906-1919: Won three League Titles and two World Series in fourteen years.
- 2000-2008: Won three Division Titles, one League Division Series, one League Championship Series, and one World Series in nine years.

Extra Bases

- On April 24th, 1901 Chicago beat Cleveland 8-2 at home in the first professional American League game.
- In 1917 the White Sox won 100 games for the first and only time.

Scoring Opportunities

1900's

- The White Sox were in a close race for the American League pennant with the Philadelphia Athletics in 1905. The two teams were tied on September 28th when they met in Philadelphia for a three game series. Chicago lost the first two games 3-2 and 11-1 and won the third game 4-3 and trailed the A's by one game after the series. The rest of the year the White Sox went 4-3 but Philadelphia went 5-2 and Chicago finished in second place two games behind the A's.
- In 1908 Chicago trailed the Tigers by 2.5 games in the American League on October 3rd with three games left in the season at home against Detroit. The White Sox needed to win all three games to win the league. They won the first two games 3-1 and 6-1 but lost the third game 7-0 and finished in third place 1.5 games out.

1910's

- The White Sox trailed Detroit in the American League by a half game on September 16th in 1916, with Boston 1.5 games back. The rest of the year Chicago went 8-5 while Detroit went 5-7. But the Red Sox went 12-4 and won the pennant and the White Sox finished in second place two games behind Boston.
- In 1919 the White Sox won the American League pennant and faced Cincinnati in a best of nine games World Series. Chicago lost Game 1 9-1 and trailed by two runs entering the ninth inning in Game 2. Their first batter up singled but then the next batter hit into a double play. Their third batter of the inning singled but their next batter up grounded out and they lost 4-2. The White Sox won Game 3 and trailed by two runs late in Game 4 when they had one runner on base in the seventh, eighth, and ninth innings but couldn't score any time and lost 2-0. Chicago lost Game 5 5-0 and fell down four games to one in the series but then won Games 6

63

& 7. The White Sox lost Game 8 10-5 and lost the series. There were rumors that the Chicago players were throwing the games on purpose for money throughout the series.

1920's

• A year later the truth about the 1919 World Series was revealed. With three games left in the 1920 American League regular season, eight White Sox players were suspended for the season and banned from baseball for life for receiving money from gamblers to lose the 1919 World Series on purpose. At the time, Chicago trailed Cleveland by a half game with three games left to play, but the White Sox lost two of their last three games of the year and finished the season in second place two games behind the Indians.

1950's

• In 1959 Chicago won the American League pennant and played the Dodgers in the World Series, where they won Game 1 11-0. In Game 2 the White Sox trailed by two runs in the bottom of the eighth inning when their first two batters of the inning both singled. Their third batter doubled which drove in one run, but the runner that started on first tried to score the tying run and was thrown out at home plate. Chicago had a runner on third with one out but their next two batters struck out and fouled out and the White Sox lost the game 4-3. In Game 3 Chicago trailed by two runs after seven innings and had the bases loaded in the top of the eighth with no outs. Their next batter hit into a double play, and one run scored, but the following batter popped out and left the tying run at third. The White Sox gave up a run in the bottom of the eighth and lost the game 3-1. Game 4 was tied at four heading into the bottom of the eighth, but Chicago gave up a solo home run to the first Dodgers batter of the inning. The White Sox were retired in order in the top of the ninth and lost 5-4. Chicago won Game 5 but lost Game 6 9-3 and lost the series.

1960's

• The White Sox were a close race with New York and Baltimore in 1964. Chicago was tied for the lead with the Orioles on September 16th and the Yankees were a half game out. The White Sox went 10-3 the rest of the season, and won their last nine games of the year. But New York went 14-4 the rest of the year and Chicago finished one game behind the Yankees in the standings.

• Chicago was in a very close four-team race the entire 1967 American League regular season with Boston, Detroit, and Minnesota. On September 24th the White Sox were in third place only one game behind the league leading Twins. The Red Sox were a half-game out, and Detroit was 1.5 games out. But Chicago lost their last five games of the season and finished in fourth place three games behind the pennant winner Boston. The Red Sox went 2-2 after the 24th, Minnesota went 1-4, and the Tigers went 3-3.

64

1980's

- In 1983 Chicago won the American League West Division and in the LCS they met the Orioles and won Game 1. The White Sox lost Game 2 4-0 and Game 3 11-1. Game 4 was tied at zero after eight innings. In the bottom of the ninth Chicago had runners on second and third with two outs, but their next batter up struck out. In the top of the tenth Chicago gave up three runs and they lost the game 3-0 to lose the series.

1990's

- Chicago won the American League West Division in 1993 and faced Toronto in the LCS, where they lost Game 1 7-3. In Game 2 the White Sox trailed by two runs in the bottom of the seventh when had runners on first and second with two outs, but their next batter struck out. Chicago got their first batter on base in the bottom of the ninth but their next three hitters all got out and they lost 3-1. The White Sox won Games 3 & 4 but lost Game 5 5-3. In Game 6 Chicago was only down by one run after eight innings, but they gave up three runs in the top of the ninth and lost the game 6-3 to lose the series.
- In 1996 the White Sox finished 14.5 games behind Cleveland in the American League Central Division race but were in the wild card race towards the end of the season with Baltimore. On September 24th, Chicago was only 1.5 games behind the Orioles for the wild card spot but the White Sox lost three of their last four games while Baltimore won three of their last five and Chicago finished three games back in the standings for the final playoff spot.

2000's

- The White Sox won the American League Central Division in 2000 and played Seattle in the LDS. Game 1 was tied at four after nine innings. In the top of the tenth Chicago gave up three runs on two home runs and they lost the game 7-4. The White Sox lost Game 2 5-2 and Game 3 was tied at one after eight innings. In the bottom of the ninth Chicago gave up a single, committed an error, and walked a batter. The next Mariners batter hit a bunt for a single and the White Sox lost 2-1 and lost the series in a sweep.
- In 2008 Chicago beat Minnesota in a one game playoff for the American League Central Division title. The White Sox played Tampa Bay in the LDS. In Game 1 Chicago trailed by three runs in the top of the seventh inning when they had the bases loaded with one out, but their next two batters both struck out. They hit a solo home run in the top of the ninth inning and lost the game 6-4. In Game 2 the White Sox trailed by one run in the top of the seventh when they got their first two runners on base, but their next three batters all got out. Tampa scored three runs in the bottom of the eighth inning and Chicago lost the game 6-2. The White Sox won Game 3, but lost Game 4 6-2 and lost the series.

Year-to-Year Figures

Team Name	League	Year	W	L	Win%	Fin	GB/GA	WS	Lge	LDS	Div	WC
Chicago White Sox	AL Cent	2010	88	74	0.543	2 of 5	6					
Chicago White Sox	AL Cent	2009	79	83	0.488	3 of 5	7.5					
Chicago White Sox	AL Cent	2008	89	74	0.546	1 of 5	+1				1	
Chicago White Sox	AL Cent	2007	72	90	0.444	4 of 5	24					
Chicago White Sox	AL Cent	2006	90	72	0.556	3 of 5	6					
Chicago White Sox	AL Cent	2005	99	63	0.611	1 of 5	+6	1	1	1	1	
Chicago White Sox	AL Cent	2004	83	79	0.512	2 of 5	9					
Chicago White Sox	AL Cent	2003	86	76	0.531	2 of 5	4					
Chicago White Sox	AL Cent	2002	81	81	0.500	2 of 5	13.5					
Chicago White Sox	AL Cent	2001	83	79	0.512	3 of 5	8					
Chicago White Sox	AL Cent	2000	95	67	0.586	1 of 5	+5				1	
Chicago White Sox	AL Cent	1999	75	86	0.466	2 of 5	21.5					
Chicago White Sox	AL Cent	1998	80	82	0.494	2 of 5	9					
Chicago White Sox	AL Cent	1997	80	81	0.497	2 of 5	6					
Chicago White Sox	AL Cent	1996	85	77	0.525	2 of 5	14.5					
Chicago White Sox	AL Cent	1995	68	76	0.472	3 of 5	32					
Chicago White Sox	AL Cent	1994	67	46	0.593	1 of 5	+1					
Chicago White Sox	AL West	1993	94	68	0.580	1 of 7	+8				1	
Chicago White Sox	AL West	1992	86	76	0.531	3 of 7	10					
Chicago White Sox	AL West	1991	87	75	0.537	2 of 7	8					
Chicago White Sox	AL West	1990	94	68	0.580	2 of 7	9					
Chicago White Sox	AL West	1989	69	92	0.429	7 of 7	29.5					
Chicago White Sox	AL West	1988	71	90	0.441	5 of 7	32.5					
Chicago White Sox	AL West	1987	77	85	0.475	5 of 7	8					
Chicago White Sox	AL West	1986	72	90	0.444	5 of 7	20					
Chicago White Sox	AL West	1985	85	77	0.525	3 of 7	6					
Chicago White Sox	AL West	1984	74	88	0.457	5t of 7	10					
Chicago White Sox	AL West	1983	99	63	0.611	1 of 7	+20				1	
Chicago White Sox	AL West	1982	87	75	0.537	3 of 7	6					
Chicago White Sox	AL West	1981	54	52	0.509	3, 6 of 7	2.5, 7					
Chicago White Sox	AL West	1980	70	90	0.438	5 of 7	26					
Chicago White Sox	AL West	1979	73	87	0.456	5 of 7	14					
Chicago White Sox	AL West	1978	71	90	0.441	5 of 7	20.5					
Chicago White Sox	AL West	1977	90	72	0.556	3 of 7	12					
Chicago White Sox	AL West	1976	64	97	0.398	6 of 6	25.5					
Chicago White Sox	AL West	1975	75	86	0.466	5 of 6	22.5					
Chicago White Sox	AL West	1974	80	80	0.500	4 of 6	9					
Chicago White Sox	AL West	1973	77	85	0.475	5 of 6	17					
Chicago White Sox	AL West	1972	87	67	0.565	2 of 6	5.5					
Chicago White Sox	AL West	1971	79	83	0.488	3 of 6	22.5					
Chicago White Sox	AL West	1970	56	106	0.346	6 of 6	42					
Chicago White Sox	AL West	1969	68	94	0.420	5 of 6	29					
Chicago White Sox	AL	1968	67	95	0.414	8t of 10	36					

Team Name	League	Year	W	L	Win%	Fin	GB/GA	WS	Lge	LDS	Div	WC
Chicago White Sox	AL	1967	89	73	0.549	4 of 10	3					
Chicago White Sox	AL	1966	83	79	0.512	4 of 10	15					
Chicago White Sox	AL	1965	95	67	0.586	2 of 10	7					
Chicago White Sox	AL	1964	98	64	0.605	2 of 10	1					
Chicago White Sox	AL	1963	94	68	0.580	2 of 10	10.5					
Chicago White Sox	AL	1962	85	77	0.525	5 of 10	11					
Chicago White Sox	AL	1961	86	76	0.531	4 of 10	23					
Chicago White Sox	AL	1960	87	67	0.565	3 of 8	10					
Chicago White Sox	AL	1959	94	60	0.610	1 of 8	+5		1			
Chicago White Sox	AL	1958	82	72	0.532	2 of 8	10					
Chicago White Sox	AL	1957	90	64	0.584	2 of 8	8					
Chicago White Sox	AL	1956	85	69	0.552	3 of 8	12					
Chicago White Sox	AL	1955	91	63	0.591	3 of 8	5					
Chicago White Sox	AL	1954	94	60	0.610	3 of 8	17					
Chicago White Sox	AL	1953	89	65	0.578	3 of 8	11.5					
Chicago White Sox	AL	1952	81	73	0.526	3 of 8	14					
Chicago White Sox	AL	1951	81	73	0.526	4 of 8	17					
Chicago White Sox	AL	1950	60	94	0.390	6 of 8	38					
Chicago White Sox	AL	1949	63	91	0.409	6 of 8	34					
Chicago White Sox	AL	1948	51	101	0.336	8 of 8	44.5					
Chicago White Sox	AL	1947	70	84	0.455	6 of 8	27					
Chicago White Sox	AL	1946	74	80	0.481	5 of 8	30					
Chicago White Sox	AL	1945	71	78	0.477	6 of 8	15					
Chicago White Sox	AL	1944	71	83	0.461	7 of 8	18					
Chicago White Sox	AL	1943	82	72	0.532	4 of 8	16					
Chicago White Sox	AL	1942	66	82	0.446	6 of 8	34					
Chicago White Sox	AL	1941	77	77	0.500	3 of 8	24					
Chicago White Sox	AL	1940	82	72	0.532	4t of 8	8					
Chicago White Sox	AL	1939	85	69	0.552	4 of 8	22.5					
Chicago White Sox	AL	1938	65	83	0.439	6 of 8	32					
Chicago White Sox	AL	1937	86	68	0.558	3 of 8	16					
Chicago White Sox	AL	1936	81	70	0.536	3 of 8	20					
Chicago White Sox	AL	1935	74	78	0.487	5 of 8	19.5					
Chicago White Sox	AL	1934	53	99	0.349	8 of 8	47					
Chicago White Sox	AL	1933	67	83	0.447	6 of 8	31					
Chicago White Sox	AL	1932	49	102	0.325	7 of 8	56.5					
Chicago White Sox	AL	1931	56	97	0.366	8 of 8	51					
Chicago White Sox	AL	1930	62	92	0.403	7 of 8	40					
Chicago White Sox	AL	1929	59	93	0.388	7 of 8	46					
Chicago White Sox	AL	1928	72	82	0.468	5 of 8	29					
Chicago White Sox	AL	1927	70	83	0.458	5 of 8	29.5					
Chicago White Sox	AL	1926	81	72	0.529	5 of 8	9.5					
Chicago White Sox	AL	1925	79	75	0.513	5 of 8	18.5					
Chicago White Sox	AL	1924	66	87	0.431	8 of 8	25.5					
Chicago White Sox	AL	1923	69	85	0.448	7 of 8	30					

Chicago White Sox

Team Name	League	Year	W	L	Win%	Fin	GB/GA	WS	Lge	LDS	Div	WC
Chicago White Sox	AL	1922	77	77	0.500	5 of 8	17					
Chicago White Sox	AL	1921	62	92	0.403	7 of 8	36.5					
Chicago White Sox	AL	1920	96	58	0.623	2 of 8	2					
Chicago White Sox	AL	1919	88	52	0.629	1 of 8	+3.5		1			
Chicago White Sox	AL	1918	57	67	0.460	6 of 8	17					
Chicago White Sox	AL	1917	100	54	0.649	1 of 8	+9	1	1			
Chicago White Sox	AL	1916	89	65	0.578	2 of 8	2					
Chicago White Sox	AL	1915	93	61	0.604	3 of 8	9.5					
Chicago White Sox	AL	1914	70	84	0.455	6t of 8	30					
Chicago White Sox	AL	1913	78	74	0.513	5 of 8	17.5					
Chicago White Sox	AL	1912	78	76	0.506	4 of 8	28					
Chicago White Sox	AL	1911	77	74	0.510	4 of 8	24					
Chicago White Sox	AL	1910	68	85	0.444	6 of 8	35.5					
Chicago White Sox	AL	1909	78	74	0.513	4 of 8	20					
Chicago White Sox	AL	1908	88	64	0.579	3 of 8	1.5					
Chicago White Sox	AL	1907	87	64	0.576	3 of 8	5.5					
Chicago White Sox	AL	1906	93	58	0.616	1 of 8	+3	1	1			
Chicago White Sox	AL	1905	92	60	0.605	2 of 8	2					
Chicago White Sox	AL	1904	89	65	0.578	3 of 8	6					
Chicago White Sox	AL	1903	60	77	0.438	7 of 8	30.5					
Chicago White Sox	AL	1902	74	60	0.552	4 of 8	8					
Chicago White Stockings	AL	1901	83	53	0.610	1 of 8	+4		1			
			8628	8413	0.506			3	6	1	5	0

Cincinnati Reds

Stats

History
Year of Origin 1882   Years Played 129

Score & Rank
Total Points Score .... 100.8   Average Points Score 0.78
Total Points Rank 8   Average Points Rank 12

Postseason Results

Postseason Results	No.	Years
World Series Won	5	1919, 1940, 1975, 1976, 1990
League Championship Series Won	5	1970, 1972, 1975, 1976, 1990
League Division Series Won	1	1995
World Series Lost	4	1939, 1961, 1970, 1972
League Championship Series Lost	3	1973, 1979, 1995
League Division Series Lost	1	2010

Postseason Won-Loss Records and Winning Percentages

	Postseason Games		Postseason Series	
All Postseason Series	47-42	.528	11-8	.579
World Series	26-25	.510	5-4	.556
League Championship Series	18-14	.563	5-3	.625
League Division Series	3-3	.500	1-1	.500

Regular Season Results
All-Time Won-Loss Record 9915-9619
All-Time Winning Percentage .... .508

	No.	Years
League Titles before 1969	5	1882, 1919, 1939, 1940, 1961
Division Titles	9	1970, 1972, 1973, 1975, 1976, 1979, 1990, 1995, 2010
Wild Cards	0	

Regular Season High & Low Points

		Year(s)
Most Wins in a Season	108	1975
Most Losses in a Season	101	1982
Highest Winning Percentage	.688	1882
Lowest Winning Percentage	.344	1934
Longest Streak with Won-Loss Record .500 or Higher	10 years	1972-1981
Longest Streak with Won-Loss Record Below .500	11 years	1945-1955

Years with .500 record or Better		Years Making Postseason	
1880's	7 (out of 8)	1880's	No Postseason
1890's	8	1890's	No Postseason
1900's	5	1900's	0
1910's	3	1910's	1
1920's	7	1920's	0
1930's	2	1930's	1
1940's	5	1940's	1
1950's	2	1950's	0
1960's	8	1960's	1
1970's	9	1970's	6
1980's	6	1980's	0
1990's	6	1990's	2
2000's	1	2000's	0
2010's:	1	2010's	1
70 out of 129 seasons played = 54%		13 out of 129 seasons played = 10%	

Streaks

• 1970-1979: Won two World Series, four League Championship Series, and six Division Titles in ten years.

Extra Bases

• There was a National League Cincinnati Reds team that played from 1876-1880 but that team is not connected to the present franchise. That team was kicked out of the National League after the 1880 season, and a new team was formed that played in the American Association starting in 1882.

• The Reds played in the last tripleheader in baseball history on October 2nd, 1920, beating the Pirates in two out of three games in Pittsburgh. Cincinnati won the first two games 13-4 and 7-3, and lost the third game 6-0.

• On May 24th, 1935 in Cincinnati, the Reds beat Philadelphia 2-1 in the first 'night' baseball game in history.

• In 2010 the Reds lost Game 1 of LDS against Philadelphia 4-0 and got no hits. This was the second no hitter in baseball postseason history.

• Cincinnati's 85th win in the 2011 season will be their 10,000th of their franchise history. If they win that many.

Scoring Opportunities

1920's

• In 1926 the Reds were in a close race for the National League pennant with the Cardinals as

70

the two teams were tied for first place on September 16th. The rest of the season St. Louis went 7-5 but Cincinnati lost seven of their last nine games and the Reds finished in second place two games back.

1930's

• Cincinnati won the National League pennant in 1939 and faced the Yankees in the World Series. Game 1 was tied at one heading into the bottom of the ninth. The Reds got the first Yankees batter out but then gave up a triple. Cincinnati walked the next New York batter intentionally to try to get a double play, but gave up a single to the following batter and let in the game winning run and lost 2-1. The Reds lost Game 2 4-0 and Game 3 7-3. In Game 4 Cincinnati led 4-2 after eight innings, but in the top of the ninth they gave up three hits, one error, and two runs and the game went into extra innings. In the top of the tenth the Reds gave up three errors, one hit, and three runs. In the bottom of the inning Cincinnati got their first two batters on base but their next three batters all got out and Cincinnati lost the game 7-4 and lost the World Series in a sweep.

1950's

• In 1956 the Reds were in a close race for the National League pennant with the Braves and Dodgers. Cincinnati only trailed Milwaukee and Brooklyn by two games on September 15th, but the Reds lost four games in a row, including two against the Dodgers, and fell to 4.5 games back in the standings on September 18th, with the Braves still tied with Brooklyn. Cincinnati won eight of their last nine games of the season but still finished in third place two games behind the Dodgers, who went 6-4 after the 18th. Milwaukee went 4-4 after the 18th and finished in second place one game out.

1960's

• Cincinnati won the National League pennant in 1961 and played the Yankees in the World Series. In Game 1 the Reds were held to two hits and lost the game 2-0. They won Game 2 and in Game 3 they had a 2-1 lead after seven innings. But in the top of the eighth Cincinnati gave up a home run that tied the game and they gave up another home run in the top of the ninth that gave New York the lead. In the bottom of the ninth the Reds had a runner on second base with one out, but their next two batters both grounded out and they lost 3-2. The Reds lost Game 4 7-0 and Game 5 13-5 to lose the series. They were outscored 25-7 in their four losses.

• In 1964 the Reds were in fourth place in the National League 8.5 games behind the Phillies on September 15th and appeared to be out of the pennant race. But Cincinnati won twelve of their next thirteen games and they were in first place by one game on September 27th. However, the Reds lost two out of three against Pittsburgh and lost one game to the Phillies and were tied for first place with St. Louis with one game left in the season. On the last day of the year Cincinnati lost to Philadelphia and the Cardinals beat the Mets and the Reds finished in second place tied with the Phillies one game behind St. Louis. After September 27th Cincinnati went 1-4 and the Cardinals went 4-2.

1970's

- Cincinnati won the National League West Division in 1970 and swept the Pirates in the LCS. In the World Series the Reds faced Baltimore and Game 1 was tied at three after six innings. Cincinnati gave up a home run in the top of the seventh and in the bottom of the inning they had a runner on second base with two outs, but their next batter grounded out. In the bottom of the ninth the Reds had a man on first with two outs but their next batter lined out and they lost 4-3. In Game 2 the Reds trailed by one run after six innings. They had runners on first and second with one out in the bottom of the seventh but their next two batters fouled out and grounded out. In the bottom of the ninth with two outs their batter hit a deep fly ball to center field but it stayed in the park and they lost 6-5. Cincinnati lost Game 3 9-3, won Game 4, but lost Game 5 9-3 and lost the series.

- In 1972 the Reds won the National League West Division and beat Pittsburgh again in the LCS. In the World Series Cincinnati faced Oakland and in Game 1 the Reds trailed by one run when they had runners on first and second in the bottom of the seventh inning with two outs, but their next batter fouled out. They got their first batter up on base in the bottom of the ninth but their next three hitters all got out and they lost 3-2. In Game 2 Cincinnati trailed by two runs in the bottom of the ninth inning when they scored one run and had a runner on first with two outs, but their next batter flied out and they lost 2-1. The Reds won Game 3 and led Game 4 2-1 heading into the bottom of the ninth inning. They got the first A's batter out but then gave up four straight singles and two runs and lost 3-2. Cincinnati won Games 5 and 6 to even the series. In Game 7 the Reds trailed by two runs in the bottom of the eighth inning when they had the bases loaded with one out. Their next batter hit a sacrifice fly that drove in one run. They were now down by one run and had runners on second and third and two outs, but their next batter flied out. In the bottom of the ninth Cincinnati had a runner on first with two outs but their next batter up flied out and they lost the game 3-2 and lost the series. Six of the seven games in the series and all four Cincinnati losses were decided by one run.

- Cincinnati repeated as National League West Division champs in 1973 and played the Mets in the LCS, where they won Game 1. In Game 2 the Reds only trailed by one run after eight innings. But in the top of the ninth they gave up four runs and they lost the game 5-0. Cincinnati lost Game 3 9-2, won Game 4 in twelve innings, but lost Game 5 7-2 to lose the series.

- In 1979 the Reds won the National League West Division and met the Pirates in the LCS. Game 1 was tied at two after nine innings. In the top of the eleventh Cincinnati gave up a three-run home run. In the bottom of the inning the Reds loaded the bases with two outs but their next batter struck up out and they lost 5-2. Game 2 was also tied at two after nine innings. In the top of the tenth Cincinnati gave up a single, a sacrifice bunt, and another single to the first three batters of the inning and let in the go-ahead run. The Reds were retired in order in the bottom of the inning and lost the game 3-2. Cincinnati lost Game 3 7-1 and lost the series in a sweep.

1980's

• Cincinnati finished the 1981 season with the best record in the National League but did not make the playoffs. There was a players strike in the middle of the season and the playoff format was restructured so that the winners of the first half of the season and the winners of the second half of the season of each division made the playoffs. In the National League West, the Reds finished a half game behind Los Angeles in the first half of the season, and in the second half of the season they ended the year 1.5 games behind Houston. Cincinnati had the best regular season won-loss record in the NL or AL in 1981.

1990's

• In 1995 the Reds won the National League Central Division. In the LDS they beat the Dodgers and in the LCS they played the Braves and had a one run lead after eight innings of Game 1. In the top of the ninth Cincinnati gave up singles to the first two Atlanta batters and the Braves had runners on first and third with no outs. The next Atlanta batter hit a ground ball to the second baseman and the Reds got an out at second and let the tying run score. Cincinnati did not bring the infield in because they did not want the Braves to have a big inning. The game went into extra innings and in the top of the eleventh the Reds gave up a single with two outs that drove in the go-ahead run. Cincinnati had runners on first and second with one out in the bottom of the inning but their next batter hit into a double play and they lost 2-1. Game 2 was tied at two in the bottom of the eighth inning when the Reds first batter up hit a double and then stole third to reach third base with no outs. But Cincinnati couldn't drive him in and the game went into extra innings. In the top of the tenth the Reds gave up two singles, a walk, a wild pitch, a three-run home run, and four runs and they lost the game 6-2. Cincinnati lost Game 3 5-2 and Game 4 6-0 and lost the series in a sweep.

• Cincinnati had a one game lead in the National League Central Division over Houston on September 28th in 1999 but then lost three of their last four games while the Astros won three of their final four. The Reds finished the regular season 1.5 games behind the Astros for the division, but tied the Mets for the wild card spot. A one game playoff was needed to determine the final playoff spot. Cincinnati was the home team in the playoff game, but they only got two hits in the game and lost it 5-0 and missed the playoffs.

2010's

• The Reds won the National League Central Division in 2010 and played Philadelphia in the LDS. In Game 1 Cincinnati got no hits and lost the game 4-0. It was the second no hitter ever in baseball postseason history. In Game 2 the Reds had a 4-3 lead in the bottom of the seventh inning, but they hit the first Phillies batter, and then on a fielders choice play the Philadelphia runner was called safe at second base even though he was really out. The next Phillies batter hit a fly ball to right field and the Cincinnati right fielder lost the ball in the lights and let the tying and go-ahead runs score. The Reds lost the game 7-4. In Game 3 Cincinnati only had five hits and only had two after the fourth inning. They lost the game 2-0 and lost the series in a sweep, being outscored 13-4 in the three games.

Year-to-Year Figures

Team Name	League	Year	W	L	Win%	Fin	GB/GA	WS	Lge	LDS	Div	WC
Cincinnati Reds	NL Cent	2010	91	71	0.562	1 of 6	+5				1	
Cincinnati Reds	NL Cent	2009	78	84	0.481	4 of 6	13					
Cincinnati Reds	NL Cent	2008	74	88	0.457	5 of 6	23.5					
Cincinnati Reds	NL Cent	2007	72	90	0.444	5 of 6	13					
Cincinnati Reds	NL Cent	2006	80	82	0.494	3 of 6	3.5					
Cincinnati Reds	NL Cent	2005	73	89	0.451	5 of 6	27					
Cincinnati Reds	NL Cent	2004	76	86	0.469	4 of 6	29					
Cincinnati Reds	NL Cent	2003	69	93	0.426	5 of 6	19					
Cincinnati Reds	NL Cent	2002	78	84	0.481	3 of 6	19					
Cincinnati Reds	NL Cent	2001	66	96	0.407	5 of 6	27					
Cincinnati Reds	NL Cent	2000	85	77	0.525	2 of 6	10					
Cincinnati Reds	NL Cent	1999	96	67	0.589	2 of 6	1.5					
Cincinnati Reds	NL Cent	1998	77	85	0.475	4 of 6	25					
Cincinnati Reds	NL Cent	1997	76	86	0.469	3 of 5	8					
Cincinnati Reds	NL Cent	1996	81	81	0.500	3 of 5	7					
Cincinnati Reds	NL Cent	1995	85	59	0.590	1 of 5	+9			1	1	
Cincinnati Reds	NL Cent	1994	66	48	0.579	1 of 5	+0.5*					
Cincinnati Reds	NL West	1993	73	89	0.451	5 of 7	31					
Cincinnati Reds	NL West	1992	90	72	0.556	2 of 6	8					
Cincinnati Reds	NL West	1991	74	88	0.457	5 of 6	20					
Cincinnati Reds	NL West	1990	91	71	0.562	1 of 6	+5	1	1		1	
Cincinnati Reds	NL West	1989	75	87	0.463	5 of 6	17					
Cincinnati Reds	NL West	1988	87	74	0.540	2 of 6	7					
Cincinnati Reds	NL West	1987	84	78	0.519	2 of 6	6					
Cincinnati Reds	NL West	1986	86	76	0.531	2 of 6	10					
Cincinnati Reds	NL West	1985	89	72	0.553	2 of 6	5.5					
Cincinnati Reds	NL West	1984	70	92	0.432	5 of 6	22					
Cincinnati Reds	NL West	1983	74	88	0.457	6 of 6	17					
Cincinnati Reds	NL West	1982	61	101	0.377	6 of 6	28					
Cincinnati Reds	NL West	1981	66	42	0.611	2, 2 of 6	0.5**, 1.5					
Cincinnati Reds	NL West	1980	89	73	0.549	3 of 6	3.5					
Cincinnati Reds	NL West	1979	90	71	0.559	1 of 6	+1.5				1	
Cincinnati Reds	NL West	1978	92	69	0.571	2 of 6	2.5					

Team Name	League	Year	W	L	Win%	Fin	GB/GA	WS	Lge	LDS	Div	WC
Cincinnati Reds	NL West	1977	88	74	0.543	2 of 6	10					
Cincinnati Reds	NL West	1976	102	60	0.630	1 of 6	+10	1	1		1	
Cincinnati Reds	NL West	1975	108	54	0.667	1 of 6	+20	1	1		1	
Cincinnati Reds	NL West	1974	98	64	0.605	2 of 6	4					
Cincinnati Reds	NL West	1973	99	63	0.611	1 of 6	+3.5				1	
Cincinnati Reds	NL West	1972	95	59	0.617	1 of 6	+10.5		1		1	
Cincinnati Reds	NL West	1971	79	83	0.488	4t of 6	11					
Cincinnati Reds	NL West	1970	102	60	0.630	1 of 6	+14.5		1		1	
Cincinnati Reds	NL West	1969	89	73	0.549	3 of 6	4					
Cincinnati Reds	NL	1968	83	79	0.512	4 of 10	14					
Cincinnati Reds	NL	1967	87	75	0.537	4 of 10	14.5					
Cincinnati Reds	NL	1966	76	84	0.475	7 of 10	18					
Cincinnati Reds	NL	1965	89	73	0.549	4 of 10	8					
Cincinnati Reds	NL	1964	92	70	0.568	2t of 10	1					
Cincinnati Reds	NL	1963	86	76	0.531	5 of 10	13					
Cincinnati Reds	NL	1962	98	64	0.605	3 of 10	3.5					
Cincinnati Reds	NL	1961	93	61	0.604	1 of 8	+4		1			
Cincinnati Reds	NL	1960	67	87	0.435	6 of 8	28					
Cincinnati Redlegs	NL	1959	74	80	0.481	5t of 8	13					
Cincinnati Redlegs	NL	1958	76	78	0.494	4 of 8	16					
Cincinnati Redlegs	NL	1957	80	74	0.519	4 of 8	15					
Cincinnati Redlegs	NL	1956	91	63	0.591	3 of 8	2					
Cincinnati Redlegs	NL	1955	75	79	0.487	5 of 8	23.5					
Cincinnati Redlegs	NL	1954	74	80	0.481	5 of 8	23					
Cincinnati Reds	NL	1953	68	86	0.442	6 of 8	37					
Cincinnati Reds	NL	1952	69	85	0.448	6 of 8	27.5					
Cincinnati Reds	NL	1951	68	86	0.442	6 of 8	28.5					
Cincinnati Reds	NL	1950	66	87	0.431	6 of 8	24.5					
Cincinnati Reds	NL	1949	62	92	0.403	7 of 8	35					
Cincinnati Reds	NL	1948	64	89	0.418	7 of 8	27					
Cincinnati Reds	NL	1947	73	81	0.474	5 of 8	21					
Cincinnati Reds	NL	1946	67	87	0.435	6 of 8	30					
Cincinnati Reds	NL	1945	61	93	0.396	7 of 8	37					
Cincinnati Reds	NL	1944	89	65	0.578	3 of 8	16					
Cincinnati Reds	NL	1943	87	67	0.565	2 of 8	18					
Cincinnati Reds	NL	1942	76	76	0.500	4 of 8	29					
Cincinnati Reds	NL	1941	88	66	0.571	3 of 8	12					
Cincinnati Reds	NL	1940	100	53	0.654	1 of 8	+12	1	1			
Cincinnati Reds	NL	1939	97	57	0.630	1 of 8	+4.5		1			
Cincinnati Reds	NL	1938	82	68	0.547	4 of 8	6					
Cincinnati Reds	NL	1937	56	98	0.364	8 of 8	40					
Cincinnati Reds	NL	1936	74	80	0.481	5 of 8	18					
Cincinnati Reds	NL	1935	68	85	0.444	6 of 8	31.5					
Cincinnati Reds	NL	1934	52	99	0.344	8 of 8	42					
Cincinnati Reds	NL	1933	58	94	0.382	8 of 8	33					

75

Team Name	League	Year	W	L	Win%	Fin	GB/GA	WS	Lge	LDS	Div	WC
Cincinnati Reds	NL	1932	60	94	0.390	8 of 8	30					
Cincinnati Reds	NL	1931	58	96	0.377	8 of 8	43					
Cincinnati Reds	NL	1930	59	95	0.383	7 of 8	33					
Cincinnati Reds	NL	1929	66	88	0.429	7 of 8	33					
Cincinnati Reds	NL	1928	78	74	0.513	5 of 8	16					
Cincinnati Reds	NL	1927	75	78	0.490	5 of 8	18.5					
Cincinnati Reds	NL	1926	87	67	0.565	2 of 8	2					
Cincinnati Reds	NL	1925	80	73	0.523	3 of 8	15					
Cincinnati Reds	NL	1924	83	70	0.542	4 of 8	10					
Cincinnati Reds	NL	1923	91	63	0.591	2 of 8	4.5					
Cincinnati Reds	NL	1922	86	68	0.558	2 of 8	7					
Cincinnati Reds	NL	1921	70	83	0.458	6 of 8	24					
Cincinnati Reds	NL	1920	82	71	0.536	3 of 8	10.5					
Cincinnati Reds	NL	1919	96	44	0.686	1 of 8	+9	1	1			
Cincinnati Reds	NL	1918	68	60	0.531	3 of 8	15.5					
Cincinnati Reds	NL	1917	78	76	0.506	4 of 8	20					
Cincinnati Reds	NL	1916	60	93	0.392	7t of 8	33.5					
Cincinnati Reds	NL	1915	71	83	0.461	7 of 8	20					
Cincinnati Reds	NL	1914	60	94	0.390	8 of 8	34.5					
Cincinnati Reds	NL	1913	64	89	0.418	7 of 8	37.5					
Cincinnati Reds	NL	1912	75	78	0.490	4 of 8	29					
Cincinnati Reds	NL	1911	70	83	0.458	6 of 8	29					
Cincinnati Reds	NL	1910	75	79	0.487	5 of 8	29					
Cincinnati Reds	NL	1909	77	76	0.503	4 of 8	33.5					
Cincinnati Reds	NL	1908	73	81	0.474	5 of 8	26					
Cincinnati Reds	NL	1907	66	87	0.431	6 of 8	41.5					
Cincinnati Reds	NL	1906	64	87	0.424	6 of 8	51.5					
Cincinnati Reds	NL	1905	79	74	0.516	5 of 8	26					
Cincinnati Reds	NL	1904	88	65	0.575	3 of 8	18					
Cincinnati Reds	NL	1903	74	65	0.532	4 of 8	16.5					
Cincinnati Reds	NL	1902	70	70	0.500	4 of 8	33.5					
Cincinnati Reds	NL	1901	52	87	0.374	8 of 8	38					
Cincinnati Reds	NL	1900	62	77	0.446	7 of 8	21.5					
Cincinnati Reds	NL	1899	83	67	0.553	6 of 12	19					
Cincinnati Reds	NL	1898	92	60	0.605	3 of 12	11.5					
Cincinnati Reds	NL	1897	76	56	0.576	4 of 12	17					
Cincinnati Reds	NL	1896	77	50	0.606	3 of 12	12					
Cincinnati Reds	NL	1895	66	64	0.508	8 of 12	21					
Cincinnati Reds	NL	1894	55	75	0.423	10 of 12	35					
Cincinnati Reds	NL	1893	65	63	0.508	6t of 12	20.5					
Cincinnati Reds	NL	1892	82	68	0.547	4, 8 of 12	8.5, 14.5					
Cincinnati Reds	NL	1891	56	81	0.409	7 of 8	30.5					
Cincinnati Reds	NL	1890	77	55	0.583	4 of 8	10.5					
Cincinnati Red Stockings	AA	1889	76	63	0.547	4 of 8	18					
Cincinnati Red Stockings	AA	1888	80	54	0.597	4 of 8	11.5					

Baseball Franchise Rankings

Team Name	League	Year	W	L	Win%	Fin	GB/GA	WS	Lge	LDS	Div	WC
Cincinnati Red Stockings	AA	1887	81	54	0.600	2 of 8	14					
Cincinnati Red Stockings	AA	1886	65	73	0.471	5 of 8	27.5					
Cincinnati Red Stockings	AA	1885	63	49	0.563	2 of 8	16					
Cincinnati Red Stockings	AA	1884	68	41	0.624	5 of 13	8					
Cincinnati Red Stockings	AA	1883	61	37	0.622	3 of 8	5					
Cincinnati Red Stockings	AA	1882	55	25	0.688	1 of 6	+11.5		1			
			9915	9619	0.508			5	10	1	9	0

* In 1994 the regular season ended early because of players' strike that started on August 12th. At that point in the season Cincinnati and Houston had played an uneven amount of games, and the Reds led the Astros by 0.5 games on that date.

** The 1981 season was divided into two halves due to a players strike in the middle of the season. The strike began on June 12 and up to that point in the season Cincinnati and Los Angeles had played an uneven amount of games and the Dodgers led the Reds by 0.5 games on that date.

Cleveland Indians

Stats

History

Year of Origin	1901	Years Played	110

Score & Rank

Total Points Score	58.9	Average Points Score	0.54
Total Points Rank	16	Average Points Rank	21 tied

Postseason Results

	No.	Years
World Series Won	2	1920, 1948
League Championship Series Won	2	1995, 1997
League Division Series Won	4	1995, 1997, 1998, 2007
World Series Lost	3	1954, 1995, 1997
League Championship Series Lost	2	1998, 2007
League Division Series Lost	3	1996, 1999, 2001

Postseason Won-Loss Records and Winning Percentages

	Postseason Games		Postseason Series	
All Postseason Series	44-41	.518	8-8	.500
World Series	14-16	.467	2-3	.400
League Championship Series	13-12	.520	2-2	.500
League Division Series	17-13	.567	4-3	.571

Regular Season Results

All-Time Won-Loss Record	8691-8367
All-Time Winning Percentage	.509

	No.	Years
League Titles before 1969	3	1920, 1948, 1954
Division Titles	7	1995, 1996, 1997, 1998, 1999, 2001, 2007
Wild Cards	0	

Regular Season High & Low Points

		Year(s)
Most Wins in a Season	111	1954
Most Losses in a Season	105	1991
Highest Winning Percentage	.721	1954
Lowest Winning Percentage	.333	1914
Longest Streak with Won-Loss Record .500 or Higher	10 years	1947-1956
Longest Streak with Won-Loss Record Below .500	7 years	1969-1975, 1987-1993

Years with .500 record or Better

1900's	6 (out of 9)
1910's	6
1920's	6
1930's	9
1940's	6
1950's	9
1960's	3
1970's	2
1980's	2
1990's	6
2000's	5
2010's	0

60 out of 110 seasons played = 55%

Years Making Postseason

1900's	0
1910's	0
1920's	1
1930's	0
1940's	1
1950's	1
1960's	0
1970's	0
1980's	0
1990's	5
2000's	2
2010's	0

10 out of 110 seasons played = 9%

Streaks

- 1948-1956: Won one World Series and two League Titles in nine years.
- 1995-2001: Won six Division Titles, including five in a row from 1995-1999, three League Division Series, and two League Championship Series in the seven year period.

Extra Bases

- On April 24th, 1901 the Cleveland Blues lost to the Chicago White Stockings 8-2 in the first professional American League game. Three other games scheduled for that day were all rained out.
- In 1939, the Indians played the Philadelphia A's in the first American League 'night' game and won 8-3.
- From 1951-1956 Cleveland won a league title and finished in second place five times, each time behind the Yankees. In three of those years Cleveland finished within five games of first place.

Scoring Opportunities

1900's

- In 1908 the Cleveland Naps were in fourth place in the American League 5.5 games behind Detroit on September 8th. Cleveland won fourteen of its next fifteen games and was in first place by 1.5 games on September 23rd. The rest of the season the Naps went 7-4, but the Tigers went 11-2 and won the pennant by a half game, the difference occurring because Detroit did not have to make up a previous game that was rained out. If the Tigers had played that game and lost they would have had the same record as the Naps. Both teams had ninety wins, but Cleveland played one more game and one more loss. The Naps protested but their argument had no affect for that season. After the season it led to a change in the rules so that games that were rained out had to be replayed if they affected the pennant outcome.

1920's

• The Indians were tied for first place in the American League with the Yankees on September 23rd in 1921 when the two teams met in New York for a four game series. But Cleveland lost three out of the four games and lost six of their last eight games of the season while New York went 7-2 over the same period. The Indians finished in second place 4.5 games behind the Yankees.

1940's

• In 1940 Cleveland was tied for first place in the American League with the Tigers on September 20th when the two teams met for a three game series in Detroit. The Indians lost two of the three games and trailed by one game in the standings. Two games later Cleveland was two games behind the Tigers with their last three games of the season at home against Detroit. The Indians needed to win all three games to win the pennant. Cleveland lost the first game 2-0 and was eliminated from winning the league title. They won the next two games and only finished one game back in the standings.

1950's

• Cleveland was in a very close race with the Yankees throughout the 1951 season. The two teams traded first and second place six times in the final two months and were tied for the lead at six different times. On September 20th they were tied for first but then the Indians lost five of their last six games of the year while New York went 8-2 and Cleveland finished in second place five games behind the Yankees.

• In 1952 the Indians were in another close pennant race with the Yankees as they never trailed New York by more than four games over the final two months of the season. On September 3rd the Indians were 3.5 games out and went 18-3 the rest of the season. They got within a half game on September 12th but could not take over first place as the Yankees finished the season going 16-4 after the September 3rd and Cleveland finished two games back in the standings.

• Cleveland won the American League pennant in 1954 and became the first AL team to win as many as 111 games in the regular season. In the World Series the Indians played the New York Giants and Game 1 was tied at two after nine innings. In the top of the tenth Cleveland had runners on first and third with one out, but their next two batters struck out and lined out. In the bottom of the inning the Indians got the first Giants batter out but then gave up two walks and a three-run home run and lost the game 5-2. In Game 2 Cleveland trailed by two runs in the top of the ninth inning when they got their first two batters on base but then their next three hitters all got out and they lost 3-1. The Indians lost Game 3 6-2 and Game 4 7-4 and were swept in the series, being outscored 21-9.

• In 1955 the Indians had a two game lead over New York on September 13th but then lost four games in a row and six out of their final nine games while the Yankees went 9-2 over the same period. Cleveland finished in second place three games behind New York.

1990's

• Cleveland won the American League Central Division in 1995, swept the Red Sox in the LDS, and beat Seattle in the LCS. In the World Series the Indians met Atlanta and Game 1 was tied at one after six innings. In the bottom of the seventh Cleveland walked the first three Braves batters and gave up a fielder's choice and a sacrifice bunt and let in two runs. In the bottom of the ninth the Indians scored one run on an Atlanta error but lost the game 3-2. Game 2 was tied at two after five innings but Cleveland gave up a two-run homer in the bottom of the sixth. The Indians scored one run in the top of the seventh and had runners on first and third with two outs, but their next batter up popped out. In the top of the ninth they had the tying run on second base with two outs, but their next batter popped out and they lost the game 4-3. Cleveland won Game 3 in eleven innings, lost Game 4 5-2, and won Game 5. In Game 6 the Indians gave up a solo home run in the bottom of the sixth inning. They had a man on first with two outs in the top of the seventh, but their next batter up flied out. Their last six batters were retired in order in the eighth and ninth innings and they lost the game 1-0 and lost the series. Three of Cleveland's four losses in the series were by one run.

• In 1996 Cleveland won the American League Central Division again and played the Orioles in the LDS. The Indians lost Game 1 10-4 and Game 2 was tied at four heading into the bottom of the eighth inning. But Cleveland gave up one error, two hits, four walks, and three runs in the inning and lost the game 7-4. The Indians won Game 3 and had a 3-2 lead after eight innings in Game 4, but gave up a run in the top of the ninth with two outs. In the bottom of the inning they had runners on first and second with one out, but their next two batters grounded out and struck out and the game went into extra innings. In the top of the twelfth, Cleveland gave up a solo home run to the first Orioles batter and the Indians lost the game 4-3 and lost the series.

• The Indians won the American League Central Division in 1997, beat the Yankees in the LDS, and the Orioles in the LCS. In the World Series against Florida Cleveland lost Game 1 7-4 and won Game 2. Game 3 was tied at seven after eight innings, but in the top of the ninth the Indians gave up seven runs. In the bottom of the inning Cleveland scored four runs and lost the game 14-11. The Indians won Game 4 and trailed by four runs in Game 5 in the bottom of the ninth inning. They rallied and scored three runs and had a runner on first with two outs, but their next batter up flied out to deep right field to end the game and they lost 8-7. Cleveland won Game 6 and had a 2-1 lead going into the bottom of the ninth inning in Game 7 but they gave up a run on a sacrifice fly that tied the score. In the bottom of the eleventh the Indians had two Marlins out but the bases were loaded. The next Florida batter hit a ground ball up the middle of the infield that got through for a single and the game winning run scored. Cleveland lost the game 3-2 and lost the series even though they outscored the Marlins 39-37 in the series.

- In 1998 the Indians won the American League Central Division again and beat Boston in the LDS. In the LCS they faced the Yankee team that won 114 regular season games. Cleveland gave up five runs in the first inning of Game 1 and lost the game 7-2, then won Games 2 & 3. In Game 4 the Indians only got four hits and lost the game 4-0. In Game 5 they trailed by two runs in the top of the eighth inning when they had runners on first and second with one out, but their next batter hit into a double play and they lost the game 5-3. Cleveland lost Game 6 9-5 and lost the series.

- Cleveland won their fifth American League Central Division title in a row in 1999 and met Boston in the LDS. The Indians won the first two games of the series outscoring the Red Sox 14-3. Game 3 was tied at three in the top of the seventh inning but Cleveland gave up six runs in the inning and lost the game 9-3. Then they lost Game 4 23-7. After two innings in Game 5 Cleveland had a 5-2 lead but then gave up five runs in the top of the third. They scored three runs in the bottom of the inning to take an 8-7 lead, and the game was tied at eight after six innings. In the top of the seventh Cleveland gave up a three run home run and they didn't get any hits in their final three at bats and lost the game 12-8, blowing their two game to none series lead. In the last three games the Indians were outscored 44-18.

2000's

- In 2000 the Indians were not close in the American League Central Division race with Chicago but they were in the AL Wild Card race. Cleveland had the wild card lead on September 20th by half a game over the A's but had to play three double headers in one week and went 3-4 over their next seven games. Oakland went 4-1 over the same period and the Indians were 1.5 games behind the A's on September 25th. Cleveland won five of their last six games but so did Oakland and the Indians finished the season one game behind Seattle for the wild card spot as the A's overtook the Mariners for the AL West Division title.

- The Indians won the American League Central Division in 2001 and played the Mariners team that won 116 regular season games in the LDS. Cleveland won Game 1 but gave up four runs in the first inning of Game 2 and lost the game 5-1. The Indians won Game 3 17-2 and had a 1-0 lead after six innings in Game 4 but gave up three runs in the top of the seventh with two outs and lost the game 6-2. In Game 5 Cleveland had only four hits, and only one after the third inning, and they lost the game 3-1 and lost the series that they led two games to one.

- In 2005 Cleveland went 17-2 from September 5th to 24th and trailed the White Sox by 1.5 games on September 24th. The Indians also led the wild card spot by 1.5 games over Boston. But Cleveland lost six out of their last seven games and finished six games behind Chicago in the division and two games behind Boston in the wild card. The White Sox went 6-2 after the 24th and the Red Sox went 5-3.

• The Indians won the American League Central Division in 2007 and beat the Yankees in the LDS. In the LCS Cleveland faced the Red Sox and lost Game 1 10-3. The Indians won the next three games to take a three game to one series lead with Game 5 at home. But Cleveland lost Game 5 7-1 and lost Games 6 & 7 in Boston 12-2 and 11-2 and lost the series. The Indians were outscored 30-5 in the final three games.

Year-to-Year Figures

Team Name	League	Year	W	L	Win%	Fin	GB/GA	WS	Lge	LDS	Div	WC
Cleveland Indians	AL Cent	2010	69	93	0.426	4 of 5	25					
Cleveland Indians	AL Cent	2009	65	97	0.401	4t of 5	21.5					
Cleveland Indians	AL Cent	2008	81	81	0.500	3 of 5	7.5					
Cleveland Indians	AL Cent	2007	96	66	0.593	1 of 5	+8			1	1	
Cleveland Indians	AL Cent	2006	78	84	0.481	4 of 5	18					
Cleveland Indians	AL Cent	2005	93	69	0.574	2 of 5	6					
Cleveland Indians	AL Cent	2004	80	82	0.494	3 of 5	12					
Cleveland Indians	AL Cent	2003	68	94	0.420	4 of 5	22					
Cleveland Indians	AL Cent	2002	74	88	0.457	3 of 5	20.5					
Cleveland Indians	AL Cent	2001	91	71	0.562	1 of 5	+6				1	
Cleveland Indians	AL Cent	2000	90	72	0.556	2 of 5	5					
Cleveland Indians	AL Cent	1999	97	65	0.599	1 of 5	+21.5				1	
Cleveland Indians	AL Cent	1998	89	73	0.549	1 of 5	+9			1	1	
Cleveland Indians	AL Cent	1997	86	75	0.534	1 of 5	+6		1	1	1	
Cleveland Indians	AL Cent	1996	99	62	0.615	1 of 5	+14.5				1	
Cleveland Indians	AL Cent	1995	100	44	0.694	1 of 5	+30		1	1	1	
Cleveland Indians	AL Cent	1994	66	47	0.584	2 of 5	1					
Cleveland Indians	AL East	1993	76	86	0.469	6 of 7	19					
Cleveland Indians	AL East	1992	76	86	0.469	4t of 7	20					
Cleveland Indians	AL East	1991	57	105	0.352	7 of 7	34					
Cleveland Indians	AL East	1990	77	85	0.475	4 of 7	11					
Cleveland Indians	AL East	1989	73	89	0.451	6 of 7	16					
Cleveland Indians	AL East	1988	78	84	0.481	6 of 7	11					
Cleveland Indians	AL East	1987	61	101	0.377	7 of 7	37					
Cleveland Indians	AL East	1986	84	78	0.519	5 of 7	11.5					
Cleveland Indians	AL East	1985	60	102	0.370	7 of 7	39.5					
Cleveland Indians	AL East	1984	75	87	0.463	6 of 7	29					
Cleveland Indians	AL East	1983	70	92	0.432	7 of 7	28					
Cleveland Indians	AL East	1982	78	84	0.481	6t of 7	17					
Cleveland Indians	AL East	1981	52	51	0.505	6, 5 of 7	5, 5					
Cleveland Indians	AL East	1980	79	81	0.494	6 of 7	23					
Cleveland Indians	AL East	1979	81	80	0.503	6 of 7	22					
Cleveland Indians	AL East	1978	69	90	0.434	6 of 7	29					
Cleveland Indians	AL East	1977	71	90	0.441	5 of 7	28.5					
Cleveland Indians	AL East	1976	81	78	0.509	4 of 6	16					

Team Name	League	Year	W	L	Win%	Fin	GB/GA	WS	Lge	LDS	Div	WC
Cleveland Indians	AL East	1975	79	80	0.497	4 of 6	15.5					
Cleveland Indians	AL East	1974	77	85	0.475	4 of 6	14					
Cleveland Indians	AL East	1973	71	91	0.438	6 of 6	26					
Cleveland Indians	AL East	1972	72	84	0.462	5 of 6	14					
Cleveland Indians	AL East	1971	60	102	0.370	6 of 6	43					
Cleveland Indians	AL East	1970	76	86	0.469	5 of 6	32					
Cleveland Indians	AL East	1969	62	99	0.385	6 of 6	46.5					
Cleveland Indians	AL	1968	86	75	0.534	3 of 10	16.5					
Cleveland Indians	AL	1967	75	87	0.463	8 of 10	17					
Cleveland Indians	AL	1966	81	81	0.500	5 of 10	17					
Cleveland Indians	AL	1965	87	75	0.537	5 of 10	15					
Cleveland Indians	AL	1964	79	83	0.488	6t of 10	20					
Cleveland Indians	AL	1963	79	83	0.488	5t of 10	25.5					
Cleveland Indians	AL	1962	80	82	0.494	6 of 10	16					
Cleveland Indians	AL	1961	78	83	0.484	5 of 10	30.5					
Cleveland Indians	AL	1960	76	78	0.494	4 of 8	21					
Cleveland Indians	AL	1959	89	65	0.578	2 of 8	5					
Cleveland Indians	AL	1958	77	76	0.503	4 of 8	14.5					
Cleveland Indians	AL	1957	76	77	0.497	6 of 8	21.5					
Cleveland Indians	AL	1956	88	66	0.571	2 of 8	9					
Cleveland Indians	AL	1955	93	61	0.604	2 of 8	3					
Cleveland Indians	AL	1954	111	43	0.721	1 of 8	+8		1			
Cleveland Indians	AL	1953	92	62	0.597	2 of 8	8.5					
Cleveland Indians	AL	1952	93	61	0.604	2 of 8	2					
Cleveland Indians	AL	1951	93	61	0.604	2 of 8	5					
Cleveland Indians	AL	1950	92	62	0.597	4 of 8	6					
Cleveland Indians	AL	1949	89	65	0.578	3 of 8	8					
Cleveland Indians	AL	1948	97	58	0.626	1 of 8	+1	1	1			
Cleveland Indians	AL	1947	80	74	0.519	4 of 8	17					
Cleveland Indians	AL	1946	68	86	0.442	6 of 8	36					
Cleveland Indians	AL	1945	73	72	0.503	5 of 8	11					
Cleveland Indians	AL	1944	72	82	0.468	5t of 8	17					
Cleveland Indians	AL	1943	82	71	0.536	3 of 8	15.5					
Cleveland Indians	AL	1942	75	79	0.487	4 of 8	28					
Cleveland Indians	AL	1941	75	79	0.487	4t of 8	26					
Cleveland Indians	AL	1940	89	65	0.578	2 of 8	1					
Cleveland Indians	AL	1939	87	67	0.565	3 of 8	20.5					
Cleveland Indians	AL	1938	86	66	0.566	3 of 8	13					
Cleveland Indians	AL	1937	83	71	0.539	4 of 8	19					
Cleveland Indians	AL	1936	80	74	0.519	5 of 8	22.5					
Cleveland Indians	AL	1935	82	71	0.536	3 of 8	12					
Cleveland Indians	AL	1934	85	69	0.552	3 of 8	16					
Cleveland Indians	AL	1933	75	76	0.497	4 of 8	23.5					
Cleveland Indians	AL	1932	87	65	0.572	4 of 8	19					
Cleveland Indians	AL	1931	78	76	0.506	4 of 8	30					

Baseball Franchise Rankings

Team Name	League	Year	W	L	Win%	Fin	GB/GA	WS	Lge	LDS	Div	WC
Cleveland Indians	AL	1930	81	73	0.526	4 of 8	21					
Cleveland Indians	AL	1929	81	71	0.533	3 of 8	24					
Cleveland Indians	AL	1928	62	92	0.403	7 of 8	39					
Cleveland Indians	AL	1927	66	87	0.431	6 of 8	43.5					
Cleveland Indians	AL	1926	88	66	0.571	2 of 8	3					
Cleveland Indians	AL	1925	70	84	0.455	6 of 8	27.5					
Cleveland Indians	AL	1924	67	86	0.438	6 of 8	24.5					
Cleveland Indians	AL	1923	82	71	0.536	3 of 8	16.5					
Cleveland Indians	AL	1922	78	76	0.506	4 of 8	16					
Cleveland Indians	AL	1921	94	60	0.610	2 of 8	4.5					
Cleveland Indians	AL	1920	98	56	0.636	1 of 8	+2	1	1			
Cleveland Indians	AL	1919	84	55	0.604	2 of 8	3.5					
Cleveland Indians	AL	1918	73	54	0.575	2 of 8	2.5					
Cleveland Indians	AL	1917	88	66	0.571	3 of 8	12					
Cleveland Indians	AL	1916	77	77	0.500	6 of 8	14					
Cleveland Indians	AL	1915	57	95	0.375	7 of 8	44.5					
Cleveland Naps	AL	1914	51	102	0.333	8 of 8	48.5					
Cleveland Naps	AL	1913	86	66	0.566	3 of 8	9.5					
Cleveland Naps	AL	1912	75	78	0.490	5 of 8	30.5					
Cleveland Naps	AL	1911	80	73	0.523	3 of 8	22					
Cleveland Naps	AL	1910	71	81	0.467	5 of 8	32					
Cleveland Naps	AL	1909	71	82	0.464	6 of 8	27.5					
Cleveland Naps	AL	1908	90	64	0.584	2 of 8	0.5*					
Cleveland Naps	AL	1907	85	67	0.559	4 of 8	8					
Cleveland Naps	AL	1906	89	64	0.582	3 of 8	5					
Cleveland Naps	AL	1905	76	78	0.494	5 of 8	19					
Cleveland Naps	AL	1904	86	65	0.570	4 of 8	7.5					
Cleveland Naps	AL	1903	77	63	0.550	3 of 8	15					
Cleveland Bronchos	AL	1902	69	67	0.507	5 of 8	14					
Cleveland Blues	AL	1901	54	82	0.397	7 of 8	29					
			8691	8367	0.509			2	5	4	7	0

* In 1908 Cleveland finished the season 0.5 game behind Detroit because the Tigers did not have to make up a game that was rained out and there was no rule in place that forced them to do so in the affect of a pennant outcome.

Colorado Rockies

Stats

History
Year of Origin 1993

Years Played 18

Score & Rank
Total Points Score 6.8

Total Points Rank 27

Average Points Score 0.38

Average Points Rank 25

Postseason Results

Postseason Results	No.	Years
World Series Won	0	
League Championship Series Won	1	2007
League Division Series Won	1	2007
World Series Lost	1	2007
League Championship Series Lost	0	
League Division Series Lost	2	1995, 2009

Postseason Won-Loss Records and Winning Percentages

	Postseason Games		Postseason Series	
All Postseason Series	9-10	.474	2-3	.400
World Series	0-4	.000	0-1	.000
League Championship Series	4-0	1.000	1-0	1.000
League Division Series	5-6	.455	1-2	.333

Regular Season Results
All-Time Won-Loss Record 1364-1490

All-Time Winning Percentage .... .478

	No.	Years
League Titles before 1969	0	
Division Titles	0	
Wild Cards	3	1995, 2007, 2009

Regular Season High & Low Points

		Year(s)
Most Wins in a Season	92	2009
Most Losses in a Season	95	1993, 2005
Highest Winning Percentage	.568	2009
Lowest Winning Percentage	.414	1993, 2005
Longest Streak with Won-Loss Record .500 or Higher	3 years	1995-1997
Longest Streak with Won-Loss Record Below .500	6 years	2001-2006

Years with .500 record or Better
1990's .... 3 (out of 7)

2000's 3

2010's 1

7 out of 18 seasons played = 39%

Years Making Postseason
1990's 1

2000's 2

2010's 0

3 out of 18 seasons played = 17%

Streaks

- 2007-2009: Won one League Championship Series, one League Division Series, and two Wild Cards in three years.

Extra Bases

- The Rockies sixty-seven wins in their expansion year of 1993 set a new National League record for wins by an expansion team.
- In 1995 Colorado made the postseason in their third year of existence. They were the quickest expansion team in history to make the playoffs until Arizona made the playoffs in their second year of existence in 1999.

Scoring Opportunities

1990's

- In 1995 the Rockies won the National League wild card by one game over Houston and faced Atlanta in the LDS. Game 1 was tied at four after eight innings but in the top of the ninth Colorado gave up a solo home run with two outs. In the bottom of the inning the Rockies had the bases loaded with one out but their next two batters both struck out and they lost 5-4. In Game 2 the Rockies had a 4-3 lead after eight innings but gave up four runs in the top of the ninth and lost the game 7-4. Colorado won Game 3 in extra innings but lost Game 4 10-4 and lost the series.

2000's

- The Rockies trailed Arizona by 6.5 games in the National League West Division on September 15th in 2007 and were in fourth place. They won thirteen out of their final fourteen regular season games and tied the Padres for the wild card spot as both teams trailed the Diamondbacks by one game at the end of the season. In the one game playoff against San Diego the Rockies scored three runs in the bottom of the thirteenth inning and won the game 9-8. In the LDS Colorado swept the Phillies and in the LCS the Rockies swept the Diamondbacks. In the World Series Colorado met the Red Sox and lost Game 1 13-1. In Game 2 the Rockies trailed by one run in the bottom of the eighth and had a runner on first base with two outs, but he was picked off and they were retired in order in the ninth and lost 2-1. Colorado lost Game 3 10-5 and in Game 4 they hit a two run home run in the bottom of the eighth and trailed by one run with one out, but their next two batters grounded out and flied out and the Rockies were retired in order in the ninth and lost 4-3 to lose the series.
- Colorado won the National League Wild Card spot in 2009, which was their third wild card appearance and is the most by any NL team. In the LDS they faced the Phillies, lost Game

1 5-1, and won Game 2. Game 3 was tied going into the ninth inning but the Rockies gave up the go ahead run on a sacrifice fly in the top of the inning. In the bottom of the inning Colorado had runners on first and second with two outs but their next batter up flied out and they lost 6-5. In Game 4 Colorado had a 4-2 lead entering the top of the ninth and had two outs with a Phillies runner on first. But then they gave up a walk, a double, and a single, and three runs scored which gave Philadelphia the lead. In the bottom of the inning the Rockies had runners on first and second with two outs, just like in Game 3, but their next batter struck out and they lost the game 5-4 and lost the series.

Year-to-Year Figures

Team Name	League	Year	W	L	Win%	Fin	GB/GA	WS	Lge	LDS	Div	WC
Colorado Rockies	NL West	2010	83	79	0.512	3 of 5	9					
Colorado Rockies	NL West	2009	92	70	0.568	2 of 5	3					1
Colorado Rockies	NL West	2008	74	88	0.457	3 of 5	10					
Colorado Rockies	NL West	2007	90	73	0.552	2 of 5	0.5*		1	1		1
Colorado Rockies	NL West	2006	76	86	0.469	4t of 5	12					
Colorado Rockies	NL West	2005	67	95	0.414	5 of 5	15					
Colorado Rockies	NL West	2004	68	94	0.420	4 of 5	25					
Colorado Rockies	NL West	2003	74	88	0.457	4 of 5	26.5					
Colorado Rockies	NL West	2002	73	89	0.451	4 of 5	25					
Colorado Rockies	NL West	2001	73	89	0.451	5 of 5	19					
Colorado Rockies	NL West	2000	82	80	0.506	4 of 5	15					
Colorado Rockies	NL West	1999	72	90	0.444	5 of 5	28					
Colorado Rockies	NL West	1998	77	85	0.475	4 of 5	21					
Colorado Rockies	NL West	1997	83	79	0.512	3 of 4	7					
Colorado Rockies	NL West	1996	83	79	0.512	3 of 4	8					
Colorado Rockies	NL West	1995	77	67	0.535	2 of 4	1					1
Colorado Rockies	NL West	1994	53	64	0.453	3 of 4	6.5					
Colorado Rockies	NL West	1993	67	95	0.414	6 of 7	37					
			1364	1490	0.478			0	1	1	0	3

* In 2007 Colorado and San Diego tied for second place in the National League West Division one game behind Arizona and tied for the National League Wild Card spot. In the one game playoff Colorado won 9-8 and therefore only finished 0.5 games behind the Diamondbacks because they played one extra game.

Detroit Tigers

Stats

History

Year of Origin 1901   Years Played...110

Score & Rank

Total Points Score .... 81.6   Average Points Score...0.74
Total Points Rank 11   Average Points Rank.. 13

Postseason Results   **No.**   **Years**
World Series Won...4.. 1935, 1945, 1968, 1984
League Championship Series Won ....2..1984, 2006
League Division Series Won..................................1... 2006

World Series Lost ....6...............................1907, 1908, 1909, 1934, 1940 2006
League Championship Series Lost.......................2..1972, 1987
League Division Series Lost ....0..

Postseason Won-Loss Records and Winning Percentages

	Postseason Games		**Postseason Series**	
All Postseason Series	40-41	.494	7-8	.467
World Series	27-33	.450	4-6	.400
League Championship Series	10-7	.588	2-2	.500
League Division Series	3-1	.750	1-0	1.000

Regular Season Results

All-Time Won-Loss Record 8645-8437
All-Time Winning Percentage .... .506

	No.	**Years**
League Titles before 1969	8	1907, 1908, 1909, 1934, 1935, 1940, 1945, 1968
Division Titles	3	1972, 1984, 1987
Wild Cards	1	2006

Regular Season High & Low Points   **Year(s)**

Most Wins in a Season	104	1984
Most Losses in a Season	119	2003
Highest Winning Percentage	.656	1934
Lowest Winning Percentage	.265	2003
Longest Streak with Won-Loss Record .500 or Higher	11 years	1978-1988
Longest Streak with Won-Loss Record Below .500	12 years	1994-2005

Years with .500 record or Better

1900's	5 (out of 9)
1910's	7
1920's	6
1930's	7
1940's	8
1950's	5
1960's	8
1970's	5
1980's	9
1990's	2
2000's	2
2010's	1

66 out of 110 seasons played = 60%

Years Making Postseason

1900's	3
1910's	0
1920's	0
1930's	2
1940's	2
1950's	0
1960's	1
1970's	1
1980's	2
1990's	0
2000's	1
2010's	0

12 out of 110 seasons played = 11%

Streaks

- 1907-1909: Won three straight League Titles in three years.
- 1934-1945: Won two World Series and four League Titles in twelve years.
- 1968-1972: Won a League Title and World Series in one season and won a Division Title in another season over the five-year period.
- 1984-1987: Won two Division Titles, one League Title, and one World Series in four years.

Extra Bases

- The Tigers finished in last place for the first time in 1952, their fifty-second season at that point.
- The Tigers had 16 losing seasons in their first 50 years, 24 in their first 70 years, and 30 in their first 90 years. In their last 17 years, since 1994, they have had 13 losing seasons.
- Detroit is the only team out of the sixteen original American League or National League teams that has not changed its team name or moved cities. They have played in Detroit, and been named the Tigers, since 1901.

Scoring Opportunities

1900's

- In 1907 the Tigers won the American League pennant by 1.5 games over the Philadelphia Athletics. It helped that two late season games against the A's were cancelled due to rain. In the World Series Detroit played the Cubs and had a 3-1 lead in Game 1 entering the bottom of the ninth inning. But the Tigers gave up a single, a hit batter, two errors, and let in two runs and the game went into extra innings. After twelve innings the game was stopped due to darkness and declared a tie at 3-3. In Game 2 Detroit trailed by two runs in the top of the eighth inning when they had runners on first and second with two outs, but their runner on second was caught stealing third, which ended the inning and the Tigers, lost the game 3-1. Detroit lost Game 3 5-1 and Game 4 6-1. In Game 5 the Tigers gave up one run in each of the first and second innings and had one runner on base in the sixth, seventh, and ninth innings but couldn't score in any inning and lost the game 2-0 to lose the series. Detroit only scored three runs in their four losses, after scoring three runs in the first game that was ruled a tie.

• Detroit won the 1908 American League pennant by a half game over Cleveland. Just like the year before they did not have to make up one rained out game. In the World Series they faced the Cubs and led Game 1 6-5 after eight innings, but in the top of the ninth they gave up five runs and lost the game 10-6. Game 2 was tied at zero after seven innings, but the Tigers gave up six runs in the bottom of the eighth and lost the game 6-1. Detroit won Game 3 but only had four hits in Game 4 and lost the game 3-0. In Game 5 the Tigers only had three hits and were shut out again, losing 2-0 and losing the series. In their four losses Detroit was outscored 21-7.

• Detroit won the American League pennant for the third straight year in 1909 and played Pittsburgh in the World Series. The Tigers lost Game 1 4-1 and won Game 2. In Game 3 Detroit only trailed by two runs after eight innings but they gave up two runs in the top of the ninth. In the bottom of the inning the Tigers scored two runs and had a runner on second with two outs, but their next batter lined out and they lost 8-6. Detroit won Game 4, lost Game 5 8-4, and won Game 6 to tie the series up. But in Game 7 the Tigers were shut out and lost the game 8-0 and lost the series.

1910's

• In 1915 the Tigers only trailed Boston by one game on September 16th but lost their next three games to the Red Sox and fell to four games back in the standings on September 20th. Detroit went 9-3 the rest of the year but Boston went 8-5 and Detroit finished in second place 2.5 games behind the Red Sox. The Tigers played three more games in the regular season than Boston. Detroit's record at the end of the year was 100-54 and the Red Sox was 101-50.

• Detroit was in first place in the American League in 1916 by one game over Boston on September 17th, but then lost four games in a row, including three against the Red Sox, and fell to third place in the standings three games behind Boston. The rest of the season the Tigers went 4-3 while the Red Sox went 7-4 and Detroit finished in third place four games behind Boston. The Tigers went 4-7 after September 17th while the Red Sox went 11-4 over the same period.

1930's

• The Tigers won the American League pennant in 1934 with 101 wins and had a .656 winning percentage, their best ever. In the World Series they played St. Louis and lost Game 1 8-3. Detroit won Game 2, lost Game 3 4-1, and won Games 4 & 5 to take a three games to two lead in the series with the last two games to be played at home. Game 6 was tied at three after six innings. The Tigers got the first Cardinals batter out in the top of the seventh, but then gave up a double and a single and let in the go ahead run. In the bottom of the inning Detroit had the tying run thrown out at home plate on a fielders' choice. In the bottom of the eighth the Tigers had runners on first and third with one out, but their next two batters flied out and fouled out and they lost the game 4-3. In Game 7 Detroit gave up seven runs in the third inning and lost the game 11-0 to lose the series.

1940's

• In 1940 Detroit won the American League pennant and won Game 1 of the World Series against Cincinnati. In Game 2 Detroit was held to three hits and their last nine batters were retired in order and they lost the game 5-3. The Tigers won Game 3, lost Game 4 5-2, and won Game 5 to take a three games to two series lead. In Game 6 Detroit only had five hits and lost the game 4-0. In Game 7 the Tigers had a 1-0 lead after six innings, but then gave up two doubles, a sacrifice bunt, and a sacrifice fly, and let in two runs in bottom of the seventh. In the top of the eighth Detroit's first batter singled but their next three batters all got out and they lost the game 2-1 and lost the series.

• The Tigers were in first place in 1944 from September 17th to September 30th either by themselves or tied with the St. Louis Browns. On the last day of the season on October 1st the two teams were tied and the Browns beat the Yankees 5-2. Detroit played Washington and lost 4-1 and missed winning the pennant by one game. The Tigers lost two of their last three games of the year. St. Louis won eleven of their last twelve games of the year.

1950's

• In 1950 Detroit was tied for first place in the American League with the Yankees on September 21st but lost four games in a row and lost six of their final ten games of the year. The Tigers finished the season three games behind New York, who went 7-3 after the 21st.

1960's

• The 1967 pennant race came down to the final day of the season. Boston and Minnesota were tied for first place and Detroit was a half-game back. On the last day of the year the Red Sox and Twins were playing each other and the Tigers had two games left against the Angels. Detroit would have to win both of its games to tie the winner of the Boston/Minnesota game for the first place. The Tigers won Game 1 of their doubleheader 6-4 and the Red Sox beat the Twins. In the second game of their doubleheader Detroit gave up eight runs to the Angels in the first five innings and lost the game 8-5. The Tigers finished tied for second place with Minnesota one game behind Boston.

1970's

• Detroit won the American League East Division in 1972 by winning two of three games against second place Boston in the final series of the season. The Tigers benefitted from a players strike earlier in the year that cancelled an unequal amount of games for the two teams. Both teams had seventy losses, but Detroit played one more game and had one more win. In the LCS against Oakland Game 1 went into extra innings tied at one. The Tigers hit a solo home run in the top of the eleventh, but in the bottom of the inning they gave up three singles and let in two runs with the second run scoring on a throwing error by the right fielder to third base. The Tigers lost 3-2 and only had three hits in Game 2 and lost that game 5-0. Detroit won Games 3 & 4 to even the series. In Game 5 the Tigers trailed by one run after four innings and had a runner on base in the seventh, eighth, and ninth innings, but couldn't score in any inning and lost the game 2-1 to lose the series.

1980's

- In 1987 the Tigers swept the Blue Jays in the final series of the year to pass them in the standings and win the American League East Division. In the LCS Detroit played the Twins and had a 5-4 lead in Game 1 heading into the bottom of the eighth. But the Tigers gave up four hits, two walks, and four runs in the half inning and lost the game 8-5. Detroit lost Game 2 6-3 and won Game 3. In Game 4 the Tigers trailed by two runs in the bottom of the ninth when their first batter up singled, but the next three hitters all got out and they lost 5-3. In Game 5 Detroit was only down by two runs after eight innings, but they gave up three runs in the top of the ninth and lost the game 9-5 to lose the series.
- The Tigers looked like they were out of the American League East Division race in 1988 as they were six games behind Boston on September 19th and were in fourth place in the standings. But Detroit won six of their next seven games and nine of their last twelve. However, they ended up one game short of the Red Sox for the division title and finished in second place.

2000's

- In 2006 Detroit won the American League Wild Card spot, beat the Yankees in the LDS, and the A's in the LCS. In the World Series the Tigers played St. Louis and got only four hits in Game 1 and lost the game 7-2. Detroit won Game 2 but got only three hits in Game 3 and lost the game 5-0. Game 4 was tied at four heading into the bottom of the eighth inning, but the Tigers gave up a walk, a wild pitch, and a double, and let in the go-ahead run and lost the game 5-4. In Game 5 Detroit trailed by two runs after eight innings. In the top of the ninth they had runners on first and third with two outs, but their next batter struck out and the Tigers lost the game 4-2 and lost the series. Detroit was outscored 22-11 in the series.

Year-to-Year Figures

Team Name	League	Year	W	L	Win%	Fin	GB/GA	WS	Lge	LDS	Div	WC
Detroit Tigers	AL Cent	2010	81	81	0.500	3 of 5	13					
Detroit Tigers	AL Cent	2009	86	77	0.528	2 of 5	1					
Detroit Tigers	AL Cent	2008	74	88	0.457	5 of 5	14.5					
Detroit Tigers	AL Cent	2007	88	74	0.543	2 of 5	8					
Detroit Tigers	AL Cent	2006	95	67	0.586	2 of 5	1		1	1		1
Detroit Tigers	AL Cent	2005	71	91	0.438	4 of 5	28					
Detroit Tigers	AL Cent	2004	72	90	0.444	4 of 5	20					
Detroit Tigers	AL Cent	2003	43	119	0.265	5 of 5	47					
Detroit Tigers	AL Cent	2002	55	106	0.342	5 of 5	39					
Detroit Tigers	AL Cent	2001	66	96	0.407	4 of 5	25					
Detroit Tigers	AL Cent	2000	79	83	0.488	3 of 5	16					
Detroit Tigers	AL Cent	1999	69	92	0.429	3 of 5	27.5					
Detroit Tigers	AL Cent	1998	65	97	0.401	5 of 5	24					
Detroit Tigers	AL East	1997	79	83	0.488	3 of 5	19					
Detroit Tigers	AL East	1996	53	109	0.327	5 of 5	39					
Detroit Tigers	AL East	1995	60	84	0.417	4 of 5	26					
Detroit Tigers	AL East	1994	53	62	0.461	5 of 5	18					
Detroit Tigers	AL East	1993	85	77	0.525	3t of 7	10					
Detroit Tigers	AL East	1992	75	87	0.463	6 of 7	21					
Detroit Tigers	AL East	1991	84	78	0.519	2t of 7	7					
Detroit Tigers	AL East	1990	79	83	0.488	3 of 7	9					
Detroit Tigers	AL East	1989	59	103	0.364	7 of 7	30					
Detroit Tigers	AL East	1988	88	74	0.543	2 of 7	1					
Detroit Tigers	AL East	1987	98	64	0.605	1 of 7	+2				1	
Detroit Tigers	AL East	1986	87	75	0.537	3 of 7	8.5					
Detroit Tigers	AL East	1985	84	77	0.522	3 of 7	15					
Detroit Tigers	AL East	1984	104	58	0.642	1 of 7	+15	1	1		1	
Detroit Tigers	AL East	1983	92	70	0.568	2 of 7	6					
Detroit Tigers	AL East	1982	83	79	0.512	4 of 7	12					
Detroit Tigers	AL East	1981	60	49	0.550	4, 2t of 7	3.5, 1.5					
Detroit Tigers	AL East	1980	84	78	0.519	5 of 7	19					
Detroit Tigers	AL East	1979	85	76	0.528	5 of 7	18					
Detroit Tigers	AL East	1978	86	76	0.531	5 of 7	13.5					
Detroit Tigers	AL East	1977	74	88	0.457	4 of 7	26					
Detroit Tigers	AL East	1976	74	87	0.460	5 of 6	24					
Detroit Tigers	AL East	1975	57	102	0.358	6 of 6	37.5					
Detroit Tigers	AL East	1974	72	90	0.444	6 of 6	19					
Detroit Tigers	AL East	1973	85	77	0.525	3 of 6	12					
Detroit Tigers	AL East	1972	86	70	0.551	1 of 6	+0.5*				1	
Detroit Tigers	AL East	1971	91	71	0.562	2 of 6	12					
Detroit Tigers	AL East	1970	79	83	0.488	4 of 6	29					
Detroit Tigers	AL East	1969	90	72	0.556	2 of 6	19					
Detroit Tigers	AL	1968	103	59	0.636	1 of 10	+12	1	1			

Team Name	League	Year	W	L	Win%	Fin	GB/GA	WS	Lge	LDS	Div	WC
Detroit Tigers	AL	1967	91	71	0.562	2t of 10	1					
Detroit Tigers	AL	1966	88	74	0.543	3 of 10	10					
Detroit Tigers	AL	1965	89	73	0.549	4 of 10	13					
Detroit Tigers	AL	1964	85	77	0.525	4 of 10	14					
Detroit Tigers	AL	1963	79	83	0.488	5t of 10	25.5					
Detroit Tigers	AL	1962	85	76	0.528	4 of 10	10.5					
Detroit Tigers	AL	1961	101	61	0.623	2 of 10	8					
Detroit Tigers	AL	1960	71	83	0.461	6 of 8	26					
Detroit Tigers	AL	1959	76	78	0.494	4 of 8	18					
Detroit Tigers	AL	1958	77	77	0.500	5 of 8	15					
Detroit Tigers	AL	1957	78	76	0.506	4 of 8	20					
Detroit Tigers	AL	1956	82	72	0.532	5 of 8	15					
Detroit Tigers	AL	1955	79	75	0.513	5 of 8	17					
Detroit Tigers	AL	1954	68	86	0.442	5 of 8	43					
Detroit Tigers	AL	1953	60	94	0.390	6 of 8	40.5					
Detroit Tigers	AL	1952	50	104	0.325	8 of 8	45					
Detroit Tigers	AL	1951	73	81	0.474	5 of 8	25					
Detroit Tigers	AL	1950	95	59	0.617	2 of 8	3					
Detroit Tigers	AL	1949	87	67	0.565	4 of 8	10					
Detroit Tigers	AL	1948	78	76	0.506	5 of 8	18.5					
Detroit Tigers	AL	1947	85	69	0.552	2 of 8	12					
Detroit Tigers	AL	1946	92	62	0.597	2 of 8	12					
Detroit Tigers	AL	1945	88	65	0.575	1 of 8	+1.5	1	1			
Detroit Tigers	AL	1944	88	66	0.571	2 of 8	1					
Detroit Tigers	AL	1943	78	76	0.506	5 of 8	20					
Detroit Tigers	AL	1942	73	81	0.474	5 of 8	30					
Detroit Tigers	AL	1941	75	79	0.487	4t of 8	26					
Detroit Tigers	AL	1940	90	64	0.584	1 of 8	+1		1			
Detroit Tigers	AL	1939	81	73	0.526	5 of 8	26.5					
Detroit Tigers	AL	1938	84	70	0.545	4 of 8	16					
Detroit Tigers	AL	1937	89	65	0.578	2 of 8	13					
Detroit Tigers	AL	1936	83	71	0.539	2 of 8	19.5					
Detroit Tigers	AL	1935	93	58	0.616	1 of 8	+3	1	1			
Detroit Tigers	AL	1934	101	53	0.656	1 of 8	+7		1			
Detroit Tigers	AL	1933	75	79	0.487	5 of 8	25					
Detroit Tigers	AL	1931	61	93	0.396	7 of 8	47					
Detroit Tigers	AL	1930	75	79	0.487	5 of 8	27					
Detroit Tigers	AL	1929	70	84	0.455	6 of 8	36					
Detroit Tigers	AL	1928	68	86	0.442	6 of 8	33					
Detroit Tigers	AL	1927	82	71	0.536	4 of 8	27.5					
Detroit Tigers	AL	1926	79	75	0.513	6 of 8	12					
Detroit Tigers	AL	1925	81	73	0.526	4 of 8	16.5					
Detroit Tigers	AL	1924	86	68	0.558	3 of 8	6					
Detroit Tigers	AL	1923	83	71	0.539	2 of 8	16					
Detroit Tigers	AL	1922	79	75	0.513	3 of 8	15					

Team Name	League	Year	W	L	Win%	Fin	GB/GA	WS	Lge	LDS	Div	WC
Detroit Tigers	AL	1921	71	82	0.464	6 of 8	27					
Detroit Tigers	AL	1920	61	93	0.396	7 of 8	37					
Detroit Tigers	AL	1919	80	60	0.571	4 of 8	8					
Detroit Tigers	AL	1918	55	71	0.437	7 of 8	20					
Detroit Tigers	AL	1917	78	75	0.510	4 of 8	21.5					
Detroit Tigers	AL	1916	87	67	0.565	3 of 8	4					
Detroit Tigers	AL	1915	100	54	0.649	2 of 8	2.5					
Detroit Tigers	AL	1914	80	73	0.523	4 of 8	19.5					
Detroit Tigers	AL	1913	66	87	0.431	6 of 8	30					
Detroit Tigers	AL	1912	69	84	0.451	6 of 8	36.5					
Detroit Tigers	AL	1911	89	65	0.578	2 of 8	13.5					
Detroit Tigers	AL	1910	86	68	0.558	3 of 8	18					
Detroit Tigers	AL	1909	98	54	0.645	1 of 8	+3.5		1			
Detroit Tigers	AL	1908	90	63	0.588	1 of 8	+0.5**		1			
Detroit Tigers	AL	1907	92	58	0.613	1 of 8	+1.5		1			
Detroit Tigers	AL	1906	71	78	0.477	6 of 8	21					
Detroit Tigers	AL	1905	79	74	0.516	3 of 8	15.5					
Detroit Tigers	AL	1904	62	90	0.408	7 of 8	32					
Detroit Tigers	AL	1903	65	71	0.478	5 of 8	25					
Detroit Tigers	AL	1902	52	83	0.385	7 of 8	30.5					
Detroit Tigers	AL	1901	74	61	0.548	3 of 8	8.5					
			8645	8437	0.506			4	10	1	3	1

* In 1972 the Tigers finished 0.5 games ahead of the Red Sox. There was a 13-day player strike at the beginning of that season cancelling an uneven amount of games. The owners refused to make up the games because they did not want to pay the players for the time they were on strike. Therefore, Detroit played one more game than Boston and finished the season with one more win and the same amount of losses.

** In 1908 Detroit finished the season 0.5 game ahead of Cleveland because the Tigers did not have to make up a game that was rained out and there was no rule in place that forced them to do so in the affect of a pennant outcome.

Florida Marlins

Stats

History
Year of Origin 1993

Years Played 18

Score & Rank
Total Points Score 27.9

Total Points Rank 21

Average Points Score.................................1.55

Average Points Rank...3

Postseason Results

	No.	Years
World Series Won	2	1997, 2003
League Championship Series Won	2	1997, 2003
League Division Series Won	2	1997, 2003
World Series Lost	0	
League Championship Series Lost	0	
League Division Series Lost	0	

Postseason Won-Loss Records and Winning Percentages

	Postseason Games		Postseason Series	
All Postseason Series	22-12	.647	6-0	1.000
World Series	8-5	.615	2-0	1.000
League Championship Series	8-5	.615	2-0	1.000
League Division Series	6-2	.750	2-0	1.000

Regular Season Results
All-Time Won-Loss Record 1363-1485

All-Time Winning Percentage .... .479

	No.	Years
League Titles before 1969	0	
Division Titles	0	
Wild Cards	2	1997, 2003

Regular Season High & Low Points

		Year(s)
Most Wins in a Season	92	1997
Most Losses in a Season	108	1998
Highest Winning Percentage	.568	1997
Lowest Winning Percentage	.333	1998
Longest Streak with Won-Loss Record .500 or Higher	3 years	2003-2005
Longest Streak with Won-Loss Record Below .500	5 years	1998-2002

Years with .500 record or Better
1990's .... 1 (out of 7)

2000's 5

2010's 0

6 out of 18 seasons played = 33%

Years Making Postseason
1990's...1

2000's...1

2010's...0

2 out of 18 seasons played = 11%

Streaks

• 1997-2003: Won two World Series, two League Championship Series, two League Division Series, and two Wild Cards in seven years.

Extra Bases

• Florida became the fastest expansion team to win the World Series, doing so in their fifth year in 1997. However, in 2001 Arizona took over this honor, as they won the World Series that year in their fourth year of existence.

• A year after winning the World Series, the 1998 Marlins finished the season with a 54-108 won-loss record. They lost two out of every three games and their poor record is the worst regular season record ever by a team the year after they won the World Series.

• Florida has not won a Division Title, they won both of their World Series Titles as the wild card team, and they have never lost a playoff series.

• The Marlins will change their official team name to the Miami Marlins prior to the 2012 season.

Scoring Opportunities

2000's

• In 2005 the Marlins had the National League Wild Card lead on September 13th by one game over Philadelphia and 1.5 games over Houston. But Florida lost two out of three games in their next two series, which were against the Astros and the Phillies. After the 13th the Marlins lost twelve of their next fourteen games, and on September 28th they were five games behind Philadelphia for the wild card spot. Florida won their last three games of the season but finished six games behind Houston for the wild card spot, who won it by one game over Philadelphia.

Year-to-Year Figures

Team	League	Year	W	L	Win%	Fin	GB/GA	WS	Lge	LDS	Div	WC
Florida Marlins	NL East	2010	80	82	0.494	3 of 5	17					
Florida Marlins	NL East	2009	87	75	0.537	2 of 5	6					
Florida Marlins	NL East	2008	84	77	0.522	3 of 5	7.5					
Florida Marlins	NL East	2007	71	91	0.438	5 of 5	18					
Florida Marlins	NL East	2006	78	84	0.481	4 of 5	19					
Florida Marlins	NL East	2005	83	79	0.512	3t of 5	7					
Florida Marlins	NL East	2004	83	79	0.512	3 of 5	13					
Florida Marlins	NL East	2003	91	71	0.562	2 of 5	10	1	1	1		1
Florida Marlins	NL East	2002	79	83	0.488	4 of 5	23					
Florida Marlins	NL East	2001	76	86	0.469	4 of 5	12					
Florida Marlins	NL East	2000	79	82	0.491	3 of 5	15.5					
Florida Marlins	NL East	1999	64	98	0.395	5 of 5	39					
Florida Marlins	NL East	1998	54	108	0.333	5 of 5	52					
Florida Marlins	NL East	1997	92	70	0.568	2 of 5	9	1	1	1		1
Florida Marlins	NL East	1996	80	82	0.494	3 of 5	16					
Florida Marlins	NL East	1995	67	76	0.469	4 of 5	22.5					
Florida Marlins	NL East	1994	51	64	0.443	5 of 5	23.5					
Florida Marlins	NL East	1993	64	98	0.395	6 of 7	33					
			1363	1485	0.479			2	2	2	0	2

Houston Astros

Stats

History
Year of Origin 1962

Years Played 49

Score & Rank
Total Points Score 23.8

Total Points Rank 22

Average Points Score..0.49

Average Points Rank 23

Postseason Results

Postseason Results	No.	Years
World Series Won	0	
League Championship Series Won	1	2005
League Division Series Won	2	2004, 2005
World Series Lost	1	2005
League Championship Series Lost	3	1980, 1986, 2004
League Division Series Lost	5	1981, 1997, 1998, 1999, 2001

Postseason Won-Loss Records and Winning Percentages

	Postseason Games		Postseason Series	
All Postseason Series	21-35	.375	3-9	.250
World Series	0-4	.000	0-1	.000
League Championship Series	11-13	.458	1-3	.250
League Division Series	10-18	.357	2-5	.286

Regular Season Results
All-Time Won-Loss Record 3888-3921

All-Time Winning Percentage .... .498

	No.	Years
League Titles before 1969	0	
Division Titles	7	1980, 1981, 1986, 1997, 1998, 1999, 2001
Wild Cards	2	2004, 2005

Regular Season High & Low Points

		Year(s)
Most Wins in a Season	102	1998
Most Losses in a Season	97	1965, 1975, 1991
Highest Winning Percentage	.630	1998
Lowest Winning Percentage	.398	1975
Longest Streak with Won-Loss Record .500 or Higher	7 years	1993-1999
Longest Streak with Won-Loss Record Below .500	7 years	1962-1968

Years with .500 record or Better
1960's	1 (out of 8)
1970's	5
1980's	7
1990's	8
2000's	7
2010's	0

28 out of 49 seasons played = 57%

Years Making Postseason
1960's	0
1970's	0
1980's	3
1990's	3
2000's	3
2010's	0

9 out of 49 seasons played = 18%

Streaks

- 1980-1986: Won three Division Titles in seven years.
- 1997-2005: Won two Wild Cards, four Division Titles, two League Division Series, and one League Championship Series in nine years.

Extra Bases

- In 1965 the Astros became the first professional baseball team to play indoors as they moved into the stadium known as the Astrodome.
- In 1966 Houston introduced the baseball world to plastic grass, which was called Astroturf.
- The Astros have the distinction of being the only National League expansion team to not finish in last place in their inaugural season, but this is also because they began play in the league the same year as the Mets in 1962 when New York lost 120 games.
- In four postseason appearances from 1997-2001 Houston lost all four times in the League Division Series, three times to Atlanta.
- The Astros became the first team to be swept in their first World Series appearance, which was in 2005.

Scoring Opportunities

1970's

- In 1979 the Astros led the National League West Division from May 30th to August 27th. On September 9th Houston had a half game lead over Cincinnati, but the rest of the season the Astros went 8-11, which included losing five of their last eight games, and they finished 1.5 games behind the Reds, who went 9-8 after the 9th. Houston had a 10.5 game lead on July 4th but lost thirteen of its next fifteen games.

1980's

- Houston beat the Dodgers in a one game playoff in 1980 to win the National League West Division. In the LCS the Astros faced Philadelphia and trailed by two runs after eight innings of Game 1. In the top of the ninth Houston got their first batter on base but their next three hitters all got out and they lost 3-1. The Astros won Games 2 & 3 both in extra innings to take a two game to one lead in the series with the last two games being played at home. Houston led Game 4 2-0 after seven innings, but gave up singles to the first four Phillies batters in the top of the eighth, as well as a sacrifice fly, and let in three runs. In the bottom of the ninth the

Astros tied the score but in the top of the tenth they gave up two doubles with two outs and let in two runs and lost the game 5-3. In Game 5 Houston had a 5-2 lead after seven innings but gave up five hits, one walk, and five runs in the top of the eighth. The Astros tied the score at seven in the bottom of the inning and the game went into extra innings. Houston gave up two doubles and let in one run with outs in the top of the tenth and lost the game 8-7 to lose the series. There were four extra innings games in the series.

- In 1981 the Astros won the second half of the National League West season in the strike split year by 1.5 games over Cincinnati. Houston met the Dodgers in the first round of the playoffs and won Games 1 & 2 at home, each on their last at bat. The Astros only needed to win one more game out of the next three to advance to the LCS, but lost Game 3 6-1. In Game 4 Houston trailed by one run in the top of the ninth when they had a runner on first with two outs, but their next batter up popped out and they lost 2-1. In Game 5 Houston only had five hits and lost the game 4-0 to lose the series they led two games to none.

- Houston won the National League West Division in 1986 and faced the Mets in the LCS. The Astros won Game 1 but lost Game 2 5-1. In Game 3 Houston had a 5-4 lead in the bottom of the ninth but gave up a two-run home run with one out and lost 6-5. The Astros won Game 4 and Game 5 was tied at one after nine innings. Houston had runners on first and second with two outs in the top of the tenth, but their next batter flied out. In the bottom of the twelfth the Astros got the first Mets batter out, but gave up a walk and two singles and let in the game winning run and lost 2-1. In Game 6 Houston led 3-0 in the top of the ninth but gave up three walks, three hits, and three runs and the game went into extra innings. In the fourteenth inning each team scored one run. In the top of the sixteenth the Astros gave up one walk, three hits, and two wild pitches, and let in three runs. In the bottom of the inning Houston scored two runs and had runners on first and second with two outs, but their next batter up struck out and Astros lost the game 7-6 and lost the series. The series featured four one run games and two extra innings games.

1990's

- In 1995 the Astros were out of the National League Central Division race behind Cincinnati but they were close in the NL Wild Card race with Colorado and Los Angeles. On September 26th Houston was only a half game behind the Dodgers but lost there next three games. The Astros won their final two games of the year but finished one game behind the Rockies for the final playoff spot. LA won the NL West Division by one game over Colorado. The Dodgers went 3-1 after the 26th and the Rockies went 2-3.

- Houston won the National League Central Division in 1997 with only 84 wins and faced Atlanta in the LDS. In Game 1 the Astros trailed by one run in the top of the eighth when they had the tying run on second base with two outs, but their next batter up struck out and they lost the game 2-1. Houston lost Game 2 13-3 and in Game 3 the Astros only had three hits and lost the game 4-1 and were swept in the series.

102

- In 1998 the Astros repeated as National League Central Division champs and won 102 regular season games, their most ever. In the LDS they faced San Diego and trailed by two runs entering the bottom of the ninth inning of Game 1. Houston scored one run and had the tying run on first base with two outs, but their next batter up flied out and they lost 2-1. The Astros won Game 2 and Game 3 was tied at one in the bottom of the seventh, but Houston gave up a solo home run with one out. In the top of the eighth the Astros had a runner on first with one out, but their next batter hit into a double play to end the inning and they lost the game 2-1. In Game 4 Houston only trailed by one run after seven innings, but in the bottom of the eighth they gave up a double, a walk, a triple, and a two run homer run, and they let in four runs and lost the game 6-1 to lose the series.
- The Astros won the National League Central Division in 1999 by one game over Cincinnati and met Atlanta in the LDS. Houston won Game 1 but only got one hit in Game 2 and lost the game 5-1. Game 3 was tied at three after nine innings. The Astros had the bases loaded with no outs in the bottom of the tenth, but their next two batters both hit ground balls that forced the runner on third out at home plate. With two outs their next batter up struck out. In the top of the twelfth the Astros gave up two singles and a double that drove in two runs and they lost the game 5-3. Houston lost Game 4 7-5 and lost the series.

2000's

- In 2001 Houston tied the Cardinals for the best record in the National League Central Division at 93-69. Both teams qualified for the playoffs and the Astros were given the division title because they won the head-to-head regular season series against St. Louis. In the LDS Houston played Atlanta and had a 3-2 lead after seven innings in Game 1. But in the top of the eighth the Astros gave up an error, three hits, and four runs and they lost the game 7-4. In Game 2 Houston gave up one run in the second inning and had a runner on second with two outs in the bottom of the eighth, but their next batter up flied out. In the bottom of the ninth inning the Astros first batter got on base, but their next batter hit into a double play and they lost the game 1-0. Houston lost Game 3 6-2 and lost the series in a sweep.
- The Astros were in a close race for the National League Central Division title with the Cubs in 2003. The two teams were tied for first place on September 25th with three games left to play in the season. Chicago won two out of three against Pittsburgh and Houston lost two of three to Milwaukee and the Astros lost the division by one game. Houston finished the season four games behind Florida for the wild card spot.
- In 2004 the Astros won the National League Wild Card by one game over the Giants and beat Atlanta in the LDS. In the LCS Houston faced the Cardinals and lost Game 1 10-7. Game 2 was tied at four after seven innings but the Astros gave up back-to-back solo home runs in the bottom of the eighth. They had runners on first and second with two outs in the top of the ninth, but their next batter up flied out and Houston lost 6-4. The Astros won the

next three games at home and only needed to win one of the next two games in St. Louis to advance to the World Series. In Game 6 the Astros tied the score at four in the top of the ninth and had runners on second and third with two outs, but their next batter up struck out. The game went into extra innings and in the bottom of the twelfth Houston gave up a walk and a two-run home run and lost 6-4. In Game 7 the Astros only got three hits and didn't have any after the fourth inning and lost the game 5-2 and lost the series.

- The Astros won the National League Wild Card spot in 2005 by one game over the Phillies. Houston beat Atlanta in the LDS and beat St. Louis in the LCS. In the World Series the Astros played the White Sox. In Game 1 Houston trailed by one run in the top of the seventh when they had runners on first and second with one out, but their next two batters both grounded out. In the top of the eighth the Astros had runners on first and third with no outs, but their next three batters all struck out. Houston gave up a run in the bottom of the eighth and lost the game 5-3. In Game 2 the Astros led 4-2 after six innings, but gave up a grand slam in the bottom of the seventh. Houston tied the score at six in the top of the ninth but gave up a solo home run in the bottom of the inning and lost 7-6. In Game 3 the Astros tied the score at five in the bottom of the eighth and had runners on second and third with two outs, but their next batter up struck out. Houston had the bases loaded in the bottom of the ninth with two outs, but their next batter up struck out and the game went into extra innings. The Astros had chances to score in extra innings but left two runners on in the bottom of the tenth and eleventh innings, grounding out each time with two outs and with runners on first and second base. In the top of the fourteenth Houston gave up a solo home run with two outs and gave up two singles and two walks and walked in a second run in the inning. In the bottom of the inning they had runners on first and third with two outs, but their next batter popped up and they lost 7-5. Game 4 was tied at zero in the bottom of the sixth inning when the Astros had the bases loaded with two outs, but their next batter up struck out. In the top of the eighth Houston gave up a single, got two outs that advanced the runner to third, and gave up another single that drove in the go-ahead run. In the bottom of the inning they had runners on first and second with one out, but their next two batters flied out and struck out. In the bottom of the ninth the Astros first batter up singled but their next three hitters all got out and they lost 1-0 and lost the series in a sweep.
- In 2006 the Astros trailed St. Louis by 8.5 games on September 19th. But Houston won nine games in a row and was only a half game behind the Cardinals on September 28th. The Astros had three games left to play against Atlanta and St. Louis had four games left in their season. But Houston lost two of their last three games to the Braves and the Cardinals won two of three and did not have to make up a rained out game. Houston finished in second place 1.5 games behind St. Louis.

Year-to-Year Figures

Team Name	League	Year	W	L	Win%	Fin	GB/GA	WS	Lge	LDS	Div	WC
Houston Astros	NL Cent	2010	76	86	0.469	4 of 6	15					
Houston Astros	NL Cent	2009	74	88	0.457	5 of 6	17					
Houston Astros	NL Cent	2008	86	75	0.534	3 of 6	11					
Houston Astros	NL Cent	2007	73	89	0.451	4 of 6	12					
Houston Astros	NL Cent	2006	82	80	0.506	2 of 6	1.5					
Houston Astros	NL Cent	2005	89	73	0.549	2 of 6	11		1	1		1
Houston Astros	NL Cent	2004	92	70	0.568	2 of 6	13			1		1
Houston Astros	NL Cent	2003	87	75	0.537	2 of 6	1					
Houston Astros	NL Cent	2002	84	78	0.519	2 of 6	13					
Houston Astros	NL Cent	2001	93	69	0.574	1t of 6	0*				1	
Houston Astros	NL Cent	2000	72	90	0.444	4 of 6	23					
Houston Astros	NL Cent	1999	97	65	0.599	1 of 6	+1.5				1	
Houston Astros	NL Cent	1998	102	60	0.630	1 of 6	+12.5				1	
Houston Astros	NL Cent	1997	84	78	0.519	1 of 5	+5				1	
Houston Astros	NL Cent	1996	82	80	0.506	2 of 5	6					
Houston Astros	NL Cent	1995	76	68	0.528	2 of 5	9					
Houston Astros	NL Cent	1994	66	49	0.574	2 of 5	0.5**					
Houston Astros	NL West	1993	85	77	0.525	3 of 7	19					
Houston Astros	NL West	1992	81	81	0.500	4 of 6	17					
Houston Astros	NL West	1991	65	97	0.401	6 of 6	29					
Houston Astros	NL West	1990	75	87	0.463	4t of 6	16					
Houston Astros	NL West	1989	86	76	0.531	3 of 6	6					
Houston Astros	NL West	1988	82	80	0.506	5 of 6	12.5					
Houston Astros	NL West	1987	76	86	0.469	3 of 6	14					
Houston Astros	NL West	1986	96	66	0.593	1 of 6	+10				1	
Houston Astros	NL West	1985	83	79	0.512	3t of 6	12					
Houston Astros	NL West	1984	80	82	0.494	2t of 6	12					
Houston Astros	NL West	1983	85	77	0.525	3 of 6	6					
Houston Astros	NL West	1982	77	85	0.475	5 of 6	12					
Houston Astros	NL West	1981	61	49	0.555	3, 1 of 6	8, +1.5				1	
Houston Astros	NL West	1980	93	70	0.571	1 of 6	+1				1	
Houston Astros	NL West	1979	89	73	0.549	2 of 6	1.5					
Houston Astros	NL West	1978	74	88	0.457	5 of 6	21					
Houston Astros	NL West	1977	81	81	0.500	3 of 6	17					
Houston Astros	NL West	1976	80	82	0.494	3 of 6	22					
Houston Astros	NL West	1975	64	97	0.398	6 of 6	43.5					
Houston Astros	NL West	1974	81	81	0.500	4 of 6	21					
Houston Astros	NL West	1973	82	80	0.506	4 of 6	17					
Houston Astros	NL West	1972	84	69	0.549	2 of 6	10.5					
Houston Astros	NL West	1971	79	83	0.488	4t of 6	11					
Houston Astros	NL West	1970	79	83	0.488	4 of 6	23					
Houston Astros	NL West	1969	81	81	0.500	5 of 6	12					
Houston Astros	NL	1968	72	90	0.444	10 of 10	25					

Team Name	League	Year	W	L	Win%	Fin	GB/GA	WS	Lge	LDS	Div	WC
Houston Astros	NL	1967	69	93	0.426	9 of 10	32.5					
Houston Astros	NL	1966	72	90	0.444	8 of 10	23					
Houston Astros	NL	1965	65	97	0.401	9 of 10	32					
Houston Colt .45's	NL	1964	66	96	0.407	9 of 10	27					
Houston Colt .45's	NL	1963	66	96	0.407	9 of 10	33					
Houston Colt .45's	NL	1962	64	96	0.400	8 of 10	36.5					
			3888	3921	0.498			0	1	2	7	2

* In 2001 the Astros and Cardinals finished the regular season with the same won-loss record. Since both teams made the playoffs and the Astros won the regular season series between the two teams, they won the NL Central Division Title and St. Louis won the NL Wild Card.

** In 1994 the regular season ended early because of players' strike that started on August 12th. At that point in the season Cincinnati and Houston had played an uneven amount of games, and the Reds led the Astros by 0.5 games on that date.

Kansas City Royals

Stats

History

Year of Origin 1969   Years Played 42

Score & Rank

Total Points Score .... 28.2   Average Points Score 0.67
Total Points Rank 20   Average Points Rank 17

Postseason Results	No.	Years
World Series Won	1	 1985
League Championship Series Won	2	.... 1980, 1985
League Division Series Won	0	
World Series Lost	1	 1980
League Championship Series Lost	4	.... 1976, 1977, 1978, 1984
League Division Series Lost	1	 1981

Postseason Won-Loss Records and Winning Percentages

	Postseason Games		Postseason Series	
All Postseason Series	18-25	.419	3-6	.333
World Series	6-7	.462	1-1	.500
League Championship Series	12-15	.444	2-4	.333
League Division Series	0-3	.000	0-1	.000

Regular Season Results

All-Time Won-Loss Record 3210-3455
All-Time Winning Percentage .... .482

	No.	Years
League Titles before 1969	0	
Division Titles	7	1976, 1977, 1978, 1980, 1981, 1984, 1985
Wild Cards	0	

Regular Season High & Low Points

		Year(s)
Most Wins in a Season	102	1977
Most Losses in a Season	106	2005
Highest Winning Percentage	.630	1977
Lowest Winning Percentage	.346	2005
Longest Streak with Won-Loss Record .500 or Higher	6 years	1975-1980
Longest Streak with Won-Loss Record Below .500	8 years	1995-2002

Years with .500 record or Better

1960's .... 0 (out of 1)
1970's 7
1980's 7
1990's 3
2000's 1
2010's 0
18 out of 42 seasons played = 43%

Years Making Postseason

1960's 0
1970's 3
1980's 4
1990's 0
2000's 0
2010's 0
7 out of 42 seasons played = 17%

Streaks

• 1976-1985: Won one World Series, two League Championship Series, and seven Division Titles in ten years.

Extra Bases

• Kansas City finished the regular season in first or second place in the American League West Division in fifteen of their first twenty-one seasons.

• It took the Royals twenty-eight years to finish in last place. The first time they did it was in 1996. Including 1996, from 1996-2010 they finished in last place nine times, occurring in 1996, 1997, 2001, 2004, 2005, 2006, 2007, 2009(tied), and 2010.

• From 1995-2010 the Royals only had one winning season in sixteen years. 2003 was their only year with a won-loss record above .500.

Scoring Opportunities

1970's

• In 1976 the Royals won the American League West Division and faced the Yankees in the LCS. In Game 1 Kansas City only trailed by one run after eight innings, but in the top of the ninth they gave up two singles and a double and let in two runs and lost the game 4-1. The Royals won Game 2 and scored three runs in the top of the first inning of Game 3. But they gave up a two-run home run in the bottom of the fourth and gave up three hits, three walks, and three runs in the bottom of the sixth. Kansas City didn't get any hits after the sixth inning and they lost the game 5-3. The Royals won Game 4 and Game 5 was tied at six in the top of the ninth inning. Kansas City had runners on first and second with two outs, but their next batter grounded out. In the bottom of the inning, the Royals gave up a home run to the first New York batter and lost the game 7-6 to lose the series.

• Kansas City won the American League West Division in 1977 and won 102 regular season games, their most ever as a franchise. They met the Yankees again in the LCS and won Game 1. In Game 2 the Royals only got three hits and lost the game 6-2. Kansas City won Game 3 to take a two game to one series lead with the last two games of the series at home. In Game 4 the Royals only trailed by one run after four innings but they only got two hits the rest of the game and lost it 6-4. In Game 5 Kansas City had a 3-2 lead after eight innings and only needed three outs to advance to the World Series. But in the top of the ninth they gave up two hits, a walk, a sacrifice fly, an error, and let in three runs. The Royals were retired in order in the bottom of the inning and lost the game 5-3 to lose the series.

- In 1978 the Royals won their third straight American League West Division title, and once again played the Yankees in the LCS. In Game 1 Kansas City only got two hits and lost the game 7-1. The Royals won Game 2 and had a 5-4 lead in the bottom of the eighth inning of Game 3 but gave up a two-run home run and lost the game 6-5. Game 4 was tied at one after five innings. In the bottom of the sixth inning Kansas City gave up a solo home run. In the top of the ninth the Royals first batter up doubled, but their next three batters all got out and they lost 2-1 and lost the series.

1980's

- Kansas City won their fourth American League West Division in five years in 1980. The Royals swept the Yankees in the LCS and faced the Phillies in the World Series. In Game 1 Kansas City trailed by one run in the top of the eighth inning when they had a runner on first with one out, but their next batter hit into a double play and they lost the game 7-6. In Game 2 the Royals had a 4-2 lead after seven innings but gave up a walk, two doubles, two singles, and four runs in the bottom of the eighth inning and lost the game 6-4. Kansas City won Games 3 & 4 to tie the series up. In Game 5 the Royals had a 3-2 lead after eight innings but gave up a single, a double, a sacrifice bunt, and another single, and let in two runs in the top of the ninth. In the bottom of the inning they loaded the bases with two outs, but their next batter struck out and they lost 4-3. In Game 6 Kansas City trailed by four runs in the top of the eighth inning when they loaded the bases with one out. They scored one run on a sacrifice fly and reloaded the bases with a single, but their next batter grounded out. The Royals had the bases loaded in the top of the ninth with one out, but their next two batters fouled out and struck out and they lost 4-1 and lost the series.
- In 1981 the Royals won the second half of the American League West Division in the strike split season. Kansas City faced Oakland in the first round of the playoffs and only had four hits in Game 1 and lost the game 4-0. Game 2 was tied at one after seven innings but the Royals gave up a single, a sacrifice bunt, and a double and let in the go ahead run in the top of the eighth. In the bottom of the inning Kansas City got their first two batters on base but their next three hitters all got out and they lost the game 2-1. In Game 3 the Royals trailed by three runs in the bottom of the eighth inning. They had runners on first and second with one out, but their next two batters struck out and flied out and they lost the game 4-1 to lose the series in a sweep.
- On September 15th in 1982 Kansas City had a two game lead over the Angels in the American League West Division. But the Royals lost ten of their next eleven games, including four to California and fell to 4.5 games behind the Angels on September 27th. Kansas City won five of their last six games of the year but California won three out of their last five and the Royals finished the season in second place three games behind the Angels.
- Kansas City won the American League West Division in 1984 and faced Detroit in the LCS.

The Royals gave up fourteen hits in Game 1 and lost the game 8-1. Game 2 was tied at three after nine innings. In the bottom of the tenth the Royals had runners on first and second with two outs, but their next batter flied out. In the top of the eleventh Kansas City gave up an error and two hits and let in two runs. In the bottom of the inning the Royals had runners on first and second with two outs and their next batter hit a fly ball to deep right field, but it stayed in the park and Kansas City lost the game 5-3. In Game 3 the Royals gave up a run in the second inning and only had one hit through seven innings. In the top of the eighth they had a runner on first with one out, but their next two batters fouled out and grounded out. In the top of the ninth Kansas City had a runner on first with two outs, but their next batter fouled out and they lost the game 1-0, and lost the series in a sweep.

Year-to-Year Figures

Team Name	League	Year	W	L	Win%	Fin	GB/GA	WS	Lge	LDS	Div	WC
Kansas City Royals	AL Cent	2010	67	95	0.414	5 of 5	27					
Kansas City Royals	AL Cent	2009	65	97	0.401	4t of 5	21.5					
Kansas City Royals	AL Cent	2008	75	87	0.463	4 of 5	13.5					
Kansas City Royals	AL Cent	2007	69	93	0.426	5 of 5	27					
Kansas City Royals	AL Cent	2006	62	100	0.383	5 of 5	34					
Kansas City Royals	AL Cent	2005	56	106	0.346	5 of 5	43					
Kansas City Royals	AL Cent	2004	58	104	0.358	5 of 5	34					
Kansas City Royals	AL Cent	2003	83	79	0.512	3 of 5	7					
Kansas City Royals	AL Cent	2002	62	100	0.383	4 of 5	32.5					
Kansas City Royals	AL Cent	2001	65	97	0.401	5 of 5	26					
Kansas City Royals	AL Cent	2000	77	85	0.475	4 of 5	18					
Kansas City Royals	AL Cent	1999	64	97	0.398	4 of 5	32.5					
Kansas City Royals	AL Cent	1998	72	89	0.447	3 of 5	16.5					
Kansas City Royals	AL Cent	1997	67	94	0.416	5 of 5	19					
Kansas City Royals	AL Cent	1996	75	86	0.466	5 of 5	24					
Kansas City Royals	AL Cent	1995	70	74	0.486	2 of 5	30					
Kansas City Royals	AL Cent	1994	64	51	0.557	3 of 5	4					
Kansas City Royals	AL West	1993	84	78	0.519	3 of 7	10					
Kansas City Royals	AL West	1992	72	90	0.444	5t of 7	24					
Kansas City Royals	AL West	1991	82	80	0.506	6 of 7	13					
Kansas City Royals	AL West	1990	75	86	0.466	6 of 7	27.5					
Kansas City Royals	AL West	1989	92	70	0.568	2 of 7	7					
Kansas City Royals	AL West	1988	84	77	0.522	3 of 7	19.5					
Kansas City Royals	AL West	1987	83	79	0.512	2 of 7	2					
Kansas City Royals	AL West	1986	76	86	0.469	3t of 7	16					
Kansas City Royals	AL West	1985	91	71	0.562	1 of 7	+1	1	1		1	
Kansas City Royals	AL West	1984	84	78	0.519	1 of 7	+3				1	
Kansas City Royals	AL West	1983	79	83	0.488	2 of 7	20					
Kansas City Royals	AL West	1982	90	72	0.556	2 of 7	3					
Kansas City Royals	AL West	1981	50	53	0.485	5, 1 of 7	12, +1				1	
Kansas City Royals	AL West	1980	97	65	0.599	1 of 7	+14		1		1	
Kansas City Royals	AL West	1979	85	77	0.525	2 of 7	3					
Kansas City Royals	AL West	1978	92	70	0.568	1 of 7	+5				1	
Kansas City Royals	AL West	1977	102	60	0.630	1 of 7	+8				1	
Kansas City Royals	AL West	1976	90	72	0.556	1 of 6	+2.5				1	
Kansas City Royals	AL West	1975	91	71	0.562	2 of 6	7					
Kansas City Royals	AL West	1974	77	85	0.475	5 of 6	13					
Kansas City Royals	AL West	1973	88	74	0.543	2 of 6	6					
Kansas City Royals	AL West	1972	76	78	0.494	4 of 6	16.5					
Kansas City Royals	AL West	1971	85	76	0.528	2 of 6	16					
Kansas City Royals	AL West	1970	65	97	0.401	4t of 6	33					
Kansas City Royals	AL West	1969	69	93	0.426	4 of 6	28					
			3210	3455	0.482			1	2	0	7	0

Los Angeles Angels of Anaheim

Stats

History
Year of Origin 1961

Years Played 50

Score & Rank
Total Points Score 34.8

Average Points Score 0.70

Total Points Rank 18

Average Points Rank 15

Postseason Results	No.	Years
World Series Won	1	2002
League Championship Series Won	1	2002
League Division Series Won	3	2002, 2005, 2009
World Series Lost	0	
League Championship Series Lost	5	1979, 1982, 1986, 2005, 2009
League Division Series Lost	3	2004, 2007, 2008

Postseason Won-Loss Records and Winning Percentages

	Postseason Games		Postseason Series	
All Postseason Series	27-34	.443	5-8	.385
World Series	4-3	.571	1-0	1.000
League Championship Series	13-19	.406	1-5	.167
League Division Series	10-12	.455	3-3	.500

Regular Season Results
All-Time Won-Loss Record 3967-4033

All-Time Winning Percentage 498

	No.	Years
League Titles before 1969	0	
Division Titles	8	1979, 1982, 1986, 2004, 2005, 2007, 2008, 2009
Wild Cards	1	2002

Regular Season High & Low Points		Year(s)
Most Wins in a Season	100	2008
Most Losses in a Season	95	1968, 1980
Highest Winning Percentage	.617	2008
Lowest Winning Percentage	.406	1980
Longest Streak with Won-Loss Record .500 or Higher	6 years	2004-2009
Longest Streak with Won-Loss Record Below .500	7 years	1971-1977

Years with .500 record or Better
1960's .... 3 (out of 9)

1970's 3

1980's 4

1990's 4

2000's 8

2010's 0

22 out of 50 seasons played = 44%

Years Making Postseason
1960's 0

1970's 1

1980's 2

1990's 0

2000's 6

2010's 0

9 out of 50 seasons played = 18%

Streaks

- 1979-1986: Won three Division Titles in eight years.
- 2002-2009: Won one Wild Card, five Division Titles, three League Division Series, one League Championship Series, and one World Series in eight years. This included winning five Division Titles in six years from 2004-2009.

Extra Bases

- The Angels have had four different team names in their franchise history. From 1961-1964 the franchise played in Los Angeles and was known as the Los Angeles Angels. Before the 1965 season the team moved to Anaheim and became the California Angels. In 1997 they became known as the Anaheim Angels and in 2005 their team name changed to the Los Angeles Angels of Anaheim.
- From 1995-1998 the Angels had three second place finishes in four years, finishing one, six, and three games out in 1995, 1997, and 1998, respectively.
- Through the 2010 season, the Angels have been eliminated eight times from the postseason and four of those times the team that eliminated them was the Red Sox (1986, 2004, 2007, and 2008).

Scoring Opportunities

1970's

- In 1979 the California Angels won their first American League West Division title and played Baltimore in the LCS. Game 1 was tied at three after nine innings. In the bottom of the tenth California had two Orioles out with a runner on second base. The Angels decided to walk an Orioles batter intentionally and pitch to a weaker hitter. But the weaker batter was pinch hit for and the new batter hit a three-run homer that won the game for Baltimore 6-3. In Game 2 California trailed by three runs after eight innings. In the top of the ninth the Angels scored two runs and had the bases loaded with two outs, but their next batter grounded out and they lost 9-8. California won Game 3 but lost Game 4 8-0 and lost the series.

1980's

- California won the American League West Division in 1982 and faced Milwaukee in the LCS. The Angels won Games 1 & 2 and only needed one more win to advance to their first World Series. But California lost Game 3 5-3 and Game 4 9-5. In Game 5 the Angels had a 3-2 lead after six innings. In the bottom of the seventh they had two Brewers out with the bases loaded and gave up a single to the next Milwaukee batter and let in two runs. In the top of the eighth California had a runner on first with two outs, but their next batter flied out. In the top of the ninth they got their first batter on base, but the next three hitters all got out and they lost 4-3 and lost the series.

- In 1985 the Angels led Kansas City by one game in the American League West Division on September 30th with seven games remaining when the two teams met for a four game series. California lost three of the four games and fell to one game behind the Royals in the standings. The rest of the season the Angels won two of their last three games but so did Kansas City and California finished in second place one game behind the Royals. A two-day players strike that season could have contributed to the Angels missing the playoffs. The strike cancelled two home games California had against a weak Mariners team and the makeup games were moved to Seattle as part of back-to-back doubleheaders, which the teams split.

- The Angels won the American League West Division in 1986 and faced the Red Sox in the LCS. California won Game 1, lost Game 2 9-2, and won Games 3 & 4 to take a three games to one lead in the series with Game 5 at home. In Game 5 they had a 5-2 lead after eight innings but gave up four runs in the top of the ninth on separate two-run home runs, the second coming with two outs and right after they hit a batter. In the bottom of the inning the Angels tied the score and had the bases loaded with one out, but their next two batters flied out and lined out. In the top of the eleventh California hit the first Red Sox batter and gave up two singles and a sacrifice fly that drove in the go-ahead run. The Angels were retired in the bottom of the inning and lost the game 7-6. California lost the next two games in Boston 10-4 and 8-1 and lost the series they were one out away from winning with a three games to one series lead.

1990's

- In 1995 the Angels were in first place in the American League West Division from July 2nd to September 20th and had an eleven game lead on August 9th. From August 21st to September 6th they went 2-14 and in the middle of September they lost nine games in a row and they fell to two games behind Seattle on September 23rd. California won six of their final seven games and tied the Mariners for first place at the end of the regular season. A one game playoff was played to determine the division champion and the Angels only had three hits in the game and lost it 9-1 to lose the division title. California also missed the wild card spot, as the Yankees had a record that was one game better then both AL West teams.

- The Anaheim Angels led the American League West Division in 1998 from August 14th to September 15th. From September 11th to the 18th Anaheim lost seven out of eight games including two to second place Texas and the Angels fell behind the Rangers in the standings on

September 17th. The two teams were tied on September 21st when they met for a three game series in Anaheim. The Angels lost all three games being outscored 25-3 (9-1, 9-1, and 7-1). Anaheim was now three games behind Texas with four games left against Oakland. The Angels split their last four games with the A's but the Rangers split a four games series with Seattle and Anaheim finished the season in second place three games behind the Rangers.

2000's

• Anaheim led the American League West Division by one game over Oakland on September 17th of the 2002 season. But the Angels lost their next two games to the A's, lost six of their next seven games, and lost seven of their final eleven games of the season. Oakland went 9-2 after the 17th and Anaheim finished in second place in the division four games behind the A's. However, the Angels won the American League Wild Card and went on to win the World Series this year.

• In 2004 the Angels won the American League West Division by one game over Oakland. Anaheim played Boston in the LDS and gave up seven runs in the fourth inning of Game 1 and lost the game 9-3. In Game 2 the Angels only trailed by one run after eight innings, but they gave up four runs in the top of the ninth and lost the game 8-3. Game 3 was tied at five after nine innings. In the top of the tenth, Anaheim had runners on first and third with two outs, but their next batter grounded out. In the bottom of the inning they gave up a two-run home run with two outs and lost 8-6 and lost the series in a sweep.

• The Los Angeles Angels of Anaheim repeated as American League West Division champs in 2005 and beat the Yankees in the LDS. In the LCS Los Angeles faced the White Sox and won Game 1. Game 2 was tied at one entering the bottom of the ninth and the Angels got the first two Chicago hitters out. The third batter appeared to strike out and the game was going to go into extra innings, but as the catcher rolled the ball back to the pitchers' mound the batter ran to first base, as he had not been called out yet. The umpire ruled that the ball hit the ground before it went into the catchers' glove, meaning that if the batter swung and missed at the third strike, the catcher had to throw the runner out at first base for the out to be recorded. Since the batter was already on first base he was ruled safe. On the next at bat the White Sox put in a pinch runner who stole second base, and then the following batter hit a double that drove in the game winning run and Los Angeles lost the game 2-1. The game should have gone into extra innings but instead the series was tied at one. In Game 3 the Angels were held to four hits and lost the game 5-2 and then lost Game 4 8-2. In Game 5 Los Angeles led 3-2 after six innings, but in the final three innings they gave up four runs and their last nine batters were retired in order and they lost the game 6-3 and lost the series.

• In 2007 the Angels won the American League West Division and met Boston in the LDS. In Game 1 Los Angeles only had four hits and they lost the game 4-0. Game 2 was tied at three in the top of the eighth when the Angels had runners on second and third with two outs, but their next batter struck out. In the bottom of the ninth Los Angeles had two Red Sox hitters out with one runner on second base when they walked a batter intentionally. The following Boston batter hit a three-run home run and the Angels lost 6-3. In Game 3 Los Angeles only trailed by two runs after seven innings, but gave up seven runs in the top of the eighth inning and lost the game 9-1 to lose the series. The Angels were outscored 19-4 in the three game sweep.

- The Angels won the American League West Division again in 2008. They had the best overall record in the American League and faced Boston again in the LDS. In Game 1 Los Angeles trailed by one run in the bottom of the eighth when they had a runner thrown out at third base with one out. In the top of the ninth the Angels gave up two runs and they lost the game 4-1. In Game 2 Los Angeles tied the score at five in the bottom of the eighth, but gave up a two-run home run in the top of the ninth and lost the game 7-5. The Angels won Game 3 and Game 4 was tied at two after eight innings. In the top of the ninth Los Angeles' first batter up doubled and got to third base with one out. But on the next at bat the Angels tried a suicide squeeze and failed and the runner from third got caught stealing home and was out. In the bottom of the inning the Angels had two Red Sox out with a runner on second base. The next Boston batter singled which drove in the game winning run and Los Angeles lost the game 3-2 and lost the series.

- In 2009 the Angels won their third straight American League West Division title and played the Red Sox in the LDS for the third year in a row. Los Angeles finally beat Boston as they swept the Red Sox in three games. In the LCS the Angels faced the Yankees and only had four hits in Game 1 and lost the game 4-1. Game 2 was tied at two after nine innings and Los Angeles scored one run in the top of the eleventh. But in the bottom of the inning the Angels closer left a 0-2 pitch over the plate to one of the better Yankees power hitters, and he hit a home run to tie the game. Los Angeles had scoring chances the next two innings but they left two runners on in the top of the twelfth and top of the thirteenth. In the bottom of the thirteenth the Angels had one Yankees batter out with runners on first and second. The next New York batter hit a ground ball to the second baseman, who should have thrown to first base to get one sure out, but he threw to second base wildly and the Yankees runner that started on second base scored and Los Angeles lost 4-3. The Angels won Games 3, lost Game 4 10-1, and won Game 5. In Game 6 Los Angeles only trailed by one run in the bottom of the eighth inning but they gave up three walks, two errors, and a sacrifice fly, and let in two runs. They lost the game 5-2 and lost the series.

Year-to-Year Figures

Team Name	League	Year	W	L	Win%	Fin	GB/GA	WS	Lge	LDS	Div	WC
LA Angels of Anaheim	AL West	2010	80	82	0.494	3 of 4	10					
LA Angels of Anaheim	AL West	2009	97	65	0.599	1 of 4	+10			1	1	
LA Angels of Anaheim	AL West	2008	100	62	0.617	1 of 4	+21				1	
LA Angels of Anaheim	AL West	2007	94	68	0.580	1 of 4	+6				1	
LA Angels of Anaheim	AL West	2006	89	73	0.549	2 of 4	4					
LA Angels of Anaheim	AL West	2005	95	67	0.586	1 of 4	+7			1	1	
Anaheim Angels	AL West	2004	92	70	0.568	1 of 4	+1				1	
Anaheim Angels	AL West	2003	77	85	0.475	3 of 4	19					
Anaheim Angels	AL West	2002	99	63	0.611	2 of 4	4	1	1	1		1
Anaheim Angels	AL West	2001	75	87	0.463	3 of 4	41					
Anaheim Angels	AL West	2000	82	80	0.506	3 of 4	9.5					
Anaheim Angels	AL West	1999	70	92	0.432	4 of 4	25					
Anaheim Angels	AL West	1998	85	77	0.525	2 of 4	3					
Anaheim Angels	AL West	1997	84	78	0.519	2 of 4	6					
California Angels	AL West	1996	70	91	0.435	4 of 4	19.5					
California Angels	AL West	1995	78	67	0.538	2 of 4	1					
California Angels	AL West	1994	47	68	0.409	4 of 4	5.5					
California Angels	AL West	1993	71	91	0.438	5t of 7	23					
California Angels	AL West	1992	72	90	0.444	5t of 7	24					
California Angels	AL West	1991	81	81	0.500	7 of 7	14					
California Angels	AL West	1990	80	82	0.494	4 of 7	23					
California Angels	AL West	1989	91	71	0.562	3 of 7	8					
California Angels	AL West	1988	75	87	0.463	4 of 7	29					
California Angels	AL West	1987	75	87	0.463	6t of 7	10					
California Angels	AL West	1986	92	70	0.568	1 of 7	+5				1	
California Angels	AL West	1985	90	72	0.556	2 of 7	1					
California Angels	AL West	1984	81	81	0.500	2t of 7	3					
California Angels	AL West	1983	70	92	0.432	5t of 7	29					
California Angels	AL West	1982	93	69	0.574	1 of 7	+3				1	
California Angels	AL West	1981	51	59	0.464	4, 7 of 7	6, 8.5					
California Angels	AL West	1980	65	95	0.406	6 of 7	31					
California Angels	AL West	1979	88	74	0.543	1 of 7	+3				1	
California Angels	AL West	1978	87	75	0.537	2t of 7	5					
California Angels	AL West	1977	74	88	0.457	5 of 7	28					
California Angels	AL West	1976	76	86	0.469	4t of 6	14					
California Angels	AL West	1975	72	89	0.447	6 of 6	25.5					
California Angels	AL West	1974	68	94	0.420	6 of 6	22					
California Angels	AL West	1973	79	83	0.488	4 of 6	15					
California Angels	AL West	1972	75	80	0.484	5 of 6	18					
California Angels	AL West	1971	76	86	0.469	4 of 6	25.5					
California Angels	AL West	1970	86	76	0.531	3 of 6	12					
California Angels	AL West	1969	71	91	0.438	3 of 6	26					
California Angels	AL	1968	67	95	0.414	8 of 10	36					

Los Angeles Angels of Anaheim

Team Name	League	Year	W	L	Win%	Fin	GB/GA	WS	Lge	LDS	Div	WC
California Angels	AL	1967	84	77	0.522	5 of 10	7.5					
California Angels	AL	1966	80	82	0.494	6 of 10	18					
California Angels	AL	1965	75	87	0.463	7 of 10	27					
Los Angeles Angels	AL	1964	82	80	0.506	5 of 10	17					
Los Angeles Angels	AL	1963	70	91	0.435	9 of 10	34					
Los Angeles Angels	AL	1962	86	76	0.531	3 of 10	10					
Los Angeles Angels	AL	1961	70	91	0.435	8 of 10	38.5					
			3967	4003	0.498			1	1	3	8	1

Los Angeles Dodgers

Stats

History
Year of Origin 1884
Years Played...127

Score & Rank
Total Points Score 168.4
Average Points Score...1.33
Total Points Rank 3
Average Points Rank...6

Postseason Results

	No.	Years
World Series Won	6	1955, 1959, 1963, 1965, 1981, 1988
League Championship Series Won	5	1974, 1977, 1978, 1981, 1988
League Division Series Won	3	1981, 2008, 2009
World Series Lost	12	1916, 1920, 1941, 1947, 1949, 1952, 1953, 1956, 1966, 1974, 1977, 1978
League Championship Series Lost	4	1983, 1985, 2008, 2009
League Division Series Lost	4	1995, 1996, 2004, 2006

Postseason Won-Loss Records and Winning Percentages

	Postseason Games		Postseason Series	
All Postseason Series	76-97	.439	14-20	.412
World Series	45-60	.429	6-12	.333
League Championship Series	21-23	.477	5-4	.555
League Division Series	10-14	.417	3-4	.429

Regular Season Results
All-Time Won-Loss Record 10135-9199
All-Time Winning Percentage .... .524

	No.	Years
League Titles before 1969	17	1889, 1890, 1899, 1900, 1916, 1920, 1941, 1947, 1949, 1952, 1953, 1955, 1956, 1959, 1963, 1965, 1966
Division Titles	11	1974, 1977, 1978, 1981, 1983, 1985, 1988, 1995, 2004, 2008, 2009
Wild Cards	2	1996, 2006

Regular Season High & Low Points

		Year(s)
Most Wins in a Season	105	1953
Most Losses in a Season	104	1905
Highest Winning Percentage	.682	1899, 1953
Lowest Winning Percentage	.316	1905
Longest Streak with Won-Loss Record .500 or Higher	13 years	1945-1957
Longest Streak with Won-Loss Record Below .500	11 years	1904-1914

Years with .500 record or Better	
1880's	3 (out of 6)
1890's	6
1900's	4
1910's	2
1920's	4
1930's	4
1940's	9
1950's	9
1960's	7
1970's	9
1980's	6
1990's	8
2000's	9
2010's	0

80 out of 127 seasons played = 63%

Years Making Postseason	
1880's	No Postseason
1890's	No Postseason
1900's	0
1910's	1
1920's	1
1930's	0
1940's	3
1950's	5
1960's	3
1970's	3
1980's	4
1990's	2
2000's	4
2010's	0

26 out of 127 seasons played = 20%

Streaks

- 1916-1920: Won two League Titles in five years.
- 1947-1966: Won ten League Titles and four World Series in twenty years.
- 1974-1988: Won seven Division Titles, one League Division Series, five League Championship Series, and two World Series in fifteen years.
- 2004-2009: Won two League Division Series, three Division Titles, and one Wild Card in six years.

Extra Bases

- In 1946, 1950, and 1951 the Dodgers lost the pennant on the final day of the season each year, three times in six years. They won the pennant in 1947 and 1949.
- The Dodgers franchise has had the worst record in the National League only twice, occurring in the 1905 and 1992 seasons.
- From 1939-2010 the Dodgers only had fourteen losing seasons in seventy-two years. The years were 1944, 1958, 1964, 1967, 1968, 1979, 1984, 1986, 1987, 1989, 1992, 1999, 2005, and 2010. From 1933-1938 they had six losing seasons in a row.
- Through the 2010 season, the Dodgers lost twelve times in the World Series. Eight of those twelve losses were against the Yankees and six of those eight occurred from 1941-1956.

Scoring Opportunities

1910's

- In 1916 the Brooklyn Robins won the National League pennant and played Boston in the World Series. In Game 1 the Robins trailed by five runs in the top of the ninth and then scored four runs and had the bases loaded with two outs, but their next batter up grounded out and they lost the game 6-5. Game 2 was tied at one in the top of the eighth when Brooklyn had runners on first and third with one out, but on a ground ball to the shortstop their runner on third was thrown out at home plate. The game went into extra innings and in the top of the thirteenth the Robins had a runner on second with one out, but their next two batters popped up and flied out. In the bottom of the fourteenth Brooklyn gave up a walk, a sacrifice bunt, and a single that drove in the winning run and they lost 2-1. The Robins won Game 3 but had only eight hits total in Games 4 & 5 and lost them 6-2 and 4-1 to lose the series.

1920's

- Brooklyn won the National League pennant in 1920 and faced Cleveland in a best of nine games World Series. In Game 1 the Robins trailed by two runs in the bottom of the eighth inning when they had runners on first and second with one out, but their next two batters popped up and grounded out and they lost the game 3-1. Brooklyn won Games 2 & 3 but lost Game 4 5-1 and Game 5 8-1. In Game 6 the Robins trailed by one run in the top of the eighth when they had a runner on second with one out, but their next two batters popped up and grounded out. In the top of the ninth Brooklyn had a runner on first with one out but their next two batters grounded out and flied out and they lost 1-0. In Game 7 the Robins were held to five hits lost the game 3-0. Brooklyn lost the series five games to two after having a two games to one series lead. They were outscored 17-2 in the four consecutive losses.
- In 1924 Brooklyn trailed the Giants by eight games in the National League on August 24th. The Robins had a fifteen game winning streak that brought them within one game of New York on September 6th. The rest of the year Brooklyn stayed within three games of the Giants, but went 10-8 to finish the season while New York went 13-7. Brooklyn was only a half a game back on September 22nd with four games left in the season but they split their final four games of the year while the Giants won four of their last five. The Robins finished in second place 1.5 games behind New York.

1930's

- Brooklyn led the National League by one game over St. Louis on September 15th in 1930 but lost their next seven games and lost eight of their last ten games of the year. The Robins fell to fourth place in the standings and finished six games behind the Cardinals, who went 10-2 after September 15th.

1940's

- The Brooklyn Dodgers won the National League pennant in 1941 and faced the Yankees in the World Series. In Game 1 Brooklyn trailed by one run in the top of the seventh inning when they had runners on first and second with no outs, but their next two batters hit into a double play and a ground out. In the top of the ninth the Dodgers had runners on first and second with one out, but their next batter hit into a double play and they lost 3-2. Brooklyn won Game 2 and Game 3 was tied at zero after seven innings. The Dodgers gave up four singles and two runs in the top of the eighth and scored one run in the bottom of the inning. They had a runner on first with two outs in the bottom of the eighth but their next batter up popped out and they lost the game 2-1. In Game 4 Brooklyn had a 4-3 lead after eight innings and got the first two Yankees batters out in the top of the ninth. They struck out the third batter of the inning, but the sharp curve ball from the pitcher got away from the catcher and the batter ran to first base as he was not ruled out due to the wild pitch. The Dodgers then gave up three hits, two walks, and four runs and lost the game 7-4 to fall behind in the series by two games instead of having the series tied at two. Brooklyn only had four hits in Game 5 and lost the game 3-1 to lose the series.

- In 1942 the Dodgers were in first place in the National League from April 19th to September 12th and had a ten game lead over the Cardinals on August 5th. Starting on August 14th, St. Louis went 38-6 the rest of the season while Brooklyn went 28-17. The Dodgers had a five game losing streak in the middle of September, which included two losses to the Cardinals, and gave St. Louis the lead. Brooklyn won their last eight games of the year and won 104 games in the season, but finished two games behind St. Louis.

- Brooklyn was in another close race with St. Louis in 1946 as the two teams were not separated by more than 2.5 games over the final two months of the regular season. On August 27th they were tied and they both went 21-11 the rest of the year. They were tied at the end of the regular season so the first best out of three game playoff series was played to determine the NL champion. In the first game in St. Louis the Dodgers trailed by two runs in the top of the eighth inning when they had runners on first and second with one out, but their next two batters grounded out and lined out and they lost the game 4-2. Brooklyn needed to win the next two games to win the NL pennant, but they lost the second game 8-4 at home and lost the pennant.

- In 1947 Brooklyn won the National League pennant and faced the Yankees in the World Series. In Game 1 the Dodges trailed by two runs in top of the ninth when they got their first batter up on base, but their next three hitters all got out and they lost 5-3. Brooklyn lost Game 2 10-3 and won Games 3 & 4 to tie the series up. In Game 5 the Dodgers trailed by one run in the bottom of the seventh inning when they had the bases loaded with two outs, but their next batter up struck out. In the bottom of the ninth Brooklyn's first batter up singled but their next three hitters all got out and they lost 2-1. The Dodgers won Game 6 but lost Game 7 5-2 and lost the series.

- The Dodgers won the National League pennant in 1949 and faced the Yankees again in the World Series. Game 1 was tied at zero after eight innings. Brooklyn was retired in order in the top of the ninth and in the bottom of the inning they gave up a home run to the first

New York batter and lost 1-0. Brooklyn won Game 2 and Game 3 was tied at one after eight innings. In the top of the ninth the Dodgers had two Yankees out with a runner on first base but gave up a walk and three singles and let in three runs. In the bottom of the inning Brooklyn scored twice on two solo home runs but lost 4-3. In Game 4 the Dodgers trailed by two runs in the bottom of the sixth inning with runners on first and third with two outs, but their next batter up struck out. Brooklyn was retired in order in the last three innings and lost the game 6-4. The Dodgers lost Game 5 10-6 and lost the series.

1950's

• In 1950 the Dodgers were 7.5 games behind Philadelphia on September 20th in the National League. But the Phillies lost seven of their next nine games and Brooklyn went 9-3 over the same period. With two games left in the season the Dodgers trailed Philadelphia by two games with two games left against the Phillies in Brooklyn. The Dodgers needed to win both games to tie Philadelphia for first place. Brooklyn won the first game 7-3 and the second game was tied at one after eight innings. In the bottom of the ninth the Dodgers first batter up walked and their second batter singled. With runners on first and second their next batter singled to center field. The runner from second base was waved home by the third base coach and stumbled a little bit around third and was thrown out at home plate by fifteen feet. Brooklyn's next batter walked which loaded the bases with one out, but their next two hitters fouled out and flied out and the game went into extra innings. In the top of the tenth the Dodgers gave up singles to the first two Phillies batters then got one out. The next Philadelphia batter hit a three-run home run and Brooklyn was retired in order in the bottom of the inning. The Dodgers lost the game 4-1 and finished two games behind the Phillies in second place.

• During the 1951 season the Dodgers led the Giants in the National League by thirteen games on August 11th and by six games on September 14th. The rest of the season, Brooklyn went 7-9 while New York went 12-1 and the two teams were tied at the end of the regular season. A best of three game playoff series was needed to determine the NL champion. In the first game the Dodgers only had five hits and did not have any after the fifth inning and they lost the game 3-1. Brooklyn had to win the next two games as the visiting team to win the pennant. The Dodgers won the second game 10-0. In the third game Brooklyn scored three runs in the top of the eighth and took a 4-1 lead. In the bottom of the ninth the Dodgers gave up two singles before getting the first out. The Giants next batter doubled which drove in one run. Then Brooklyn gave up a three-run home run and lost the game 5-4. The Dodgers lost the pennant in the last inning of the season in consecutive seasons in 1950 & 1951.

• In 1952 Brooklyn won the National League pennant and faced the Yankees in the World Series. The Dodgers won Game 1, lost Game 2 7-1 in which they only had three hits, and won Game 3. In Game 4 Brooklyn trailed by one run when they got their first batter on base in the top of the seventh. But their next batter struck out and the following batter hit into a double play.

In the top of the eighth the Dodgers got their first hitter of the inning on base again but their next three batters all got out and they lost the game 2-0. Brooklyn won Game 5 to take a three games to two series lead with Games 6 & 7 at home. In Game 6 the Dodgers led 1-0 after six innings but gave up a solo home run, a single, a balk, and another single that drove in another run in the top of the seventh, and gave up another solo home run in the top of the eighth. In the bottom of the eighth Brooklyn scored one run and had the tying run on second base with two outs, but their next batter up struck out and they lost the game 3-2. Game 7 was tied at two after five innings. The Dodgers gave up a solo home run in the top of the sixth and gave up a single, a sacrifice bunt, and another single in the top of the seventh. In the bottom of the seventh Brooklyn trailed by two runs and had the bases loaded with one out, but their next two batters both popped up and they lost the game 4-2, and lost the series.

- The Dodgers repeated as National League champions in 1953 and met the Yankees again in the World Series. Game 1 was tied at five in the top of the seventh when Brooklyn had runners on first and second with no outs. The Dodgers next two batters both tried to advance the runners with a bunt, but both times the lead runner was thrown out at third base and the next Brooklyn batter up fouled out. In the bottom of the seventh inning the Dodgers gave up a home run and in they gave up three runs in the eighth inning and lost the game 9-5. In Game 2 Brooklyn led 2-1 after six innings but gave up a solo home run in the bottom of the seventh and a two-run home run in the bottom of the eighth. In the top of the ninth the Dodgers had runners on first and second with two outs, but their next batter up grounded out and they lost 4-2. Brooklyn won Games 3 & 4 to even the series, but lost Game 5 11-7. In Game 6 the Dodgers tied the score at three in the top of the ninth with at two-run home run. But in the bottom of the inning they walked the first batter and with one out they gave up two singles and let in the game winning run and lost 4-3 to lose the series.

- Brooklyn won the National League pennant in 1956 and faced the Yankees again in the World Series. The Dodgers won Games 1 & 2 at home and had a 2-1 lead in Game 3 in the bottom of the sixth inning, but with two outs they gave up a three run home run. In the top of the seventh Brooklyn scored one run and had runners on first and second with one out, but their next two batters flied out and grounded out. The Dodgers gave up another run in the bottom of the eighth and they lost the game 5-3. Brooklyn lost Game 4 6-2 and in Game 5 they didn't get any hits or runners on base as the Yankees pitcher threw a perfect game and the Dodgers lost the game 2-0. Brooklyn won Game 6 1-0 in ten innings to even the series, but only had three hits in Game 7 and lost the game 9-0 to lose the series.

1960's

- In 1962 the Los Angeles Dodgers led the National League by four games over San Francisco on September 22nd. But the Dodgers lost six of their last seven games of the year while the Giants went 5-2 and the two teams were tied for first place at the end of the season. A best of three game series was played to determine the pennant winner. In the first game Los Angeles only had three hits and lost the game 8-0. The Dodgers won the second game and in the third game they had a 4-2 lead in the top of the ninth, but gave up four walks, two hits, one error, one wild pitch, and four runs. Los Angeles was retired in order in the bottom of the inning and lost the game 6-4 to lose the pennant.

- LA won the National League pennant in 1966 and played Baltimore in the World Series. The Dodgers had the first two games at home but lost Game 1 5-2 and Game 2 6-0, getting only seven hits total in the two games. In Game 3 Los Angeles gave up a run in the bottom of the fifth inning on a home run. The Dodgers had one runner on base in the sixth, seventh, and eighth innings but couldn't score and lost the game 1-0. In Game 4 Los Angeles gave up a solo home run in the bottom of the fourth inning. They got their first batter on base in the top of the fifth and sixth innings but hit into double plays after the hits each inning. In the top of the ninth the Dodgers had runners on first and second with one out, but their next two batters lined out and flied out. LA lost 1-0 for the second straight game and lost the series in a sweep. The Dodgers scored two runs the whole series and were shut out three times. They only had seventeen hits in the four games and were outscored 13-2 in the series.

1970's

- In 1971 the Dodgers were eight games behind the Giants in the National League West Division on September 5th but won eight games in a row and were only one game back on September 14th. Five of those wins were against San Francisco. LA lost their next four games and lost six out of their next eight games and was 2.5 games behind the Giants on September 22nd. The Dodgers won five of their last six games but San Francisco went 4-3 over the same period and LA finished one game back in the standings at the end of the season.
- The Dodgers won the National League West Division in 1974 and beat Pittsburgh in the LCS. In the World Series LA faced Oakland and trailed by two runs in the bottom of the eighth inning of Game 1 when they had runners on first and third with two outs, but their next batter grounded out. The Dodgers hit a solo home run in the bottom of the ninth but lost the game 3-2. LA won Game 2 and trailed by two runs in the top of ninth inning of Game 3. Their first batter up hit a home run and the next batter reached on an error. They had a runner on first with no outs but their next batter stuck out and the following batter grounded into a double play that ended the game. The Dodgers lost 3-2 and lost Game 4 5-2. Game 5 was tied at two after six innings, but in the bottom of the seventh LA gave up a solo home run. In the top of the eighth the Dodgers first batter up singled and advanced to second base on an error, but he tried to extend his hit to third and was thrown out. The Dodgers lost the game 3-2 and lost the series. They had three losses by the score of 3-2 in the series.
- In 1977 LA won the National League West Division, beat the Phillies in the LCS, and faced the Yankees in the World Series. In Game 1 the Dodgers tied the score at three in the top

of the ninth and had runners on first and second with one out, but their next two batters flied out and lined out. The game went into extra innings and Los Angeles was retired in order in the top of the tenth, eleventh, and twelfth innings. In the bottom of the twelfth the Dodgers gave up a double, a walk, and single that drove in the game winning run and they lost 4-3. LA won Game 2 and only trailed by two runs after five innings in Game 3. They had a runner on first with one out in the bottom of the sixth, but their next two batters both grounded out. They went down in order in the seventh, eighth, and ninth innings and lost the game 5-3. In Game 4 the Dodgers trailed by two runs after six innings. They had runners on first and second with two outs in the bottom of the seventh, but their next batter up grounded out. In the bottom of the ninth LA had a runner on second with one out, but their next two batters grounded out and flied out and they lost 4-2. The Dodgers won Game 5 but lost Game 6 8-4 and lost the series.

• The Dodgers repeated as National League West Division champs in 1978 and beat the Phillies again in the LCS. In the World Series LA played the Yankees again and won Games 1 & 2. In Game 3 the Dodgers only trailed by one run after six innings, but gave up three runs in the bottom of the seventh and lost the game 5-1. In Game 4 LA had a 3-2 lead after seven innings, but gave up a single, a sacrifice bunt, and a double that drove in the tying run in the bottom of the eighth and the game went into extra innings. In the bottom of the tenth inning the Dodgers had two Yankees out with a runner on first base, but gave up two singles in a row and let in the game winning run and lost 4-3, which tied the series. LA lost Game 5 12-2 and Game 6 7-2 and lost the series.

1980's

• In 1980 the National League West Division title came down to the final series of the season as the Dodgers trailed Houston by three games and the two teams met in LA for a three game series. The Dodgers needed to win all three games and they did. This forced a one game playoff which was also played in Los Angeles. Unfortunately, the Dodgers gave up seven runs in the first four innings and lost the game 7-1, losing the division.

• Los Angeles led the National League West Division in 1982 by 3.5 games over Atlanta on September 17th but lost nine of their next ten games and fell to two games behind the Braves in the standings on September 29th. The Dodgers won three of their last four games of the year, but Atlanta split its remaining four games of the year and LA finished in second place one game behind the Braves.

• In 1983 the Dodgers won the National League West Division and played the Phillies in the LCS. In Game 1 LA gave up one run in the top of the first inning. They had the bases loaded in the bottom of the eighth with two outs, but their next batter flied out. In the bottom of the ninth the Dodgers had a runner on second base with two outs, but their next batter up grounded out and they lost 1-0. LA won Game 2 but lost Games 3 & 4 both by the score of 7-2 and lost the series.

- LA won the National League West Division in 1985 and played St. Louis in the LCS in the first year of the best of seven game LCS format. The Dodgers won Games 1 & 2 and in Game 3 they trailed by two runs when they had one runner on base in the seventh, eighth, and ninth innings but couldn't score any time and lost the game 4-2. In Game 4 Los Angeles gave up nine runs in the second inning and lost the game 12-2. Game 5 was tied at two in the bottom of the ninth inning, but the Dodgers gave up a game winning solo home run and lost 3-2. In Game 6 LA was ahead 5-4 in the top of the ninth inning and had two Cardinals out with St. Louis runners on second and third base. A Cardinals power hitter was up and first base was open. But the Dodgers manager chose to pitch to the batter instead of walking him and LA gave up a three-run home run and lost the game 7-5 to lose the series. The Dodgers lost four straight games after winning the first two games of the series.

1990's

- In 1991 the Dodgers led Atlanta by one game in the National League West Division on October 1st with four games left to play in the season. But LA lost three of their last four games while the Braves won three out of their last four and the Dodgers finished in second place one game behind Atlanta.
- Los Angeles won the National League West Division in 1995 by one game over Colorado who was the wild card team. In the LDS the Dodgers played the Reds and lost Game 1 7-2. Game 2 was tied at two after seven innings but LA gave up a single in the top of the eighth with two outs and let in the go-ahead run. The Dodgers gave up two more runs in the top of the ninth and in the bottom of the inning LA hit a two-run home run but lost the game 5-4. The Dodgers lost Game 3 10-1 and were swept in the series.
- In 1996 the Dodgers finished one game behind San Diego in the National League West Division but were the NL Wild Card team. LA led the division by two games over the Padres with three games left to play against San Diego but lost all three games and finished in second place. If the Dodgers had won the division they would have played St. Louis in the LDS instead of Atlanta. In the LDS LA met the Braves and Game 1 went into extra innings tied at one. In the top of the tenth the Dodgers gave up a home run to the first Atlanta batter. In the bottom of the inning LA had a runner on first with one out, but their next two batters struck out and popped out and they lost 2-1. In Game 2 the Dodgers led 2-1 after six innings but gave up two solo home runs in the top of the seventh and were retired in order in the bottom of the seventh, eighth, and ninth innings and lost the game 3-2. The Dodgers lost Game 3 5-2 and lost the series in a sweep.
- LA had a two game lead over San Francisco in the National League West Division on September 16th in 1997 but lost five straight games and fell to two games behind the Giants on September 21st. The Dodgers won four of their last six games of the year but so did San Francisco and LA

finished two games behind the Giants for the division. The Dodgers also finished four games behind Florida for the wild card.

2000's

- In 2004 Los Angeles won the National League West Division and played St. Louis in the LDS. The Dodgers lost Games 1 & 2 both by the score of 8-3. They won Game 3 but only got three hits in Game 4 and lost the game 6-2 to lose the series.

- The Dodgers tied the Padres for the National League West Division in 2006 but were given the wild card spot as the Padres won the regular season series. In the LDS LA faced the Mets and trailed by two runs in the top of the ninth inning of Game 1. The Dodgers scored one run and had the tying runner on second base with two outs, but their next batter struck out and they lost 6-5. LA lost Game 2 4-1 and Game 3 9-5 and lost the series in a sweep.

- In 2008 Los Angeles won the National League West Division and swept the Cubs in the LDS. In the LCS the Dodgers played the Phillies and led Game 1 2-0 after five innings. In the bottom of the sixth LA committed an error and gave up two home runs and three runs in the inning. The Dodgers trailed by one run and had a runner on first in the top of the eighth inning and were down by one run, but their next batter grounded out and they lost the game 3-2. LA lost Game 2 8-5 and won Game 3. The Dodgers had a 5-3 lead after seven innings in Game 4, but in the top of the eighth they gave up four runs on two two-run home runs and lost the game 7-5. Then they lost Game 5 5-1 and lost the series.

- The Dodgers repeated as National League West Division champs in 2009 and beat the Cardinals in the LDS. In the LCS LA played the Phillies again. In Game 1 the Dodgers trailed by two runs in the bottom of the ninth and got their first batter up on base, but their next batter hit into a double play. They got another runner to second base in the inning but their next batter up popped out and they lost 8-6. LA won Game 2 but lost Game 3 11-0. In Game 4 the Dodgers had a 4-3 lead in the bottom of the ninth. They got one Phillies batter out but then walked a batter and a hit a batter. Then they got the second out. The next Philadelphia batter hit a double which drove in two runs and the LA lost 5-4. The Dodgers lost Game 5 10-4 and lost the series

Year-to-Year Figures

Team Name	League	Year	W	L	Win%	Fin	GB/GA	WS	Lge	LDS	Div	WC
Los Angeles Dodgers	NL West	2010	80	82	0.494	4 of 5	12					
Los Angeles Dodgers	NL West	2009	95	67	0.586	1 of 5	+3			1	1	
Los Angeles Dodgers	NL West	2008	84	78	0.519	1 of 5	+2			1	1	
Los Angeles Dodgers	NL West	2007	82	80	0.506	4 of 5	8					
Los Angeles Dodgers	NL West	2006	88	74	0.543	1t of 5	0*					1
Los Angeles Dodgers	NL West	2005	71	91	0.438	4 of 5	11					
Los Angeles Dodgers	NL West	2004	93	69	0.574	1 of 5	+2				1	
Los Angeles Dodgers	NL West	2003	85	77	0.525	2 of 5	15.5					
Los Angeles Dodgers	NL West	2002	92	70	0.568	3 of 5	6					
Los Angeles Dodgers	NL West	2001	86	76	0.531	3 of 5	6					
Los Angeles Dodgers	NL West	2000	86	76	0.531	2 of 5	11					
Los Angeles Dodgers	NL West	1999	77	85	0.475	3 of 5	23					
Los Angeles Dodgers	NL West	1998	83	79	0.512	3 of 5	15					
Los Angeles Dodgers	NL West	1997	88	74	0.543	2 of 4	2					
Los Angeles Dodgers	NL West	1996	90	72	0.556	2 of 4	1					1
Los Angeles Dodgers	NL West	1995	78	66	0.542	1 of 4	+1				1	
Los Angeles Dodgers	NL West	1994	58	56	0.509	1 of 4	3.5+					
Los Angeles Dodgers	NL West	1993	81	81	0.500	4 of 7	23					
Los Angeles Dodgers	NL West	1992	63	99	0.389	6 of 6	35					
Los Angeles Dodgers	NL West	1991	93	69	0.574	2 of 6	1					
Los Angeles Dodgers	NL West	1990	86	76	0.531	2 of 6	5					
Los Angeles Dodgers	NL West	1989	77	83	0.481	4 of 6	14					
Los Angeles Dodgers	NL West	1988	94	67	0.584	1 of 6	+7	1	1		1	
Los Angeles Dodgers	NL West	1987	73	89	0.451	4 of 6	17					
Los Angeles Dodgers	NL West	1986	73	89	0.451	5 of 6	23					
Los Angeles Dodgers	NL West	1985	95	67	0.586	1 of 6	+5.5				1	
Los Angeles Dodgers	NL West	1984	79	83	0.488	4 of 6	13					
Los Angeles Dodgers	NL West	1983	91	71	0.562	1 of 6	+3				1	
Los Angeles Dodgers	NL West	1982	88	74	0.543	2 of 6	1					
Los Angeles Dodgers	NL West	1981	63	47	0.573	1,4 of 6	+0.5**,6	1	1	1	1	
Los Angeles Dodgers	NL West	1980	92	71	0.564	2 of 6	1					
Los Angeles Dodgers	NL West	1979	79	83	0.488	3 of 6	11.5					
Los Angeles Dodgers	NL West	1978	95	67	0.586	1 of 6	+2.5		1		1	
Los Angeles Dodgers	NL West	1977	98	64	0.605	1 of 6	+10		1		1	
Los Angeles Dodgers	NL West	1976	92	70	0.568	2 of 6	10					
Los Angeles Dodgers	NL West	1975	88	74	0.543	2 of 6	20					
Los Angeles Dodgers	NL West	1974	102	60	0.630	1 of 6	+4		1		1	
Los Angeles Dodgers	NL West	1973	95	66	0.590	2 of 6	3.5					
Los Angeles Dodgers	NL West	1972	85	70	0.548	3 of 6	10.5					
Los Angeles Dodgers	NL West	1971	89	73	0.549	2 of 6	1					
Los Angeles Dodgers	NL West	1970	87	74	0.540	2 of 6	14.5					
Los Angeles Dodgers	NL West	1969	85	77	0.525	4 of 6	8					
Los Angeles Dodgers	NL	1968	76	86	0.469	7t of 10	21					

Los Angeles Dodgers

Team Name	League	Year	W	L	Win%	Fin	GB/GA	WS	Lge	LDS	Div	WC
Los Angeles Dodgers	NL	1967	73	89	0.451	8 of 10	28.5					
Los Angeles Dodgers	NL	1966	95	67	0.586	1 of 10	+1.5		1			
Los Angeles Dodgers	NL	1965	97	65	0.599	1 of 10	+2	1	1			
Los Angeles Dodgers	NL	1964	80	82	0.494	6t of 10	13					
Los Angeles Dodgers	NL	1963	99	63	0.611	1 of 10	+6	1	1			
Los Angeles Dodgers	NL	1962	102	63	0.618	2 of 10	1					
Los Angeles Dodgers	NL	1961	89	65	0.578	2 of 8	4					
Los Angeles Dodgers	NL	1960	82	72	0.532	4 of 8	13					
Los Angeles Dodgers	NL	1959	88	68	0.564	1 of 8	+2	1	1			
Los Angeles Dodgers	NL	1958	71	83	0.461	7 of 8	21					
Brooklyn Dodgers	NL	1957	84	70	0.545	3 of 8	11					
Brooklyn Dodgers	NL	1956	93	61	0.604	1 of 8	+1		1			
Brooklyn Dodgers	NL	1955	98	55	0.641	1 of 8	+13.5	1	1			
Brooklyn Dodgers	NL	1954	92	62	0.597	2 of 8	5					
Brooklyn Dodgers	NL	1953	105	49	0.682	1 of 8	+13		1			
Brooklyn Dodgers	NL	1952	96	57	0.627	1 of 8	+4.5		1			
Brooklyn Dodgers	NL	1951	97	60	0.618	2 of 8	1					
Brooklyn Dodgers	NL	1950	89	65	0.578	2 of 8	2					
Brooklyn Dodgers	NL	1949	97	57	0.630	1 of 8	+1		1			
Brooklyn Dodgers	NL	1948	84	70	0.545	3 of 8	7.5					
Brooklyn Dodgers	NL	1947	94	60	0.610	1 of 8	+5		1			
Brooklyn Dodgers	NL	1946	96	60	0.615	2 of 8	2					
Brooklyn Dodgers	NL	1945	87	67	0.565	3 of 8	11					
Brooklyn Dodgers	NL	1944	63	91	0.409	7 of 8	42					
Brooklyn Dodgers	NL	1943	81	72	0.529	3 of 8	23.5					
Brooklyn Dodgers	NL	1942	104	50	0.675	2 of 8	2					
Brooklyn Dodgers	NL	1941	100	54	0.649	1 of 8	+2.5		1			
Brooklyn Dodgers	NL	1940	88	65	0.575	2 of 8	12					
Brooklyn Dodgers	NL	1939	84	69	0.549	3 of 8	12.5					
Brooklyn Dodgers	NL	1938	69	80	0.463	7 of 8	18.5					
Brooklyn Dodgers	NL	1937	62	91	0.405	6 of 8	33.5					
Brooklyn Dodgers	NL	1936	67	87	0.435	7 of 8	25					
Brooklyn Dodgers	NL	1935	70	83	0.458	5 of 8	29.5					
Brooklyn Dodgers	NL	1934	71	81	0.467	6 of 8	23.5					
Brooklyn Dodgers	NL	1933	65	88	0.425	6 of 8	26.5					
Brooklyn Dodgers	NL	1932	81	73	0.526	3 of 8	9					
Brooklyn Robins	NL	1931	79	73	0.520	4 of 8	21					
Brooklyn Robins	NL	1930	86	68	0.558	4 of 8	6					
Brooklyn Robins	NL	1929	70	83	0.458	6 of 8	28.5					
Brooklyn Robins	NL	1928	77	76	0.503	6 of 8	17.5					
Brooklyn Robins	NL	1927	65	88	0.425	6 of 8	28.5					
Brooklyn Robins	NL	1926	71	82	0.464	6 of 8	17.5					
Brooklyn Robins	NL	1925	68	85	0.444	6t of 8	27					
Brooklyn Robins	NL	1924	92	62	0.597	2 of 8	1.5					
Brooklyn Robins	NL	1923	76	78	0.494	6 of 8	19.5					

Team Name	League	Year	W	L	Win%	Fin	GB/GA	WS	Lge	LDS	Div	WC
Brooklyn Robins	NL	1922	76	78	0.494	6 of 8	17					
Brooklyn Robins	NL	1921	77	75	0.507	5 of 8	16.5					
Brooklyn Robins	NL	1920	93	61	0.604	1 of 8	+7		1			
Brooklyn Robins	NL	1919	69	71	0.493	5 of 8	27					
Brooklyn Robins	NL	1918	57	69	0.452	5 of 8	25.5					
Brooklyn Robins	NL	1917	70	81	0.464	7 of 8	26.5					
Brooklyn Robins	NL	1916	94	60	0.610	1 of 8	+2.5		1			
Brooklyn Robins	NL	1915	80	72	0.526	3 of 8	10					
Brooklyn Robins	NL	1914	75	79	0.487	5 of 8	19.5					
Brooklyn Superbas	NL	1913	65	84	0.436	6 of 8	34.5					
Brooklyn Dodgers	NL	1912	58	95	0.379	7 of 8	46					
Brooklyn Dodgers	NL	1911	64	86	0.427	7 of 8	33.5					
Brooklyn Superbas	NL	1910	64	90	0.416	6 of 8	40					
Brooklyn Superbas	NL	1909	55	98	0.359	6 of 8	55.5					
Brooklyn Superbas	NL	1908	53	101	0.344	7 of 8	46					
Brooklyn Superbas	NL	1907	65	83	0.439	5 of 8	40					
Brooklyn Superbas	NL	1906	66	86	0.434	5 of 8	50					
Brooklyn Superbas	NL	1905	48	104	0.316	8 of 8	56.5					
Brooklyn Superbas	NL	1904	56	97	0.366	6 of 8	50					
Brooklyn Superbas	NL	1903	70	66	0.515	5 of 8	19					
Brooklyn Superbas	NL	1902	75	63	0.543	2 of 8	27.5					
Brooklyn Superbas	NL	1901	79	57	0.581	3 of 8	9.5					
Brooklyn Superbas	NL	1900	82	54	0.603	1 of 8	+4.5		1			
Brooklyn Superbas	NL	1899	101	47	0.682	1 of 12	+8		1			
Brooklyn Bridgegrooms	NL	1898	54	91	0.372	10 of 12	46					
Brooklyn Bridgegrooms	NL	1897	61	71	0.462	6t of 12	32					
Brooklyn Bridgegrooms	NL	1896	58	73	0.443	9t of 12	33					
Brooklyn Grooms	NL	1895	71	60	0.542	5t of 12	16.5					
Brooklyn Grooms	NL	1894	70	61	0.534	5 of 12	20.5					
Brooklyn Grooms	NL	1893	65	63	0.508	6t of 12	20.5					
Brooklyn Grooms	NL	1892	95	59	0.617	2, 3 of 12	2.5, 9.5					
Brooklyn Grooms	NL	1891	61	76	0.445	6 of 8	25.5					
Brooklyn Bridgegrooms	NL	1890	86	43	0.667	1 of 8	+6		1			
Brooklyn Bridgegrooms	AA	1889	93	44	0.679	1 of 8	+2		1			
Brooklyn Bridgegrooms	AA	1888	88	52	0.629	2 of 8	6.5					
Brooklyn Grays	AA	1887	60	74	0.448	6 of 8	34.5					
Brooklyn Grays	AA	1886	76	61	0.555	3 of 8	16					
Brooklyn Grays	AA	1885	53	59	0.473	5t of 8	26					
Brooklyn Atlantics	AA	1884	40	64	0.385	9 of 13	33.5					
			10135	9199	0.524			6	22	3	11	2

* In 2006 the Dodgers and Padres finished the regular season with the same won-loss record. Since both teams made the playoffs and San Diego won the regular season series between the two teams, they won the NL West Division Title and Los Angeles won the NL Wild Card.

** The 1981 season was divided into two halves due to a players strike in the middle of the season. The strike began on June 12 and up to that point in the season Cincinnati and Los Angeles had played an uneven amount of games and the Dodgers led the Reds by 0.5 games on that date.

Milwaukee Brewers

Stats

History
Year of Origin 1969   Years Played 42

Score & Rank
Total Points Score .... 6.5   Average Points Score 0.15
Total Points Rank 28   Average Points Rank 29

Postseason Results

	No.	Years
World Series Won	0	
League Championship Series Won	1	1982
League Division Series Won	0	
World Series Lost	1	1982
League Championship Series Lost	0	
League Division Series Lost	2	1981, 2008

Postseason Won-Loss Records and Winning Percentages

	Postseason Games		Postseason Series	
All Postseason Series	9-12	.429	1-3	.250
World Series	3-4	.429	0-1	.000
League Championship Series	3-2	.600	1-0	1.000
League Division Series	3-6	.333	0-2	.000

Regular Season Results
All-Time Won-Loss Record 3166-3505
All-Time Winning Percentage .... .475

	No.	Years
League Titles before 1969	0	
Division Titles	2	1981, 1982
Wild Cards	1	2008

Regular Season High & Low Points

		Year(s)
Most Wins in a Season	95	1979, 1982
Most Losses in a Season	106	2002
Highest Winning Percentage	.590	1979
Lowest Winning Percentage	.346	2002
Longest Streak with Won-Loss Record .500 or Higher	6 years	1978–1983
Longest Streak with Won-Loss Record Below .500	12 years	1993–2004

Years with .500 record or Better
1960's	0 (out of 1)
1970's	2
1980's	7
1990's	2
2000's	3
2010's:	0

14 out of 42 seasons played = 33%

Years Making Postseason
1960's	0
1970's	0
1980's	2
1990's	0
2000's	1
2010's	0

3 out of 42 seasons played = 7%

Streaks

• 1981-1982: Won two Division Titles and one League Championship Series in two years.

Extra Bases

• The Brewers have played in four different divisions in their franchise history. They started in the AL West when they originated as the Seattle Pilots in 1969. In 1972 they moved to the AL East as they switched places with the Washington Senators, who were moving to Texas and becoming the Rangers. In 1994 Milwaukee moved to the AL Central as baseball changed its league format to have three divisions in each league. In 1998 the Brewers moved to the NL Central because baseball was adding the Diamondbacks and Devil Rays as expansion teams and did not want an odd number of teams in each league, and did not want both expansion teams to go to the same league. Milwaukee's move marked the first time a team switched leagues in the twentieth century.

• In the 1982 ALCS Milwaukee trailed California zero games to two before coming back to win the next three games and the pennant. They became the first team in baseball history to accomplish this feat.

Scoring Opportunities

1980's

• In 1981 the Brewers won the second half of the American League East Division in the strike split season. In the first round of the playoffs Milwaukee played the Yankees. In Game 1 the Brewers trailed by one run in the bottom of the fifth when they had runners on first and second with one out, but their next two batters struck out and flied out. Milwaukee only had one hit the rest of the game and they lost the game 5-3. In Game 2 the Brewers trailed by one run in the bottom of the seventh inning when they had the bases loaded with one out, but their next two batters popped out and struck out and Milwaukee lost the game 3-0. The Brewers won Games 3 & 4 to tie the series, but they lost Game 5 7-3 and lost the series.

• Milwaukee won the American League East Division in 1982 by beating Baltimore on the final day of the season. In the LCS the Brewers beat the Angels by winning the last three games of the series after losing the first two. Milwaukee became the first team in baseball history to come back from a 0-2 game deficit in the playoffs and win the series. In the World Series the Brewers played St. Louis and won Game 1 10-0. In Game 2 Milwaukee had a 4-2 lead in the bottom of the sixth inning and had two Cardinals out with a runner on second base. But the Brewers gave up a walk and a double and let in two runs that tied the game. In the top of the seventh Milwaukee had runners on first and second with two outs, but their next batter grounded out. In the bottom of the eighth the Brewers gave up three walks and a single and let in the go-ahead run. They got their first batter up on base in the top of the ninth, but he was caught stealing second and Milwaukee lost the game 5-4. The Brewers lost Game 3 6-2 and won Games 4 & 5 to take a three games to two lead in the series. Needing only one more win to become World Series champs the Brewers lost Game 6 13-1. In Game 7 Milwaukee had a 3-1 lead in the bottom of the sixth but gave up four hits, one walk, and three runs in the inning. They gave up fifteen hits in the game and lost it 6-3 to lose the series.

1990's

• In 1992 the Brewers won fifteen out of seventeen games from September 11th to September 29th and closed the gap in the standings with Toronto from being back by six games to trailing by 2.5. The rest of the season Milwaukee went 2-3 and the Blue Jays went 3-1 and the Brewers finished in second place four games behind Toronto.

2000's

• Milwaukee was tied for first place with Chicago in the National League Central Division on September 18th in 2007. But the Brewers lost seven of their next ten games and were eliminated with two games left in the season. Milwaukee won their last two games of the year and finished in second place two games behind the Cubs. After the 18th the Cubs went 6-4 the rest of the season while Milwaukee went 5-7.

• In 2008 the Brewers won the National League Wild Card and played the Phillies in the LDS. In Game 1 Milwaukee gave up three runs in the third inning and had no runs and only two hits through eight innings. In the top of the ninth the Brewers scored one run and had runners on second and third with two outs, but their next batter up struck out and they lost 3-1. In Game 2 Milwaukee gave up five runs in the second inning and only had three hits in the game and lost it 5-2. The Brewers won Game 3 but lost Game 4 6-2 and lost the series.

Year-to-Year Figures

Team	League	Year	W	L	Win%	Fin	GB/GA	WS	Lge	LDS	Div	WC
Milwaukee Brewers	NL Cent	2010	77	85	0.475	3 of 6	14					
Milwaukee Brewers	NL Cent	2009	80	82	0.494	3 of 6	11					
Milwaukee Brewers	NL Cent	2008	90	72	0.556	2 of 6	7.5					1
Milwaukee Brewers	NL Cent	2007	83	79	0.512	2 of 6	2					
Milwaukee Brewers	NL Cent	2006	75	87	0.463	4 of 6	8.5					
Milwaukee Brewers	NL Cent	2005	81	81	0.500	3 of 6	19					
Milwaukee Brewers	NL Cent	2004	67	94	0.416	6 of 6	37.5					
Milwaukee Brewers	NL Cent	2003	68	94	0.420	6 of 6	20					
Milwaukee Brewers	NL Cent	2002	56	106	0.346	6 of 6	41					
Milwaukee Brewers	NL Cent	2001	68	94	0.420	4 of 6	25					
Milwaukee Brewers	NL Cent	2000	73	89	0.451	3 of 6	22					
Milwaukee Brewers	NL Cent	1999	74	87	0.460	5 of 6	22.5					
Milwaukee Brewers	NL Cent	1998	74	88	0.457	5 of 6	28					
Milwaukee Brewers	AL Cent	1997	78	83	0.484	3 of 5	8					
Milwaukee Brewers	AL Cent	1996	80	82	0.494	3 of 5	19.5					
Milwaukee Brewers	AL Cent	1995	65	79	0.451	4 of 5	35					
Milwaukee Brewers	AL Cent	1994	53	62	0.461	5 of 5	15					
Milwaukee Brewers	AL East	1993	69	93	0.426	7 of 7	26					
Milwaukee Brewers	AL East	1992	92	70	0.568	2 of 7	4					
Milwaukee Brewers	AL East	1991	83	79	0.512	4 of 7	8					
Milwaukee Brewers	AL East	1990	74	88	0.457	6 of 7	14					
Milwaukee Brewers	AL East	1989	81	81	0.500	4 of 7	8					
Milwaukee Brewers	AL East	1988	87	75	0.537	3t of 7	2					
Milwaukee Brewers	AL East	1987	91	71	0.562	3t of 7	7					
Milwaukee Brewers	AL East	1986	77	84	0.478	6 of 7	18					
Milwaukee Brewers	AL East	1985	71	90	0.441	6 of 7	28					
Milwaukee Brewers	AL East	1984	67	94	0.416	7 of 7	36.5					
Milwaukee Brewers	AL East	1983	87	75	0.537	5 of 7	11					
Milwaukee Brewers	AL East	1982	95	67	0.586	1 of 7	+1		1		1	
Milwaukee Brewers	AL East	1981	62	47	0.569	3, 1 of 7	3, +1.5				1	
Milwaukee Brewers	AL East	1980	86	76	0.531	3 of 7	17					
Milwaukee Brewers	AL East	1979	95	66	0.590	2 of 7	8					
Milwaukee Brewers	AL East	1978	93	69	0.574	3 of 7	6.5					
Milwaukee Brewers	AL East	1977	67	95	0.414	6 of 7	33					
Milwaukee Brewers	AL East	1976	66	95	0.410	6 of 6	32					
Milwaukee Brewers	AL East	1975	68	94	0.420	5 of 6	28					
Milwaukee Brewers	AL East	1974	76	86	0.469	5 of 6	15					
Milwaukee Brewers	AL East	1973	74	88	0.457	5 of 6	23					
Milwaukee Brewers	AL East	1972	65	91	0.417	6 of 6	21					
Milwaukee Brewers	AL West	1971	69	92	0.429	6 of 6	32					
Milwaukee Brewers	AL West	1970	65	97	0.401	4t of 6	33					
Seattle Pilots	AL West	1969	64	98	0.395	6 of 6	33					
			3166	3505	0.475			0	1	0	2	1

Minnesota Twins

Stats

History

Year of Origin 1901   Years Played...110

Score & Rank

Total Points Score .... 68.3   Average Points Score...0.62
Total Points Rank 14   Average Points Rank... 19

Postseason Results   **No.**   **Years**

World Series Won...3...1924, 1987, 1991
League Championship Series Won ....2...1987, 1991
League Division Series Won..1...2002

World Series Lost ....3 ....1925, 1933, 1965
League Championship Series Lost.........................3 ....1969, 1970, 2002
League Division Series Lost ....5................................2003, 2004, 2006, 2009, 2010

Postseason Won-Loss Records and Winning Percentages

	Postseason Games		Postseason Series	
All Postseason Series	33-50	.398	6-11	.353
World Series	19-21	.475	3-3	.500
League Championship Series	9-12	.429	2-3	.400
League Division Series	5-17	.227	1-5	.167

Regular Season Results

All-Time Won-Loss Record 8232-8816
All-Time Winning Percentage .... .483

	No.	Years
League Titles before 1969	4	1924, 1925, 1933, 1965
Division Titles	10	1969, 1970, 1987, 1991, 2002, 2003, 2004, 2006, 2009, 2010
Wild Cards	0	

Regular Season High & Low Points   **Year(s)**

Most Wins in a Season .... 102................................... 1965
Most Losses in a Season... 113.................................... 1904
Highest Winning Percentage .... .651................................... 1933
Lowest Winning Percentage.. .252................................... 1904
Longest Streak with Won-Loss Record .500 or Higher ....6 years...................2001-2006
Longest Streak with Won-Loss Record Below .500.............................. 11 years...................1901-1911

Years with .500 record or Better

1900's	0 (out of 9)
1910's	5
1920's	5
1930's	5
1940's	2
1950's	2
1960's	6
1970's	7
1980's	3
1990's	2
2000's	8
2010's	1

46 out of 110 seasons played = 42%

Years Making Postseason

1900's	0
1910's	0
1920's	2
1930's	1
1940's	0
1950's	0
1960's	2
1970's	1
1980's	1
1990's	1
2000's	5
2010's	1

14 out of 110 seasons played = 13%

Streaks

- 1924-1933: Won one World Series and three League Titles in ten years.
- 1965-1970: Won a League Title in one season and won Division Titles in two other seasons over the six year period.
- 1987-1991: Won two World Series, two League Championship Series, and two Division Titles in five years.
- 2002-2010: Won six Division Titles and one League Division Series in nine years.

Extra Bases

- The 1987 World Series was the first championship to be played with some of the games indoors.
- Minnesota was undefeated in their eight World Series home games in 1987 and 1991.
- The Twins lost twelve straight postseason games from 2004-2010, which is currently the second longest streak of all time. As of this printing, the longest belongs to the Red Sox who lost thirteen straight postseason games from 1986 to 1995. Minnesota is in jeopardy of overtaking the top spot if they lose more playoff games without winning any.

Scoring Opportunities

1920's

- The Washington Senators won the American League pennant in 1925 and faced Pittsburgh in the World Series. The Senators won Game 1 and Game 2 was tied at one in the bottom of the eighth inning. But Washington let the first Pirates batter reach base on an error, and with one out the Senators gave up a two-run home run. In the top of the ninth Washington had the bases loaded and scored one run on a sacrifice fly. They had runners on first and second with one out, but their next two batters struck out and grounded out and they lost 3-2. The Senators won Games 3 & 4 to take a three games to one series lead. Game 5 was tied at two until the Senators gave up a walk and three straight singles and let in two runs in the top of the seventh. In the bottom of the inning Washington scored one run and had runners on first and third with two outs but their next batter flied out. The Senators gave up one run each in eighth and ninth innings and were retired in order in the bottom of those innings and lost the game 6-3. In Game 6 Washington trailed by one run in the top of the eighth when they had the tying run on second with no outs, but their next three batters all got out. In the top of the ninth the Senators had a runner on second with one out, but their next two batters popped out and struck out and they lost 3-2. In Game 7 Washington had a 7-6 lead in the bottom of the eighth. They got the first two Pirates batters out, but gave up two doubles and a walk and let in one run that tied the score. The next Pittsburgh batter reached base on an error which loaded the bases, and the following batter hit a ground rule double which drove in two runs. In the top of the ninth Washington was retired in order and lost the game 9-7, losing the series. The Senators gave up fifteen hits in Game 7.

1930's

• In 1933 the Senators won the American League pennant and had their highest winning percentage and their most wins while the team was in Washington. In the World Series they played the New York Giants. In Game 1 the Senators trailed by two runs in the top of the ninth when they had runners on second and third with one out, but their next two batters struck out and grounded out and they lost 4-2. Washington lost Game 2 6-1 and won Game 3. Game 4 was tied at one after nine innings. In the bottom of the tenth the Senators had runners on first and second with two outs but their next batter grounded out. In the top of the eleventh Washington gave up a single, a sacrifice bunt, and another single and let in the go-ahead run. In the bottom of the inning the Senators had the bases loaded with one out but their next batter hit into a double play to end the game and they lost 2-1. Game 5 was tied at three after nine innings and Washington gave up a solo home run with two outs in the top of the eleventh. In the bottom of the inning the Senators had runners on first and second with two outs but their next batter up struck out and they lost the game 4-3 and lost the series.

1940's

• Washington only trailed the Tigers by a half game in the American League on September 15th in 1945 when the two teams met in Washington for a five game series. The Senators lost three out of the five games and fell to 1.5 games behind Detroit. The rest of the year the Tigers went 3-4 but Washington went 2-3 and finished 1.5 games behind Detroit.

1960's

• In the franchise's fifth season in Minnesota in 1965 the Twins won the American League pennant with a franchise record 102 wins. This is the only year the franchise won 100 or more games. In the World Series against the Dodgers Minnesota won Games 1 & 2 but lost the next three games 4-0, 7-2, and 7-0. The Twins only had a total of two runs and fourteen hits in the three games. Minnesota won Game 6 and Game 7 was played in Minnesota, but the Twins were held to three hits and were shutout for the third time in the series, losing 2-0 to lose the series.

• In 1967 the Twins had a one game lead over the Red Sox and Tigers on September 30th and had two games left in the season at Boston. Minnesota lost the first game 6-4 and the second game 5-3 and finished the year one game behind the Red Sox, tied for second place with Detroit. The Twins lost five of their last seven games of the year.

• Minnesota won the American League West Division in 1969 and met Baltimore in the first ALCS. In Game 1 the Twins had a 3-2 lead in the bottom of the ninth inning, but gave up a home run to the first Orioles batter. In the top of the twelfth Minnesota had the bases loaded with one out, but their next two batters struck out and flied out. In the bottom of the inning the Twins had two Orioles out with a runner on third base. The next Baltimore batter singled which drove in the game winning run and Minnesota lost 4-3. Game 2 was tied at zero after nine innings. In the top of the eleventh the Twins had runners on first and second with two outs, but their next batter lined out. In the bottom of the inning Minnesota had two Orioles out, but there were runners on first and second base. The next Baltimore batter up singled and the game winning run scored. The Twins lost the game 1-0 and then lost Game 3 11-2 to lose the series in a sweep. Two of Minnesota's losses in the series were by one run and were in extra innings.

1970's

• The Twins repeated as American League West Division champs in 1970 and faced Baltimore again in the LCS. In Game 1 Minnesota gave up seven runs in the fourth inning and lost the game 10-6. In Game 2 the Twins only trailed by one run in the top of the ninth inning, but gave up seven runs and lost the game 11-3. In Game 3 Minnesota trailed 5-0 after three innings and lost the game 6-1. The Twins were outscored 27-10 in the series.

1980's

• In 1984 the Twins were tied for the American League West Division lead with Kansas City on September 23rd but lost six out of their final seven games and finished in second place three games behind the Royals. Kansas City went 4-3 after September 23rd.

2000's

• Minnesota won the American League Central Division in 2002 and beat Oakland in the LDS. In the LCS the Twins faced the Angels, won Game 1, and lost Game 2 6-3. In Game

3 Minnesota tied the score at one in the top of the seventh, but gave up a solo home run to the Angels first batter in the bottom of the eighth. The Twins were retired in order in the top of the ninth and lost the game 2-1. Minnesota lost Game 4 7-1 and led Game 5 5-3 in the bottom of the seventh inning, but gave up ten runs in the half inning and lost the game 13-5, to lose the series.

- In 2003 the Twins repeated as American League Central Division champs and played the Yankees in the LDS. Minnesota won Game 1 and Game 2 was tied at one after six innings. But in the bottom of the seventh the Twins gave up a hit batter, a sacrifice bunt, and error, and three singles, and let in three runs and they lost the game 4-1. In Game 3 Minnesota only had five hits and their last twelve batters were retired in order and they lost the game 3-1. The Twins lost Game 4 8-1 and lost the series. They were outscored 15-3 in the three losses.

- Minnesota won their third American League Central Division in a row in 2004, faced the Yankees again in the LDS, and won Game 1, just like the previous year. Game 2 was tied at five after nine innings. In the top of the twelfth the Twins hit a solo home run to take the lead. In the bottom of the inning they got the first Yankees batter out, but then gave up two walks and a ground rule double and let in the tying run. Minnesota intentionally walked the next New York batter and then gave up a sacrifice fly which drove in the game winning run and they lost 7-6. The Twins lost Game 3 8-4 and led Game 4 5-1 after seven innings. But in the top of the eighth they gave up two singles, a wild pitch, a walk, a three-run home run, and let in four runs which tied the score. The game went into extra innings and in the top of the eleventh Minnesota had one Yankees batter out with a runner on third base when their pitcher threw a wild pitch that let in the go-ahead run. The Twins were retired in order in the bottom of the inning and lost 6-5 to lose the series.

- In 2006 the Twins won the American League Central Division on the last day of the season by one game over Detroit. In the LDS Minnesota played Oakland and in Game 1 they trailed by one run in the bottom of the eighth inning when they had a runner on second with no outs, but their next three batters all got out. In the top of the ninth the A's hit a solo home run and in the bottom of the inning the Twins scored one run but they lost the game 3-2. Game 2 was tied at two after six innings. In the top of the seventh Minnesota had two A's batters out with a runner on first base. The next Oakland batter hit a line drive to center field and the Twins outfielder made a poor defensive play and dove for the ball. The ball went passed him and went all the way to the wall and the runner on first scored and the batter had an inside the park home run when he should have only had a single. The Twins lost the game 5-2 and lost Game 3 8-3 to lose the series in a sweep.

- In 2008 Minnesota and Chicago were tied at the end of the regular season and needed a one game playoff to determine the American League Central Division winner. The Twins won the head-to-head regular season matchup between the two teams, but the home field of the playoff was decided by a coin toss, which was won by the White Sox. The Twins only had two hits in the game and gave up a solo home run in the seventh inning. Minnesota had a runner on first with one out in the top of the eighth, but their next batter hit into a double play. They were retired in order in the top of the ninth and lost the playoff 1-0 and lost the division.

• Minnesota won the American League Central Division in 2009 by beating Detroit in a one game playoff in twelve innings. In the LDS they played the Yankees and lost Game 1 7-2. The Twins had a 3-1 lead in Game 2 entering the bottom of the ninth inning but gave up a single to the first New York batter and gave up a home run that tied to score. The game went into extra innings and Minnesota had the bases loaded with no outs in the top of the eleventh, but their next three batters got out without driving in a run. Unfortunately, the Twins first batter of the inning hit a ball down the left field line for a double that was a fair ball, but was called foul by the umpire. If that hit had been called correctly and the next two batters singled as they did, then Minnesota most likely would have taken the lead. In the bottom of the inning the Twins gave up a home run to the first Yankee batter and lost 4-3. In Game 3 Minnesota had a 1-0 lead after six innings but gave up two solo home runs in the bottom of the seventh inning. In the bottom of the eighth the Twins first batter up doubled and their second batter hit an infield single to the shortstop, but the runner that was on second base advanced to far past third base and was thrown out. Minnesota gave up two more runs in the top of the ninth and lost the game 4-1 and lost the series in a sweep.

2010's

• In 2010 the Twins won the American League Central Division and played the Yankees in the LDS. Minnesota led Game 1 3-0 after five innings, but in the top of the sixth the Twins gave up four hits, a wild pitch, a walk, and let four runs score. Minnesota tied the game in the bottom of the sixth but gave up a two-run home run in the top of the seventh. In the bottom of the seventh, the Twins had runners on first and second with two outs, but their next batter up struck out. In the bottom of the eighth, Minnesota had runners on second and third with one out, but their next two batters up both grounded out and they lost the game 6-4. The Twins lost Game 2 5-2 and Game 3 6-1 and lost the series in a sweep. They were outscored 17-7 in the three games.

Year-to-Year Figures

Team Name	League	Year	W	L	Win%	Fin	GB/GA	WS	Lge	LDS	Div	WC
Minnesota Twins	AL Cent	2010	94	68	0.580	1 of 5	+6				1	
Minnesota Twins	AL Cent	2009	87	76	0.534	1 of 5	+1				1	
Minnesota Twins	AL Cent	2008	88	75	0.540	2 of 5	1					
Minnesota Twins	AL Cent	2007	79	83	0.488	3 of 5	17					
Minnesota Twins	AL Cent	2006	96	66	0.593	1 of 5	+1				1	
Minnesota Twins	AL Cent	2005	83	79	0.512	3 of 5	16					
Minnesota Twins	AL Cent	2004	92	70	0.568	1 of 5	+9				1	
Minnesota Twins	AL Cent	2003	90	72	0.556	1 of 5	+4				1	
Minnesota Twins	AL Cent	2002	94	67	0.584	1 of 5	+13.5			1	1	
Minnesota Twins	AL Cent	2001	85	77	0.525	2 of 5	6					
Minnesota Twins	AL Cent	2000	69	93	0.426	5 of 5	26					
Minnesota Twins	AL Cent	1999	63	97	0.394	5 of 5	33					
Minnesota Twins	AL Cent	1998	70	92	0.432	4 of 5	19					
Minnesota Twins	AL Cent	1997	68	94	0.420	4 of 5	18.5					
Minnesota Twins	AL Cent	1996	78	84	0.481	4 of 5	21.5					
Minnesota Twins	AL Cent	1995	56	88	0.389	5 of 5	44					
Minnesota Twins	AL Cent	1994	53	60	0.469	4 of 5	14					
Minnesota Twins	AL West	1993	71	91	0.438	5t of 7	23					
Minnesota Twins	AL West	1992	90	72	0.556	2 of 7	6					
Minnesota Twins	AL West	1991	95	67	0.586	1 of 7	+8	1	1		1	
Minnesota Twins	AL West	1990	74	88	0.457	7 of 7	29					
Minnesota Twins	AL West	1989	80	82	0.494	5 of 7	19					
Minnesota Twins	AL West	1988	91	71	0.562	2 of 7	13					
Minnesota Twins	AL West	1987	85	77	0.525	1 of 7	+2	1	1		1	
Minnesota Twins	AL West	1986	71	91	0.438	6 of 7	21					
Minnesota Twins	AL West	1985	77	85	0.475	4t of 7	14					
Minnesota Twins	AL West	1984	81	81	0.500	2t of 7	3					
Minnesota Twins	AL West	1983	70	92	0.432	5t of 7	29					
Minnesota Twins	AL West	1982	60	102	0.370	7 of 7	33					
Minnesota Twins	AL West	1981	41	68	0.376	7, 4 of 7	18, 6					
Minnesota Twins	AL West	1980	77	84	0.478	3 of 7	19.5					
Minnesota Twins	AL West	1979	82	80	0.506	4 of 7	6					
Minnesota Twins	AL West	1978	73	89	0.451	4 of 7	19					
Minnesota Twins	AL West	1977	84	77	0.522	4 of 7	17.5					
Minnesota Twins	AL West	1976	85	77	0.525	3 of 6	5					
Minnesota Twins	AL West	1975	76	83	0.478	4 of 6	20.5					
Minnesota Twins	AL West	1974	82	80	0.506	3 of 6	8					
Minnesota Twins	AL West	1973	81	81	0.500	3 of 6	13					
Minnesota Twins	AL West	1972	77	77	0.500	3 of 6	15.5					
Minnesota Twins	AL West	1971	74	86	0.463	5 of 6	26.5					
Minnesota Twins	AL West	1970	98	64	0.605	1 of 6	+9				1	
Minnesota Twins	AL West	1969	97	65	0.599	1 of 6	+9				1	
Minnesota Twins	AL	1968	79	83	0.488	7 of 10	24					

Team Name	League	Year	W	L	Win%	Fin	GB/GA	WS	Lge	LDS	Div	WC
Minnesota Twins	AL	1967	91	71	0.562	2t of 10	1					
Minnesota Twins	AL	1966	89	73	0.549	2 of 10	9					
Minnesota Twins	AL	1965	102	60	0.630	1 of 10	+7		1			
Minnesota Twins	AL	1964	79	83	0.488	6t of 10	20					
Minnesota Twins	AL	1963	91	70	0.565	3 of 10	13					
Minnesota Twins	AL	1962	91	71	0.562	2 of 10	5					
Minnesota Twins	AL	1961	70	90	0.438	7 of 10	38					
Washington Senators	AL	1960	73	81	0.474	5 of 8	24					
Washington Senators	AL	1959	63	91	0.409	8 of 8	31					
Washington Senators	AL	1958	61	93	0.396	8 of 8	31					
Washington Senators	AL	1957	55	99	0.357	8 of 8	43					
Washington Senators	AL	1956	59	95	0.383	7 of 8	38					
Washington Senators	AL	1955	53	101	0.344	8 of 8	43					
Washington Senators	AL	1954	66	88	0.429	6 of 8	45					
Washington Senators	AL	1953	76	76	0.500	5 of 8	23.5					
Washington Senators	AL	1952	78	76	0.506	5 of 8	17					
Washington Senators	AL	1951	62	92	0.403	7 of 8	36					
Washington Senators	AL	1950	67	87	0.435	5 of 8	31					
Washington Senators	AL	1949	50	104	0.325	8 of 8	47					
Washington Senators	AL	1948	56	97	0.366	7 of 8	40					
Washington Senators	AL	1947	64	90	0.416	7 of 8	33					
Washington Senators	AL	1946	76	78	0.494	4 of 8	28					
Washington Senators	AL	1945	87	67	0.565	2 of 8	1.5					
Washington Senators	AL	1944	64	90	0.416	8 of 8	25					
Washington Senators	AL	1943	84	69	0.549	2 of 8	13.5					
Washington Senators	AL	1942	62	89	0.411	7 of 8	39.5					
Washington Senators	AL	1941	70	84	0.455	6t of 8	31					
Washington Senators	AL	1940	64	90	0.416	7 of 8	26					
Washington Senators	AL	1939	65	87	0.428	6 of 8	41.5					
Washington Senators	AL	1938	75	76	0.497	5 of 8	23.5					
Washington Senators	AL	1937	73	80	0.477	6 of 8	28.5					
Washington Senators	AL	1936	82	71	0.536	4 of 8	20					
Washington Senators	AL	1935	67	86	0.438	6 of 8	27					
Washington Senators	AL	1934	66	86	0.434	7 of 8	34					
Washington Senators	AL	1933	99	53	0.651	1 of 8	+7		1			
Washington Senators	AL	1932	93	61	0.604	3 of 8	14					
Washington Senators	AL	1931	92	62	0.597	3 of 8	16					
Washington Senators	AL	1930	94	60	0.610	2 of 8	8					
Washington Senators	AL	1929	71	81	0.467	5 of 8	34					
Washington Senators	AL	1928	75	79	0.487	4 of 8	26					
Washington Senators	AL	1927	85	69	0.552	3 of 8	25					
Washington Senators	AL	1926	81	69	0.540	4 of 8	8					
Washington Senators	AL	1925	96	55	0.636	1 of 8	+8.5		1			
Washington Senators	AL	1924	92	62	0.597	1 of 8	+2	1	1			
Washington Senators	AL	1923	75	78	0.490	4 of 8	23.5					

Team Name	League	Year	W	L	Win%	Fin	GB/GA	WS	Lge	LDS	Div	WC
Washington Senators	AL	1922	69	85	0.448	6 of 8	25					
Washington Senators	AL	1921	80	73	0.523	4 of 8	18					
Washington Senators	AL	1920	68	84	0.447	6 of 8	29					
Washington Senators	AL	1919	56	84	0.400	7 of 8	32					
Washington Senators	AL	1918	72	56	0.563	3 of 8	4					
Washington Senators	AL	1917	74	79	0.484	5 of 8	25.5					
Washington Senators	AL	1916	76	77	0.497	7 of 8	14.5					
Washington Senators	AL	1915	85	68	0.556	4 of 8	17					
Washington Senators	AL	1914	81	73	0.526	3 of 8	19					
Washington Senators	AL	1913	90	64	0.584	2 of 8	6.5					
Washington Senators	AL	1912	91	61	0.599	2 of 8	14					
Washington Senators	AL	1911	64	90	0.416	7 of 8	38.5					
Washington Senators	AL	1910	66	85	0.437	7 of 8	36.5					
Washington Senators	AL	1909	42	110	0.276	8 of 8	56					
Washington Senators	AL	1908	67	85	0.441	7 of 8	22.5					
Washington Senators	AL	1907	49	102	0.325	8 of 8	43.5					
Washington Senators	AL	1906	55	95	0.367	7 of 8	37.5					
Washington Senators	AL	1905	64	87	0.424	7 of 8	29.5					
Washington Senators	AL	1904	38	113	0.252	8 of 8	55.5					
Washington Senators	AL	1903	43	94	0.314	8 of 8	47.5					
Washington Senators	AL	1902	61	75	0.449	6 of 8	22					
Washington Senators	AL	1901	61	72	0.459	6 of 8	20.5					
			8232	8816	0.483			3	6	1	10	0

New York Mets

Stats

History

Year of Origin	1962	Years Played	49

Score & Rank

Total Points Score	47.9	Average Points Score	0.98
Total Points Rank	17	Average Points Rank	11

Postseason Results

	No.	Years
World Series Won	2	1969, 1986
League Championship Series Won	4	1969, 1973, 1986, 2000
League Division Series Won	3	1999, 2000, 2006
World Series Lost	2	1973, 2000
League Championship Series Lost	3	1988, 1999, 2006
League Division Series Lost	0	

Postseason Won-Loss Records and Winning Percentages

	Postseason Games		Postseason Series	
All Postseason Series	43-31	.581	9-5	.643
World Series	12-12	.500	2-2	.500
League Championship Series	22-17	.564	4-3	.571
League Division Series	9-2	.818	3-0	1.000

Regular Season Results

All-Time Won-Loss Record	3734-4064
All-Time Winning Percentage	.479

	No.	Years
League Titles before 1969	0	
Division Titles	5	1969, 1973, 1986, 1988, 2006
Wild Cards	2	1999, 2000

Regular Season High & Low Points

		Year(s)
Most Wins in a Season	108	1986
Most Losses in a Season	120	1962
Highest Winning Percentage	.667	1986
Lowest Winning Percentage	.250	1962
Longest Streak with Won-Loss Record .500 or Higher	7 years	1984-1990
Longest Streak with Won-Loss Record Below .500	7 years	1962-1968, 1977-1983

Years with .500 record or Better

1960's	1 (out of 8)
1970's	6
1980's	6
1990's	4
2000's	6
2010's	0
23 out of 49 seasons played = 47%	

Years Making Postseason

1960's	1
1970's	1
1980's	2
1990's	1
2000's	2
2010's	0
7 out of 49 seasons played = 14%	

Streaks

- 1969-1973: Won two Division Titles, two League Championship Series, and one World Series in five years.
- 1984-1988: Won one World Series, one League Championship Series, and two Division Titles in three years.
- 1999-2006: Won one League Championship Series, three League Division Series, one Division Title, and two Wild Cards in eight years.

Extra Bases

- In their inaugural season of 1962 New York went 40-120, which is a winning percentage of .250. Another way to look at this is that they lost three out of every four games.
- In their championship year of 1986 New York won two of every three games in the regular season (108-54 won-loss record = .667 winning percentage). This was the most wins in the National League since the 1975 Reds and no National League team has won as many games in the regular season since.

Scoring Opportunities

1970's

- New York won the National League East Division in 1973 with an 82-79 record and beat the Reds, who had 99 wins, in the LCS. In the World Series the Mets played Oakland. In Game 1 New York trailed by one run in the top of the sixth inning when they had runners on first and third with two outs, but their next batter struck out. The Mets had a runner on first in the top of the eighth and ninth innings but couldn't score in either inning and lost the game 2-1. New York won Game 2 and led Game 3 2-1 after seven innings. But in the top of the eighth they gave up a single, a stolen base, and another single and let in the tying run. The Mets had runners on first and second with two outs in the bottom of the ninth, but their next batter flied out. In the top of the eleventh New York had one out and there was an A's runner on first base. The next Oakland batter struck out but a passed ball by the Mets catcher let the A's runner on first advance to second. The next Oakland batter singled and drove in the go-ahead run. New York got their first batter up on base in the bottom of the inning, but their next three batters all got out and they lost 3-2. The Mets won Games 4 & 5 to take a three game to two lead in the series. In Game 6 New York trailed by two runs after seven innings. They scored one run in the top of the eighth and had runners on first and third with one out, but their next two batters struck out and flied out. The Mets gave up one run in the bottom of the inning and lost the game 3-1. Then they lost Game 7 5-2 and lost the series, blowing their three games to two series lead.

1980's

- In 1985 the Mets trailed St. Louis by one game in the National League East Division on October 2nd with four games left to play, and their next game was against the Cardinals. If New York won the next game the two teams would have been tied, but the Mets lost the game 4-3, and lost two of their last three games against Montreal while St. Louis won two of their last three games against the Cubs. New York ended the season with 98 wins, but finished in second place three games behind the Cardinals.
- New York was in close race with St. Louis for the 1987 National League East Division title. On September 28th the Mets were two games behind the Cardinals with five games left, and their last three against St. Louis. Before the two teams met in the final series of the year, New York lost two games to Philadelphia and was eliminated from division contention with three games to go. The Mets won two out of their final three games against the Cardinals and finished in second place three games behind St. Louis, just like in 1985.
- In 1988 the Mets won 100 games and won the National League East Division title. In the LCS they faced the Dodgers and won two of the first three games, winning Games 1 & 3 and losing Game 2 6-3. In Game 4 New York had a 4-2 lead after eight innings. But in the top of the ninth they gave up a walk to the first Dodgers batter and then a two-run home run that tied the game. The game went into extra innings and in the top of the twelfth the Mets got the first two Dodgers batters out but then gave up a solo home run. In the bottom of the inning New York got their first two batters on base and had the bases loaded with one out, but their next two hitters both popped out and they lost 5-4. Instead of having a 3-1 series lead, the series was tied at two games apiece. The Mets lost Game 5 7-4 and won Game 6. In Game 7 New York gave up five runs in the second inning and only had five hits in the game. They lost the game 6-0 and lost the series.

1990's

- New York had a one game lead over Chicago for the National League Wild Card spot on September 20th of the 1998 season. But the Mets lost their last five games of the year and finished one game behind the Cubs and Giants, who tied for the wild card spot. If New York had won just one more game there would have been the first three team tie for a playoff spot ever.
- In 1999 the Mets beat Cincinnati in a one game playoff for the National League Wild Card spot and beat Arizona in the LDS. In the LCS New York played Atlanta and lost Game 1 4-2. In Game 2 the Mets led 2-0 after five innings but gave up two two-run home runs in the bottom of the sixth. In the top of the eighth New York scored one run and had runners on first and second with two outs, but their next batter up struck out and they lost the game 4-3. In Game

3 the Mets gave up one run in the first inning and only gave up three hits the whole game. But New York only got a runner to third base twice, in the second and fourth innings, and did not get a runner to second base after the fourth inning. In the bottom of the ninth the Mets first batter up reached base on an error, but the next three batters all got out and New York lost 1-0. The Mets were down three games to zero in the series but won Games 4 & 5. Game 6 went into extra innings tied at eight. In the top of the tenth New York scored one run and had a runner on third with two outs but their next batter up struck out. In the bottom of the inning the Mets gave up a single, a walk, and another single and let in the tying run. In the bottom of the eleventh New York gave up a double to the first Atlanta batter who advanced to third on a sacrifice bunt. The Mets decided to walk the next two Braves batters intentionally and load the bases. The New York pitcher walked the following Atlanta batter and walked in a run and they lost the game 10-9 and lost the series.

2000's

- New York won the National League Wild Card again in 2000, making the playoffs in back to back years for the first time ever. They beat the Giants in the LDS and the Cardinals in the LCS. In the World Series the Mets played the Yankees in the 'subway series.' The Mets had a 3-2 lead in Game 1 in the bottom of the ninth. They got the first Yankees batter out but then gave up a walk and two singles. The next Yankees batter hit a sacrifice fly that tied the score and the game went into extra innings. The Mets were retired in order in the top of the tenth, eleventh, and twelfth innings and in the bottom of the twelfth they gave up a single, a double, an intentional walk, and with two outs another single that drove in the game winning run. They lost the game 4-3. In Game 2 the Mets trailed 6-0 after eight innings but scored five runs in the top of the ninth on two home runs. With the bases empty their next batter up struck out and the Mets lost 6-5. The Mets won Game 3 and in Game 4 they trailed by one run after three innings. They got a runner to first base in the fourth, sixth, seventh, and eighth innings, but couldn't score in any inning and lost the game 3-2. Game 5 was tied at two after eight innings and the Mets got the first two Yankees out in the top of the ninth. But then they gave up a walk and two singles and let in two runs. The Mets lost the game 4-2 and lost the series.
- In 2006 the Mets won the National League East Division and swept the Dodgers in the LDS. In the LCS New York played St. Louis and won Game 1. The Mets had a 6-4 lead in Game 2 in the top of the seventh and got the first two Cardinals batters out, but then gave up a single, a walk, and a triple that drove in two runs and tied the score. In the bottom of the eighth New York had runners on first and second with one out, but their next batter up hit into a double play. In the top of the ninth they gave up a home run to the first St. Louis batter and gave up two more runs in the inning and lost the game 9-6. The Mets only had three hits in Game 3 and lost the game 5-0. New York won Game 4 to tie the series up. In Game 5 the Mets trailed by two runs in the top of the eighth inning when they had runners on second and third with one

out, but their next two batters flied out and struck out and they lost the game 4-2. New York won Game 6 to even the series again and Game 7 was tied at one after eight innings. In the top of the ninth the Mets gave up a single and a home run with one out. In the bottom of the inning New York got their first two batters on base and had the bases loaded with two outs, but their next batter struck out and they lost 3-1 and lost the series.

- The Mets looked like they were going to win the National League East Division in 2007 as they had a seven game lead over the Phillies on September 12th. But New York lost five games in a row including three games against Philadelphia. The Mets still had a 2.5 game lead on September 23rd, but lost six of their last seven games of the year. New York went 5-12 after the 12th while the Phillies went 13-4 and the Mets lost the division by one game. New York lost five games in a row twice during that time. The Mets also missed the wild card spot as they finished the year one game behind San Diego and Colorado, who tied for the final playoff spot and played a one game playoff, which was won by the Rockies.
- In 2008 New York led the National League East Division by 3.5 games over the Phillies on September 10th. But just like the year before the Mets had another late season collapse. They went 7-10 the rest of the year while Philadelphia went 13-3. New York still led the division by a half a game on September 19th but went 3-6 the rest of the season from that point while the Phillies went 6-2. On September 23rd the Mets led Milwaukee by one game for the wild card spot, but the rest of the season New York went 2-3 and the Brewers went 4-1. The Mets finished three games behind Philadelphia for the division and one game behind Milwaukee for the wild card.

Year-to-Year Figures

Team Name	League	Year	W	L	Win%	Fin	GB/GA	WS	Lge	LDS	Div	WC
New York Mets	NL East	2010	79	83	0.488	4 of 5	18					
New York Mets	NL East	2009	70	92	0.432	4 of 5	23					
New York Mets	NL East	2008	89	73	0.549	2 of 5	3					
New York Mets	NL East	2007	88	74	0.543	2 of 5	1					
New York Mets	NL East	2006	97	65	0.599	1 of 5	+12			1	1	
New York Mets	NL East	2005	83	79	0.512	3t of 5	7					
New York Mets	NL East	2004	71	91	0.438	4 of 5	25					
New York Mets	NL East	2003	66	95	0.410	5 of 5	34.5					
New York Mets	NL East	2002	75	86	0.466	5 of 5	26.5					
New York Mets	NL East	2001	82	80	0.506	3 of 5	6					
New York Mets	NL East	2000	94	68	0.580	2 of 5	1		1	1		1
New York Mets	NL East	1999	97	66	0.595	2 of 5	6.5			1		1
New York Mets	NL East	1998	88	74	0.543	2 of 5	18					
New York Mets	NL East	1997	88	74	0.543	3 of 5	13					
New York Mets	NL East	1996	71	91	0.438	4 of 5	25					
New York Mets	NL East	1995	69	75	0.479	2t of 5	21					
New York Mets	NL East	1994	55	58	0.487	3 of 5	18.5					

Team Name	League	Year	W	L	Win%	Fin	GB/GA	WS	Lge	LDS	Div	WC
New York Mets	NL East	1993	59	103	0.364	7 of 7	38					
New York Mets	NL East	1992	72	90	0.444	5 of 6	24					
New York Mets	NL East	1991	77	84	0.478	5 of 6	20.5					
New York Mets	NL East	1990	91	71	0.562	2 of 6	4					
New York Mets	NL East	1989	87	75	0.537	2 of 6	6					
New York Mets	NL East	1988	100	60	0.625	1 of 6	+15				1	
New York Mets	NL East	1987	92	70	0.568	2 of 6	3					
New York Mets	NL East	1986	108	54	0.667	1 of 6	+21.5	1	1		1	
New York Mets	NL East	1985	98	64	0.605	2 of 6	3					
New York Mets	NL East	1984	90	72	0.556	2 of 6	6.5					
New York Mets	NL East	1983	68	94	0.420	6 of 6	22					
New York Mets	NL East	1982	65	97	0.401	6 of 6	27					
New York Mets	NL East	1981	41	62	0.398	5, 4 of 6	15, 5.5					
New York Mets	NL East	1980	67	95	0.414	5 of 6	24					
New York Mets	NL East	1979	63	99	0.389	6 of 6	35					
New York Mets	NL East	1978	66	96	0.407	6 of 6	24					
New York Mets	NL East	1977	64	98	0.395	6 of 6	37					
New York Mets	NL East	1976	86	76	0.531	3 of 6	15					
New York Mets	NL East	1975	82	80	0.506	3t of 6	10.5					
New York Mets	NL East	1974	71	91	0.438	5 of 6	17					
New York Mets	NL East	1973	82	79	0.509	1 of 6	+1.5		1		1	
New York Mets	NL East	1972	83	73	0.532	3 of 6	13.5					
New York Mets	NL East	1971	83	79	0.512	3t of 6	14					
New York Mets	NL East	1970	83	79	0.512	3 of 6	6					
New York Mets	NL East	1969	100	62	0.617	1 of 6	+8	1	1		1	
New York Mets	NL	1968	73	89	0.451	9 of 10	24					
New York Mets	NL	1967	61	101	0.377	10 of 10	40.5					
New York Mets	NL	1966	66	95	0.410	9 of 10	28.5					
New York Mets	NL	1965	50	112	0.309	10 of 10	47					
New York Mets	NL	1964	53	109	0.327	10 of 10	40					
New York Mets	NL	1963	51	111	0.315	10 of 10	48					
New York Mets	NL	1962	40	120	0.250	10 of 10	60.5					
			3734	4064	0.479			2	4	3	5	2

New York Yankees

Stats

History

Year of Origin 1901   Years Played..110

Score & Rank

Total Points Score ....438.8   Average Points Score....................................3.99
Total Points Rank 1   Average Points Rank...1

Postseason Results	No.	Years
World Series Won.. 27		1923, 1927, 1928, 1932, 1936, 1937, 1938, 1939, 1941, 1943, 1947, 1949, 1950, 1951, 1952, 1953, 1956, 1958, 1961, 1962, 1977, 1978, 1996, 1998, 1999, 2000, 2009
League Championship Series Won 11		1976, 1977, 1978, 1981, 1996, 1998, 1999, 2000, 2001, 2003, 2009
League Division Series Won.................... 10		1981, 1996, 1998, 1999, 2000, 2001, 2003, 2004, 2009, 2010
World Series Lost 13		1921, 1922, 1926, 1942, 1955, 1957, 1960, 1963, 1964, 1976, 1981, 2001, 2003
League Championship Series Lost............3		1980, 2004, 2010
League Division Series Lost 6		1995, 1997, 2002, 2005, 2006, 2007

Postseason Won-Loss Records and Winning Percentages

	Postseason Games		Postseason Series	
All Postseason Series....................	218-145	.601	48-22	.686
World Series..................................	134-90	.598	27-13	.675
League Championship Series	45-28	.616	11-3	.786
League Division Series..................	39-27	.591	10-6	.625

Regular Season Results

All-Time Won-Loss Record 9670-7361
All-Time Winning Percentage 568

	No.	Years
League Titles before 1969	29	1921, 1922, 1923, 1926, 1927, 1928, 1932, 1936, 1937, 1938, 1939, 1941, 1942, 1943, 1947, 1949, 1950, 1951, 1952, 1953, 1955, 1956, 1957, 1958, 1960, 1961, 1962, 1963, 1964
Division Titles.......................................	16	1976, 1977, 1978, 1980, 1981, 1996, 1998, 1999, 2000, 2001, 2002, 2003, 2004, 2005, 2006, 2009
Wild Cards	4	1995, 1997, 2007, 2010

Regular Season High & Low Points		Year(s)
Most Wins in a Season	114	1998
Most Losses in a Season.....................................	103	1908
Highest Winning Percentage	.714	1927
Lowest Winning Percentage..............................	.329	1912
Longest Streak with Won-Loss Record .500 or Higher	39 years	1926 - 1964
Longest Streak with Won-Loss Record Below .500	4 years	1912-1915, 1989-1992

Years with .500 record or Better

1900's	4 (out of 9)
1910's	4
1920's	9
1930's	10
1940's	10
1950's	10
1960's	6
1970's	9
1980's	8
1990's	7
2000's	10
2010's	1

88 out of 110 seasons played = 80%

Years Making Postseason

1900's	0
1910's	0
1920's	6
1930's	5
1940's	5
1950's	8
1960's	5
1970's	3
1980's	2
1990's	5
2000's	9
2010's	1

49 out of 110 seasons played = 45%

Streaks

- 1921-1928: Won three World Series and six League Titles in eight years.
- 1936-1943: Won seven League Titles and six World Series in eight years.
- 1947-1964: Won ten World Series and fifteen League Titles in eighteen years. Went to the World Series in every year except three over this period.
- 1976-1981: Won five Division Titles, one League Division Series, four League Championship Series, and two World Series in six years.
- 1995–2010: Won five World Series, seven League Championship Series, nine League Division Series, eleven Division Titles, and four Wild Cards in sixteen years. This included winning nine straight Division Titles from 1998-2006. From 1996-2003 they appeared in the World Series six times in eight years.

Extra Bases

- From 1926-1964 New York had thirty-nine consecutive winning seasons.
- From 1936-1964 the Yankees appeared in twenty-two World Series and won sixteen of them over the twenty-nine year period. From 1949-1964 they went to the World Series fourteen times in sixteen years, winning nine of them.
- New York dominated the 1941 regular season by so much that they clinched the pennant in 136 games, which is an American League record.
- In 1953 the Yankees won their fifth World Series in a row. No other team has even won five league pennants in a row.
- In 1965 New York finished the regular season with a record under .500 for the first time since 1925 and in 1966 they finished in last place for the first time since 1912.
- From 1989-1992 the Yankees had four straight losing seasons, which they had not done

since 1912-1915.

- When New York won the World Series in 2000 they became the third Yankee team and fourth baseball team ever to win three or more World Series in a row. Oakland is the only non-Yankee team to do it, winning three in a row from 1972-1974. New York won four in a row from 1936-1939 and five in a row from 1949-1953.

- In 2004 the Yankees became the first and only baseball playoff team to blow a 3-0 series lead when they lost to the Red Sox in the ALCS in seven games by losing the final four games of the series.

Scoring Opportunities

1900's

- In 1904 the New York Highlanders had a half-game lead over the Boston Americans on October 7th with four games remaining against Boston. New York lost the next three games with the loss in the third game occurring because of wild pitch in the top of the ninth inning that let in the go-ahead run. The Highlanders won the last game of the season and finished a game and a half behind Boston. The two teams had the same amount of losses, but New York played three less games, and had three less wins.

- New York had a one game lead over Chicago on September 23rd in 1906 but lost four games in a row and fell to three games behind the White Sox on September 27th. The Highlanders went 5-3 the rest of the season but so did Chicago and New York finished the season in second place 3.5 games behind the White Sox.

1920's

- In 1920 the Yankees led the American League by 1.5 games over Cleveland on September 14th. But New York lost four games in a row and fell to three games behind the Indians on September 19th. The Yankees went 7-2 the rest of the season but the Indians went 9-4 and New York finished in third place three games behind Cleveland.

- New York won its first American League pennant in 1921 and played the Giants in a best of nine games World Series. The Yankees won Games 1 & 2 and Game 3 was tied at four after six innings. But in the bottom of the seventh the Yankees gave up eight hits and eight runs and they lost the game 13-5. The Yankees led Game 4 1-0 after seven innings but gave up four hits and three runs in the top of the eighth and lost the game 4-2. The Yankees won Game 5 but lost Game 6 8-5. Game 7 was tied at one after six innings. In the top of the seventh the Yankees had runners on second and third with two outs, but their next batter grounded out. In the bottom of the inning the Yankees retired the first two Giants batters, but then committed an error that let a runner on base. The next Giants batter doubled and drove in the go-ahead run. The Yankees had a runner on first in each of the top of the eighth and ninth innings with two outs, but couldn't score in either inning and lost the game 2-1. In Game 8 the Yankees walked two batters and committed an error with two outs in the top of the first inning that let in one run. The Yankees had the bases loaded in the fourth inning with two outs, but their next batter flied out. In the bottom of the ninth inning the Yankees had a runner on first with one out, but their next batter hit into a double play to end the game. The Yankees lost 1-0 and lost the series five games to three after leading it three games to two, losing the last three games of the series.

- New York won the American League pennant in 1922 by one game over the St. Louis Browns and had a rematch with the Giants in the World Series. In Game 1 the Yankees led 2-0 in the bottom of the eighth inning, but gave up four straight singles and a sacrifice fly to start the inning and let in three runs. In the top of the ninth the Yankees first batter singled but with one out their next batter hit into a double play and they lost 3-2. Game 2 was tied at three after ten innings when the game was called due to darkness. In Game 3 the Yankees trailed by two runs in the top of the seventh when they had runners on second and third with one out, but their next two batters struck out and grounded out and they lost the game 3-0. In Game 4 the Yankees trailed by one run in the bottom of the eighth when they had a runner on base second with one out, but their next two batters flied out and popped out. In the bottom of the ninth the Yankees first batter up doubled, but their next batter grounded to third and the runner on second was thrown out at third base in a rundown. The next Yankees batter singled, advancing the runner who reached on the rundown from first base to third, but the hitter was thrown out trying to get to second base. With two outs and a runner on third the next Yankees batter flied out and they lost 4-3. In Game 5 the Yankees had a 3-2 lead in the bottom of the eighth but gave up four hits and three runs. The runs all scored with two outs and the Yankees lost the game 5-3 and lost the series.

- In 1924 New York was tied with Washington on September 18th but lost three games in a row and fell to two games behind the Senators on September 21st. The Yankees won four of their last five games of the season, but Washington went 5-2 over the same period and New York finished the year in second place two games behind the Senators.

- The Yankees won the American League pennant in 1926 and won Game 1 in the World Series against the Cardinals. Game 2 was tied at two after six innings but New York gave up a three-run home run with two outs in the top of the seventh and lost the game 6-2. The Yankees only had five hits in Game 3 and did not get a runner to third base the entire game and they lost the game 4-0. New York won Games 4 & 5, and Games 6 & 7 were going to be played at home, but the Yankees lost Game 6 10-2. In Game 7 New York made two errors in the top of the fourth inning that let in three runs. The Yankees trailed by one run in the bottom of the seventh inning when they had the bases loaded with two outs, but their next batter up struck out and they lost the game 3-2 and lost the series.

1940's

- In 1940 New York only trailed the Tigers by one game on September 11th but lost six of their next seven games, including two in a three game series to Detroit, and fell to four games behind the Tigers on September 16th. The Yankees went 11-3 the rest of the year but Detroit went 9-4 and New York finished in third place two games behind the Tigers.

- New York won the American League pennant in 1942 and played St. Louis in the World Series. The Yankees won Game 1 and Game 2 was tied at three in the bottom of the eighth. New York got the first two Cardinals batters out but gave up a double and made an error letting the runner on second advance to third. The next St. Louis batter singled and drove in the go-ahead run. In the top of the ninth the first two Yankees batters singled, but on the second hit, the runner that started on first was thrown out trying to reach third base, and the next two batters flied out and grounded out and New York lost the game 4-3. In Game 3 the Yankees only got one runner past first base and it occurred in the first inning and they lost the game 2-0. Game 4 was tied at six after six innings but in the top of the seventh the Yankees gave up three walks, one hit, and one error, and let in two runs and lost the game 9-6. Game 5 was tied at two after eight innings but in the top of the ninth New York gave up a two-run home run with one out. In the bottom of the inning the Yankee got their first two batters on base, but their runner on second was picked off. Their next two batters popped out and grounded out and the Yankees lost 4-2 and lost the series.

- In 1948 the Yankees were tied for first place with Boston and Cleveland on September 24th with seven games left in the season. New York went 3-2 in their next five games and was tied with the Red Sox for second place on September 30th, 1.5 games behind the Indians with two games left against Boston. The Yankees lost both games to Boston 5-1 and 10-5 and finished two games behind the Indians and Red Sox, who tied for first place at the end of the regular season. The Indians won a one game playoff against Boston and beat the Boston Braves in the World Series.

1950's

- The Yankees won the American League pennant in 1955 and faced the Dodgers in the World Series. New York won Games 1 & 2 at home, but lost the next three games on the road 8-3, 8-5 and 5-3. The Yankees won Game 6 and trailed by two runs in the bottom of the sixth inning of Game 7. They got their first two batters of the inning on base, but their next two batters hit into a double play and a ground out. In the bottom of the eighth New York had runners on first and third with one out, but their next two hitters both flied out and they lost the game 2-0 and lost the series.

- In 1957 New York won the American League pennant and played the Milwaukee Braves in the World Series. The Yankees won Game 1 and in Game 2 they trailed by two runs in the bottom of the sixth inning when they had runners on second and third with one out. But their next two batters both grounded out. In the bottom of the ninth New York had runners on first and second with two outs, but their next batter up grounded out and they lost 4-2. The Yankees won Game 3 and Game 4 was tied at four after nine innings. In the top of the tenth New York scored one run but in the bottom of the inning they hit a batter, gave up a sacrifice bunt, a double that drove in the tying run, and a two run home run and they lost the game 7-5. In Game 5 the Yankees had a runner on base in every inning except the fifth and sixth, with their best chance to score coming in the top of the fourth inning when they had runners on first and second with one out. But their next batter up hit into a double play. New York had two Braves batters out in the bottom of the sixth but gave up three singles in a row and let in one run and lost the game 1-0. The Yankees won Game 6 to even the series but lost Game 7 5-0 and lost the series.

1960's

• New York won the American League pennant in 1960 and faced Pittsburgh in the World Series. The Yankees lost Game 1 6-4 and won Games 2 & 3 by a combined score of 26-3. In Game 4 New York trailed by one in the bottom of the seventh when they had runners on first and second with one out, but their next two batters flied out and grounded out and they lost the game 3-2. The Yankees lost Game 5 5-2 and won Game 6. In Game 7 New York led 7-4 in the bottom of the eighth but gave up five hits and let in five runs. The Yankees scored two runs in the top of the ninth to tie the score at nine, but in the bottom of the inning New York gave up a home run to the Pirates first batter of the inning and lost the game 10-9. New York outscored Pittsburgh 55-27 in the series.

• In 1963 the Yankees won the American League pennant and played the Dodgers in the World Series, where they lost Game 1 5-2 and Game 2 4-1. In the first inning of Game 3 New York gave up a walk with one out and a wild pitch and a single with two outs and let in one run. The Yankees had the bases loaded with two outs in the top of the second inning, but their next batter up struck out. In the top of the sixth New York had a runner on third base with two outs, but their next batter up struck out and they lost the game 1-0. Game 4 was tied at one in the bottom of the seventh. The Yankees committed an error on the first Dodgers batter of the inning and the hitter got all the way to third base. The following batter hit a sacrifice fly and drove in the go-ahead run. In the top of the ninth New York had runners on first and second with two outs, but their next batter grounded out and they lost 3-2 and lost the series in a sweep.

• The Yankees won the 1964 American League pennant by one game over the White Sox. In the World Series New York played St. Louis, lost Game 1 9-5, and won Games 2 & 3. In Game 4 the Yankees had a three run lead after five innings but gave up a grand slam in the top of the sixth inning. New York only got one runner on base the rest of the game and lost the game 4-3. In Game 5 the Yankees tied the score at two in the bottom of the ninth inning by hitting a two-run home run with two outs. But in the top of the tenth they gave up a walk, a single, and a three run home run with one out and they lost the game 5-2. New York won Game 6 but trailed 6-0 after five innings in Game 7 and lost the game 7-5 to lose the series.

1970's

• New York led the American League East Division by one game over Baltimore on September 22nd in 1974. The rest of the year the Yankees went 5-3 but the Orioles won their last eight games of the season and New York finished in second place two games behind Baltimore.

• In 1976 the Yankees won the American League East Division and beat the Royals in the LCS on a home run in the bottom of the ninth inning of Game 5. In the World Series New York played Cincinnati and lost Game 1 5-1. Game 2 was tied at three after eight innings. In the bottom of the ninth the Yankees got the first two Reds hitters out. The next Cincinnati batter hit a ground ball to the New York shortstop who committed a throwing error to first base that let the Reds player reach second base. The Yankees walked the next Cincinnati hitter intentionally and the following batter hit a single that drove in the game winning run and New York lost 4-3. The Yankees lost Game 3 6-2 and Game 4 7-2 and lost the series in a sweep. They were outscored 22-8 in the four games.

1980's

• The Yankees won the American League East Division in 1980, and played the Royals in the LCS. New York lost Game 1 7-2 and trailed by one run in the top of the eighth inning in Game 2. They had a runner on first with two outs and their next batter hit a double to left field. But the runner from first tried to score the tying run and was thrown out at home plate. In the top of the ninth the Yankees had runners on first and second with one out, but their next batter hit into a double play and they lost 3-2. New York led Game 3 2-1 after six innings and got the first two Royals hitters out in the top of the seventh. But then they gave up a double, a single, and a three-run home run. In the bottom of the eighth the Yankees had the bases loaded with no outs, but hit into a double play and a ground out and they lost the game 4-2 and lost the series in a sweep.

• In 1981 New York made the playoffs by winning the first half of the season in the American League East Division in the strike split season. The Yankees beat the Brewers in the first round of the playoffs and swept the A's in the LCS. In the World Series against the Dodgers the Yankees won Games 1 & 2 at home. In Game 3 New York trailed by one run in the top of the eighth when they got their first two batters on base, but they hit into a double play and a ground out and they lost the game 5-4. The Yankees trailed by one run in Game 4 in the top of the ninth inning when they had runners on first and second with two outs. Their next batter hit a fly ball to deep center field but it stayed in the park and they lost 8-7. In Game 5 New York led 1-0 after six innings but gave up two solo home runs in the bottom of the seventh. In the top of the ninth they had a runner on first with one out, but their next two batters flied out and struck out and they lost 2-1. The Yankees lost Game 6 9-2 and lost the series they led two games to none. Three of their four losses were by one run.

1990's

• The Yankees won the American League Wild Card in 1995 and played Seattle in the LDS. New York won Games 1 & 2 at home but lost Game 3 7-4. Game 4 was tied at six in the bottom of the eighth but the Yankees gave up a grand slam and a solo home run. New York scored two runs in the top of the ninth but lost the game 11-8. In Game 5 the Yankees led 4-2 in the bottom of the eighth, but gave up a solo home run, three walks, a single, and let in two runs and the game went into extra innings. New York scored one run in the top of the eleventh but in the bottom of the inning they gave up two singles and a double and the game winning run for Seattle scored all the way from first base just beating the throw at home plate. The Yankees lost the game 5-4 and lost the series in which they led two games to zero.

• In 1997 New York won the American League Wild Card and played Cleveland in the LDS. The Yankees won Game 1, lost Game 2 7-5, and won Game 3. In Game 4 New York led 2-1 entering the bottom of the eighth inning. They got the first two Indians batters out, but then gave up a solo home run that tied the game. In the bottom of the ninth the Yankees gave up a single to the first Cleveland hitter, followed by a sacrifice bunt. The next Indians batter hit a ball that deflected off of the New York pitcher and rolled past their shortstop and the game winning run scored and the Yankees lost 3-2. In Game 5 New York trailed by one run after six innings. They had runners on first and third in the top of the eighth with two outs, but their next batter grounded out. The Yankees had a runner on second base with two outs in the top of the ninth and their next batter hit a deep fly ball to left center field, but it stayed in the park and New York lost the game 4-3 and lost the series.

2000's

• New York won the American League East Division in 2001 and beat the A's in the LDS by winning the final three games of the series after losing the first two. In the LCS the Yankees beat the Mariners team that won 116 regular season games. New York played Arizona in the World Series and lost the first two games on the road 9-1 and 4-0, getting only six hits total in the two games. The Yankees won the next three games at home with come from behind wins in Games 4 & 5. Both games were tied by the Yankees in the bottom of the ninth inning and won in extra innings. In Game 6 New York had their worst World Series loss ever, getting beaten 15-2. In Game 7 the Yankees had a 2-1 lead entering the Diamondbacks at bat in the bottom of the ninth. The first Arizona batter singled and the New York pitcher made a throwing error to second base on the second batter. After a bunt advanced the runners to second and third the Yankees gave up a double that drove in one run and tied the score at two. The next Arizona batter was hit by a pitch that loaded the bases, and there was still only one out. New York brought their infield in and the Diamondbacks next batter hit a blooper over the Yankees shortstop and the game-winning run scored and New York lost 3-2 and lost the series.

- In 2002 the Yankees won the American League East Division and played the Angels in the LDS. New York won Game 1 and led Game 2 5-4 after seven innings. But in the top of the eighth they gave up solo home runs to the first two Angels batters and gave up three runs in the inning. In the bottom of the eighth the Yankees had the bases loaded with two outs but their next batter up struck out. New York trailed by two runs in the bottom of the ninth when they had runners on first and second with one out, but their next two batters struck out and popped out and they lost 8-6. In Game 3 the Yankees had a 6-5 lead in the bottom of the seventh but gave up a single with two outs that drove in the tying run. In the bottom of the eighth they gave up two doubles and a three-run home run and let in three runs. New York lost the game 9-6 and gave up eight runs in the fifth inning of Game 4 and lost the game 9-5 to lose the series.

- New York won the American League East Division in 2003 and beat the Twins in the LDS. In the LCS against Boston the Yankees trailed 5-2 in the eighth inning of Game 7 but rallied to tie the score and they won the game and the series in the bottom of the eleventh inning on a solo home run. In the World Series New York played Florida and trailed by one run in the bottom of the eighth inning of Game 1. The Yankees had runners on first and third with two outs, but their next batter up struck out. In the bottom of the ninth New York had runners on first and second with one out, but their next two batters struck out and flied out and they lost 3-2. The Yankees won Games 2 & 3 and Game 4 was tied at three after nine innings. In the top of the eleventh New York had the bases loaded with one out, but their next two batters struck out and popped out. In the bottom of the twelfth the first Florida batter hit a home run and the Yankees lost 4-3. New York lost Game 5 6-4 and only had five hits in Game 6 and lost the game 2-0 to lose the series. They lost the series by losing three games in a row after leading two games to one.

- The Yankees won the American League East Division again in 2004 and beat the Twins again the LDS. In the LCS New York played Boston and had a three game to zero series lead. In Game 4 the Yankees had a 4-3 lead entering the bottom of the ninth. But they walked the first Red Sox batter, gave up a stolen base to a pinch runner, and gave up a single that drove in the tying run. In extra innings the Yankees loaded the bases in the top of the eleventh with two outs, but their next batter flied out. In the bottom of the twelfth New York gave up a single and a two-run home run and lost 6-4. In Game 5 the Yankees led 4-2 in the bottom of the eighth but gave up a solo home run, a walk, a single, and a sacrifice fly that drove in the tying run. In the top of the ninth New York had a runner on first with two outs when their next batter hit a ball down the right field foul line for a ground rule double. If the ball hadn't gone into the stands their runner on first would have scored the go-ahead run. Instead, their next batter up fouled out and the game went into extra innings. In the top of the thirteenth the Yankees had runners on second and third with two outs, but their next

159

batter up struck out. In the bottom of the fourteenth New York walked two Boston batters and gave up a single with two outs that drove in the game winning run and the Yankees lost 5-4. New York still had a three games to two lead with the next two games being played at home, but they lost Game 6 4-2. Then they lost Game 7 10-3 and became the first and only baseball playoff team to blow a 3-0 series lead.

- In 2005 New York tied Boston for the same record in the American League East Division. The Yankees won the division title as they won the regular season series against the Red Sox and Boston made the playoffs as the wild card team. In the LDS New York played the Angels and won Game 1. Game 2 was tied at two after six innings. In the bottom of the seventh the Yankees committed an error with one Angels runner on base that could have been the first out of the inning. New York got the next two Angels batters out but then gave up a single that drove in two runs and they lost the game 5-3. In Game 3 the Yankees trailed by one run when they had the bases loaded in the bottom of the sixth with two outs, but their next batter up flied out. New York gave up four runs the rest of the game and scored one and lost the game 11-7. The Yankees won Game 4 to even the series. In Game 5 New York gave up five runs in the first three innings and trailed by two runs in the top of the ninth when they had runners on first and second with two outs, but their next batter grounded out and they lost 5-3 and lost the series.

- New York won their ninth straight American League East Division in 2006 and played the Tigers in the LDS. The Yankees won Game 1 and led Game 2 3-1 after four innings. But they gave up one run in each of the fifth, sixth, and seventh innings and lost the game 4-3. Then they lost Games 3 6-0 and Game 4 8-3 and lost the series.

- In 2007 New York won the American League Wild Card and faced the Indians in the LDS, where they lost Game 1 12-3. In Game 2 the Yankees led 1-0 in the bottom of the eighth, but gave up a walk, a wild pitch, a sacrifice bunt, and another wild pitch that let in the tying run. The game went into extra innings and New York was retired in order in the tenth and eleventh innings. In the bottom of the eleventh the Yankees gave up two walks and a single and the bases loaded were loaded with two outs. The next Indians batter singled and New York lost 2-1. The Yankees won Game 3 but gave up six runs in the first four innings of Game 4 and lost 6-4 to lose the series.

2010's

- The Yankees won the American League Wild Card in 2010, and swept the Twins in LDS. In the LCS New York played Texas and won Game 1 6-5. In Game 2 the Yankees gave up five runs in the first three innings and lost the game 7-2. In Game 3 New York only trailed by two after eight innings, but they only had two hits in the game and they gave up six runs in the top of the ninth and lost the game 8-0. The Yankees led Game 4 3-2 after five innings but gave up eight runs the rest of the game and lost 10-3. New York won Game 5 but only had three hits in Game 6 and lost it 6-1 to lose the series. The Yankees were outscored 31-6 in their four losses.

Year-to-Year Figures

Team Name	League	Year	W	L	Win%	Fin	GB/GA	WS	Lge	LDS	Div	WC
New York Yankees	AL East	2010	95	67	0.586	2 of 5	1			1		1
New York Yankees	AL East	2009	103	59	0.636	1 of 5	+8	1	1	1	1	
New York Yankees	AL East	2008	89	73	0.549	3 of 5	8					
New York Yankees	AL East	2007	94	68	0.580	2 of 5	2					1
New York Yankees	AL East	2006	97	65	0.599	1 of 5	+10				1	
New York Yankees	AL East	2005	95	67	0.586	1 of 5	0*				1	
New York Yankees	AL East	2004	101	61	0.623	1 of 5	+3			1	1	
New York Yankees	AL East	2003	101	61	0.623	1 of 5	+6		1	1	1	
New York Yankees	AL East	2002	103	58	0.640	1 of 5	+10.5				1	
New York Yankees	AL East	2001	95	65	0.594	1 of 5	+13.5		1	1	1	
New York Yankees	AL East	2000	87	74	0.540	1 of 5	+2.5	1	1	1	1	
New York Yankees	AL East	1999	98	64	0.605	1 of 5	+4	1	1	1	1	
New York Yankees	AL East	1998	114	48	0.704	1 of 5	+22	1	1	1	1	
New York Yankees	AL East	1997	96	66	0.593	2 of 5	2					1
New York Yankees	AL East	1996	92	70	0.568	1 of 5	+4	1	1	1	1	
New York Yankees	AL East	1995	79	65	0.549	2 of 5	7					1
New York Yankees	AL East	1994	70	43	0.619	1 of 5	+6.5					
New York Yankees	AL East	1993	88	74	0.543	2 of 7	7					
New York Yankees	AL East	1992	76	86	0.469	4t of 7	20					
New York Yankees	AL East	1991	71	91	0.438	5 of 7	20					
New York Yankees	AL East	1990	67	95	0.414	7 of 7	21					
New York Yankees	AL East	1989	74	87	0.460	5 of 7	14.5					
New York Yankees	AL East	1988	85	76	0.528	5 of 7	3.5					
New York Yankees	AL East	1987	89	73	0.549	4 of 7	9					
New York Yankees	AL East	1986	90	72	0.556	2 of 7	5.5					
New York Yankees	AL East	1985	97	64	0.602	2 of 7	2					
New York Yankees	AL East	1984	87	75	0.537	3 of 7	17					
New York Yankees	AL East	1983	91	71	0.562	3 of 7	7					
New York Yankees	AL East	1982	79	83	0.488	5 of 7	16					
New York Yankees	AL East	1981	59	48	0.551	1,6 of 7	+2,5		1	1	1	
New York Yankees	AL East	1980	103	59	0.636	1 of 7	+3				1	
New York Yankees	AL East	1979	89	71	0.556	4 of 7	13.5					
New York Yankees	AL East	1978	100	63	0.613	1 of 7	+1	1	1		1	
New York Yankees	AL East	1977	100	62	0.617	1 of 7	+2.5	1	1		1	
New York Yankees	AL East	1976	97	62	0.610	1 of 6	+10.5		1		1	
New York Yankees	AL East	1975	83	77	0.519	3 of 6	12					
New York Yankees	AL East	1974	89	73	0.549	2 of 6	2					
New York Yankees	AL East	1973	80	82	0.494	4 of 6	17					
New York Yankees	AL East	1972	79	76	0.510	4 of 6	6.5					
New York Yankees	AL East	1971	82	80	0.506	4 of 6	21					
New York Yankees	AL East	1970	93	69	0.574	2 of 6	15					
New York Yankees	AL East	1969	80	81	0.497	5 of 6	28.5					
New York Yankees	AL	1968	83	79	0.512	5 of 10	20					

Team Name	League	Year	W	L	Win%	Fin	GB/GA	WS	Lge	LDS	Div	WC
New York Yankees	AL	1967	72	90	0.444	9 of 10	20					
New York Yankees	AL	1966	70	89	0.440	10 of 10	26.5					
New York Yankees	AL	1965	77	85	0.475	6 of 10	25					
New York Yankees	AL	1964	99	63	0.611	1 of 10	+1		1			
New York Yankees	AL	1963	104	57	0.646	1 of 10	+10.5		1			
New York Yankees	AL	1962	96	66	0.593	1 of 10	+5	1	1			
New York Yankees	AL	1961	109	53	0.673	1 of 10	+8	1	1			
New York Yankees	AL	1960	97	57	0.630	1 of 8	+8		1			
New York Yankees	AL	1959	79	75	0.513	3 of 8	15					
New York Yankees	AL	1958	92	62	0.597	1 of 8	+10	1	1			
New York Yankees	AL	1957	98	56	0.636	1 of 8	+8		1			
New York Yankees	AL	1956	97	57	0.630	1 of 8	+9	1	1			
New York Yankees	AL	1955	96	58	0.623	1 of 8	+3		1			
New York Yankees	AL	1954	103	51	0.669	2 of 8	8					
New York Yankees	AL	1953	99	52	0.656	1 of 8	+8.5	1	1			
New York Yankees	AL	1952	95	59	0.617	1 of 8	+2	1	1			
New York Yankees	AL	1951	98	56	0.636	1 of 8	+5	1	1			
New York Yankees	AL	1950	98	56	0.636	1 of 8	+3	1	1			
New York Yankees	AL	1949	97	57	0.630	1 of 8	+1	1	1			
New York Yankees	AL	1948	94	60	0.610	3 of 8	2.5					
New York Yankees	AL	1947	97	57	0.630	1 of 8	+12	1	1			
New York Yankees	AL	1946	87	67	0.565	3 of 8	17					
New York Yankees	AL	1945	81	71	0.533	4 of 8	6.5					
New York Yankees	AL	1944	83	71	0.539	3 of 8	6					
New York Yankees	AL	1943	98	56	0.636	1 of 8	+13.5	1	1			
New York Yankees	AL	1942	103	51	0.669	1 of 8	+9		1			
New York Yankees	AL	1941	101	53	0.656	1 of 8	+17	1	1			
New York Yankees	AL	1940	88	66	0.571	3 of 8	2					
New York Yankees	AL	1939	106	45	0.702	1 of 8	+17	1	1			
New York Yankees	AL	1938	99	53	0.651	1 of 8	+9.5	1	1			
New York Yankees	AL	1937	102	52	0.662	1 of 8	+13	1	1			
New York Yankees	AL	1936	102	51	0.667	1 of 8	+19.5	1	1			
New York Yankees	AL	1935	89	60	0.597	2 of 8	3					
New York Yankees	AL	1934	94	60	0.610	2 of 8	7					
New York Yankees	AL	1933	91	59	0.607	2 of 8	7					
New York Yankees	AL	1932	107	47	0.695	1 of 8	+13	1	1			
New York Yankees	AL	1931	94	59	0.614	2 of 8	13.5					
New York Yankees	AL	1930	86	68	0.558	3 of 8	16					
New York Yankees	AL	1929	88	66	0.571	2 of 8	18					
New York Yankees	AL	1928	101	53	0.656	1 of 8	+2.5	1	1			
New York Yankees	AL	1927	110	44	0.714	1 of 8	+19	1	1			
New York Yankees	AL	1926	91	63	0.591	1 of 8	+3		1			
New York Yankees	AL	1925	69	85	0.448	7 of 8	30					
New York Yankees	AL	1924	89	63	0.586	2 of 8	2					
New York Yankees	AL	1923	98	54	0.645	1 of 8	+16	1	1			

Baseball Franchise Rankings

Team Name	League	Year	W	L	Win%	Fin	GB/GA	WS	Lge	LDS	Div	WC
New York Yankees	AL	1922	94	60	0.610	1 of 8	+1		1			
New York Yankees	AL	1921	98	55	0.641	1 of 8	+4.5		1			
New York Yankees	AL	1920	95	59	0.617	3 of 8	3					
New York Yankees	AL	1919	80	59	0.576	3 of 8	7.5					
New York Yankees	AL	1918	60	63	0.488	4 of 8	13.5					
New York Yankees	AL	1917	71	82	0.464	6 of 8	28.5					
New York Yankees	AL	1916	80	74	0.519	4 of 8	11					
New York Yankees	AL	1915	69	83	0.454	5 of 8	32.5					
New York Yankees	AL	1914	70	84	0.455	6t of 8	30					
New York Yankees	AL	1913	57	94	0.377	7 of 8	38					
New York Highlanders	AL	1912	50	102	0.329	8 of 8	55					
New York Highlanders	AL	1911	76	76	0.500	6 of 8	25.5					
New York Highlanders	AL	1910	88	63	0.583	2 of 8	14.5					
New York Highlanders	AL	1909	74	77	0.490	5 of 8	23.5					
New York Highlanders	AL	1908	51	103	0.331	8 of 8	39.5					
New York Highlanders	AL	1907	70	78	0.473	5 of 8	21					
New York Highlanders	AL	1906	90	61	0.596	2 of 8	3					
New York Highlanders	AL	1905	71	78	0.477	6 of 8	21.5					
New York Highlanders	AL	1904	92	59	0.609	2 of 8	1.5					
New York Highlanders	AL	1903	72	62	0.537	4 of 8	17					
Baltimore Orioles	AL	1902	50	88	0.362	8 of 8	34					
Baltimore Orioles	AL	1901	68	65	0.511	5 of 8	13.5					
			9670	7361	0.568			27	40	10	16	4

* In 2005 Boston and New York finished the regular season tied with the same won-loss record. Since both teams made the playoffs and the Yankees won the regular season series between the two teams, they won the AL East Division Title and Boston won the AL Wild Card.

Oakland Athletics

Stats

History
Year of Origin 1901

Years Played 110

Score & Rank
Total Points Score 163.6
Total Points Rank 4

Average Points Score 1.49
Average Points Rank 5

Postseason Results	No.	Years
World Series Won	9	1910, 1911, 1913, 1929, 1930, 1972, 1973, 1974, 1989
League Championship Series Won	6	1972, 1973, 1974, 1988, 1989, 1990
League Division Series Won	2	1981, 2006
World Series Lost	5	1905, 1914, 1931, 1988, 1990
League Championship Series Lost	5	1971, 1975, 1981, 1992, 2006
League Division Series Lost	4	2000, 2001, 2002, 2003

Postseason Won-Loss Records and Winning Percentages

	Postseason Games		Postseason Series	
All Postseason Series	78-69	.531	17-14	.548
World Series	41-34	.547	9-5	.643
League Championship Series	23-23	.500	6-5	.545
League Division Series	14-12	.538	2-4	.333

Regular Season Results
All-Time Won-Loss Record 8270-8752
All-Time Winning Percentage .... .486

	No.	Years
League Titles before 1969	9	1902, 1905, 1910, 1911, 1913, 1914, 1929, 1930, 1931
Division Titles	14	1971, 1972, 1973, 1974, 1975, 1981, 1988, 1989, 1990, 1992, 2000, 2002, 2003, 2006
Wild Cards	1	2001

Regular Season High & Low Points		Years(s)
Most Wins in a Season	107	1931
Most Losses in a Season	117	1916
Highest Winning Percentage	.704	1931
Lowest Winning Percentage	.235	1916
Longest Streak with Won-Loss Record .500 or Higher	9 years	1925-1933, 1968-1976
Longest Streak with Won-Loss Record Below .500	15 years	1953-1967

Years with .500 record or Better		**Years Making Postseason**	
1900's	8 (out of 9)	1900's	1
1910's	5	1910's	4
1920's	5	1920's	1
1930's	4	1930's	2
1940's	3	1940's	0
1950's	1	1950's	0
1960's	2	1960's	0
1970's	7	1970's	5
1980's	5	1980's	3
1990's	4	1990's	2
2000's	7	2000's	5
2010's	1	2010's	0
52 out of 110 seasons played = 47%		23 out of 110 seasons played = 21%	

Streaks

- 1910-1914: Won three World Series and four League Titles in five years.
- 1929-1931: Won three League Titles and two World Series in three years.
- 1971-1975: Won five Division Titles in five years and won three League Championship Series and three World Series in a row from 1972-1974.
- 1988-1992: Won one World Series, three League Championship Series, and four Division Titles in five years which included winning the LCS in three straight years from 1988-1990.
- 2000-2006: Won one League Division Series, four Division Titles, and one Wild Card in seven years, and appeared in the playoffs in four straight years from 2000-2003.

Extra Bases

- From 1953-1967 while the franchise was in Kansas City they had fifteen straight losing seasons, every year that they played there.
- The 1974 World Series was the first championship ever played entirely on the west coast. The A's beat the Dodgers and it was Oakland's third championship in a row. This championship gave the franchise the distinction of being the only franchise besides the Yankees to win three World Series in a row.
- The 2001 A's were the first team ever to finish with 100 or more wins after being below .500 by ten games at one point in the season.
- In 2002 Oakland won an American League record twenty games in a row from August 13th to September 4th.
- From 2000-2003 the A's lost in the League Division Series each time in four straight years.
- The Oakland franchise has finished last in a league or division twenty-seven times and has lost 100 games or more sixteen times, both American League worsts.

Scoring Opportunities

1900's

• The Philadelphia Athletics won the American League pennant in 1905 and played the Giants in the World Series. Philadelphia lost Game 1 3-0, won Game 2, and lost Game 3 9-0. The A's only had four hits in each of their two losses. In Game 4 Philadelphia committed an error that let the first Giants batter of the bottom of the fourth inning reach base. The A's got the next two New York hitters out but the following batter singled and drove in the runner from second. Philadelphia had runners on first and third with two outs in the top of the eighth, but their next batter up struck out and they lost the game 1-0. In Game 5 Philadelphia only gave up two runs, but they only had two hits after the second inning and they were retired in order in their last three at bats of the game and lost the game 2-0 to lose the series. The A's were shutout in all four of their losses.

• In 1907 Philadelphia led the American League by 2.5 games over Chicago on September 14th, with Detroit three games behind. The rest of the season the A's went 8-7 and the White Sox went 8-10, but the Tigers went 15-5 and won the pennant. Philadelphia finished in second place 1.5 games behind Detroit.

1910's

• The A's won their fourth American League pennant in five years in 1914 and played the Boston Braves in the World Series. Philadelphia lost Game 1 7-1 and Game 2 was tied at zero after eight innings. In the top of the ninth the A's had two Braves out with a runner on third, but gave up a single that drove in the go-ahead run. In the bottom of the inning the Philadelphia had runners on first and second with one out, but their next batter hit into a double play and they lost 1-0. Game 3 was tied at two after nine innings. The A's scored two runs in the top of the tenth, but gave up a solo home run and another run on a sacrifice fly in the bottom of the inning. In the top of the twelfth Philadelphia had runners on first and second with two outs, but their next batter up grounded out. In the bottom of the inning they gave up a double and an intentional walk, then committed an error on the next batter's sacrifice bunt and let in the game winning run and lost 5-4. Game 4 was tied at one in the bottom of the fifth. The A's got the first two Braves batters out but then gave up a single, a double, and a single, and let in two runs. Philadelphia didn't get any hits the rest of the game and lost the game 3-1 to lose the series in a sweep.

1920's

• In 1928 the A's led the American League by a half a game over the Yankees on September 9th when the two teams met for a four games series in New York. Philadelphia lost three out of the four games and fell to second place 1.5 games behind the Yankees on September 12th.

The A's went 8-5 the rest of the year but New York went 10-5 and Philadelphia finished the season in second place 2.5 games behind the Yankees.

1930's

- Philadelphia won the American League pennant in 1931 by winning 107 games and having a .704 winning percentage, both their all time franchise highs. In the World Series they played St. Louis and won Game 1. In Game 2 the A's trailed by two runs in the top of the ninth when they had the bases loaded with two outs, but their next batter up fouled out and they lost 2-0. The teams split the next four games as Philadelphia lost Game 3 5-2 and Game 5 5-1 and won Games 4 & 6. In Game 7 the A's trailed by two runs in the top of the ninth when they had runners on first and second with two outs, but their next batter flied out and they lost 4-2 to lose the series.

1970's

- In 1971 the Oakland A's won the American League West Division and played Baltimore in the LCS. In Game 1 Oakland had a 3-1 lead after six innings but in the bottom of the seventh the A's gave up a walk and a single and then with two outs they gave up a single and two doubles and let in four runs. Oakland lost the game 5-3, lost Game 2 5-1, and lost Game 3 5-3 to lose the series in a sweep.
- The A's won their fifth American League West Division in a row in 1975. In the LCS they played the Red Sox and only had three hits in Game 1 and lost the game 7-1. Game 2 was tied at three after five innings but Oakland gave up one run in the bottom of the sixth, seventh, and eighth innings and lost the game 6-3. In Game 3 the A's trailed by two runs in the bottom of the eighth when they had runners on first and third with one out, but their next batter up hit into a double play and Oakland lost the game 5-3 and lost the series in a sweep.
- In 1976 Oakland trailed Kansas City by six games in the American League West on September 19th and the two teams still had six games left against each other the rest of the season. Over the next nine days the A's went 5-2 and the Royals went 2-6. This included four Oakland wins over Kansas City out of five games. On September 29th the A's were only 2.5 games behind the Royals when the two means met for the final game of their second three game series. Oakland lost the game 4-0 and trailed Kansas City by 3.5 games with only three games left on the schedule with make up game if needed. The Royals lost their last three games of the year but the A's lost two out of their last three games to the Angels and did not need to play the make up game as they finished the season in second place 2.5 games behind Kansas City.

1980's

- In 1981 Oakland won the first half of the season in the American League West Division in the strike split season and beat Kansas City in the first round of the playoffs. In the LCS against the Yankees the A's trailed by two runs in the top of the eighth inning of Game 1 when they had runners on first and second with one out, but their next two batters both grounded out and Oakland lost the game 3-1. The A's lost Game 2 13-3 and Game 3 4-0 and lost the series in a sweep.

• The A's won the American League West Division in 1988 and swept Boston in the LCS. In the World Series Oakland faced Los Angeles and had a 4-3 lead in Game 1 in the bottom of the ninth inning. The A's got the first two Dodgers batters out and then walked a batter. An injured pinch hitter came up to bat next for LA and hit a game winning two run home run and Oakland lost 5-4. The A's only had three hits in Game 2 and lost 6-0, and won Game 3. In Game 4 Oakland trailed by one run in the bottom of the seventh when they had the bases loaded with two outs, but their next batter up popped out. The A's had a runner on first with two outs in the bottom of the eighth and a runner on first with one out in the bottom of the ninth, but couldn't drive in the tying run in either inning and they lost the game 4-3. Oakland had only four hits in Game 5 and lost 5-2 to lose the series.

1990's

• Oakland won the American League West Division for the third straight year in 1990 and swept Boston in the LCS. In the World Series the A's played Cincinnati and lost Game 1 7-0. In Game 2 Oakland had a 4-3 lead in the bottom of the eighth inning with one out. The Reds had runners on first and third and the A's did not bring the infield in as they were trying to get the double play. The next Cincinnati batter hit a sharp ground ball up the middle of the infield. The Oakland shortstop had a tough play but got to the ball and tagged the runner coming to second base for an out. But because of the location of the play, the Reds batter beat out his throw to first and the runner from third base scored the tying run. The game went into extra innings and in the bottom of the tenth the A's got the first Cincinnati batter out, but then gave up a three straight singles. The first was a high infield chopper and the third was hit barely inside the third base line. This hit drove in the game winning run and the A's lost 5-4. In Game 3 Oakland gave up seven runs in the third inning and lost the game 8-3. In Game 4 Oakland had a 1-0 lead after seven innings. In the top of the eighth the A's gave up singles to the first two Cincinnati hitters, the second one a bunt in which the batter beat out the throw at first base. The following Reds batter also bunted and was called safe at first as the umpire said that the pitchers throw to first was wide and pulled the fielder off the base, even though it looked like he kept his foot on the bag. This loaded the bases and with no outs the A's kept their middle infielders back in hopes to get a double play and avoid giving up a big inning. The next Cincinnati batter hit a slow ground ball to shortstop who tried to turn a double play but could only get one out at second base. The tying run scored and there were Reds runners on first and third with one out. The next batter hit a sacrifice fly that drove in the go ahead run. The A's were retired in order in their at bats in the bottom of the eighth and ninth innings and lost the game 2-1 to lose the series in a sweep.

168

• In 1992 Oakland won their fourth American League West Division in five years. The A's won Game 1 of the LCS against Toronto, but lost Game 2 3-1. In Game 3 Oakland trailed by one run in the bottom of the eighth inning when they had runners on first and third with one out, but their next batter grounded out and they lost the game 7-5. In Game 4 Oakland led 6-1 after seven innings. But they gave up five hits and three runs in the top of the eighth inning and a two-run home run in the top of the ninth inning that tied the game. In the bottom of the ninth the A's had a runner on third with one out. Their next batter hit a ground ball to second base and the runner on third was thrown out at home. In the top of the eleventh Oakland gave up a walk and a single to the first two Blue Jays batters, and with one out a sacrifice fly that drove in the game winning run and the A's lost the game 7-6. Oakland won Game 5 but lost Game 6 9-2 and lost the series.

2000's

• The A's won the 2000 American League West Division by a half game over Seattle. Oakland lost one less game then the Mariners but did not need to make the game up as Seattle was the AL Wild Card team. In the LDS the A's played the Yankees and won Game 1. Oakland lost Game 2 4-0 and in Game 3 they only had four hits and didn't have any after the fifth inning and they lost the game 4-2. The A's won Game 4 and Game 5 was played at home, but the A's gave up six runs in the first inning. After four innings they only trailed by two runs, but they only got one runner to second base the rest of the game and they lost the game 7-5 and lost the series.

• Oakland won the American League Wild Card in 2001 and played New York again in the LDS. The A's won Games 1 & 2 and only needed to win one of the last three games to advance to the LCS. In Game 3 Oakland only gave up two hits but one of them was a home run in the top of the fifth inning that gave the Yankees a 1-0 lead. The A's trailed by one run in the bottom of the seventh inning when they had a runner on first base with two outs. Their next batter doubled to right field and their runner tried to score from first. It looked like he was going to be safe but he chose not to slide into home plate and the Yankee shortstop made a terrific cut off play and got him out. In the bottom of the eighth inning Oakland had a runner on first with one out, but their next two batters filed out and lined out. In the bottom of the ninth the A's had a runner on second with one out, but their next two batters struck out and grounded out and they lost the game 1-0. Oakland lost Game 4 9-2 and lost Game 5 5-3 and lost the series that they led two games to none.

• In 2002 Oakland won the American League West Division and during the season set an American League record with twenty wins in a row from August 13th to September 4th. In the playoffs the A's played Minnesota in the LDS. Oakland lost Game 1 7-5, won Games 2 & 3 and lost Game 4 11-2. In Game 5 the A's trailed by one run after eight innings but gave up three runs in the top of the ninth. In the bottom of the inning they hit a three-run home run and had a runner on first base with two outs, but their next batter hit a foul fly out and they lost 5-4 and lost the series.

- The A's won the American League West Division in 2003 and won Games 1 & 2 in the LDS against the Red Sox. Game 3 was tied at one after nine innings and the A's were retired in order in the top of the tenth and eleventh innings. In the bottom of the eleventh Oakland got the first Red Sox batter out, but then gave up a single and a home run and lost 3-1. In Game 4 the A's had a 4-3 lead after seven innings. In the bottom of the eighth they had two Boston batters out with a runner on second base, but gave up a single and a double that drove in two runs and they lost the game 5-4. In Game 5 Oakland gave up four runs in the sixth inning on two home runs. In the bottom of the ninth they were down by one run and had the bases loaded with two outs, but their next batter up struck out to end the game and they lost 4-3 and lost the series in which they had a two games to none series lead.

- In 2004 Oakland had a three game lead in the American League West Division over Texas and Anaheim on September 24th. The A's lost their next two games against the Angels and then split a four game series with Seattle, while Anaheim won those two games against Oakland and then three out of four against Texas. On October 1st the A's and Angels were tied for first place with three games left to play against each other in Oakland. The A's lost the first game 10-0. In the second game the A's had a 4-2 lead after seven innings but gave up four hits, one walk, and three runs in the top of the eighth inning. Oakland lost the game 5-4 and was eliminated from the AL West Division race. They won the last game of the year and finished one game behind Anaheim in the standings. After September 24th the A's went 3-6 the rest of the season while the Angels went 7-2. Four of Oakland's six losses were against the Anaheim.

- The A's won their fourth American League West Division in seven years in 2006, and finally won in the LDS by beating the Twins. In the LCS Oakland played the Tigers and was outplayed. The A's lost Game 1 5-1, Game 2 8-5, and Game 3 3-0. Game 4 was tied at three in the bottom of the ninth. The A's got the first two Tigers batters out but then gave up two straight singles. The next Detroit batter hit a three-run home run to win the game and the A's lost 6-3 and were swept in the series, being outscored 22-9 in the four games.

Year-to-Year Figures

Team Name	League	Year	W	L	Win%	Fin	GB/GA	WS	Lge	LDS	Div	WC
Oakland Athletics	AL West	2010	81	81	0.500	2 of 4	9					
Oakland Athletics	AL West	2009	75	87	0.463	4 of 4	22					
Oakland Athletics	AL West	2008	75	86	0.466	3 of 4	24.5					
Oakland Athletics	AL West	2007	76	86	0.469	3 of 4	18					
Oakland Athletics	AL West	2006	93	69	0.574	1 of 4	+4			1	1	
Oakland Athletics	AL West	2005	88	74	0.543	2 of 4	7					
Oakland Athletics	AL West	2004	91	71	0.562	2 of 4	1					
Oakland Athletics	AL West	2003	96	66	0.593	1 of 4	+3				1	
Oakland Athletics	AL West	2002	103	59	0.636	1 of 4	+4				1	
Oakland Athletics	AL West	2001	102	60	0.630	2 of 4	14					1
Oakland Athletics	AL West	2000	91	70	0.565	1 of 4	+0.5*				1	
Oakland Athletics	AL West	1999	87	75	0.537	2 of 4	8					
Oakland Athletics	AL West	1998	74	88	0.457	4 of 4	14					
Oakland Athletics	AL West	1997	65	97	0.401	4 of 4	25					
Oakland Athletics	AL West	1996	78	84	0.481	3 of 4	12					
Oakland Athletics	AL West	1995	67	77	0.465	4 of 4	11.5					
Oakland Athletics	AL West	1994	51	63	0.447	2 of 4	1					
Oakland Athletics	AL West	1993	68	94	0.420	7 of 7	26					
Oakland Athletics	AL West	1992	96	66	0.593	1 of 7	+6				1	
Oakland Athletics	AL West	1991	84	78	0.519	4 of 7	11					
Oakland Athletics	AL West	1990	103	59	0.636	1 of 7	+9		1		1	
Oakland Athletics	AL West	1989	99	63	0.611	1 of 7	+7	1	1		1	
Oakland Athletics	AL West	1988	104	58	0.642	1 of 7	+13		1		1	
Oakland Athletics	AL West	1987	81	81	0.500	3 of 7	4					
Oakland Athletics	AL West	1986	76	86	0.469	3t of 7	16					
Oakland Athletics	AL West	1985	77	85	0.475	4t of 7	14					
Oakland Athletics	AL West	1984	77	85	0.475	4 of 7	7					
Oakland Athletics	AL West	1983	74	88	0.457	4 of 7	25					
Oakland Athletics	AL West	1982	68	94	0.420	5 of 7	25					
Oakland Athletics	AL West	1981	64	45	0.587	1, 2 of 7	+1.5, 1			1	1	
Oakland Athletics	AL West	1980	83	79	0.512	2 of 7	14					
Oakland Athletics	AL West	1979	54	108	0.333	7 of 7	34					
Oakland Athletics	AL West	1978	69	93	0.426	6 of 7	23					
Oakland Athletics	AL West	1977	63	98	0.391	7 of 7	38.5					
Oakland Athletics	AL West	1976	87	74	0.540	2 of 6	2.5					
Oakland Athletics	AL West	1975	98	64	0.605	1 of 6	+7				1	
Oakland Athletics	AL West	1974	90	72	0.556	1 of 6	+5	1	1		1	
Oakland Athletics	AL West	1973	94	68	0.580	1 of 6	+6	1	1		1	
Oakland Athletics	AL West	1972	93	62	0.600	1 of 6	+5.5	1	1		1	
Oakland Athletics	AL West	1971	101	60	0.627	1 of 6	+16				1	
Oakland Athletics	AL West	1970	89	73	0.549	2 of 6	9					
Oakland Athletics	AL West	1969	88	74	0.543	2 of 6	9					
Oakland Athletics	AL	1968	82	80	0.506	6 of 10	21					

Team Name	League	Year	W	L	Win%	Fin	GB/GA	WS	Lge	LDS	Div	WC
Kansas City Athletics	AL	1967	62	99	0.385	10 of 10	29.5					
Kansas City Athletics	AL	1966	74	86	0.463	7 of 10	23					
Kansas City Athletics	AL	1965	59	103	0.364	10 of 10	43					
Kansas City Athletics	AL	1964	57	105	0.352	10 of 10	42					
Kansas City Athletics	AL	1963	73	89	0.451	8 of 10	31.5					
Kansas City Athletics	AL	1962	72	90	0.444	9 of 10	24					
Kansas City Athletics	AL	1961	61	100	0.379	9t of 10	47.5					
Kansas City Athletics	AL	1960	58	96	0.377	8 of 8	39					
Kansas City Athletics	AL	1959	66	88	0.429	7 of 8	28					
Kansas City Athletics	AL	1958	73	81	0.474	7 of 8	19					
Kansas City Athletics	AL	1957	59	94	0.386	7 of 8	38.5					
Kansas City Athletics	AL	1956	52	102	0.338	8 of 8	45					
Kansas City Athletics	AL	1955	63	91	0.409	6 of 8	33					
Philadelphia Athletics	AL	1954	51	103	0.331	8 of 8	60					
Philadelphia Athletics	AL	1953	59	95	0.383	7 of 8	41.5					
Philadelphia Athletics	AL	1952	79	75	0.513	4 of 8	16					
Philadelphia Athletics	AL	1951	70	84	0.455	6 of 8	28					
Philadelphia Athletics	AL	1950	52	102	0.338	8 of 8	46					
Philadelphia Athletics	AL	1949	81	73	0.526	5 of 8	16					
Philadelphia Athletics	AL	1948	84	70	0.545	4 of 8	12.5					
Philadelphia Athletics	AL	1947	78	76	0.506	5 of 8	19					
Philadelphia Athletics	AL	1946	49	105	0.318	8 of 8	55					
Philadelphia Athletics	AL	1945	52	98	0.347	8 of 8	34.5					
Philadelphia Athletics	AL	1944	72	82	0.468	5t of 8	17					
Philadelphia Athletics	AL	1943	49	105	0.318	8 of 8	49					
Philadelphia Athletics	AL	1942	55	99	0.357	8 of 8	48					
Philadelphia Athletics	AL	1941	64	90	0.416	8 of 8	37					
Philadelphia Athletics	AL	1940	54	100	0.351	8 of 8	36					
Philadelphia Athletics	AL	1939	55	97	0.362	7 of 8	51.5					
Philadelphia Athletics	AL	1938	53	99	0.349	8 of 8	46					
Philadelphia Athletics	AL	1937	54	97	0.358	7 of 8	46.5					
Philadelphia Athletics	AL	1936	53	100	0.346	8 of 8	49					
Philadelphia Athletics	AL	1935	58	91	0.389	8 of 8	34					
Philadelphia Athletics	AL	1934	68	82	0.453	5 of 8	31					
Philadelphia Athletics	AL	1933	79	72	0.523	3 of 8	19.5					
Philadelphia Athletics	AL	1932	94	60	0.610	2 of 8	13					
Philadelphia Athletics	AL	1931	107	45	0.704	1 of 8	+13.5		1			
Philadelphia Athletics	AL	1930	102	52	0.662	1 of 8	+8	1	1			
Philadelphia Athletics	AL	1929	104	46	0.693	1 of 8	+18	1	1			
Philadelphia Athletics	AL	1928	98	55	0.641	2 of 8	2.5					
Philadelphia Athletics	AL	1927	91	63	0.591	2 of 8	19					
Philadelphia Athletics	AL	1926	83	67	0.553	3 of 8	6					
Philadelphia Athletics	AL	1925	88	64	0.579	2 of 8	8.5					
Philadelphia Athletics	AL	1924	71	81	0.467	5 of 8	20					
Philadelphia Athletics	AL	1923	69	83	0.454	6 of 8	29					

Team Name	League	Year	W	L	Win%	Fin	GB/GA	WS	Lge	LDS	Div	WC
Philadelphia Athletics	AL	1922	65	89	0.422	7 of 8	29					
Philadelphia Athletics	AL	1921	53	100	0.346	8 of 8	45					
Philadelphia Athletics	AL	1920	48	106	0.312	8 of 8	50					
Philadelphia Athletics	AL	1919	36	104	0.257	8 of 8	52					
Philadelphia Athletics	AL	1918	52	76	0.406	8 of 8	24					
Philadelphia Athletics	AL	1917	55	98	0.359	8 of 8	44.5					
Philadelphia Athletics	AL	1916	36	117	0.235	8 of 8	54.5					
Philadelphia Athletics	AL	1915	43	109	0.283	8 of 8	58.5					
Philadelphia Athletics	AL	1914	99	53	0.651	1 of 8	+8.5		1			
Philadelphia Athletics	AL	1913	96	57	0.627	1 of 8	+6.5	1	1			
Philadelphia Athletics	AL	1912	90	62	0.592	3 of 8	15					
Philadelphia Athletics	AL	1911	101	50	0.669	1 of 8	+13.5	1	1			
Philadelphia Athletics	AL	1910	102	48	0.680	1 of 8	+14.5	1	1			
Philadelphia Athletics	AL	1909	95	58	0.621	2 of 8	3.5					
Philadelphia Athletics	AL	1908	68	85	0.444	6 of 8	22					
Philadelphia Athletics	AL	1907	88	57	0.607	2 of 8	1.5					
Philadelphia Athletics	AL	1906	78	67	0.538	4 of 8	12					
Philadelphia Athletics	AL	1905	92	56	0.622	1 of 8	+2		1			
Philadelphia Athletics	AL	1904	81	70	0.536	5 of 8	12.5					
Philadelphia Athletics	AL	1903	75	60	0.556	2 of 8	14.5					
Philadelphia Athletics	AL	1902	83	53	0.610	1 of 8	+5		1			
Philadelphia Athletics	AL	1901	74	62	0.544	4 of 8	9					
			8270	8752	0.486			9	15	2	14	1

* In 2000 Oakland finished the season 0.5 game ahead of Seattle in the AL West Division but the Mariners won the AL Wild Card spot. Seattle played one less game than Oakland and decided not to make up that game, because even if they won it they would have lost the tiebreaker to Oakland and still been the AL Wild Card team because the A's won the regular season series between the two teams.

Philadelphia Phillies

Stats

History

Year of Origin 1883

Years Played 128

Score & Rank

Total Points Score 69.2

Average Points Score 0.54

Total Points Rank 13

Average Points Rank .... 21 tied

Postseason Results	No.	Years
World Series Won	2	1980, 2008
League Championship Series Won	5	1980, 1983, 1993, 2008, 2009
League Division Series Won	3	2008, 2009, 2010
World Series Lost	5	1915, 1950, 1983, 1993, 2009
League Championship Series Lost	4	1976, 1977, 1978, 2010
League Division Series Lost	2	1981, 2007

Postseason Won-Loss Records and Winning Percentages

	Postseason Games		Postseason Series	
All Postseason Series	47-51	.480	10-11	.476
World Series	14-23	.378	2-5	.286
League Championship Series	22-20	.524	5-4	.556
League Division Series	11-8	.579	3-2	.600

Regular Season Results

All-Time Won-Loss Record 9135-10233

All-Time Winning Percentage .... .472

	No.	Years
League Titles before 1969	2	1915, 1950
Division Titles	11	1976, 1977, 1978, 1980, 1981, 1983, 1993, 2007, 2008, 2009, 2010
Wild Cards	0	

Regular Season High & Low Points

		Year(s)
Most Wins in a Season	101	1976, 1977
Most Losses in a Season	111	1941
Highest Winning Percentage	.623	1886, 1976, 1977
Lowest Winning Percentage	.173	1883
Longest Streak with Won-Loss Record .500 or Higher	10 years	1975-1984
Longest Streak with Won-Loss Record Below .500	16 years	1933-1948

Years with .500 record or Better

1880's	4 (out of 7)
1890's	7
1900's	5
1910's	6
1920's	0
1930's	1
1940's	1
1950's	5
1960's	6
1970's	5
1980's	6
1990's	1
2000's	8
2010's	1

54 out of 128 seasons played = 42%

Years Making Postseason

1880's	No Postseason
1890's	No Postseason
1900's	0
1910's	1
1920's	0
1930's	0
1940's	0
1950's	1
1960's	0
1970's	3
1980's	3
1990's	1
2000's	3
2010's	1

13 out of 128 seasons played = 10%

Streaks

- 1976-1983: Won six Division Titles, two League Championship Series, and one World Series in eight years including three Division Titles in a row from 1976-1978..
- 2007-2010: Won one World Series, two League Championship Series, three League Division Series, and four Division Titles in a row in the four year period.

Extra Bases

- It took the Phillies franchise ninety-seven years to win their first championship, occurring in 1980.
- The Phillies have finished last in their league or division thirty times, which on average is almost one in every four seasons. (30 times / 128 seasons = 23.44%)

Scoring Opportunities

1910's

- The Phillies won the National League pennant in 1915 and won Game 1 of the World Series against Boston. Game 2 was tied at one after eight innings. In the top of the ninth the Phillies had two Red Sox batters out with a runner on second base. The next Boston batter singled and drove in the go-ahead run and Philadelphia lost the game 2-1. Game 3 was also tied at one after eight innings. In the bottom of the ninth the Phillies had two Red Sox batters out and there were runners on second and third. The next Boston batter singled in the winning run and Philadelphia lost 2-1 again. In Game 4 the Phillies trailed by one run in the top of the eighth with two outs and a runner on second. Their next batter grounded out and they lost a third game by the score of 2-1. In Game 5 the Phillies had a 4-2 lead after seven innings. In the top of the eighth they gave up a two-run home run that tied the game. In the bottom of the inning Philadelphia had runners on first and second with two outs, but their next batter grounded out. In the top of the ninth they gave up a solo home run and they lost the game 5-4 and lost the series. All four of the Phillies losses were by one run and three of them were by the score of 2-1.

- In 1916 the Phillies only trailed the Brooklyn Robins by a half game for the National League pennant on September 30th. But Philadelphia lost five of their last seven games of the year while the Robins won four of their last five. The Phillies finished in second place 2.5 games behind Brooklyn.

1950's

- Philadelphia won the National League pennant in 1950 and faced the Yankees in the World Series. In Game 1 the Phillies only had two hits, which were both in the bottom of the fifth inning. Their last eleven batters were retired in order and they lost the game 1-0. Game 2 was tied at one in the bottom of the ninth when Philadelphia had runners on first and second with one out, but their next batter hit into a double play and the game went into extra innings. In the top of the tenth the Phillies gave up a solo home run to the first Yankees batter and they lost the game 2-1. In Game 3 Philadelphia had a 2-1 lead after seven innings. In the bottom of the eighth they got the first two Yankees batters out, but gave up three straight walks and made an error that let in the tying run. In the top of the ninth the Phillies had runners on first and third with one out, but their next batter hit a ground ball to first base and the go ahead run was thrown out at home. Their next batter flied out and the game remained tied. In the bottom of the inning Philadelphia got the first two Yankee batters out but then gave up three straight singles and let in the game winning run and lost 3-2. The Phillies lost Game 4 5-2 to lose the series in a sweep. Three of their four losses were by one run.

1960's

- In 1964 the Phillies led the National League from July 21st to September 26th and had a 6.5 game lead over the Reds and Cardinals on September 20th. But Philadelphia lost ten games in a row and fell to third place 2.5 games behind the Cardinals on September 30th. Their last three losses in that streak were against St. Louis. The Phillies won their next game against the Reds and St. Louis lost two games against the Mets and Philadelphia trailed the Cardinals by one game with one game left in the season. On the last day of the year the Phillies beat Cincinnati but St. Louis beat New York and Philadelphia finished the season tied for second place with the Reds, one game behind the Cardinals.

1970's

- The Phillies won the National League East Division in 1976 and played the Reds in the LCS.

Philadelphia lost Game 1 6-3 and Game 2 6-2. In Game 3 the Phillies had a 6-4 lead in the bottom of the ninth, but gave up solo home runs to the first two Cincinnati batters which tied the game, and gave up two walks and two singles and let in the game winning run. The Phillies lost 7-6 and lost the series in a sweep.

- In 1977 Philadelphia repeated as National League East Division champs and faced the Dodgers in the LCS. The Phillies won Game 1 but lost Game 2 7-1. In Game 3 Philadelphia had a 5-3 lead after eight innings and got the first two Los Angeles batters out in the top of the ninth. But the Phillies gave up two singles and a double and let in two runs that tied the game. During the next at bat, the Philadelphia pitcher tried to pick the Dodgers runner off of first base, but he threw wildly and the runner advanced to second. The next LA batter singled and drove in the go-ahead run and the Phillies lost the game 6-5. Philadelphia lost Game 4 4-1 and lost the series.

- The Phillies won their third National League East Division title in a row in 1978 and played Los Angeles again in the LCS. Philadelphia lost Game 1 9-5 and Game 2 4-0, and won Game 3. Game 4 was tied at three after nine innings. The Phillies had a runner on first base in the top of the tenth inning with one out, but their next two batters struck out and grounded out. In the bottom of the inning Philadelphia got the first two Dodgers batters out, but then walked a batter and let another hitter reach base on an error. The next LA batter singled and drove in the game winning run and the Phillies lost the game 4-3 and lost the series.

1980's

- In 1981 the Phillies won the first half of the season in the National League East Division in the strike split season and played the Montreal Expos in the first round of the playoffs. In Game 1 Philadelphia trailed by two runs in the top of the ninth when they had runners on first and second with two outs, but their next batter up lined out and they lost 3-1. In Game 2 the Phillies trailed by two runs in the top of the eighth inning when they had the bases loaded with two outs, but their next batter up hit a foul pop out and they lost the game by the same score of 3-1. Philadelphia won Games 3 & 4 but in Game 5 they only had two hits after the fourth inning and they lost the game 3-0 and lost the series.

- Philadelphia won the National League East Division in 1983 and beat the Dodgers in the LCS. In the World Series the Phillies played the Orioles and won Game 1. In Game 2 Philadelphia only had three hits and lost the game 4-1. The Phillies led Game 3 2-1 after six innings. In the top of the seventh they got the first two Orioles batters out, but then gave up three hits, a wild pitch, an error, and let in two runs and they lost the game 3-2. In Game 4 Philadelphia led 3-2 after five innings but gave up two walks, two hits, a sacrifice fly, and two runs in the top of the sixth. In the bottom of the ninth they trailed by one run and had a runner on first with two outs, but their next batter lined out and they lost 5-4. The Phillies lost Game 5 5-0 and lost the series.

177

1990's

- In 1993 the Phillies won the National League East Division and beat the Braves in the LCS. In the World Series against the Blue Jays Philadelphia lost Game 1 8-5, won Game 2, and lost Game 3 10-3. In Game 4 the Phillies had a 14-9 lead after seven innings. In the top of the eighth they got the first Toronto batter out, and then gave up five hits, two walks, and six runs and they lost the game 15-14. Philadelphia won Game 5 and led Game 6 6-5 in the bottom of the ninth inning. The Phillies walked the first Toronto batter, got one out, and gave up a single. The next Blue Jays batter hit a three-run home run and the Philadelphia lost the game 8-6 and lost the series.

2000's

- Philadelphia and Atlanta were tied for first place in the National League East Division in 2001 on September 1st. The Phillies stayed within 3.5 games the rest of the year and were one game behind the Braves on October 2nd with five games left to play. Their next two games were against Atlanta but Philadelphia lost both games and fell to three games back in the standings with three games left to play. The Phillies won their final three games against the Reds but Atlanta won two out of three against the Marlins and Philadelphia finished in second place two games behind the Braves.
- In 2005 the Phillies were not close in the National League East Division race but were in a close race with the Astros for the NL Wild Card. On September 2nd Philadelphia had a half-game lead over Houston but then lost five games in a row that included three losses to the Astros. This brought the Phillies to 2.5 games behind Houston in the wild card standings. The rest of the season Philadelphia had the best record in the National League going 15-7, but the Astros went 14-9 and the Phillies finished the season one game behind Houston for the final playoff spot.
- Philadelphia was not in contention for the National League East Division title in 2006 but they led the NL Wild Card spot on September 24th by a half game over the Dodgers. The rest of the year the Phillies went 3-4 and LA went 6-0 and Philadelphia finished three games behind the Dodgers for the wild card spot.
- In 2007 Philadelphia won the National League East Division by one game over the Mets. In the LDS Philadelphia faced Colorado who won fourteen out of there last fifteen regular season games. In Game 1 the Phillies had only four hits and didn't have any after the fifth inning and lost the game 4-2. Philadelphia lost Game 2 10-5 and Game 3 was tied at one after seven innings. In the bottom of the eighth the Phillies got the first two Rockies batters out but then gave up three straight singles and let in the go-ahead run. Philadelphia lost the game 2-1 and lost the series in a sweep.
- Philadelphia won the National League East Division in 2009, beat Colorado in the LDS, and beat the Dodgers in the LCS. The Phillies faced the Yankees in the World Series and won

Game 1. In Game 2 Philadelphia trailed by two runs in the top of the eighth when they had runners on first and second with one out, but their next batter hit into a double play and they lost the game 3-1. The Phillies lost Game 3 8-5 and Game 4 was tied at four after eight innings. In the top of the ninth Philadelphia got the first two Yankee batters out, but then gave up a single, two stolen bases, a hit batter, a double, and another single. The Yankees scored three runs and Philadelphia lost the game 7-4. The Phillies won Game 5 but lost Game 6 7-3 and lost the series.

2010's

• The Phillies won the National League East Division in 2010, swept Cincinnati in the LDS, and played San Francisco in the LCS. In Game 1 Philadelphia trailed by one run after six innings. In the bottom of the eighth inning they had a runner on first base with two outs, but their next batter struck out. In the bottom of the ninth they had a runner on first base with one out, but their next two batters both struck out and they lost the game 4-3. The Phillies won Game 2 but only had three hits in Game 3 and lost the game 3-0. Game 4 was tied at five entering the Giants at bat in the bottom of the ninth inning. Philadelphia got the first San Francisco batter out, but gave up two singles and a sacrifice fly and let in the game winning run and lost the game 6-5. The Phillies won Game 5 and Game 6 was tied at two after seven innings. In the top of the eighth inning Philadelphia got the first two Giants batters out, but then gave up a solo home run. In the bottom of the eighth the Phillies had runners on first and second with one out but their next batter hit into a double play. In the bottom of the ninth Philadelphia had runners on first and second with two outs, but their next batter up struck out and they lost the game 3-2 and lost the series. The Phillies outscored San Francisco 20-19 in the series.

Year-to-Year Figures

Team Name	League	Year	W	L	Win%	Fin	GB/GA	WS	Lge	LDS	Div	WC
Philadelphia Phillies	NL East	2010	97	65	0.599	1 of 5	+6			1	1	
Philadelphia Phillies	NL East	2009	93	69	0.574	1 of 5	+6		1	1	1	
Philadelphia Phillies	NL East	2008	92	70	0.568	1 of 5	+3	1	1	1	1	
Philadelphia Phillies	NL East	2007	89	73	0.549	1 of 5	+1				1	
Philadelphia Phillies	NL East	2006	85	77	0.525	2 of 5	12					
Philadelphia Phillies	NL East	2005	88	74	0.543	2 of 5	2					
Philadelphia Phillies	NL East	2004	86	76	0.531	2 of 5	10					
Philadelphia Phillies	NL East	2003	86	76	0.531	3 of 5	15					
Philadelphia Phillies	NL East	2002	80	81	0.497	3 of 5	21.5					
Philadelphia Phillies	NL East	2001	86	76	0.531	2 of 5	2					
Philadelphia Phillies	NL East	2000	65	97	0.401	5 of 5	30					
Philadelphia Phillies	NL East	1999	77	85	0.475	3 of 5	26					
Philadelphia Phillies	NL East	1998	75	87	0.463	3 of 5	31					
Philadelphia Phillies	NL East	1997	68	94	0.420	5 of 5	33					
Philadelphia Phillies	NL East	1996	67	95	0.414	5 of 5	29					
Philadelphia Phillies	NL East	1995	69	75	0.479	2t of 5	21					
Philadelphia Phillies	NL East	1994	54	61	0.470	4 of 5	20.5					
Philadelphia Phillies	NL East	1993	97	65	0.599	1 of 7	+3		1		1	
Philadelphia Phillies	NL East	1992	70	92	0.432	6 of 6	26					
Philadelphia Phillies	NL East	1991	78	84	0.481	3 of 6	20					
Philadelphia Phillies	NL East	1990	77	85	0.475	4t of 6	18					
Philadelphia Phillies	NL East	1989	67	95	0.414	6 of 6	26					
Philadelphia Phillies	NL East	1988	65	96	0.404	6 of 6	35.5					
Philadelphia Phillies	NL East	1987	80	82	0.494	4t of 6	15					
Philadelphia Phillies	NL East	1986	86	75	0.534	2 of 6	21.5					
Philadelphia Phillies	NL East	1985	75	87	0.463	5 of 6	26					
Philadelphia Phillies	NL East	1984	81	81	0.500	4 of 6	15.5					
Philadelphia Phillies	NL East	1983	90	72	0.556	1 of 6	+6		1		1	
Philadelphia Phillies	NL East	1982	89	73	0.549	2 of 6	3					
Philadelphia Phillies	NL East	1981	59	48	0.551	1, 3 of 6	+1.5, 4.5				1	
Philadelphia Phillies	NL East	1980	91	71	0.562	1 of 6	+1	1	1		1	
Philadelphia Phillies	NL East	1979	84	78	0.519	4 of 6	14					
Philadelphia Phillies	NL East	1978	90	72	0.556	1 of 6	+1.5				1	
Philadelphia Phillies	NL East	1977	101	61	0.623	1 of 6	+5				1	
Philadelphia Phillies	NL East	1976	101	61	0.623	1 of 6	+9				1	
Philadelphia Phillies	NL East	1975	86	76	0.531	2 of 6	6.5					
Philadelphia Phillies	NL East	1974	80	82	0.494	3 of 6	8					
Philadelphia Phillies	NL East	1973	71	91	0.438	6 of 6	11.5					
Philadelphia Phillies	NL East	1972	59	97	0.378	6 of 6	37.5					
Philadelphia Phillies	NL East	1971	67	95	0.414	6 of 6	30					
Philadelphia Phillies	NL East	1970	73	88	0.453	5 of 6	15.5					
Philadelphia Phillies	NL East	1969	63	99	0.389	5 of 6	37					
Philadelphia Phillies	NL	1968	76	86	0.469	7t of 10	21					

Team Name	League	Year	W	L	Win%	Fin	GB/GA	WS	Lge	LDS	Div	WC
Philadelphia Phillies	NL	1967	82	80	0.506	5 of 10	19.5					
Philadelphia Phillies	NL	1966	87	75	0.537	4 of 10	8					
Philadelphia Phillies	NL	1965	85	76	0.528	6 of 10	11.5					
Philadelphia Phillies	NL	1964	92	70	0.568	2t of 10	1					
Philadelphia Phillies	NL	1963	87	75	0.537	4 of 10	12					
Philadelphia Phillies	NL	1962	81	80	0.503	7 of 10	20					
Philadelphia Phillies	NL	1961	47	107	0.305	8 of 8	46					
Philadelphia Phillies	NL	1960	59	95	0.383	8 of 8	36					
Philadelphia Phillies	NL	1959	64	90	0.416	8 of 8	23					
Philadelphia Phillies	NL	1958	69	85	0.448	8 of 8	23					
Philadelphia Phillies	NL	1957	77	77	0.500	5 of 8	19					
Philadelphia Phillies	NL	1956	71	83	0.461	5 of 8	22					
Philadelphia Phillies	NL	1955	77	77	0.500	4 of 8	21.5					
Philadelphia Phillies	NL	1954	75	79	0.487	4 of 8	22					
Philadelphia Phillies	NL	1953	83	71	0.539	3t of 8	22					
Philadelphia Phillies	NL	1952	87	67	0.565	4 of 8	9.5					
Philadelphia Phillies	NL	1951	73	81	0.474	5 of 8	23.5					
Philadelphia Phillies	NL	1950	91	63	0.591	1 of 8	+2		1			
Philadelphia Phillies	NL	1949	81	73	0.526	3 of 8	16					
Philadelphia Phillies	NL	1948	66	88	0.429	6 of 8	25.5					
Philadelphia Phillies	NL	1947	62	92	0.403	7t of 8	32					
Philadelphia Phillies	NL	1946	69	85	0.448	5 of 8	28					
Philadelphia Phillies	NL	1945	46	108	0.299	8 of 8	52					
Philadelphia Blue Jays	NL	1944	61	92	0.399	8 of 8	43.5					
Philadelphia Blue Jays	NL	1943	64	90	0.416	7 of 8	41					
Philadelphia Phillies	NL	1942	42	109	0.278	8 of 8	62.5					
Philadelphia Phillies	NL	1941	43	111	0.279	8 of 8	57					
Philadelphia Phillies	NL	1940	50	103	0.327	8 of 8	50					
Philadelphia Phillies	NL	1939	45	106	0.298	8 of 8	50.5					
Philadelphia Phillies	NL	1938	45	105	0.300	8 of 8	43					
Philadelphia Phillies	NL	1937	61	92	0.399	7 of 8	34.5					
Philadelphia Phillies	NL	1936	54	100	0.351	8 of 8	38					
Philadelphia Phillies	NL	1935	64	89	0.418	7 of 8	35.5					
Philadelphia Phillies	NL	1934	56	93	0.376	7 of 8	37					
Philadelphia Phillies	NL	1933	60	92	0.395	7 of 8	31					
Philadelphia Phillies	NL	1932	78	76	0.506	4 of 8	12					
Philadelphia Phillies	NL	1931	66	88	0.429	6 of 8	35					
Philadelphia Phillies	NL	1930	52	102	0.338	8 of 8	40					
Philadelphia Phillies	NL	1929	71	82	0.464	5 of 8	27.5					
Philadelphia Phillies	NL	1928	43	109	0.283	8 of 8	51					
Philadelphia Phillies	NL	1927	51	103	0.331	8 of 8	43					
Philadelphia Phillies	NL	1926	58	93	0.384	8 of 8	29.5					
Philadelphia Phillies	NL	1925	68	85	0.444	6t of 8	27					
Philadelphia Phillies	NL	1924	55	96	0.364	7 of 8	37					
Philadelphia Phillies	NL	1923	50	104	0.325	8 of 8	45.5					

181

Philadelphia Phillies

Team Name	League	Year	W	L	Win%	Fin	GB/GA	WS	Lge	LDS	Div	WC
Philadelphia Phillies	NL	1922	57	96	0.373	7 of 8	35.5					
Philadelphia Phillies	NL	1921	51	103	0.331	8 of 8	43.5					
Philadelphia Phillies	NL	1920	62	91	0.405	8 of 8	30.5					
Philadelphia Phillies	NL	1919	47	90	0.343	8 of 8	47.5					
Philadelphia Phillies	NL	1918	55	68	0.447	6 of 8	26					
Philadelphia Phillies	NL	1917	87	65	0.572	2 of 8	10					
Philadelphia Phillies	NL	1916	91	62	0.595	2 of 8	2.5					
Philadelphia Phillies	NL	1915	90	62	0.592	1 of 8	+7		1			
Philadelphia Phillies	NL	1914	74	80	0.481	6 of 8	20.5					
Philadelphia Phillies	NL	1913	88	63	0.583	2 of 8	12.5					
Philadelphia Phillies	NL	1912	73	79	0.480	5 of 8	30.5					
Philadelphia Phillies	NL	1911	79	73	0.520	4 of 8	19.5					
Philadelphia Phillies	NL	1910	78	75	0.510	4 of 8	25.5					
Philadelphia Phillies	NL	1909	74	79	0.484	5 of 8	36.5					
Philadelphia Phillies	NL	1908	83	71	0.539	4 of 8	16					
Philadelphia Phillies	NL	1907	83	64	0.565	3 of 8	21.5					
Philadelphia Phillies	NL	1906	71	82	0.464	4 of 8	45.5					
Philadelphia Phillies	NL	1905	83	69	0.546	4 of 8	21.5					
Philadelphia Phillies	NL	1904	52	100	0.342	8 of 8	53.5					
Philadelphia Phillies	NL	1903	49	86	0.363	7 of 8	39.5					
Philadelphia Phillies	NL	1902	56	81	0.409	7 of 8	46					
Philadelphia Phillies	NL	1901	83	57	0.593	2 of 8	7.5					
Philadelphia Phillies	NL	1900	75	63	0.543	3 of 8	8					
Philadelphia Phillies	NL	1899	94	58	0.618	3 of 12	9					
Philadelphia Phillies	NL	1898	78	71	0.523	6 of 12	24					
Philadelphia Phillies	NL	1897	55	77	0.417	10 of 12	38					
Philadelphia Phillies	NL	1896	62	68	0.477	8 of 12	28.5					
Philadelphia Phillies	NL	1895	78	53	0.595	3 of 12	9.5					
Philadelphia Phillies	NL	1894	71	57	0.555	4 of 12	18					
Philadelphia Phillies	NL	1893	72	57	0.558	4 of 12	14					
Philadelphia Phillies	NL	1892	87	66	0.569	3, 5 of 12	7, 12.5					
Philadelphia Phillies	NL	1891	68	69	0.496	4 of 8	18.5					
Philadelphia Phillies	NL	1890	78	54	0.591	3 of 8	9.5					
Philadelphia Quakers	NL	1889	63	64	0.496	4 of 8	20.5					
Philadelphia Quakers	NL	1888	69	61	0.531	3 of 8	14.5					
Philadelphia Quakers	NL	1887	75	48	0.610	2 of 8	3.5					
Philadelphia Quakers	NL	1886	71	43	0.623	4 of 8	14					
Philadelphia Quakers	NL	1885	56	54	0.509	3 of 8	30					
Philadelphia Quakers	NL	1884	39	73	0.348	6 of 8	45					
Philadelphia Quakers	NL	1883	17	81	0.173	8 of 8	46					
			9135	10233	0.472			2	7	3	11	0

Pittsburgh Pirates

Stats

History
Year of Origin 1882   Years Played 129

Score & Rank
Total Points Score .... 94.3   Average Points Score 0.73
Total Points Rank 10   Average Points Rank 14

Postseason Results	**No.**	**Years**
World Series Won	5	1909, 1925, 1960, 1971, 1979
League Championship Series Won	2	1971, 1979
League Division Series Won	0	
World Series Lost	2	1903. 1927
League Championship Series Lost	7	1970, 1972, 1974, 1975, 1990, 1991, 1992
League Division Series Lost	0	

Postseason Won-Loss Records and Winning Percentages

	Postseason Games		**Postseason Series**	
All Postseason Series	40-49	.449	7-9	.438
World Series	23-24	.489	5-2	.714
League Championship Series	17-25	.405	2-7	.222
League Division Series	0-0	.000	0-0	.000

Regular Season Results
All-Time Won-Loss Record 9810-9684
All-Time Winning Percentage .... .503

	No.	**Years**
League Titles before 1969	7	1901, 1902, 1903, 1909, 1925, 1927, 1960
Division Titles	9	1970, 1971, 1972, 1974, 1975, 1979, 1990, 1991, 1992
Wild Cards	0	

Regular Season High & Low Points		**Year(s)**
Most Wins in a Season	110	1909
Most Losses in a Season	113	1890
Highest Winning Percentage	.741	1902
Lowest Winning Percentage	.169	1890
Longest Streak with Won-Loss Record .500 or Higher	15 years	1899-1913
Longest Streak with Won-Loss Record Below .500	18 years	1993-2010

Years with .500 record or Better

1880's	3 (out of 8)
1890's	6
1900's	10
1910's	6
1920's	10
1930's	7
1940's	6
1950's	2
1960's	6
1970's	9
1980's	4
1990's	3
2000's	0
2010's	0

72 out of 129 seasons played = 56%

Years Making Postseason

1880's	No Postseason
1890's	No Postseason
1900's	2
1910's	0
1920's	2
1930's	0
1940's	0
1950's	0
1960's	1
1970's	6
1980's	0
1990's	3
2000's	0
2010's	0

14 out of 129 seasons played = 11%

Streaks

- 1901-1903: Won three League Titles in three years.
- 1925-1927: Won one World Series and two League Titles in three years.
- 1970-1979: Won two World Series, two League Championship Series, and six Division Titles in ten years. Five of their six Division Titles occurred in the six year span of 1970-1975.
- 1990-1992: Won three Division Titles in three years.

Extra Bases

- The Pirates played the Reds in the last tripleheader in baseball history in 1920. It was on October 2nd and Cincinnati won the first two games 13-4 and 7-3 and Pittsburgh won the third game 6-0.
- Pittsburgh became the first team to come back from being down three games to one in the World Series when they won Games 5, 6, & 7 in the 1925 World Series against the Washington Senators.
- A historic occurrence took place at Forbes Field in 1935. On May 25th, on the visiting Boston Braves team, Babe Ruth hit three home runs, and they were #'s 712, 713, and 714 for his career, just before he retired.
- In 1957 the Pittsburgh was the last road team to play in the Polo Grounds and in Ebbets Field, the historic ballparks of the Giants and Dodgers who each moved to California after the season.
- The 1971 World Series featured the first World Series night game, played on October 13th in Pittsburgh. It was for Game 4 of the series and the Pirates beat Baltimore 4-3.
- In 1927 and 1972 the Pirates were eliminated from the postseason on a wild pitch in both seasons.

- Pittsburgh fell behind three games to one in the 1979 World Series just like they did in the 1925 series. When they beat Baltimore in Games 5, 6, & 7 and won the series they became the only major league team to accomplish this twice. No other National League franchise has ever done it, and only three American League teams have done it, once each. The three AL teams are the 1958 Yankees, the 1968 Tigers, and the 1985 Royals.
- The Pirates had eighteen consecutive losing seasons from 1993-2010. This is the longest consecutive season losing streak any U.S. major professional sports franchise has ever had.

Scoring Opportunities

1900's

- Pittsburgh won the National League regular season for the third straight year in 1903 and played Boston in the first World Series, which was a best of nine game series. The Pirates won Game 1 but were held to three hits in Game 2 and lost the game 3-0. Pittsburgh won Games 3 & 4 but lost Games 5, 6, & 7 11-2, 6-3, and 7-3. In Game 8 Pittsburgh was held to four hits and lost the game 3-0 to lose the series five games to three after leading three games to one. In the last four games they were outscored 27-8.
- In 1908 the Pirates were in a close race for the National League pennant all season long with the Cubs and Giants. On October 3rd Pittsburgh had a half game lead over Chicago and a 1.5 game lead over New York with one game left to play against the Cubs. The Pirates lost the game 5-2 and fell to a half game behind Chicago and finished the season tied for second place with the Giants, one game behind the Cubs.

1920's

- The Pirates were in first place in the National League in 1921 either tied or by themselves for every day of the season except two from April 19th to September 5th. They had a 7.5 game lead over the Giants on August 22nd, but lost six games in a row, ten of their next twelve, and went 14-23 the rest of the year. Five of the losses in their six games losing streak in late August were against the Giants. Pittsburgh finished the season in second place four games behind New York. The Giants went 24-10 after August 22nd.
- In 1927 Pittsburgh won the National League pennant and faced the Murderers Row Yankees team in the World Series. In Game 1 the Pirates trailed by one run in the bottom of the eighth inning when they had runners at first and third, but their next batter grounded out and they lost the game 5-4. Pittsburgh lost Game 2 6-2 and Game 3 8-1. Game 4 was tied at three in the bottom of the ninth. The Pirates gave up two walks and a single to the first three New York batters and struck out the next two Yankees. During the next at bat the Pittsburgh pitcher threw a wild pitch and the game winning run scored. The Pirates lost the game 4-3 and lost the series in a sweep.

1930's

• Pittsburgh led the National League in 1938 from July 18th to September 27th and had a seven game lead over Chicago and Cincinnati on September 1st. But the Pirates lost eight of their next eleven games, including two against the Cubs, and their lead was down to 2.5 games over Chicago on September 14th. The Pirates had a two game lead over the Cubs on September 25th with seven games left in the season, but lost six of their last seven games, including three against Chicago, and finished the season in second place two games behind the Cubs. Pittsburgh went 12-16 after September 1st while Chicago went 21-7.

1960's

• In 1966 the Pirates led the National League by 1.5 games over the Dodgers and Giants on September 9th. Pittsburgh lost four of their next five games, including two against Los Angeles, and fell out of first place. The Pirates were only 1.5 games behind the Dodgers on September 24th with seven games left in the season, but they lost five of their last seven games and finished the season in third place three games behind the Dodgers. Pittsburgh went 9-11 after September 9th while LA went 15-8. The Dodgers went 4-4 after September 24th.

1970's

• Pittsburgh won the National League East Division in 1970 and played Cincinnati in the LCS. In Game 1 the score was tied at zero in the bottom of the seventh when the Pirates had runners on first and second with two outs, but their next batter grounded out. In the bottom of the eighth Pittsburgh had runners on first and second with one out, but their next two batters both struck out. The game went into extra innings and in the top of the tenth the Pirates gave up three hits, a walk, and three runs and lost the game 3-0. In Game 2 Pittsburgh trailed by one run in the bottom of the sixth inning when they had runners on first and second with one out, but their next two batters grounded out and flied out and they lost the game 3-1. Game 3 was tied at two after seven innings. In the bottom of the eighth the Pirates got the first two Reds batters out but then walked a batter and gave up two singles and let in the go-ahead run. In the top of the ninth Pittsburgh had runners on first and third with two outs, but their next batter up grounded out and they lost 3-2 and lost the series in a sweep.

• The Pirates won the National League East Division in 1972 and won Game 1 of the LCS against Cincinnati. In Game 2 the Pirates only trailed by one run after six innings, but they didn't get any hits the rest of the game and lost the game 5-3. Pittsburgh won Game 3 but lost Game 4 7-1. In Game 5 the Pirates had a 3-2 lead in the bottom of the ninth inning, but gave up a home run to the first Cincinnati batter that tied the game. The next two Reds batters both singled, then Pittsburgh got two outs. With runners on first and third the Pirates pitcher threw a wild pitch during the next at bat that let in the game winning run and Pittsburgh lost the game 4-3 and lost the series.

- In 1973 the Pirates led the National League East Division on September 17th by one game over the Expos and 3.5 games over the Mets. Pittsburgh lost their next four games to New York and fell to second place a half game behind the Mets on September 21st. The rest of the season the Pirates went 5-6 while New York went 5-2 and Pittsburgh finished the season in third place 2.5 games behind the Mets in the standings.

- Pittsburgh won the National League East Division in 1974 on the last day of the season by winning a game against the Cubs in the bottom of the tenth inning. In the LCS the Pirates played the Dodgers and in Game 1 they only had four hits and lost the game 3-0. Game 2 was tied at two after seven innings. But Pittsburgh gave up five straight hits to start the top of the eighth and they let in three runs and lost the game 5-2. The Pirates won Game 3 but in Game 4 they only had three hits and they lost the game 12-1 and lost the series.

- The Pirates won the National League East Division again in 1975 and played the Reds in the LCS. Pittsburgh lost Game 1 8-3 and Game 2 6-1. In Game 3 the Pirates tied the game at three in the bottom of the ninth, and had the bases loaded with two outs, but their next batter up flied out. In the top of the tenth Pittsburgh gave up three hits, a balk, a sacrifice fly, and let in two runs. In the bottom of the inning they were retired in order and they lost the game 5-3 and lost the series in a sweep.

- In 1978 the Pirates trailed the Phillies by 11.5 games on August 12th. Pittsburgh was 51-61 and then went 37-12 the rest of the year with separate seven, ten, and eleven game winning streaks. With four games remaining in the season, the Pirates trailed Philadelphia by 3.5 games and the two teams met for a four games series in Pittsburgh. The Pirates would need to win all four games, and then win a make up game they had not replayed yet. Pittsburgh won the first two games of the series but lost the third game 10-8 and was eliminated from division title contention. The Pirates won the last game of the series and finished the season in second place 1.5 behind the Phillies.

1990's

- Pittsburgh won the National League East Division in 1990 and faced Cincinnati in the LCS, where they won Game 1. Game 2 was tied at one in the bottom of the fifth inning when the Pirates gave up a stolen base and then a double that drove in the go ahead run with two outs. In the top of the sixth Pittsburgh had runners on first and second with no outs, but their next batter hit into a double play and the following batter struck out. The Pirates didn't get any hits the rest of the game and lost the game 2-1. Pittsburgh lost Game 3 6-3 and Game 4 was tied at two after six innings. In the top of the seventh the Pirates gave up a two-run home run. In the bottom of the eighth they hit a solo home run, and with one out a batter hit a double but was thrown out at third base trying to stretch it into a triple. The next Pittsburgh hitter singled so if the runner had stayed on second he could have scored the tying run. The batter that singled stole second, but the next batter struck out to end the inning. The Pirates lost the game 5-3 and won Game 5. Game 6 was tied at one after six innings. In the top of the seventh Pittsburgh got their first two batters on base, but their next three hitters all got out. In the bottom of the inning they gave up three hits and the go-ahead run and they lost the game 2-1 and lost the series.

- The Pirates repeated as National League East Division champs in 1991 and played the Braves in the LCS, where they won Game 1. In Game 2 Pittsburgh gave up one run in the top of the sixth inning and had runners on first and third with two outs in the bottom of the eighth, but their next batter up grounded out. In the bottom of the ninth the Pirates had the tying run at third base with one out, but their next two batters grounded out and struck out and they lost 1-0. Pittsburgh lost Game 3 10-3 but won Games 4 & 5 to take a three games to two series lead. The Pirates needed only one more win to reach the World Series and they had the last two games at home. Game 6 was tied at zero after eight innings. In the top of the ninth Pittsburgh had two Braves out and a runner was on first base. The Pirates gave up a stolen base, and the next Atlanta batter doubled which drove in the go-ahead run. In the bottom of the inning Pittsburgh had the tying run on third base with two outs but their next batter up struck out and they lost 1-0 for the second time in the series. In Game 7 the Pirates gave up three runs in the top of the first and left two runners on base in the first, fourth, and eighth innings. They lost the game 4-0 and were shut out in back to back games, and the third time in the series. They lost the series they led three games to two with the last two games at home.

- In 1992 Pittsburgh won their third straight National League East Division and met Atlanta again in the LCS. The Pirates lost Game 1 5-1 and Game 2 13-5. They won Game 3 but lost Game 4 6-4 to fall behind in the series three games to one. Pittsburgh won Games 5 & 6 to tie the series and in Game 7 they had a 2-0 lead in the bottom of the ninth. They were three outs away from the World Series, but gave up a double, an error, and a walk to load the bases. The next Atlanta batter flied out which drove in one run. The Pirates walked the next batter, which reloaded the bases, and the next Braves hitter popped out for the second out. The next batter was the Atlanta pitchers' spot in the lineup and the pinch hitter who came up was the Braves backup catcher. The batter hit a ground ball single into left field and the tying run scored easily from third base. The potential game winning run went around third base and raced the left fielders throw at home plate. The throw was a little bit up the first base line and the base runner was safe, just beating the tag from the catcher. Pittsburgh lost the game 3-2 and lost the NLCS in Game 7 against the Braves for the second straight year.

Year-to-Year Figures

Team Name	League	Year	W	L	Win%	Fin	GB/GA	WS	Lge	LDS	Div	WC
Pittsburgh Pirates	NL Cent	2010	57	105	0.352	6 of 6	34					
Pittsburgh Pirates	NL Cent	2009	62	99	0.385	6 of 6	28.5					
Pittsburgh Pirates	NL Cent	2008	67	95	0.414	6 of 6	30.5					
Pittsburgh Pirates	NL Cent	2007	68	94	0.420	6 of 6	17					
Pittsburgh Pirates	NL Cent	2006	67	95	0.414	5 of 6	16.5					
Pittsburgh Pirates	NL Cent	2005	67	95	0.414	6 of 6	33					
Pittsburgh Pirates	NL Cent	2004	72	89	0.447	5 of 6	32.5					
Pittsburgh Pirates	NL Cent	2003	75	87	0.463	4 of 6	13					
Pittsburgh Pirates	NL Cent	2002	72	89	0.447	4 of 6	24.5					
Pittsburgh Pirates	NL Cent	2001	62	100	0.383	6 of 6	31					
Pittsburgh Pirates	NL Cent	2000	69	93	0.426	5 of 6	26					
Pittsburgh Pirates	NL Cent	1999	78	83	0.484	3 of 6	18.5					
Pittsburgh Pirates	NL Cent	1998	69	93	0.426	6 of 6	33					
Pittsburgh Pirates	NL Cent	1997	79	83	0.488	2 of 5	5					
Pittsburgh Pirates	NL Cent	1996	73	89	0.451	5 of 5	15					
Pittsburgh Pirates	NL Cent	1995	58	86	0.403	5 of 5	27					
Pittsburgh Pirates	NL Cent	1994	53	61	0.465	3t of 5	13					
Pittsburgh Pirates	NL East	1993	75	87	0.463	5 of 7	22					
Pittsburgh Pirates	NL East	1992	96	66	0.593	1 of 6	+9				1	
Pittsburgh Pirates	NL East	1991	98	64	0.605	1 of 6	+14				1	
Pittsburgh Pirates	NL East	1990	95	67	0.586	1 of 6	+4				1	
Pittsburgh Pirates	NL East	1989	74	88	0.457	5 of 6	19					
Pittsburgh Pirates	NL East	1988	85	75	0.531	2 of 6	15					
Pittsburgh Pirates	NL East	1987	80	82	0.494	4t of 6	15					
Pittsburgh Pirates	NL East	1986	64	98	0.395	6 of 6	44					
Pittsburgh Pirates	NL East	1985	57	104	0.354	6 of 6	43.5					
Pittsburgh Pirates	NL East	1984	75	87	0.463	6 of 6	21.5					
Pittsburgh Pirates	NL East	1983	84	78	0.519	2 of 6	6					
Pittsburgh Pirates	NL East	1982	84	78	0.519	4 of 6	8					
Pittsburgh Pirates	NL East	1981	46	56	0.451	4, 6 of 6	5.5, 9.5					
Pittsburgh Pirates	NL East	1980	83	79	0.512	3 of 6	8					
Pittsburgh Pirates	NL East	1979	98	64	0.605	1 of 6	+2	1	1		1	
Pittsburgh Pirates	NL East	1978	88	73	0.547	2 of 6	1.5					
Pittsburgh Pirates	NL East	1977	96	66	0.593	2 of 6	5					
Pittsburgh Pirates	NL East	1976	92	70	0.568	2 of 6	9					
Pittsburgh Pirates	NL East	1975	92	69	0.571	1 of 6	+6.5				1	
Pittsburgh Pirates	NL East	1974	88	74	0.543	1 of 6	+1.5				1	
Pittsburgh Pirates	NL East	1973	80	82	0.494	3 of 6	2.5					
Pittsburgh Pirates	NL East	1972	96	59	0.619	1 of 6	+11				1	
Pittsburgh Pirates	NL East	1971	97	65	0.599	1 of 6	+7	1	1		1	
Pittsburgh Pirates	NL East	1970	89	73	0.549	1 of 6	+5				1	
Pittsburgh Pirates	NL East	1969	88	74	0.543	3 of 6	12					
Pittsburgh Pirates	NL	1968	80	82	0.494	6 of 10	17					

Team Name	League	Year	W	L	Win%	Fin	GB/GA	WS	Lge	LDS	Div	WC
Pittsburgh Pirates	NL	1967	81	81	0.500	6 of 10	20.5					
Pittsburgh Pirates	NL	1966	92	70	0.568	3 of 10	3					
Pittsburgh Pirates	NL	1965	90	72	0.556	3 of 10	7					
Pittsburgh Pirates	NL	1964	80	82	0.494	6t of 10	13					
Pittsburgh Pirates	NL	1963	74	88	0.457	8 of 10	25					
Pittsburgh Pirates	NL	1962	93	68	0.578	4 of 10	8					
Pittsburgh Pirates	NL	1961	75	79	0.487	6 of 8	18					
Pittsburgh Pirates	NL	1960	95	59	0.617	1 of 8	+7	1	1			
Pittsburgh Pirates	NL	1959	78	76	0.506	4 of 8	9					
Pittsburgh Pirates	NL	1958	84	70	0.545	2 of 8	8					
Pittsburgh Pirates	NL	1957	62	92	0.403	7t of 8	33					
Pittsburgh Pirates	NL	1956	66	88	0.429	7 of 8	27					
Pittsburgh Pirates	NL	1955	60	94	0.390	8 of 8	38.5					
Pittsburgh Pirates	NL	1954	53	101	0.344	8 of 8	44					
Pittsburgh Pirates	NL	1953	50	104	0.325	8 of 8	55					
Pittsburgh Pirates	NL	1952	42	112	0.273	8 of 8	54.5					
Pittsburgh Pirates	NL	1951	64	90	0.416	7 of 8	32.5					
Pittsburgh Pirates	NL	1950	57	96	0.373	8 of 8	33.5					
Pittsburgh Pirates	NL	1949	71	83	0.461	6 of 8	26					
Pittsburgh Pirates	NL	1948	83	71	0.539	4 of 8	8.5					
Pittsburgh Pirates	NL	1947	62	92	0.403	7t of 8	32					
Pittsburgh Pirates	NL	1946	63	91	0.409	7 of 8	34					
Pittsburgh Pirates	NL	1945	82	72	0.532	4 of 8	16					
Pittsburgh Pirates	NL	1944	90	63	0.588	2 of 8	14.5					
Pittsburgh Pirates	NL	1943	80	74	0.519	4 of 8	25					
Pittsburgh Pirates	NL	1942	66	81	0.449	5 of 8	36.5					
Pittsburgh Pirates	NL	1941	81	73	0.526	4 of 8	19					
Pittsburgh Pirates	NL	1940	78	76	0.506	4 of 8	22.5					
Pittsburgh Pirates	NL	1939	68	85	0.444	6 of 8	28.5					
Pittsburgh Pirates	NL	1938	86	64	0.573	2 of 8	2					
Pittsburgh Pirates	NL	1937	86	68	0.558	3 of 8	10					
Pittsburgh Pirates	NL	1936	84	70	0.545	4 of 8	8					
Pittsburgh Pirates	NL	1935	86	67	0.562	4 of 8	13.5					
Pittsburgh Pirates	NL	1934	74	76	0.493	5 of 8	19.5					
Pittsburgh Pirates	NL	1933	87	67	0.565	2 of 8	5					
Pittsburgh Pirates	NL	1932	86	68	0.558	2 of 8	4					
Pittsburgh Pirates	NL	1931	75	79	0.487	5 of 8	26					
Pittsburgh Pirates	NL	1930	80	74	0.519	5 of 8	12					
Pittsburgh Pirates	NL	1929	88	65	0.575	2 of 8	10.5					
Pittsburgh Pirates	NL	1928	85	67	0.559	4 of 8	9					
Pittsburgh Pirates	NL	1927	94	60	0.610	1 of 8	+1.5		1			
Pittsburgh Pirates	NL	1926	84	69	0.549	3 of 8	4.5					
Pittsburgh Pirates	NL	1925	95	58	0.621	1 of 8	+8.5	1	1			
Pittsburgh Pirates	NL	1924	90	63	0.588	3 of 8	3					
Pittsburgh Pirates	NL	1923	87	67	0.565	3 of 8	8.5					

Team Name	League	Year	W	L	Win%	Fin	GB/GA	WS	Lge	LDS	Div	WC
Pittsburgh Pirates	NL	1922	85	69	0.552	3t of 8	8					
Pittsburgh Pirates	NL	1921	90	63	0.588	2 of 8	4					
Pittsburgh Pirates	NL	1920	79	75	0.513	4 of 8	14					
Pittsburgh Pirates	NL	1919	71	68	0.511	4 of 8	24.5					
Pittsburgh Pirates	NL	1918	65	60	0.520	4 of 8	17					
Pittsburgh Pirates	NL	1917	51	103	0.331	8 of 8	47					
Pittsburgh Pirates	NL	1916	65	89	0.422	6 of 8	29					
Pittsburgh Pirates	NL	1915	73	81	0.474	5 of 8	18					
Pittsburgh Pirates	NL	1914	69	85	0.448	7 of 8	25.5					
Pittsburgh Pirates	NL	1913	78	71	0.523	4 of 8	21.5					
Pittsburgh Pirates	NL	1912	93	58	0.616	2 of 8	10					
Pittsburgh Pirates	NL	1911	85	69	0.552	3 of 8	14.5					
Pittsburgh Pirates	NL	1910	86	67	0.562	3 of 8	17.5					
Pittsburgh Pirates	NL	1909	110	42	0.724	1 of 8	+6.5	1	1			
Pittsburgh Pirates	NL	1908	98	56	0.636	2t of 8	1					
Pittsburgh Pirates	NL	1907	91	63	0.591	2 of 8	17					
Pittsburgh Pirates	NL	1906	93	60	0.608	3 of 8	23.5					
Pittsburgh Pirates	NL	1905	96	57	0.627	2 of 8	9					
Pittsburgh Pirates	NL	1904	87	66	0.569	4 of 8	19					
Pittsburgh Pirates	NL	1903	91	49	0.650	1 of 8	+6.5		1			
Pittsburgh Pirates	NL	1902	103	36	0.741	1 of 8	+27.5		1			
Pittsburgh Pirates	NL	1901	90	49	0.647	1 of 8	+7.5		1			
Pittsburgh Pirates	NL	1900	79	60	0.568	2 of 8	4.5					
Pittsburgh Pirates	NL	1899	76	73	0.510	7 of 12	25.5					
Pittsburgh Pirates	NL	1898	72	76	0.486	8 of 12	29.5					
Pittsburgh Pirates	NL	1897	60	71	0.458	8 of 12	32.5					
Pittsburgh Pirates	NL	1896	66	63	0.512	6 of 12	24					
Pittsburgh Pirates	NL	1895	71	61	0.538	7 of 12	17					
Pittsburgh Pirates	NL	1894	65	65	0.500	7 of 12	25					
Pittsburgh Pirates	NL	1893	81	48	0.628	2 of 12	5					
Pittsburgh Pirates	NL	1892	80	73	0.523	6, 4 of 12	16, 10.5					
Pittsburgh Pirates	NL	1891	55	80	0.407	8 of 8	30.5					
Pittsburgh Alleghenys	NL	1890	23	113	0.169	8 of 8	66.5					
Pittsburgh Alleghenys	NL	1889	61	71	0.462	5 of 8	25					
Pittsburgh Alleghenys	NL	1888	66	68	0.493	6 of 8	19.5					
Pittsburgh Alleghenys	NL	1887	55	69	0.444	6 of 8	24					
Pittsburgh Alleghenys	AA	1886	80	57	0.584	2 of 8	12					
Pittsburgh Alleghenys	AA	1885	56	55	0.505	3 of 8	22.5					
Pittsburgh Alleghenys	AA	1884	30	78	0.278	11 of 13	45.5					
Pittsburgh Alleghenys	AA	1883	31	67	0.316	7 of 8	35					
Pittsburgh Alleghenys	AA	1882	39	39	0.500	4 of 6	15					
			9810	9684	0.503			5	9	0	9	0

St. Louis Cardinals

Stats

History
Year of Origin 1882

Years Played 129

Score & Rank
Total Points Score 198.8
Total Points Rank 2

Average Points Score 1.54
Average Points Rank 4

Postseason Results	**No.**	**Years**
World Series Won	10	1926, 1931, 1934, 1942, 1944, 1946, 1964, 1967, 1982, 2006
League Championship Series Won	5	1982, 1985, 1987, 2004, 2006
League Division Series Won	6	1996, 2000, 2002, 2004, 2005, 2006
World Series Lost	7	1928, 1930, 1943, 1968, 1985, 1987, 2004
League Championship Series Lost	4	1996, 2000, 2002, 2005
League Division Series Lost	2	2001, 2009

Postseason Won-Loss Records and Winning Percentages

	Postseason Games		**Postseason Series**	
All Postseason Series	98-88	.527	21-13	.618
World Series	52-53	.495	10-7	.588
League Championship Series	26-27	.491	5-4	.555
League Division Series	20-8	.714	6-2	.750

Regular Season Results
All-Time Won-Loss Record 10107-9419
All-Time Winning Percentage .... .518

	No.	**Years**
League Titles before 1969	16	1885, 1886, 1887 1888, 1926, 1928, 1930, 1931, 1934, 1942, 1943, 1944, 1946, 1964, 1967, 1968
Division Titles	10	1982, 1985, 1987, 1996, 2000, 2002, 2004, 2005, 2006, 2009
Wild Cards	1	2001

Regular Season High & Low Points		**Year(s)**
Most Wins a Season	106	1942
Most Losses in a Season	111	1898
Highest Winning Percentage	.705	1885
Lowest Winning Percentage	.221	1897
Longest Streak with Won-Loss Record .500 or Higher	15 years	1939-1953
Longest Streak with Won-Loss Record Below .500	9 years	1902-1910

Years with .500 record or Better		**Years Making Postseason**	
1880's	7 (out of 8)	1880's	No Postseason
1890's	3	1890's	No Postseason
1900's	1	1900's	0
1910's	3	1910's	0
1920's	8	1920's	2
1930's	8	1930's	3
1940's	10	1940's	4
1950's	5	1950's	0
1960's	9	1960's	3
1970's	6	1970's	0
1980's	6	1980's	3
1990's	5	1990's	1
2000's	9	2000's	7
2010's	1	2010's	0
80 out of 129 seasons played = 62%		23 out of 129 seasons played = 18%	

Streaks

- 1885-1888: Won four League Titles in four years.
- 1926-1934: Won three World Series and five League Titles in nine years.
- 1942-1946: Won four League Titles and three World Series in five years.
- 1964-1968: Won two World Series and three League Titles in five years.
- 1982-1987: Won three Division Titles, three League Championship Series, and one World Series in six years.
- 2000-2009: Won one World Series, two League Championship Series, five League Division Series, six Division Titles, and one Wild Card in ten years.

Extra Bases

- St. Louis is the last National League team to win three consecutive league titles, doing so from 1942-1944.
- In the seven World Series that St. Louis played in from 1946-1987 all seven of them went the full seven games. The Cardinals won in 1946, 1964, 1967, and 1982. They lost in 1968, 1985, and 1987.

Scoring Opportunities

1880's

- In the 1883 American Association the St. Louis Browns led the league by half a game over the Philadelphia A's on September 3rd. But the Browns lost their next three games in a row to the A's and fell to 2.5 games back in the standings on September 6th. St. Louis went 9-4 the rest of the year, but two of those losses were against Philadelphia, who went 8-6 the rest of the season, and the Browns finished the year in second place one game behind the A's.

- In 1889 St. Louis either was tied for first place or led the American Association by themselves from April 17th to August 31st. On August 28th the Browns led the Brooklyn Bridegrooms by three games but lost their next four games while Brooklyn went 6-1 over the same period. St. Louis fell to second place, 1.5 games behind the Bridegrooms on September 3rd. The rest of the year the Browns went 19-7 and had a ten game winning streak, but Brooklyn went 20-7 the rest of the season and St. Louis finished in second place two games behind the Bridegrooms.

1920's

- The Cardinals were in a close race for the National League title with the Pirates and Giants in 1927. St. Louis was 5.5 games behind Pittsburgh on September 16th and won twelve of their final fourteen games of the year. But the Pirates went 9-7 and held on to their lead and the Cardinals finished in second place 1.5 games behind Pittsburgh.
- In 1928 St. Louis won the National League pennant and faced the Yankees in the World Series. In Games 1 & 2 in New York the Cardinals only had seven hits total in the two games and lost them by the scores of 4-1 and 9-3. St. Louis lost Games 3 & 4 at home both by the score of 7-3 and lost the series in a sweep. They were outscored 27-10 in the series and outhit 39-25.

1930's

- St. Louis won the National League pennant in 1930 and faced the Philadelphia Athletics in the World Series. The Cardinals lost Game 1 5-2 and Game 2 6-1 and won Games 3 & 4. Game 5 was tied at zero after eight innings. In the top of the ninth St. Louis walked the first A's hitter and then got one out. The next Philadelphia batter hit a two-run home run and the Cardinals lost the game 2-0. St. Louis lost Game 6 7-1 and lost the series.
- In 1935 the Cardinals were in second place in the National League on September 24th three games behind Chicago with their five remaining games at home against the Cubs. St. Louis needed to win all five games to win the pennant or win four of the five to tie Chicago for first place. But the Cardinals lost the first three games in the series and were eliminated from league title contention. They won the last two games of the year and finished the season four games behind the Cubs.

1940's

- St. Louis was in a close race for the National League pennant with Brooklyn in 1941. The Cardinals trailed the Dodgers by one game on September 11th when the two teams met for a three game series in St. Louis. The Cardinals lost two out of the three games and fell to two games behind Brooklyn in the standings. St. Louis went 10-5 the rest of the season, but the Dodgers went 10-4 and the Cardinals finished in second place 2.5 games behind Brooklyn.

- In 1943 St. Louis won the National League pennant and played the Yankees in the World Series. Game 1 was tied at two in the bottom of the sixth inning. The Cardinals gave up singles to the first two New York batters and then the St. Louis pitcher threw a wild pitch that let the runner from second base score the go ahead run. The Cardinals trailed by two runs in the top of the eighth when they had runners on first and second with two outs, but their next batter grounded out and they lost the game 4-2. The Cardinals won Game 2 and led Game 3 2-1 after seven innings. But in the bottom of the eighth they gave up five hits, two walks, two errors, and five runs and they lost the game 6-2. Game 4 was tied at one after seven innings but in the top of the eighth St. Louis gave up a double, a sacrifice bunt, a sacrifice fly, and let in the go-ahead run. In the bottom of the inning the Cardinals had runners on first and second with one out, but their next two batters flied out and grounded out. In the bottom of the ninth they had a runner on second with one out, but their next two batters grounded out and flied out and they lost 2-1. Game 5 was scoreless until St. Louis gave up a two-run home run in the top of the sixth inning. The Cardinals had runners on first and second with two outs in the bottom of the eighth, but their next hitter grounded out. They had runners on first and second in the bottom of the ninth with one out, but their next two batters struck out and grounded out and they lost the game 2-0 and lost the series.
- St. Louis was in a close race for the National League pennant with the Cubs in 1945. On September 2nd the Cardinals were 1.5 games behind Chicago in the standings but lost three of their next four games and fell to 4.5 games behind the Cubs on September 6th. The rest of the year St. Louis went 18-6 and beat Chicago three times in their five remaining games against each other, but the Cubs went 16-8 over the same period and the Cardinals finished the season in second place three games behind the Chicago.
- In 1949 the Cardinals led the National League from August 20th to September 27th and had a 1.5 game lead over the Dodgers on September 25th with five games left in the season. But St. Louis lost four of their last five games while Brooklyn won three of its last four and the Cardinals finished the season in second place one game behind the Dodgers. The Cardinals had a 2.5 game lead on September 16th but went 6-8 the rest of the season from that point, including losing two out of three in a series against the Dodgers, who went 9-4 after September 16th.

1960's

- The Cardinals were in a close race for the National League pennant in 1963 as they only trailed Los Angeles by one game on September 16th when the two teams met in St. Louis for a three game series. The Cardinals lost all three games of the series and then lost five of their last seven games of the year. They finished the season in second place six games behind the Dodgers St. Louis went 2-8 after September 15th while LA went 8-4.
- In 1968 St. Louis won the National League pennant and played the Tigers in the World Series. The Cardinals won Game 1, lost Game 2 8-1, and won Games 3 & 4. They had a

three game to one lead in the series and Games 6 & 7 would be played at home if necessary. In Game 5 St. Louis had a 3-2 lead after six innings. In the bottom of the seventh they got the first Tigers hitter out but then gave up four singles, one walk, and three runs. In the top of the ninth the Cardinals trailed by two runs when they had runners on first and second with one out, but their next two batters struck out and grounded out and they lost 5-3. In Game 6 St. Louis gave up ten runs in the third inning and lost the game 13-1. Game 7 was tied at zero after six innings. In the top of the seventh the Cardinals got the first two Detroit batters out, but gave up four straight hits and let in three runs. St. Louis lost the game 4-1 and lost the series in which they had a three games to one series lead.

1970's

- St. Louis was in first place in the National League East Division in 1973 from July 22nd to September 11th either tied or by themselves. They led the division on September 5th by three games over Pittsburgh with Montreal 3.5 games back, and Chicago and New York 5.5 games back. The Cardinals lost their next seven games, including three against Chicago, two against Montreal, and two against the Pirates, and fell to third place three games behind Pittsburgh on September 15th. The rest of the year St. Louis went 9-6 and won their last five games of the year while Pittsburgh went 6-11. But the Mets went 10-3 and the Cardinals finished in second place 1.5 games behind New York in the standings.

- In 1974 St. Louis was in a close race with the Pirates for the National League East Division title. The Cardinals had a 1.5 game lead on September 23rd when the two teams met in St. Louis for a three game series, but the Cardinals lost two out of the three games. The two teams were tied on October 1st. St. Louis played the Expos in their last game of the year and had a 2-1 lead in the bottom of the eighth inning. They got the first two Montreal batters out but then gave up a single and a home run and they lost the game 3-2. Pittsburgh had two games left and beat the Cubs in their last two games of the year. The Cardinals did not have to make up a cancelled game and finished the season in second place 1.5 games behind the Pirates.

1980's

- The Cardinals had the best overall record in the National League East Division in 1981 but did not make the playoffs. The season was split into two halves due to a players strike and playoff spots were given to the teams that won the first half and the second half of the season in each division. In the first half St. Louis finished 1.5 games behind Philadelphia and in the second half they finished a half a game behind Montreal.

- In 1985 St. Louis won the National League East Division and beat the Dodgers in the LCS. In the World Series the Cardinals faced Kansas City and won Games 1 & 2. St. Louis lost Game 3 6-1 and won Game 4 to take a three games to one lead in the series. The Cardinals lost Game 5 6-1 at home. In Game 6 St. Louis had a 1-0 lead in the bottom of the ninth inning. The first Kansas City batter hit a ground ball to the first basemen who flipped the ball to pitcher at first base for what looked like an out. But the umpire called the runner safe, even though the runner was clearly out. The next Royals batter singled, and then the Cardinals got one out. On the next batter the St. Louis pitcher threw a passed ball that let the runners advance to second and third. St. Louis walked the following batter intentionally to try to get a force out or double play. But the next Kansas City batter singled and drove in two runs and the Cardinals lost 2-1. St. Louis lost Game 7 11-0 and lost the series in which they had a three game to one series lead.

- St. Louis won the National League East Division in 1987 and beat the Giants in the LCS. The Cardinals played the Twins in the World Series and lost the Game 1 10-1 and Game 2 8-4. St. Louis won the next three games at home to take a three games to two lead in the series, but lost Game 6 11-5. Game 7 was tied at two after five innings. In the bottom of the sixth the Cardinals walked three Minnesota batters and gave up a single with two outs that let in the go-ahead run. In the top of the seventh St. Louis had a runner on third base with two outs, but their next batter flied out. The Cardinals were retired in order in the top of the eighth and ninth innings and lost the game 4-2 to lose the series.

1990's

- In 1996 the Cardinals won the National League Central Division and swept the Padres in the LDS. In the LCS St. Louis faced the Braves and Game 1 was tied at two after seven innings. In the bottom of the eighth the Cardinals gave up two walks, two singles, and two runs and they lost the game 4-2. St. Louis won the next three games to take a three game to one series lead. In Game 5 they gave up twenty-two hits and lost 14-0. In Game 6 the Cardinals trailed by one run in the top of the eighth when they had a runner on second with two outs, but the next batter up flied out and they lost the game 3-1. Then they lost Game 7 15-0 in which they gave up seventeen hits and they lost the series in which they had a three game to one series lead. In the last three games St. Louis gave up thirty-two runs and forty-six hits. In the first four games they gave up twelve runs and thirty-one hits.

2000's

- The Cardinals won the National League Central Division in 2000 and swept the Braves in the LDS. In the LCS St. Louis played the Mets and lost Game 1 6-2. Game 2 was tied at five in the bottom of the eighth when the Cardinals had runners on first and second with two outs, but their next batter struck out. In the top of the ninth St. Louis let the first Mets batter reach base on an error. The next New York hitter sacrificed bunted to advance the runner to second, and the following batter hit a single that drove in the go-ahead run and the Cardinals lost the game 6-5. St. Louis won Game 3 but in Game 4 they gave up seven runs in the first two innings and lost the game 10-6. Then they lost Game 5 7-0 and lost the series.
- In 2001 St. Louis tied Houston for the best record in the National League Central Division.

Since Houston won the regular season series, the Astros won the Division Title and the Cardinals got the Wild Card spot as both teams qualified for the playoffs. In the LDS St. Louis faced Arizona. In Game 1 the Cardinals only had three hits and only had one after the fifth inning and they lost the game 1-0. St. Louis won Game 2 and had a 2-1 lead after six innings in Game 3. But in the top of the seventh they gave up four hits, one walk, and four runs. In the bottom of the eighth the Cardinals had the bases loaded with two outs and their next batter hit a deep fly ball to center field but it stayed in the park. In the bottom of the ninth St. Louis had runners on first and second with no outs, but their next two batters struck out and grounded into a double play and they lost 5-3. The Cardinals won Game 4 to even the series and Game 5 was tied after eight innings. In the top of the ninth their first batter up singled but their next three hitters all got out. In the bottom of the inning Arizona had runners on first and third with one out and St. Louis caught a runner stealing home that prevented the go ahead run from scoring. But the Diamondbacks runner on first advanced to second on the play and on the next at bat he was singled in for the game winning run the Cardinals lost the game 2-1 and lost the series.

- St. Louis won the National League Central Division in 2002 and swept Arizona in the LDS. In the LCS the Cardinals played San Francisco and lost Game 1 9-6 and Game 2 4-1. St. Louis won Game 3 and Game 4 was tied at two after seven innings. In the bottom of the eighth the Cardinals got the first two Giants batters out and then intentionally walked San Francisco's best hitter, but the next San Francisco batter hit a two-run home run. In the top of the ninth St. Louis scored one run and had runners on first and third with one out, but their next two batters both struck out and they lost 4-3. The Cardinals led Game 5 1-0 after seven innings. In the bottom of the eighth they got the first Giants batter out but then gave up two singles and hit a batter. The next San Francisco batter hit a sacrifice fly that drove in the tying run. In the bottom of the ninth St. Louis got the first two Giants batters out but then gave up three straight singles and let in the game winning run and lost 2-1 to lose the series.

- In 2004 the Cardinals repeated as National League Central Division champs, beat the Dodgers in the LDS, and beat the Astros the LCS. In the World Series the Cardinals faced the Red Sox and Game 1 was tied at nine in the eighth inning. St. Louis had the bases loaded with one out but their next two batters popped out and struck out. In the bottom of the inning the Cardinals got the first Red Sox hitter out and then committed an error that let a runner on base. The next Boston batter hit a two-run home run off the right field foul pole and St. Louis lost the game 11-9. The Cardinals only had five hits in Game 2 and lost the game 6-2. In Games 3 & 4 in St. Louis the Cardinals only had four hits in each game and lost Game 3 4-1 and Game 4 3-0 and lost the series in a sweep. St. Louis never had a lead in any game in the series.

- The Cardinals won their third straight National League Central Division title in 2005 and swept San Diego in the LDS. In the LCS St. Louis played Houston, won Game 1, and lost

Game 2 4-1. In Game 3 the Cardinals trailed by one run in the top of the ninth when they had a runner on second with two outs, but their next batter flied out and they lost 4-3. Game 4 was tied at one after six innings. In the bottom of the seventh St. Louis walked two batters and committed an error that loaded the bases. The next Astros batter hit a sacrifice fly that drove in the go-ahead run. In the top of the ninth the Cardinals first two batters singled and they had runners on first and third with no outs. Their next batter hit a ground ball to third and the tying run was thrown out at home plate. Their following batter hit into a double play that ended the game and they lost 2-1. St. Louis won Game 5 but had only four hits in Game 6 and lost it 5-1 to lose the series.

• St. Louis won the National League Central Division in 2009 and faced Los Angeles in the LDS. The Cardinals lost Game 1 5-3 and led Game 2 2-1 in the bottom of the ninth. They got the first two Dodgers batters out and the third batter hit a routine fly ball to left field, but the St. Louis left fielder dropped the ball and the batter reached base. Then the Cardinals gave up a walk and a single that drove in the tying run. During the next at bat there was a passed ball and St. Louis walked the batter, which loaded the bases. The next LA batter hit a single that drove in the game winning run and St. Louis lost 3-2. The Cardinals lost Game 3 5-1 and lost the series in a sweep. They only scored six runs in the three games.

Year-to-Year Figures

Team	League	Year	W	L	Win%	Fin	GB/GA	WS	Lge	LDS	Div	WC
St. Louis Cardinals	NL Cent	2010	86	76	0.531	2 of 6	5					
St. Louis Cardinals	NL Cent	2009	91	71	0.562	1 of 6	+7.5				1	
St. Louis Cardinals	NL Cent	2008	86	76	0.531	4 of 6	11.5					
St. Louis Cardinals	NL Cent	2007	78	84	0.481	3 of 6	7					
St. Louis Cardinals	NL Cent	2006	83	78	0.516	1 of 6	+1.5	1	1	1	1	
St. Louis Cardinals	NL Cent	2005	100	62	0.617	1 of 6	+11			1	1	
St. Louis Cardinals	NL Cent	2004	105	57	0.648	1 of 6	+13		1	1	1	
St. Louis Cardinals	NL Cent	2003	85	77	0.525	3 of 6	3					
St. Louis Cardinals	NL Cent	2002	97	65	0.599	1 of 6	+13			1	1	
St. Louis Cardinals	NL Cent	2001	93	69	0.574	1t of 6	0*					1
St. Louis Cardinals	NL Cent	2000	95	67	0.586	1 of 6	+10			1	1	
St. Louis Cardinals	NL Cent	1999	75	86	0.466	4 of 6	21.5					
St. Louis Cardinals	NL Cent	1998	83	79	0.512	3 of 6	19					
St. Louis Cardinals	NL Cent	1997	73	89	0.451	4 of 5	11					
St. Louis Cardinals	NL Cent	1996	88	74	0.543	1 of 5	+6			1	1	
St. Louis Cardinals	NL Cent	1995	62	81	0.434	4 of 5	22.5					
St. Louis Cardinals	NL Cent	1994	53	61	0.465	3t of 5	13					
St. Louis Cardinals	NL East	1993	87	75	0.537	3 of 7	10					
St. Louis Cardinals	NL East	1992	83	79	0.512	3 of 6	13					
St. Louis Cardinals	NL East	1991	84	78	0.519	2 of 6	14					
St. Louis Cardinals	NL East	1990	70	92	0.432	6 of 6	25					
St. Louis Cardinals	NL East	1989	86	76	0.531	3 of 6	7					
St. Louis Cardinals	NL East	1988	76	86	0.469	5 of 6	25					
St. Louis Cardinals	NL East	1987	95	67	0.586	1 of 6	+3		1		1	
St. Louis Cardinals	NL East	1986	79	82	0.491	3 of 6	28.5					
St. Louis Cardinals	NL East	1985	101	61	0.623	1 of 6	+3		1		1	
St. Louis Cardinals	NL East	1984	84	78	0.519	3 of 6	12.5					
St. Louis Cardinals	NL East	1983	79	83	0.488	4 of 6	11					
St. Louis Cardinals	NL East	1982	92	70	0.568	1 of 6	+3	1	1		1	
St. Louis Cardinals	NL East	1981	59	43	0.578	2, 2 of 6	1.5, 0.5**					
St. Louis Cardinals	NL East	1980	74	88	0.457	4 of 6	17					
St. Louis Cardinals	NL East	1979	86	76	0.531	3 of 6	12					
St. Louis Cardinals	NL East	1978	69	93	0.426	5 of 6	21					
St. Louis Cardinals	NL East	1977	83	79	0.512	3 of 6	18					
St. Louis Cardinals	NL East	1976	72	90	0.444	5 of 6	29					
St. Louis Cardinals	NL East	1975	82	80	0.506	3t of 6	10.5					
St. Louis Cardinals	NL East	1974	86	75	0.534	2t of 6	1.5					
St. Louis Cardinals	NL East	1973	81	81	0.500	2t of 6	1.5					
St. Louis Cardinals	NL East	1972	75	81	0.481	4 of 6	21.5					
St. Louis Cardinals	NL East	1971	90	72	0.556	2t of 6	7					
St. Louis Cardinals	NL East	1970	76	86	0.469	4 of 6	13					
St. Louis Cardinals	NL East	1969	87	75	0.537	4 of 6	13					
St. Louis Cardinals	NL	1968	97	65	0.599	1 of 10	+9		1			

Team	League	Year	W	L	Win%	Fin	GB/GA	WS	Lge	LDS	Div	WC
St. Louis Cardinals	NL	1967	101	60	0.627	1 of 10	+10.5	1	1			
St. Louis Cardinals	NL	1966	83	79	0.512	6 of 10	12					
St. Louis Cardinals	NL	1965	80	81	0.497	7 of 10	16.5					
St. Louis Cardinals	NL	1964	93	69	0.574	1 of 10	+1	1	1			
St. Louis Cardinals	NL	1963	93	69	0.574	2 of 10	6					
St. Louis Cardinals	NL	1962	84	78	0.519	6 of 10	17.5					
St. Louis Cardinals	NL	1961	80	74	0.519	5 of 8	13					
St. Louis Cardinals	NL	1960	86	68	0.558	3 of 8	9					
St. Louis Cardinals	NL	1959	71	83	0.461	7 of 8	16					
St. Louis Cardinals	NL	1958	72	82	0.468	5t of 8	20					
St. Louis Cardinals	NL	1957	87	67	0.565	2 of 8	8					
St. Louis Cardinals	NL	1956	76	78	0.494	4 of 8	17					
St. Louis Cardinals	NL	1955	68	86	0.442	7 of 8	30.5					
St. Louis Cardinals	NL	1954	72	82	0.468	6 of 8	25					
St. Louis Cardinals	NL	1953	83	71	0.539	3t of 8	22					
St. Louis Cardinals	NL	1952	88	66	0.571	3 of 8	8.5					
St. Louis Cardinals	NL	1951	81	73	0.526	3 of 8	15.5					
St. Louis Cardinals	NL	1950	78	75	0.510	5 of 8	12.5					
St. Louis Cardinals	NL	1949	96	58	0.623	2 of 8	1					
St. Louis Cardinals	NL	1948	85	69	0.552	2 of 8	6.5					
St. Louis Cardinals	NL	1947	89	65	0.578	2 of 8	5					
St. Louis Cardinals	NL	1946	98	58	0.628	1 of 8	+2	1	1			
St. Louis Cardinals	NL	1945	95	59	0.617	2 of 8	3					
St. Louis Cardinals	NL	1944	105	49	0.682	1 of 8	+14.5	1	1			
St. Louis Cardinals	NL	1943	105	49	0.682	1 of 8	+18		1			
St. Louis Cardinals	NL	1942	106	48	0.688	1 of 8	+2	1	1			
St. Louis Cardinals	NL	1941	97	56	0.634	2 of 8	2.5					
St. Louis Cardinals	NL	1940	84	69	0.549	3 of 8	16					
St. Louis Cardinals	NL	1939	92	61	0.601	2 of 8	4.5					
St. Louis Cardinals	NL	1938	71	80	0.470	6 of 8	17.5					
St. Louis Cardinals	NL	1937	81	73	0.526	4 of 8	15					
St. Louis Cardinals	NL	1936	87	67	0.565	2t of 8	5					
St. Louis Cardinals	NL	1935	96	58	0.623	2 of 8	4					
St. Louis Cardinals	NL	1934	95	58	0.621	1 of 8	+2	1	1			
St. Louis Cardinals	NL	1933	82	71	0.536	5 of 8	9.5					
St. Louis Cardinals	NL	1932	72	82	0.468	6t of 8	18					
St. Louis Cardinals	NL	1931	101	53	0.656	1 of 8	+13	1	1			
St. Louis Cardinals	NL	1930	92	62	0.597	1 of 8	+2		1			
St. Louis Cardinals	NL	1929	78	74	0.513	4 of 8	20					
St. Louis Cardinals	NL	1928	95	59	0.617	1 of 8	+2		1			
St. Louis Cardinals	NL	1927	92	61	0.601	2 of 8	1.5					
St. Louis Cardinals	NL	1926	89	65	0.578	1 of 8	+2	1	1			
St. Louis Cardinals	NL	1925	77	76	0.503	4 of 8	18					
St. Louis Cardinals	NL	1924	65	89	0.422	6 of 8	28.5					
St. Louis Cardinals	NL	1923	79	74	0.516	5 of 8	16					

Team	League	Year	W	L	Win%	Fin	GB/GA	WS	Lge	LDS	Div	WC
St. Louis Cardinals	NL	1922	85	69	0.552	3t of 8	8					
St. Louis Cardinals	NL	1921	87	66	0.569	3 of 8	7					
St. Louis Cardinals	NL	1920	75	79	0.487	5t of 8	18					
St. Louis Cardinals	NL	1919	54	83	0.394	7 of 8	40.5					
St. Louis Cardinals	NL	1918	51	78	0.395	8 of 8	33					
St. Louis Cardinals	NL	1917	82	70	0.539	3 of 8	15					
St. Louis Cardinals	NL	1916	60	93	0.392	7t of 8	33.5					
St. Louis Cardinals	NL	1915	72	81	0.471	6 of 8	18.5					
St. Louis Cardinals	NL	1914	81	72	0.529	3 of 8	13					
St. Louis Cardinals	NL	1913	51	99	0.340	8 of 8	49					
St. Louis Cardinals	NL	1912	63	90	0.412	6 of 8	41					
St. Louis Cardinals	NL	1911	75	74	0.503	5 of 8	22					
St. Louis Cardinals	NL	1910	63	90	0.412	7 of 8	40.5					
St. Louis Cardinals	NL	1909	54	98	0.355	7 of 8	56					
St. Louis Cardinals	NL	1908	49	105	0.318	8 of 8	50					
St. Louis Cardinals	NL	1907	52	101	0.340	8 of 8	55.5					
St. Louis Cardinals	NL	1906	52	98	0.347	7 of 8	63					
St. Louis Cardinals	NL	1905	58	96	0.377	6 of 8	47.5					
St. Louis Cardinals	NL	1904	75	79	0.487	5 of 8	31.5					
St. Louis Cardinals	NL	1903	43	94	0.314	8 of 8	46.5					
St. Louis Cardinals	NL	1902	56	78	0.418	6 of 8	44.5					
St. Louis Cardinals	NL	1901	76	64	0.543	4 of 8	14.5					
St. Louis Cardinals	NL	1900	65	75	0.464	5t of 8	19					
St. Louis Perfectos	NL	1899	84	67	0.556	5 of 12	18.5					
St. Louis Browns	NL	1898	39	111	0.260	12 of 12	63.5					
St. Louis Browns	NL	1897	29	102	0.221	12 of 12	63.5					
St. Louis Browns	NL	1896	40	90	0.308	11 of 12	50.5					
St. Louis Browns	NL	1895	39	92	0.298	11 of 12	48.5					
St. Louis Browns	NL	1894	56	76	0.424	9 of 12	35					
St. Louis Browns	NL	1893	57	75	0.432	10 of 12	30.5					
St. Louis Browns	NL	1892	56	94	0.373	9, 11 of 12	20.5, 28.5					
St. Louis Browns	AA	1891	86	52	0.623	2 of 9	8.5					
St. Louis Browns	AA	1890	78	58	0.574	3 of 9	12					
St. Louis Browns	AA	1889	90	45	0.667	2 of 8	2					
St. Louis Browns	AA	1888	92	43	0.681	1 of 8	+6.5		1			
St. Louis Browns	AA	1887	95	40	0.704	1 of 8	+14		1			
St. Louis Browns	AA	1886	93	46	0.669	1 of 8	+12		1			
St. Louis Browns	AA	1885	79	33	0.705	1 of 8	+16		1			
St. Louis Browns	AA	1884	67	40	0.626	4 of 13	8					
St. Louis Browns	AA	1883	65	33	0.663	2 of 8	1					
St. Louis Brown Stockings	AA	1882	37	43	0.463	5 of 6	18					
			10107	9419	0.518			10	21	6	10	1

* In 2001 the Astros and Cardinals finished the regular season with the same won-loss record. Since both teams made the playoffs and the Astros won the regular season series between the two teams, they won the NL Central Division Title and St. Louis won the NL Wild Card.

** The 1981 season was divided into two halves due to a players strike in the middle of the season. Both halves were played with teams playing an uneven amount of games. In the second half of the season the Montreal Expos played one more game than the Cardinals and beat St. Louis for the division by 0.5 games.

San Diego Padres

Stats

History
Year of Origin 1969   Years Played 42

Score & Rank
Total Points Score .... 16.6   Average Points Score 0.40
Total Points Rank 24   Average Points Rank 24

Postseason Results

Postseason Results	No.	Years
World Series Won	0	
League Championship Series Won	2	1984, 1998
League Division Series Won	1	1998
World Series Lost	2	1984, 1998
League Championship Series Lost	0	
League Division Series Lost	3	1996, 2005, 2006

Postseason Won-Loss Records and Winning Percentages

	Postseason Games		Postseason Series	
All Postseason Series	12-22	.353	3-5	.375
World Series	1-8	.111	0-2	.000
League Championship Series	7-4	.636	2-0	1.000
League Division Series	4-10	.286	1-3	.250

Regular Season Results
All-Time Won-Loss Record 3098-3580
All-Time Winning Percentage .... .464

	No.	Years
League Titles before 1969	0	
Division Titles	5	1984, 1996, 1998, 2005, 2006
Wild Cards	0	

Regular Season High & Low Points

		Year(s)
Most Wins in a Season	98	1998
Most Losses in a Season	111	1969
Highest Winning Percentage	.605	1998
Lowest Winning Percentage	.321	1969
Longest Streak with Won-Loss Record .500 or Higher	4 years	1982-1985, 2004-2007
Longest Streak with Won-Loss Record Below .500	9 years	1969-1977

Years with .500 record or Better
1960's .... 0 (out of 1)
1970's 1
1980's 6
1990's 4
2000's 4
2010's 1
16 out of 42 seasons played = 38%

Years Making Postseason
1960's 0
1970's 0
1980's 1
1990's 2
2000's 2
2010's 0
5 out of 42 seasons played = 12%

Streaks

- 1996-1998: Won two Division Titles, one League Division Series, and one League Championship Series in three years.
- 2005-2006: Won two Division Titles in two years.

Extra Bases

- San Diego has a 1-8 won-loss record in their two World Series appearances.
- The Padres won the 1996 National League West Division despite playing forty-four games in three countries and ten cities from July 22nd through September 8th, winning twenty-six games and losing eighteen.

Scoring Opportunities

1980's
- San Diego won the National League West Division in 1984 and beat the Cubs in the LCS by winning the last three games of the series after losing the first two. In the World Series the Padres faced the Tigers. In Game 1 San Diego trailed by one run in the bottom of the seventh inning. Their first batter up hit a double to right field but tried to stretch it into a triple and was thrown out at third base. The Padres lost the game 3-2 and won Game 2. In Game 3 San Diego gave up four runs in the second inning and lost the game 5-2. The Padres only had five hits in Game 4 and only had two after the third inning and they lost the game 4-2. In Game 5 San Diego only trailed by one run in the bottom of the eighth inning but they gave up a three run home run and lost the game 8-4 to lose the series.

1990's
- In 1996 the Padres won the National League West Division on the last day of the year by completing a sweep over the Dodgers in the last series of the season. In the LDS San Diego played the Cardinals and gave up a three-run home run in the first inning of Game 1. The Padres scored one run in the top of the sixth inning and had runners on first and third with two outs, but their next batter struck out. In the top of the seventh and the top of the ninth they had runners on first and second with two outs but their next batter up in each inning was retired and they lost the game 3-1. In Game 2 San Diego tied the score at four in the top of the eighth inning and had runners on first and third with two outs, but their next batter up popped out. In the bottom of the inning the Padres gave up two walks and threw a wild pitch that put St. Louis runners on second and third with one out. The next Cardinals batter

hit a line drive that went off the Padres pitcher's glove and over to the second baseman, who threw to first for an out as the St. Louis go ahead run scored from third base. San Diego was retired in order in the top of the ninth and lost 5-4. In Game 3 the Padres tied the score at five in the bottom of the eighth but in the top of the ninth they gave up a two-run home run and they lost the game 7-5 and lost the series in a sweep.

- The Padres won the National League West Division in 1998 with a franchise high 98 wins and .605 winning percentage. They beat the Astros in the LDS and the Braves in the LCS and made their second World Series appearance where they played the Yankees team that won 114 regular season games. In Game 1 San Diego had a 5-2 lead after six innings but gave up a three run home run and a grand slam in the bottom of the seventh inning and they lost the game 9-6. In Game 2 the Padres gave up sixteen hits and nine runs and lost the game 9-3. In Game 3 San Diego had a 3-0 lead after six innings but gave up a solo home run and another run on an error in the top of the seventh and gave up two walks and a three run home run in the top of the eighth. In the bottom of the eighth the Padres scored one run and in the bottom of the ninth they trailed by one and had runners on first and third with two outs, but their next batter struck out and they lost 5-4. In Game 4 San Diego trailed by three runs in the bottom of the eighth when they had the bases loaded with two outs, but their next batter flied out and they lost the game 3-0 and lost the series in a sweep.

2000's

- In 2005 San Diego won the National League West Division and played St. Louis in the LDS. The Padres were not close in any of the games and were beaten 8-5, 6-2, and 7-4. They outhit the Cardinals 32-29 but were outscored 21-11 and lost the series in a sweep.
- San Diego repeated as National League West Division champs in 2006 and faced the Cardinals again in the LDS. The Padres lost Game 1 5-1 and only had four hits in Game 2 and lost the game 2-0. San Diego won Game 3, and Game 4 was tied at two after five innings. But in the bottom of the sixth the Padres gave up three hits, one walk, a hits batsman, and one error. They let four runs score in the inning and lost the game 6-2 to lose the series.
- In 2007 the Padres had a 2.5 game lead for the National League Wild Card on September 20th. But they lost six out of their last ten regular season games, including three against Colorado, and finished the season tied with the Rockies for the final playoff spot. Colorado went 8-1 after the 20th. In the one game playoff the game went into extra innings with the score tied at six. San Diego hit a two-run home run in the top of the thirteenth to take a two run lead. But in the bottom of the inning they gave up two doubles and a triple to the first three batters which tied the score at eight. The Padres walked the next Rockies batter intentionally and then San Diego gave up a sacrifice fly to right field. The Colorado runner on third tagged up and slid head first into home plate and although it looked like he missed the plate he was called safe and the Padres lost 9-8.

2010's

• The Padres were in first place in the National League West Division in 2010 from June 18th to September 15th. On August 25th San Diego had the best record in the National League at 76-49 and led San Francisco by 6.5 games in the NL West. But the Padres lost their next ten games in a row while the Giants went 5-4 and on September 5th San Diego only led San Francisco by one game. The Padres went 14-13 the rest of the season while the Giants went 16-9. On the last day of the season on October 3rd San Diego trailed San Francisco by one game in the NL West and was tied with Atlanta for the NL Wild Card spot. The Padres last game of the season was against the Giants in San Francisco. San Diego needed to win to force a tie for the NL West Division and the NL Wild Card but they lost the game 3-0 and finished two games behind the Giants for the NL West Division title and one game behind the Braves for the NL Wild Card spot. After August 25th San Diego went 14-23, which was the worst record in the National League for that period. Over the same time San Francisco went 21-13 and Atlanta went 18-17.

Year-to-Year Figures

Team Name	League	Year	W	L	Win%	Fin	GB/GA	WS	Lge	LDS	Div	WC
San Diego Padres	NL West	2010	90	72	0.556	2 of 5	2					
San Diego Padres	NL West	2009	75	87	0.463	4 of 5	20					
San Diego Padres	NL West	2008	63	99	0.389	5 of 5	21					
San Diego Padres	NL West	2007	89	74	0.546	3 of 5	1.5					
San Diego Padres	NL West	2006	88	74	0.543	1 of 5	0*				1	
San Diego Padres	NL West	2005	82	80	0.506	1 of 5	+5				1	
San Diego Padres	NL West	2004	87	75	0.537	3 of 5	6					
San Diego Padres	NL West	2003	64	98	0.395	5 of 5	36.5					
San Diego Padres	NL West	2002	66	96	0.407	5 of 5	32					
San Diego Padres	NL West	2001	79	83	0.488	4 of 5	13					
San Diego Padres	NL West	2000	76	86	0.469	5 of 5	21					
San Diego Padres	NL West	1999	74	88	0.457	4 of 5	26					
San Diego Padres	NL West	1998	98	64	0.605	1 of 5	+9.5		1	1	1	
San Diego Padres	NL West	1997	76	86	0.469	4 of 4	14					
San Diego Padres	NL West	1996	91	71	0.562	1 of 4	+1				1	
San Diego Padres	NL West	1995	70	74	0.486	3 of 4	8					
San Diego Padres	NL West	1994	47	70	0.402	4 of 4	12.5					
San Diego Padres	NL West	1993	61	101	0.377	7 of 7	43					
San Diego Padres	NL West	1992	82	80	0.506	3 of 6	16					
San Diego Padres	NL West	1991	84	78	0.519	3 of 6	10					
San Diego Padres	NL West	1990	75	87	0.463	4t of 6	16					
San Diego Padres	NL West	1989	89	73	0.549	2 of 6	3					
San Diego Padres	NL West	1988	83	78	0.516	3 of 6	11					
San Diego Padres	NL West	1987	65	97	0.401	6 of 6	25					
San Diego Padres	NL West	1986	74	88	0.457	4 of 6	22					
San Diego Padres	NL West	1985	83	79	0.512	3t of 6	12					
San Diego Padres	NL West	1984	92	70	0.568	1 of 6	+12		1		1	
San Diego Padres	NL West	1983	81	81	0.500	4 of 6	10					
San Diego Padres	NL West	1982	81	81	0.500	4 of 6	8					
San Diego Padres	NL West	1981	41	69	0.373	6, 6 of 6	12.5, 15.5					
San Diego Padres	NL West	1980	73	89	0.451	6 of 6	19.5					
San Diego Padres	NL West	1979	68	93	0.422	5 of 6	22					
San Diego Padres	NL West	1978	84	78	0.519	4 of 6	11					
San Diego Padres	NL West	1977	69	93	0.426	5 of 6	29					
San Diego Padres	NL West	1976	73	89	0.451	5 of 6	29					
San Diego Padres	NL West	1975	71	91	0.438	4 of 6	37					
San Diego Padres	NL West	1974	60	102	0.370	6 of 6	42					
San Diego Padres	NL West	1973	60	102	0.370	6 of 6	39					
San Diego Padres	NL West	1972	58	95	0.379	6 of 6	36.5					
San Diego Padres	NL West	1971	61	100	0.379	6 of 6	28.5					
San Diego Padres	NL West	1970	63	99	0.389	6 of 6	39					
San Diego Padres	NL West	1969	52	110	0.321	6 of 6	41					
			3098	3580	0.464			0	2	1	5	0

* In 2006 the Dodgers and Padres finished the regular season with the same won-loss record. Since both teams made the playoffs and San Diego won the regular season series between the two teams, they won the NL West Division Title and Los Angeles won the NL Wild Card.

San Francisco Giants

Stats

History
Year of Origin 1883

Years Played...128

Score & Rank
Total Points Score 154.8
Total Points Rank 5

Average Points Score...1.21
Average Points Rank...8

Postseason Results	No.	Years
World Series Won.................................	6	1905, 1921, 1922, 1933, 1954, 2010
League Championship Series Won	3	1989, 2002, 2010
League Division Series Won.............................	2	2002, 2010
World Series Lost	12	1911, 1912, 1913, 1917, 1923, 1924, 1936, 1937, 1951, 1962 1989, 2002
League Championship Series Lost.......................	2	1971, 1987,
League Division Series Lost	3	1997, 2000, 2003

Postseason Won-Loss Records and Winning Percentages

	Postseason Games		Postseason Series	
All Postseason Series..............................	74-77	.490	11-17	.414
World Series...	49-54	.476	6-12	.333
League Championship Series	16-11	.593	3-2	.600
League Division Series...........................	9-12	.429	2-3	.400

Regular Season Results
All-Time Won-Loss Record 10436-8958
All-Time Winning Percentage .... .538

	No.	Years
League Titles before 1969	18	1888, 1889, 1904, 1905, 1911, 1912, 1913, 1917, 1921, 1922, 1923, 1924, 1933, 1936, 1937, 1951, 1954, 1962
Division Titles......................................	7	1971, 1987, 1989, 1997, 2000, 2003, 2010
Wild Cards	1	2002

Regular Season High & Low Points		Year(s)
Most Wins in a Season	106	1904
Most Losses in a Season..	100	1985
Highest Winning Percentage	.759	1885
Lowest Winning Percentage....................................	.353	1902
Longest Streak with Won-Loss Record .500 or Higher	14 years	1958-1971
Longest Streak with Won-Loss Record Below .500..........	4 years	1899-1902, 1974-1977, 2005-2008

Years with .500 record or Better

1880's	6
1890's	6
1900's	7
1910's	9
1920's	9
1930's	9
1940's	4
1950's	7
1960's	10
1970's	4
1980's	6
1990's	5
2000's	6
2010's	1

89 out of 128 seasons played = 70%

Years Making Postseason

1880's	No Postseason
1890's	No Postseason
1900's	1
1910's	4
1920's	4
1930's	3
1940's	0
1950's	2
1960's	1
1970's	1
1980's	2
1990's	1
2000's	3
2010's	1

23 out of 128 seasons played = 18%

Streaks

- 1911-1913: Won three League Titles in three years.
- 1921-1924: Won two World Series and four League Titles in four years.
- 1933-1937: Won three League Titles and one World Series in five years.
- 1951-1954: Won one World Series and two League Titles in four years.
- 1987-1989: Won two Division Titles and one League Championship Series in three years.
- 1997-2003: Won one League Championship Series, one League Division Series, three Division Titles, and one Wild Card in seven years.

Extra Bases

- In 1916 the New York Giants had a twenty-six game winning streak in September from the 7th to the 30th. This is the record for longest consecutive games wining streak. However, after the twelfth game there was a game that ended as a 1-1 tie.
- The Giants are the last National League team to win four league titles in a row. They did it from 1921-1924.
- In 2010 the Giants won their first World Series as a franchise in the city of San Francisco.

Scoring Opportunities

1880's
- In 1885 the New York Giants were in a close race for the National League title all season long with the Chicago White Stockings and were only two games behind Chicago on September 29th when the two teams met for a four game series in Chicago. If the Giants won all four games

they would have a two game lead, and if New York won three out of the four the teams would be tied for first place. But the Giants lost the first three games of the series and won the last one and fell to four games behind the White Stockings. New York won three of their last four games of the year and Chicago lost three of their last four games but the Giants finished in second place two games behind the White Stockings in the standings.

1900's

- The Giants should have won the National League pennant in 1908, but an apparent victory against the Cubs on September 23rd was ruled a tie, and the two teams had to make up the game at the end of the year because they were tied for first place. In the game on the 23rd the Giants had runners on first and third in the bottom of the ninth inning with two outs and their next batter singled in the game winning run. But their runner on first base did not advance to second base. He turned to go back to the dugout as he saw fans running onto the field. The Cubs retrieved a ball, it is not sure if it was the actual ball that had been hit, and touched second base therefore getting the runner out, and canceling the run that had scored. The umpire called the game a tie because of darkness. The Giants protested but the National League President and Board of Directors agreed that the game was a tie and should be replayed if needed. On October 8th the make up game was played and the Giants gave up four runs in the third inning and lost the game 4-2 to lose the pennant they technically should have won.

1910's

- In 1911 the Giants won the National League pennant and played the Philadelphia A's in the World Series. New York won Game 1 and Game 2 was tied at one after five innings. In the bottom of the sixth the Giants got the first two A's batters out but then gave up a double and a two run home run. New York's last nine batters were retired in order and they lost the game 3-1. In Game 3 the Giants led 1-0 after eight innings but in the top of the ninth with one out they gave up a solo home run that tied the game. The game went into extra innings and in the top of the eleventh New York gave up three hits and committed two errors and let in two runs. In the bottom of the inning the Giants scored one run and had a runner on first with two outs, but the runner was caught stealing second and they lost 3-2. In Game 4 New York trailed by two runs in the top of the eighth when they had runners on first and second with two outs but their next batter up fouled out to the catcher and they lost the game 4-2. The Giants won Game 5 but lost Game 6 13-2 and lost the series.
- New York repeated as National League champs in 1912 and faced the Red Sox in the World Series. The Giants led Game 1 2-1 after six innings but gave up four hits in the top of the seventh and let in three runs with two outs. In the bottom of the ninth New York scored one run and had runners on first and third with one out, but their next two batters both struck out and they lost 4-3. Game 2 ended in a 6-6 tie after eleven innings due to darkness and the

Giants won Game 3. In Game 4 New York trailed by one run when they had runners on first and third with two outs in the bottom of the eighth, but their next batter up struck out and they lost the game 3-1. In Game 5 the Giants trailed by one run in the top of the seventh when they had a runner on first with two outs, but their next batter grounded out and their final six batters were retired in order and they lost the game 2-1. New York won Games 6 & 7 to tie the series at three games apiece. Game 8 was tied at one after nine innings. The Giants scored one run in the top of the tenth and had a runner on second with one out, but their next two batters struck out and grounded out. In the bottom of the inning New York let the first Boston batter reach base on an error. They walked a batter with one out and the following Red Sox hitter singled which drove in the tying run. The Giants walked the next batter intentionally to load the bases and the next Boston batter hit a sacrifice fly that drove in the game-winning run and New York lost 3-2 and lost the series. Three of the Giants losses in the series were by one run.

- In 1913 the Giants won their third straight National League pennant and played the Philadelphia Athletics in the World Series. In Game 1 New York trailed by one run in the bottom of the seventh inning when they had runners on first and third with one out, but their next batter hit into a double play and they lost the game 6-4. The Giants won Game 2 but lost Game 3 8-2, and in Game 4 they trailed 6-0 after six innings. New York hit a three-run homer in the top of the seventh and in the top of the eighth scored two runs and had the tying run at third with two outs, but their next batter grounded out and they lost the game 6-5. In Game 5 the Giants only had two hits and their last eleven batters were retired in order and they lost the game 3-1 to lose the series.

- The Giants won the National League pennant in 1917 and met the White Sox in the World Series. In Game 1 New York only trailed by one run after five innings but only got one hit the rest of the game and lost the game 2-1. They lost Game 2 7-2, but won Games 3 & 4 to tie the series. In Game 5 the Giants had a 5-2 lead in the bottom of the seventh, but gave up three hits, one walk, one error, and let in three runs, which tied the score. In the bottom of the eighth New York gave up four hits and one error and let in three more runs and they lost the game 8-5. In Game 6 the Giants trailed by one run and had the tying run on third base with two outs in the fifth and seventh innings, but in each inning their next batter up was retired. In the bottom of the ninth New York trailed by two runs and their first batter up was hit by a pitch, but their next three hitters all got out and they lost the game 4-2 and lost the series.

1920's

- New York won the National League pennant for the third straight year in 1923 and played the Yankees in the World Series where they won Game 1. In Game 2 the Giants trailed by two runs in the bottom of the sixth when they had runners on first and second with no outs, but their next two batters grounded out and hit into a double play. In the bottom of the eighth the Giants had runners on first and second with two outs, but their next batter up flied out and they lost the game 4-2. The Giants won Game 3 to take a two games to one series lead, but then they lost Game 4 8-1 and Game 5 8-1. In Game 6 the Giants led 4-1 after seven innings but in the top of the eighth they gave up three hits, three walks, and one error, and let in five runs and lost the game 6-4 and lost the series.

• In 1924 New York won their fourth straight National League pennant and faced the Washington Senators in the World Series. The Giants won Game 1 and Game 2 was tied at three in the bottom of the ninth. New York walked the first Senators batter and the second hitter sacrificed bunted the runner to second. The following batter doubled and drove in the game winning run and the Giants lost 2-1. New York won Game 3, lost Game 4 7-4, and won Game 5. In Game 6 the Giants led 1-0 until they gave up a single with two outs in the bottom of the fifth that drove in two runs. New York had a runner on first base with one out in the top of the seventh and ninth innings, but they couldn't tie the score in either inning and they lost the game 2-1. The Giants led Game 7 3-1 after seven innings but in the bottom of the eighth they gave up a double, single, and walk with one out, and gave up single with two outs that drove in two runs and tied the game at three. In the top of the ninth New York had runners on first and third with one out, but their next two batters struck out and grounded out and the game went into extra innings. The Giants got their first batter up on base in the tenth, eleventh, and twelfth innings but they couldn't score in any inning. In the bottom of the twelfth New York gave up two errors and two doubles and let in the game winning run and lost the game 4-3 to lose the series.

• The Giants were only a half game behind St. Louis for the 1928 National League pennant on September 27th with five games left in the season. But New York lost three of their last five games and the Cardinals won three of their last four games. The Giants finished in second place two games behind St. Louis. From August 21st to 31st New York went 1-10.

1930's

• New York led the National League in 1934 from June 6th to September 26th. The Giants had a seven game lead over the Cardinals on September 7th but lost seven of their next ten games. New York still had a three game lead over St. Louis on September 22nd with seven games left in the season, but the Giants lost six of their last seven games of the year, including their last five, and finished the season in second place two games behind the Cardinals who went 7-2 over the same period. After September 6th New York went 8-13 while St. Louis went 18-5.

• In 1936 the Giants won the National League pennant and met the Yankees in the World Series. The Giants won Game 1 but gave up seventeen hits in Game 2 and lost the game 18-4. Game 3 was tied at one after seven innings. The Giants had runners on first and second with one out in the top of the eighth, but their next two batters grounded out and flied out. In the bottom of the inning they had two Yankees batters out but runners were on first and third. The next Yankees batter singled and drove in the go-ahead run. The Giants got a runner on first base in the top of the ninth with two outs, but their next batter grounded out and they lost 2-1. The Giants lost Game 4 5-2 and won Game 5. In Game 6 they only trailed 6-5 in the top of the ninth inning but gave up five hits, four walks, and seven runs and lost the game 13-5 to lose the series.

- The Giants repeated as National League champs in 1937 and faced the Yankees again in the World Series. The Giants lost Games 1 & 2 both by the score of 8-1 and lost Game 3 5-1. They won Game 4 and in Game 5 they trailed by two runs after five innings. In the bottom of the sixth the Giants first two hitters got on base, but their next three batters all got out. In the bottom of the seventh they had runners on first and second with two outs, but their next batter up grounded out and they lost the game 4-2 and lost the series.

1950's

- In 1951 New York came back from a thirteen game deficit on August 11th to tie Brooklyn for the National League pennant at the end of the regular season. The Giants won twelve of their last thirteen games and in the best of three game tiebreaker playoff series New York won the NL pennant by hitting a three-run home run in the bottom of the ninth inning of the third game. In the World Series the Giants played the Yankees and won Game 1. In Game 2 the Giants trailed by one run the top of the seventh inning when they had runners on first and third with two outs, but their next batter up fouled out and they lost the game 3-1. The Giants won Game 3 but lost Game 4 6-2 and lost Game 5 13-1. In Game 6 the Giants trailed by thee runs when they loaded the bases in the top of the eighth inning with two outs, but their next batter up struck out. In the top of the ninth the Giants first three batters singled and they scored two runs with two sacrifice flies. They had the tying run on second base with two outs, but their next batter up lined out and they lost the game 4-3 and lost the series.
- The San Francisco Giants were in first place in the National League either tied or by themselves for all but one day from July 4th to September 19th in 1959. They had a two game lead over the Braves and Dodgers on September 17th but lost three games in a row to Los Angeles and lost seven of their last eight games of the season. San Francisco ended the regular season three games behind the Dodgers and Braves who both went 6-2 after the 17th and tied for first place. LA beat Milwaukee in a best of three playoff series for the National League pennant and won the World Series.

1960's

- The Giants beat the Dodgers in a best of three games playoff for the National League pennant in 1962 and played the Yankees in the World Series. San Francisco lost Game 1 6-2, and won Game 2 to even the series. Game 3 was tied at zero after six innings. In the bottom of the seventh the Giants gave up singles to the first three Yankees batters, committed two errors, hit a batter, and gave up three runs. In the top of the ninth San Francisco hit a two-run home run but they lost the game 3-2. The Giants won Game 4 and Game 5 was tied at two after seven innings. In the bottom of the eighth San Francisco got the first Yankees batter out, but then gave up two singles and a three-run home run and the Giants lost the game 5-3. San Francisco won Game 6 to tie the series again and force Game 7. In the series finale the Giants gave up two singles and a walk to the first three Yankees batters in the top of the fifth inning. The next New York batter hit a ground ball and San Francisco turned a double play and let one run score in order to prevent a big inning. Down by one run the Giants had runners on second and third with two outs in the bottom of the ninth, but their next batter up lined out and they lost 1-0 and lost the series.

- In 1965 San Francisco had a four game lead over Los Angeles in the National League on September 20th. But the rest of the season the Giants went 5-7 and the Dodgers went 11-1 and San Francisco finished the year in second place two games behind LA.
- The Giants were in a close race for the National League pennant in 1966. They were tied for first place with Pittsburgh on August 31st with Los Angeles three games back. But San Francisco lost seven of their next ten games and twelve of their next nineteen. They won eight of their last nine games of the year but finished in second place 1.5 games behind the Dodgers. After August 31st San Francisco went 15-13, Pittsburgh went 14-15, and Los Angeles went 21-10.
- In 1969 San Francisco led the National League West Division by a half game over Atlanta on September 22nd with eight games left in the season. But the rest of the year the Giants went 3-5 while the Braves went 6-1. Atlanta won ten of their last eleven games of the season and San Francisco finished in second place three games behind the Braves.

1970's

- San Francisco won the National League West Division in 1971 by one game over the Dodgers. In the LCS the Giants played Pittsburgh, won Game 1, and lost Game 2 9-4. Game 3 was tied at one after seven innings. In the top of the eighth inning San Francisco had runners on first and second with two outs, but their next batter up grounded out. In the bottom of the inning they got the first two Pirates batters out, but then gave up a solo home run. The Giants were retired in order in the top of the ninth and lost 2-1. Then they lost Game 4 9-5 and lost the series.

1980's

- In 1982 the Giants were in a close race for the National League West Division title with the Braves and Dodgers. On September 27th San Francisco was tied with Atlanta for second place one game behind LA. The Giants next two games were against the Braves at home, but San Francisco lost them both 7-0 and 8-3. The Giants went 3-2 the rest of the year but so did the Dodgers and Atlanta, and San Francisco finished the year in third place, two games behind the Braves who won the division by one game over LA.

- The Giants won the National League West Division in 1987 and played St. Louis in the LCS. Game 1 was tied at two in the bottom of the sixth inning. San Francisco got the first Cardinals batter out but gave up four straight hits and five hits in the inning and let in three runs. In the top of the eighth the Giants trailed by two runs and had the bases loaded with two outs, but their next batter up flied out and they lost the game 5-3. San Francisco won Game 2 and had a 4-2 lead in Game 3 after six innings. But in the top of the seventh they gave up five singles in a row and let in four runs in the inning. The Giants hit a solo home run in the bottom of the ninth but lost the game 6-5. San Francisco won Games 4 & 5 to take a three game to two lead in the series. In Game 6 the Giants gave up a triple, a sacrifice fly, and one run in the bottom of the second inning. In the top of the fifth San Francisco got their first two batters on base, but their next three hitters all got out. In the top of the sixth the Giants had a runner on second base with one out, but their next two batters both flied out and they lost the game 1-0. San Francisco lost Game 7 6-0 and lost the series they led three games to two.

- In 1989 the Giants won the National League West Division and beat the Cubs in the LCS. In the World Series San Francisco met the A's in the 'Battle of the Bay' series and the Giants lost Game 1 5-0 and Game 2 5-1 and only had nine hits total in the two games. Before Game 3 in San Francisco there was an earthquake and the series was suspended for ten days. When the series resumed the Giants lost Game 3 13-7 and Game 4 9-6 and lost the series in a sweep. San Francisco was outscored 32-14 in the four games.

1990's

- San Francisco won 103 games in 1993 and led the National League West Division from May 11th to September 9th. The Giants led by 3.5 games over Atlanta on September 6th but then lost their next eight games and fell to 3.5 games behind the Braves on September 15th. The Giants won fourteen of their next sixteen games and were tied for first place with Atlanta with one game left in the season. On the last day of the year the Braves beat Colorado but the Giants lost to the Dodgers 12-1 and lost the division by one game.

- In 1997 the Giants won the National League West Division and faced Florida in the LDS. Game 1 was tied at one in the bottom of the ninth. San Francisco gave up a single, a hit batter, a sacrifice bunt, and an intentional walk that loaded the bases. The next Florida batter grounded out and the Giants got the force out at home plate for the second out of the inning. But the next Marlins hitter singled and drove in the game winning run and San Francisco lost 2-1. In Game 2 the Giants tied the score at six in the top of the ninth. But in the bottom of the inning they gave up a single, a stolen base, a walk, and another single which drove in the game winning run and they lost the game 7-6. San Francisco lost Game 3 6-2 and was swept in the series.

- The Giants tied the Cubs for the National League Wild Card in 1998 and played a one game playoff to determine the final postseason spot. San Francisco trailed by four runs in the top of the seventh inning when they had the bases loaded with two outs, but their next batter grounded out. In the top of the ninth the Giants trailed by five runs when they rallied. They started the inning with three straight singles and a walk. One run scored and the bases were loaded with no outs. Their next batter hit a sacrifice fly and the following batter hit a ground out, and each out scored one run. They were down by two runs with two outs and a runner on first, but their next batter hit a foul ball pop out and they lost 5-3 and missed the playoffs.

2000's

- San Francisco won the National League West Division in 2000 and played the Mets in the LDS. The Giants won Game 1 and in Game 2 they hit a three-run home run in the bottom of the ninth inning that tied the score at four. In the top of the tenth San Francisco got the first two Mets batters out but gave up a double and a single that drove in the go-ahead run. In the bottom of the inning the Giants had a runner on second base with one out but their base runner was thrown out at third on a ground ball to the shortstop and their next batter up struck out and they lost 5-4. In Game 3 San Francisco led 2-1 in the bottom of the eighth inning. The Giants had two Mets batters out with a runner on first, but gave up a stolen base and double that drove in the tying run. The game went into extra innings and San Francisco had two runners on in the top of the tenth, twelfth, and thirteenth innings but couldn't score in any inning. In the bottom of the thirteenth the Giants gave up a solo home run with one out and lost 3-2. In Game 4 San Francisco only had one hit and lost the game 4-0 to lose the series.
- In 2001 the Giants were in a close race for the National League West Division title with Arizona. Over the final month of the season San Francisco remained between 1.5 and three games out, but couldn't get any closer and finished the year two games behind the Diamondbacks. In the wild card race the Giants had a one game lead over St. Louis on September 9th. After the time off from the September 11th tragedy San Francisco lost three games in a row to Houston and fell to three games behind St. Louis for the wild card. The rest of the year the Giants went 10-5 but the Cardinals had the same record and San Francisco finished the season three games behind St. Louis for the final playoff spot.
- The Giants made the playoffs in 2002 as the National League Wild Card team. They beat the Braves in the LDS, and the Cardinals in the LCS. In the World Series the Giants met the Angels and won Game 1. Game 2 was tied at nine in the bottom of the eighth inning. San Francisco had two Angels batters out and there was a runner on first but the next batter hit a two-run home run. In the top of the ninth the Giants hit a solo home run but lost the game 11-10. San Francisco lost Game 3 10-4 and won Games 4 & 5 to take a three games to two series lead. In Game 6 the Giants had a 5-0 lead in the bottom of the seventh, but gave up a three-run home run with one out. They led 5-3 in the bottom of the eighth but gave up

a solo home run, two singles, and a double that drove in the tying and go ahead runs. San Francisco lost the game 6-5 and lost Game 7 4-1 to lose the series they were only six outs away from winning.

• In 2003 San Francisco won the National League West Division and played Florida in the LDS. The Giants won Game 1 but lost Game 2 9-5. Game 3 was tied at two after nine innings. In the top of the eleventh San Francisco scored the go-ahead run and had the bases loaded with one out, but their next two batters grounded out. In the bottom of the inning the Giants let the first Marlins batter reach base on an error and walked the second batter. The next Florida hitter sacrificed bunted the runners to second and third and San Francisco walked the next batter intentionally to load the bases. The next Marlins batter grounded out to the pitcher with the Giants getting the force out at home plate, but the following batter hit a single that drove in the tying and go ahead runs and San Francisco lost 4-3. Game 4 was tied at five after seven innings. In the bottom of the eighth the Giants got the first two Marlins batters out but gave up a single, a hit batter, and another singled which drove in two runs. In the top of the ninth San Francisco scored one run and had runners at first and second with two outs. Their next batter singled to left field and the runner from second tried to score the tying run, but was thrown out at home plate and the Giants lost the game 7-6 and lost the series.

• On September 22nd of the 2004 season San Francisco trailed Los Angeles by a half a game in the National League West Division and led the wild card race by half a game over Chicago, with the Astros three games back. But the Giants lost four of their next six games which included one loss to Houston and two losses to the Dodgers and they fell to three games back in the NL West and one game back in the wild card on September 29th. San Francisco won three out of their last four games, which included two wins against LA, but they finished the season two games back in the NL West and one game back in the wild card. After the 22nd the Giants went 5-5, the Dodgers went 7-4, and the Astros went 9-1.

Year-to-Year Figures

Team Name	League	Year	W	L	Win%	Fin	GB/GA	WS	Lge	LDS	Div	WC
San Francisco Giants	NL West	2010	92	70	0.568	1 of 5	+2	1	1	1	1	
San Francisco Giants	NL West	2009	88	74	0.543	3 of 5	7					
San Francisco Giants	NL West	2008	72	90	0.444	4 of 5	12					
San Francisco Giants	NL West	2007	71	91	0.438	5 of 5	19					
San Francisco Giants	NL West	2006	76	85	0.472	3 of 5	11.5					
San Francisco Giants	NL West	2005	75	87	0.463	3 of 5	7					
San Francisco Giants	NL West	2004	91	71	0.562	2 of 5	2					
San Francisco Giants	NL West	2003	100	61	0.621	1 of 5	+15.5				1	
San Francisco Giants	NL West	2002	95	66	0.590	2 of 5	2.5		1	1		1
San Francisco Giants	NL West	2001	90	72	0.556	2 of 5	2					
San Francisco Giants	NL West	2000	97	65	0.599	1 of 5	+11				1	
San Francisco Giants	NL West	1999	86	76	0.531	2 of 5	14					
San Francisco Giants	NL West	1998	89	74	0.546	2 of 5	9.5					
San Francisco Giants	NL West	1997	90	72	0.556	1 of 4	+2				1	
San Francisco Giants	NL West	1996	68	94	0.420	4 of 4	23					
San Francisco Giants	NL West	1995	67	77	0.465	4 of 4	11					
San Francisco Giants	NL West	1994	55	60	0.478	2 of 4	3.5					
San Francisco Giants	NL West	1993	103	59	0.636	2 of 7	1					
San Francisco Giants	NL West	1992	72	90	0.444	5 of 6	26					
San Francisco Giants	NL West	1991	75	87	0.463	4 of 6	19					
San Francisco Giants	NL West	1990	85	77	0.525	3 of 6	6					
San Francisco Giants	NL West	1989	92	70	0.568	1 of 6	+3		1		1	
San Francisco Giants	NL West	1988	83	79	0.512	4 of 6	11.5					
San Francisco Giants	NL West	1987	90	72	0.556	1 of 6	+6				1	
San Francisco Giants	NL West	1986	83	79	0.512	3 of 6	13					
San Francisco Giants	NL West	1985	62	100	0.383	6 of 6	33					
San Francisco Giants	NL West	1984	66	96	0.407	6 of 6	26					
San Francisco Giants	NL West	1983	79	83	0.488	5 of 6	12					
San Francisco Giants	NL West	1982	87	75	0.537	3 of 6	2					
San Francisco Giants	NL West	1981	56	55	0.505	5, 3 of 6	10, 3.5					
San Francisco Giants	NL West	1980	75	86	0.466	5 of 6	17					
San Francisco Giants	NL West	1979	71	91	0.438	4 of 6	19.5					
San Francisco Giants	NL West	1978	89	73	0.549	3 of 6	6					
San Francisco Giants	NL West	1977	75	87	0.463	4 of 6	23					
San Francisco Giants	NL West	1976	74	88	0.457	4 of 6	28					
San Francisco Giants	NL West	1975	80	81	0.497	3 of 6	27.5					
San Francisco Giants	NL West	1974	72	90	0.444	5 of 6	30					
San Francisco Giants	NL West	1973	88	74	0.543	3 of 6	11					
San Francisco Giants	NL West	1972	69	86	0.445	5 of 6	26.5					
San Francisco Giants	NL West	1971	90	72	0.556	1 of 6	+1				1	
San Francisco Giants	NL West	1970	86	76	0.531	3 of 6	16					
San Francisco Giants	NL West	1969	90	72	0.556	2 of 6	3					
San Francisco Giants	NL	1968	88	74	0.543	2 of 10	9					

Team Name	League	Year	W	L	Win%	Fin	GB/GA	WS	Lge	LDS	Div	WC
San Francisco Giants	NL	1967	91	71	0.562	2 of 10	10.5					
San Francisco Giants	NL	1966	93	68	0.578	2 of 10	1.5					
San Francisco Giants	NL	1965	95	67	0.586	2 of 10	2					
San Francisco Giants	NL	1964	90	72	0.556	4 of 10	3					
San Francisco Giants	NL	1963	88	74	0.543	3 of 10	11					
San Francisco Giants	NL	1962	103	62	0.624	1 of 10	+1		1			
San Francisco Giants	NL	1961	85	69	0.552	3 of 8	8					
San Francisco Giants	NL	1960	79	75	0.513	5 of 8	16					
San Francisco Giants	NL	1959	83	71	0.539	3 of 8	4					
San Francisco Giants	NL	1958	80	74	0.519	3 of 8	12					
New York Giants	NL	1957	69	85	0.448	6 of 8	26					
New York Giants	NL	1956	67	87	0.435	6 of 8	26					
New York Giants	NL	1955	80	74	0.519	3 of 8	18.5					
New York Giants	NL	1954	97	57	0.630	1 of 8	+5	1	1			
New York Giants	NL	1953	70	84	0.455	5 of 8	35					
New York Giants	NL	1952	92	62	0.597	2 of 8	4.5					
New York Giants	NL	1951	98	59	0.624	1 of 8	+1		1			
New York Giants	NL	1950	86	68	0.558	3 of 8	5					
New York Giants	NL	1949	73	81	0.474	5 of 8	24					
New York Giants	NL	1948	78	76	0.506	5 of 8	13.5					
New York Giants	NL	1947	81	73	0.526	4 of 8	13					
New York Giants	NL	1946	61	93	0.396	8 of 8	36					
New York Giants	NL	1945	78	74	0.513	5 of 8	19					
New York Giants	NL	1944	67	87	0.435	5 of 8	38					
New York Giants	NL	1943	55	98	0.359	8 of 8	49.5					
New York Giants	NL	1942	85	67	0.559	3 of 8	20					
New York Giants	NL	1941	74	79	0.484	5 of 8	25.5					
New York Giants	NL	1940	72	80	0.474	6 of 8	27.5					
New York Giants	NL	1939	77	74	0.510	5 of 8	18.5					
New York Giants	NL	1938	83	67	0.553	3 of 8	5					
New York Giants	NL	1937	95	57	0.625	1 of 8	+3		1			
New York Giants	NL	1936	92	62	0.597	1 of 8	+5		1			
New York Giants	NL	1935	91	62	0.595	3 of 8	8.5					
New York Giants	NL	1934	93	60	0.608	2 of 8	2					
New York Giants	NL	1933	91	61	0.599	1 of 8	+5	1	1			
New York Giants	NL	1932	72	82	0.468	6t of 8	18					
New York Giants	NL	1931	87	65	0.572	2 of 8	13					
New York Giants	NL	1930	87	67	0.565	3 of 8	5					
New York Giants	NL	1929	84	67	0.556	3 of 8	13.5					
New York Giants	NL	1928	93	61	0.604	2 of 8	2					
New York Giants	NL	1927	92	62	0.597	3 of 8	2					
New York Giants	NL	1926	74	77	0.490	5 of 8	13.5					
New York Giants	NL	1925	86	66	0.566	2 of 8	8.5					
New York Giants	NL	1924	93	60	0.608	1 of 8	+1.5		1			
New York Giants	NL	1923	95	58	0.621	1 of 8	+4.5		1			

Team Name	League	Year	W	L	Win%	Fin	GB/GA	WS	Lge	LDS	Div	WC
New York Giants	NL	1922	93	61	0.604	1 of 8	+7	1	1			
New York Giants	NL	1921	94	59	0.614	1 of 8	+4	1	1			
New York Giants	NL	1920	86	68	0.558	2 of 8	7					
New York Giants	NL	1919	87	53	0.621	2 of 8	9					
New York Giants	NL	1918	71	53	0.573	2 of 8	10.5					
New York Giants	NL	1917	98	56	0.636	1 of 8	+10		1			
New York Giants	NL	1916	86	66	0.566	4 of 8	7					
New York Giants	NL	1915	69	83	0.454	8 of 8	21					
New York Giants	NL	1914	84	70	0.545	2 of 8	10.5					
New York Giants	NL	1913	101	51	0.664	1 of 8	+12.5		1			
New York Giants	NL	1912	103	48	0.682	1 of 8	+10		1			
New York Giants	NL	1911	99	54	0.647	1 of 8	+7.5		1			
New York Giants	NL	1910	91	63	0.591	2 of 8	13					
New York Giants	NL	1909	92	61	0.601	3 of 8	18.5					
New York Giants	NL	1908	98	56	0.636	2t of 8	1					
New York Giants	NL	1907	82	71	0.536	4 of 8	25.5					
New York Giants	NL	1906	96	56	0.632	2 of 8	20					
New York Giants	NL	1905	105	48	0.686	1 of 8	+9	1	1			
New York Giants	NL	1904	106	47	0.693	1 of 8	+13		1			
New York Giants	NL	1903	84	55	0.604	2 of 8	6.5					
New York Giants	NL	1902	48	88	0.353	8 of 8	53.5					
New York Giants	NL	1901	52	85	0.380	7 of 8	37					
New York Giants	NL	1900	60	78	0.435	8 of 8	23					
New York Giants	NL	1899	60	90	0.400	10 of 12	42					
New York Giants	NL	1898	77	73	0.513	7 of 12	25.5					
New York Giants	NL	1897	83	48	0.634	3 of 12	9.5					
New York Giants	NL	1896	64	67	0.489	7 of 12	27					
New York Giants	NL	1895	66	65	0.504	9 of 12	21.5					
New York Giants	NL	1894	88	44	0.667	2 of 12	3					
New York Giants	NL	1893	68	64	0.515	5 of 12	19.5					
New York Giants	NL	1892	71	80	0.470	10,6 of 12	21, 13.5					
New York Giants	NL	1891	71	61	0.538	3 of 8	13					
New York Giants	NL	1890	63	68	0.481	6 of 8	24					
New York Giants	NL	1889	83	43	0.659	1 of 8	+1		1			
New York Giants	NL	1888	84	47	0.641	1 of 8	+9		1			
New York Giants	NL	1887	68	55	0.553	4 of 8	10.5					
New York Giants	NL	1886	75	44	0.630	3 of 8	12.5					
New York Giants	NL	1885	85	27	0.759	2 of 8	2					
New York Gothams	NL	1884	62	50	0.554	4 of 8	22					
New York Gothams	NL	1883	46	50	0.479	6 of 8	16					
			10436	8958	0.538			6	21	2	7	1

Seattle Mariners

Stats

History

Year of Origin 1977   Years Played.. 34

Score & Rank

Total Points Score ....9.9   Average Points Score..0.29
Total Points Rank 26   Average Points Rank.................................. 26 tied

Postseason Results	**No.**	**Years**
World Series Won....................................	0	
League Championship Series Won	0	
League Division Series Won........................	3	1995, 2000, 2001
World Series Lost	0	
League Championship Series Lost...............	3	1995, 2000, 2001
League Division Series Lost	1	1997

Postseason Won-Loss Records and Winning Percentages

	Postseason Games		**Postseason Series**	
All Postseason Series...............................	15-19	.441	3-4	.429
World Series..	0-0	.000	0-0	.000
League Championship Series	5-12	.294	0-3	.000
League Division Series..............................	10-7	.588	3-1	.750

Regular Season Results

All-Time Won-Loss Record 2522-2861
All-Time Winning Percentage .... .469

	No.	**Years**
League Titles before 1969	0	
Division Titles..	3	1995, 1997, 2001
Wild Cards	1	2000

Regular Season High & Low Points		**Year(s)**
Most Wins in a Season	116	2001
Most Losses in a Season............................	104	1978
Highest Winning Percentage	.716	2001
Lowest Winning Percentage.......................	.350	1978
Longest Streak with Won-Loss Record .500 or Higher	4 years	2000-2003
Longest Streak with Won-Loss Record Below .500	14 years	1977-1990

Years with .500 record or Better

1970's...0 (out of 3)
1980's... 0
1990's... 5
2000's... 6
2010's... 0
11 out of 34 seasons played = 32%

Years Making Postseason

1970's..0
1980's..0
1990's..2
2000's..2
2010's..0
4 out of 34 seasons played = 12%

Streaks

• 1995-2001: Won three League Division Series, three Division Titles, and one Wild Card in seven years.

Extra Bases

• In 2001 Seattle won an American League record 116 regular season games, which is tied with the 1906 Chicago Cubs for the major league record. The Mariners went 59-22 on the road that year, which is another AL record. Of the twenty-six series they had on the road, they won twenty-one, lost one, and tied four. Seattle went 57-24 at home that year, winning twenty-one of their home series and losing five.

• In three of their four postseason appearances, the Mariners have won the League Division Series and appeared in the League Championship Series.

Scoring Opportunities

1990's

• The Mariners beat the Angels in a one game playoff for the American League West Division in 1995. In the LDS Seattle came back from a two games to none deficit and beat the Yankees in the bottom of the eleventh inning in Game 5 to win the series. In the LCS the Mariners faced Cleveland and won Games 1 & 3 but lost Game 2 5-2 and Game 4 7-0. In Game 5 the Mariners trailed by one run in the top of the seventh inning when they had runners on first and third with one out, but their next two batters both struck out. In the top of the eighth Seattle had runners on first and second with one out, but their next batter up hit into a double play and they lost the game 3-2. In Game 6 the Mariners only had four hits and lost the game 4-0 to lose the series.

• In 1996 Seattle only trailed Texas by one game in the American League West Division and only trailed Baltimore by a half game in the AL Wild Card race on September 21st. But the Mariners lost six of their final eight games of the year and finished the season 4.5 games behind the Rangers in the division and 2.5 games behind the Orioles for the wild card. Texas went 5-2 after the 21st and Baltimore went 4-4.

• Seattle won the American League West Division in 1997 and played Baltimore in the LDS. The Mariners lost Games 1 & 2 both by the score of 9-3 and won Game 3. In Game 4 Seattle only had two hits and they were both in the second inning. They lost the game 3-1 and lost the series.

2000's

- The Mariners finished a half game behind Oakland in the American League West Division in 2000 but won the AL Wild Card spot. In the LDS Seattle beat the White Sox and faced the Yankees in the LCS. The Mariners won Game 1 and had a 1-0 lead after seven innings in Game 2. But in the bottom of the eighth they gave up eight hits, a sacrifice fly, a passed ball, and let in seven runs and lost the game 7-1. They lost Game 3 8-2 and only had one hit in Game 4 and lost the game 5-0. Seattle won Game 5 and had a 4-3 lead in Game 6 after six innings, but in the bottom of the seventh they gave up six hits, three walks, and six runs. The Mariners scored three runs in the top of the eighth, but lost the game 9-7 and lost the series.

- In 2001 the Mariners won 116 games in the regular season and tied the 1906 Chicago Cubs for most regular season wins in baseball history. They won the American League West Division and beat the Indians in the LDS. In the LCS Seattle played New York and in Game 1 the Mariners only had four hits and lost the game 4-2. In Game 2 they trailed by one run in the bottom of the seventh inning when they had runners on first and second with two outs, but their next batter up grounded out and they lost the game 3-2. Seattle won Game 3 and Game 4 was tied at one after eight innings. The Mariners were retired in order in the top of the ninth and in the bottom of the inning they got the first Yankee batter out and gave up a single. The next New York batter hit a two-run home run and Seattle lost 3-1. The Mariners lost Game 5 12-3 and lost the series.

- Seattle was in first place in the American League West Division in 2003 either tied or by themselves from April 14th to August 26th. They had a five game lead over Oakland on August 15th but then lost nine of their next twelve games, including four in a row against Boston, who knocked them out of first place. On August 28th the Mariners trailed the A's by two games in the division and were a half game behind the Red Sox for the AL Wild Card. The rest of season Seattle won five of its remaining six games against Oakland, but only went 16-12 overall while the A's went 17-11 and Boston went 18-11. The Mariners finished three games behind Oakland in the division and two games behind the Red Sox for the wild card spot.

Year-to-Year Figures

Team Name	League	Year	W	L	Win%	Fin	GB/GA	WS	Lge	LDS	Div	WC
Seattle Mariners	AL West	2010	61	101	0.377	4 of 4	29					
Seattle Mariners	AL West	2009	85	77	0.525	3 of 4	12					
Seattle Mariners	AL West	2008	61	101	0.377	4 of 4	39					
Seattle Mariners	AL West	2007	88	74	0.543	2 of 4	6					
Seattle Mariners	AL West	2006	78	84	0.481	4 of 4	15					
Seattle Mariners	AL West	2005	69	93	0.426	4 of 4	26					
Seattle Mariners	AL West	2004	63	99	0.389	4 of 4	29					
Seattle Mariners	AL West	2003	93	69	0.574	2 of 4	3					
Seattle Mariners	AL West	2002	93	69	0.574	3 of 4	10					
Seattle Mariners	AL West	2001	116	46	0.716	1 of 4	+14			1	1	
Seattle Mariners	AL West	2000	91	71	0.562	2 of 4	0.5*			1		1
Seattle Mariners	AL West	1999	79	83	0.488	3 of 4	16					
Seattle Mariners	AL West	1998	76	85	0.472	3 of 4	11.5					
Seattle Mariners	AL West	1997	90	72	0.556	1 of 4	+6				1	
Seattle Mariners	AL West	1996	85	76	0.528	2 of 4	4.5					
Seattle Mariners	AL West	1995	79	66	0.545	1 of 4	+1			1	1	
Seattle Mariners	AL West	1994	49	63	0.438	3 of 4	2					
Seattle Mariners	AL West	1993	82	80	0.506	4 of 7	12					
Seattle Mariners	AL West	1992	64	98	0.395	7 of 7	32					
Seattle Mariners	AL West	1991	83	79	0.512	5 of 7	12					
Seattle Mariners	AL West	1990	77	85	0.475	5 of 7	26					
Seattle Mariners	AL West	1989	73	89	0.451	6 of 7	26					
Seattle Mariners	AL West	1988	68	93	0.422	7 of 7	35.5					
Seattle Mariners	AL West	1987	78	84	0.481	4 of 7	7					
Seattle Mariners	AL West	1986	67	95	0.414	7 of 7	25					
Seattle Mariners	AL West	1985	74	88	0.457	6 of 7	17					
Seattle Mariners	AL West	1984	74	88	0.457	5t of 7	10					
Seattle Mariners	AL West	1983	60	102	0.370	7 of 7	39					
Seattle Mariners	AL West	1982	76	86	0.469	4 of 7	17					
Seattle Mariners	AL West	1981	44	65	0.404	6, 5 of 7	14.5, 6.5					
Seattle Mariners	AL West	1980	59	103	0.364	7 of 7	38					
Seattle Mariners	AL West	1979	67	95	0.414	6 of 7	21					
Seattle Mariners	AL West	1978	56	104	0.350	7 of 7	35					
Seattle Mariners	AL West	1977	64	98	0.395	6 of 7	38					
			2522	2861	0.469			0	0	3	3	1

* In 2000 Seattle finished the season 0.5 game behind Oakland in the AL West Division but won the AL Wild Card spot. Seattle played one less game than Oakland and decided not to make up that game, because even if they won it they would have lost the tiebreaker to Oakland and still been the AL Wild Card team because the A's won the regular season series between the two teams.

Tampa Bay Rays

Stats

History

Year of Origin 1998   Years Played 13

Score & Rank

Total Points Score ....3.8   Average Points Score................................0.29
Total Points Rank 29   Average Points Rank..................................26 tied

Postseason Results	No.	Years
World Series Won	0	
League Championship Series Won	1	2008
League Division Series Won	1	2008
World Series Lost	1	2008
League Championship Series Lost	0	
League Division Series Lost	1	2010

Postseason Won-Loss Records and Winning Percentages

	Postseason Games		Postseason Series	
All Postseason Series	10-11	.476	2-2	.500
World Series	1-4	.200	0-1	.000
League Championship Series	4-3	.571	1-0	1.000
League Division Series	5-4	.556	1-1	.500

Regular Season Results

All-Time Won-Loss Record 922-1181
All-Time Winning Percentage 438

	No.	Years
League Titles before 1969	0	
Division Titles	2	2008, 2010
Wild Cards	0	

Regular Season High & Low Points

		Year(s)
Most Wins in a Season	97	2008
Most Losses in a Season	106	2002
Highest Winning Percentage	.599	2008
Lowest Winning Percentage	.342	2002
Longest Streak with Won-Loss Record .500 or Higher	3 years	2008-2010
Longest Streak with Won-Loss Record Below .500	10 years	1998-2007

Years with .500 record or Better

1990's: .... 0 (out of 2)
2000's 2
2010's 1
3 out of 13 seasons played = 23%

Years Making Postseason

1990's..0
2000's..1
2010's..1
2 out of 13 seasons played = 15%

Streaks

• 2008-2010: Won two Division Titles, one League Division Series, and one League Championship Series in three years.

Extra Bases

• The 2010 League Division Series against Texas was the first series in baseball postseason history in which the road team won every game. Texas won the series three games to two.

Scoring Opportunities

2000's

• In 2008 the Rays won their first American League East Division Title. In the playoffs they beat the White Sox in the LDS and the Red Sox in the LCS. In the World Series Tampa Bay played the Phillies and in Game 1 the Rays only trailed by one run after five innings. But the rest of the game Tampa Bay didn't get any more hits and their last eleven batters were retired in order and they lost the game 3-2. The Rays won Game 2 and Game 3 was tied at four after eight innings. Tampa Bay was retired in order in the top of the ninth and in the bottom of the inning their pitcher hit the first Phillies batter. The Rays made a pitching change and on the next at bat their new pitcher threw a wild pitch and the Phillies base runner advanced to third base on a throwing error by the catcher. With a runner on third and no outs Tampa Bay walked the next two batters intentionally to load the bases and try to get a force out. But the next Philadelphia batter singled and drove in the game winning run and the Rays lost 5-4. Tampa Bay lost Game 4 10-2. Game 5 started on a Monday but was suspended due to rain after the top of the sixth inning with the game tied at two. The game resumed two days later on Wednesday and in the bottom of the sixth inning the Rays gave up a double, a sacrifice bunt, and a single and let in one run. In the top of the seventh Tampa Bay tied the score with a solo home run, but in the bottom of the inning they gave up a double and a single and gave up the go ahead run again. In the top of the ninth the Rays had a runner on second base with one out, but the next two batters lined out and struck out and they lost the game 4-3 and lost the series.

2010's

• The Rays won the American League East Division in 2010 and played Texas in the LDS. Tampa Bay lost the first two games at home, losing Game 1 5-1 and Game 2 6-0, getting only two hits in Game 2. The Rays won Games 3 and 4 on the road to even the series. Game 5 was at in Tampa but the Rays lost the game 5-1 and lost the series. Tampa committed five errors in their three losses. This series was the first series in baseball postseason history in which the road team won every game.

Year-to-Year Figures

Team Name	League	Year	W	L	Win%	Fin	GB/GA	WS	Lge	LDS	Div	WC
Tampa Bay Rays	AL East	2010	96	66	0.593	1 of 5	+1				1	
Tampa Bay Rays	AL East	2009	84	78	0.519	3 of 5	19					
Tampa Bay Rays	AL East	2008	97	65	0.599	1 of 5	+2		1	1	1	
Tampa Bay Devil Rays	AL East	2007	66	96	0.407	5 of 5	30					
Tampa Bay Devil Rays	AL East	2006	61	101	0.377	5 of 5	36					
Tampa Bay Devil Rays	AL East	2005	67	95	0.414	5 of 5	28					
Tampa Bay Devil Rays	AL East	2004	70	91	0.435	4 of 5	30.5					
Tampa Bay Devil Rays	AL East	2003	63	99	0.389	5 of 5	38					
Tampa Bay Devil Rays	AL East	2002	55	106	0.342	5 of 5	48					
Tampa Bay Devil Rays	AL East	2001	62	100	0.383	5 of 5	34					
Tampa Bay Devil Rays	AL East	2000	69	92	0.429	5 of 5	18					
Tampa Bay Devil Rays	AL East	1999	69	93	0.426	5 of 5	29					
Tampa Bay Devil Rays	AL East	1998	63	99	0.389	5 of 5	51					
			922	1181	0.438			0	1	1	2	0

Texas Rangers

Stats

History
Year of Origin 1961   Years Played...50

Score & Rank
Total Points Score .... 11.1   Average Points Score.......................................0.22
Total Points Rank 25   Average Points Rank.......................................28

Postseason Results	No.	Years
World Series Won	0	
League Championship Series Won	1	2010
League Division Series Won	1	2010
World Series Lost	1	2010
League Championship Series Lost	0	
League Division Series Lost	3	1996, 1998, 1999

Postseason Won-Loss Records and Winning Percentages

	Postseason Games		Postseason Series	
All Postseason Series	9-17	.346	2-4	.333
World Series	1-4	.200	0-1	.000
League Championship Series	4-2	.667	1-0	1.000
League Division Series	4-11	.267	1-3	.250

Regular Season Results
All-Time Won-Loss Record 3747-4206
All-Time Winning Percentage .... .471

	No.	Years
League Titles before 1969	0	
Division Titles	4	1996, 1998, 1999, 2010
Wild Cards	0	

Regular Season High & Low Points

		Year(s)
Most Wins in a Season	95	1999
Most Losses in a Season	106	1963
Highest Winning Percentage	.586	1999
Lowest Winning Percentage	.346	1963
Longest Streak with Won-Loss Record .500 or Higher	3 years	1977-1979, 1989-1991
Longest Streak with Won-Loss Record Below .500	8 years	1961-1968

Years with .500 record or Better
1960's .... 1 (out of 9)
1970's 4
1980's 3
1990's 7
2000's 2
2010's 1
18 out of 50 seasons played = 36%

Years Making Postseason
1960's...0
1970's...0
1980's...0
1990's...3
2000's...0
2010's...1
4 out of 50 seasons played = 8%

Streaks

• 1996-1999: Won three Division Titles in four years.

Extra Bases

• In 1997 the first interleague game was played in Texas on June 12th. The Giants beat the Rangers 4-3.
• The Rangers played the Yankees in their first three postseason appearances, in 1996, 1998, and 1999. In the 1996 series both teams scored sixteen runs but the Yankees won in four games. In 1998 & 1999 Texas was swept (3 games to 0) by New York each year and was outscored 23-2 in the six games.

Scoring Opportunities

1990's

• Texas won the American League West Division in 1996 and played the Yankees in the LDS. The Rangers won Game 1 and had a 4-2 lead in Game 2 after six innings. In the bottom of the seventh they hit the first Yankee batter, gave up a single, a sacrifice bunt, and a sacrifice fly that drove in one run. In the bottom of the eighth Texas gave up a single and then a deep fly ball along the left field line in which the New York runner tagged up from first base and advanced to second. The next Yankee batter singled and drove in the tying run. The game went into extra innings and in the top of the tenth the Rangers had runners on first and third with two outs, but their next batter flied out. In the top of the twelfth Texas had the bases loaded with two outs, but their next batter up also flied out. In the bottom of the inning the Rangers gave up a single, a walk, and then on a sacrifice bunt their third basemen made a throwing error to first base and the game winning run scored and Texas lost 5-4. In Game 3 the Rangers led 2-1 in the top of the ninth inning. Texas gave up singles to the first two Yankees batters and gave up a sacrifice fly that drove in the tying run. The Rangers got the next New York batter out and intentionally walked a batter to pitch to a weaker hitter, but he hit a single that drove in the go-ahead run. Texas had a runner on second in the bottom of the ninth with one out, but their next two batters grounded out and struck out and they lost 3-2. Game 4 was tied at four after six innings and Texas had two Yankees out with a New York runner on second base in the top of the seventh, but the Rangers gave up singles to the next two Yankees hitters and let in the go-ahead run. Texas gave up a solo home run in the top of the ninth and had runners on first and second with one out in the bottom of the inning, but their next two batters flied out and struck out and they lost 6-4 and lost the series.

- In 1998 the Rangers won the American League West Division and faced the Yankees again in the LDS. In Game 1 Texas gave up two runs in the second inning and only had five hits in the game. The Rangers trailed by two runs in the top of the seventh inning when they had runners on first and second with two outs, but their next batter struck out and they lost the game 2-0. In Game 2 Texas trailed by two runs in the top of the ninth inning. Their first batter up singled, but their next three hitters all got out and they lost 3-1. In Game 3 Texas had only three hits and lost the game 4-0 to lose the series in a sweep. They were shut out twice in the series and were outscored 9-1 in the three games.

- The Rangers repeated as American League West Division champs in 1999 and faced the Yankees in the LDS for the third time in four years. In Game 1 Texas only had two hits and lost the game 8-0. Game 2 was tied at one after six innings. In the bottom of the seventh the Rangers gave up a walk, a single, and a double that drove in the go-ahead run. In the bottom of the eighth Texas walked in one run and they lost the game 3-1. In Game 3 the Rangers gave up a three-run home run in the top of the first inning. Texas only had five hits and did not get a runner to third base the entire game. They only got a runner to second base three times and they lost the game 3-0. They were swept out of the playoffs by New York for the second straight year. This year they also were shut out twice and they were outscored 14-1 in the series.

2010's

- Texas won the American League West Division in 2010, beat Tampa Bay in the LDS, and beat the Yankees in the LCS. In the World Series the Rangers faced San Francisco and lost Game 1 11-7. In Game 2 Texas only had four hits and gave up seven runs in the bottom of the eighth inning and lost the game 9-0. The Rangers won Game 3 but only had three hits in Game 4 and only reached second base once. They lost the game 4-0. Game 5 was tied at zero after six innings. In the top of the seventh inning Texas gave up singles to the first two Giants batters and gave up a three-run home run with two outs. The Rangers only had three hits in the game and lost 3-1 to lose the series. They were outscored 29-12 in the series.

Year-to-Year Figures

Team Name	League	Year	W	L	Win%	Fin	GB/GA	WS	Lge	LDS	Div	WC
Texas Rangers	AL West	2010	90	72	0.556	1 of 4	+9		1	1	1	
Texas Rangers	AL West	2009	87	75	0.537	2 of 4	10					
Texas Rangers	AL West	2008	79	83	0.488	2 of 4	21					
Texas Rangers	AL West	2007	75	87	0.463	4 of 4	19					
Texas Rangers	AL West	2006	80	82	0.494	3 of 4	13					
Texas Rangers	AL West	2005	79	83	0.488	3 of 4	16					
Texas Rangers	AL West	2004	89	73	0.549	3 of 4	3					

Team Name	League	Year	W	L	Win%	Fin	GB/GA	WS	Lge	LDS	Div	WC
Texas Rangers	AL West	2003	71	91	0.438	4 of 4	25					
Texas Rangers	AL West	2002	72	90	0.444	4 of 4	31					
Texas Rangers	AL West	2001	73	89	0.451	4 of 4	43					
Texas Rangers	AL West	2000	71	91	0.438	4 of 4	20.5					
Texas Rangers	AL West	1999	95	67	0.586	1 of 4	+8				1	
Texas Rangers	AL West	1998	88	74	0.543	1 of 4	+3				1	
Texas Rangers	AL West	1997	77	85	0.475	3 of 4	13					
Texas Rangers	AL West	1996	90	72	0.556	1 of 4	+4.5				1	
Texas Rangers	AL West	1995	74	70	0.514	3 of 4	4.5					
Texas Rangers	AL West	1994	52	62	0.456	1 of 4	+1					
Texas Rangers	AL West	1993	86	76	0.531	2 of 7	8					
Texas Rangers	AL West	1992	77	85	0.475	4 of 7	19					
Texas Rangers	AL West	1991	85	77	0.525	3 of 7	10					
Texas Rangers	AL West	1990	83	79	0.512	3 of 7	20					
Texas Rangers	AL West	1989	83	79	0.512	4 of 7	16					
Texas Rangers	AL West	1988	70	91	0.435	6 of 7	33.5					
Texas Rangers	AL West	1987	75	87	0.463	6t of 7	10					
Texas Rangers	AL West	1986	87	75	0.537	2 of 7	5					
Texas Rangers	AL West	1985	62	99	0.385	7 of 7	28.5					
Texas Rangers	AL West	1984	69	92	0.429	7 of 7	14.5					
Texas Rangers	AL West	1983	77	85	0.475	3 of 7	22					
Texas Rangers	AL West	1982	64	98	0.395	6 of 7	29					
Texas Rangers	AL West	1981	57	48	0.543	2, 3 of 7	1.5, 4.5					
Texas Rangers	AL West	1980	76	85	0.472	4 of 7	20.5					
Texas Rangers	AL West	1979	83	79	0.512	3 of 7	5					
Texas Rangers	AL West	1978	87	75	0.537	2t of 7	5					
Texas Rangers	AL West	1977	94	68	0.580	2 of 7	8					
Texas Rangers	AL West	1976	76	86	0.469	4t of 6	14					
Texas Rangers	AL West	1975	79	83	0.488	3 of 6	19					
Texas Rangers	AL West	1974	84	76	0.525	2 of 6	5					
Texas Rangers	AL West	1973	57	105	0.352	6 of 6	37					
Texas Rangers	AL West	1972	54	100	0.351	6 of 6	38.5					
Washington Senators	AL East	1971	63	96	0.396	5 of 6	38.5					
Washington Senators	AL East	1970	70	92	0.432	6 of 6	36.5					
Washington Senators	AL East	1969	86	76	0.531	4 of 6	56					
Washington Senators	AL	1968	65	96	0.404	10 of 10	22.5					
Washington Senators	AL	1967	76	85	0.472	6t of 10	43.5					
Washington Senators	AL	1966	71	88	0.447	8 of 10	37.5					
Washington Senators	AL	1965	70	92	0.432	8 of 10	29.5					
Washington Senators	AL	1964	62	100	0.383	9 of 10	55.5					
Washington Senators	AL	1963	56	106	0.346	10 of 10	47.5					
Washington Senators	AL	1962	60	101	0.373	10 of 10	22					
Washington Senators	AL	1961	61	100	0.379	9t of 10	20.5					
			3747	4206	0.471			0	1	1	4	0

231

Toronto Blue Jays

Stats

History

Year of Origin 1977	Years Played...............34

Score & Rank

Total Points Score 33.7	Average Points Score...............0.99
Total Points Rank 19	Average Points Rank...............10

Postseason Results

Postseason Results	No.	Years
World Series Won	2	1992, 1993
League Championship Series Won	2	1992, 1993
League Division Series Won	0	
World Series Lost	0	
League Championship Series Lost	3	1985, 1989, 1991
League Division Series Lost	0	

Postseason Won-Loss Records and Winning Percentages

	Postseason Games		Postseason Series	
All Postseason Series	21-20	.512	4-3	.571
World Series	8-4	.667	2-0	1.000
League Championship Series	13-16	.448	2-3	.400
League Division Series	0-0	.000	0-0	.000

Regular Season Results

All-Time Won-Loss Record	2674-2709
All-Time Winning Percentage	.497

	No.	Years
League Titles before 1969	0	
Division Titles	5	1985, 1989, 1991, 1992, 1993
Wild Cards	0	

Regular Season High & Low Points

		Year(s)
Most Wins in a Season	99	1985
Most Losses in a Season	109	1979
Highest Winning Percentage	.615	1985
Lowest Winning Percentage	.327	1979
Longest Streak with Won-Loss Record .500 or Higher	11 years	1983-1993
Longest Streak with Won-Loss Record Below .500	6 years	1977-1982

Years with .500 record or Better

1970's	0 (out of 3)
1980's	7
1990's	6
2000's	5
2010's	1

19 out of 34 seasons played = 56%

Years Making Postseason

1970's	0
1980's	2
1990's	3
2000's	0
2010's	0

5 out of 34 seasons played = 15%

Streaks

• 1985-1993: Won two World Series, two League Championship Series, and five Division Titles in nine years.

Extra Bases

• In 1987, 1988, and 1990 Toronto finished two games out in the American League East Division race each year, behind Detroit, Boston, and Boston, respectively.
• By winning the World Series in 1992 the Blue Jays became both the first team located outside the U.S. to win the World Series, and the first Canadian team to win the World Series.
• When Toronto won the World Series in 1993 on a walk off home run in the bottom of the ninth inning it became the second World Series to end on a home run.
• By winning the 1993 World Series at home the Blue Jays became the only team to win the World Series in Canada, as their 1992 World Series championship was won in Atlanta.

Scoring Opportunities

1980's

• Toronto won the American League East Division in 1985 and played Kansas City in the LCS. The Blue Jays won Games 1 & 2 and Game 3 was tied at five after seven innings. In the bottom of the eighth Toronto had two Royals out with runners on first and third. The next Kansas City batter singled and drove in the go-ahead run and the Blue Jays lost the game 6-5. Toronto won Game 4 to take a three game to one series lead. In Game 5 the Blue Jays gave up one run in each of the first two innings and trailed by two in the top of the fifth inning when they had runners on second and third with no outs, but their next three batters all got out. In the top of the sixth Toronto had the bases loaded with two outs but their next batter grounded out. Their last nine batters were retired in order and they lost the game 2-0. In Game 6 the Blue Jays trailed by two runs in the bottom of the seventh inning when they had runners on first and second with two outs, but their next batter grounded out. In the bottom of the ninth they had runners on first and second with two outs again, but their next batter up struck out and they lost 5-3. Toronto lost Game 7 6-2 and lost the series that they led three games to one.
• In 1987 Toronto led the American League East Division by 3.5 games over the Tigers on September 26th. In the last game of a four game series against Detroit the Blue Jays blew a 2-1 lead in the ninth inning and lost the game 3-2 in thirteen innings. Then Toronto lost three games in a row to Milwaukee and was only one game ahead of the Tigers when the two teams met in Detroit for the last three games of the year. The Blue Jays needed to win one out of

three games to tie the Tigers for the division and needed to win two out of three to win the division. In the first game Toronto trailed by one run after three innings and in the top of the eighth they had runners on first and second with no outs, but their next batter hit a fielders choice that got the Blue Jays runner out at third base and their following batter grounded into a double play. They lost the game 4-3 and the second game was tied at two after nine innings. In the top of the twelfth Toronto had runners on first and second with two outs, but their next batter up struck out. In the bottom of the inning the Blue Jays got the first Tigers batter out, but then gave up two singles and a walk, which loaded the bases. The next Detroit batter singled and Toronto lost 3-2. In the third game the Blue Jays gave up a run in the second inning. In the top of the seventh Toronto had runners on first and second with two outs, but their next batter grounded out. They had one runner on second base with one out in the top of the eighth, but their next two hitters lined out and grounded out. They were retired in order in the top of the ninth and lost 1-0 and finished the season two games behind the Tigers. The Blue Jays lost their last seven games of the year after September 26th while Detroit went 6-2. Toronto's last three losses of the season against the Tigers were all by one run.

- The Blue Jays won the American League East Division in 1989 and lost Games 1 & 2 of the LCS against the A's 7-3 and 6-3. Toronto won Game 3 and trailed by one run late in Game 4. The Blue Jays had a runner on first base with two outs in each of the eighth and ninth innings but in each inning their next batter up popped out and they lost the game 6-5. In Game 5 Toronto trailed by three runs in the bottom of the ninth inning. They hit a solo home run and scored another run on a sacrifice fly, but lost the game 4-3 and lost the series.

1990's

- In 1990 Toronto led the American League East Division by 1.5 games over Boston on September 24th with eight games left in the season. The Blue Jays lost four games in a row and fell out of first place, which included two games in a three game series against the Red Sox. Toronto went 2-6 after the 24th while Boston went 6-3 and the Blue Jays finished the season in second place two games behind Boston.

- Toronto won the American League East Division in 1991 and played Minnesota in the LCS. In Game 1 the Blue Jays trailed by one run in the top of the sixth inning when they had runners on first and second with one out, but their next two batters flied out and grounded out. They only had one hit the rest of the game and lost the game 5-4. Toronto won Game 2 and Game 3 was tied at two after nine innings. In the top of the tenth the Blue Jays gave up a solo home run and were retired in order in the bottom of the inning and lost 3-2. Toronto lost Game 4 9-3 and had a 5-2 lead after five innings of Game 5. In the top of the sixth the Blue Jays gave up three hits, a stolen base, an error, and let in three runs that tied the game. In the top of the eighth Toronto had two Twins out with no runners on base but then gave up a single, a stolen base, a walk, and two more singles. The Blue Jays let in three runs and lost the game 8-5 to lose the series.

Year-to-Year Figures

Team Name	League	Year	W	L	Win%	Fin	GB/GA	WS	Lge	LDS	Div	WC
Toronto Blue Jays	AL East	2010	85	77	0.525	4 of 5	11					
Toronto Blue Jays	AL East	2009	75	87	0.463	4 of 5	28					
Toronto Blue Jays	AL East	2008	86	76	0.531	4 of 5	11					
Toronto Blue Jays	AL East	2007	83	79	0.512	3 of 5	13					
Toronto Blue Jays	AL East	2006	87	75	0.537	2 of 5	10					
Toronto Blue Jays	AL East	2005	80	82	0.494	3 of 5	15					
Toronto Blue Jays	AL East	2004	67	94	0.416	5 of 5	33.5					
Toronto Blue Jays	AL East	2003	86	76	0.531	3 of 5	15					
Toronto Blue Jays	AL East	2002	78	84	0.481	3 of 5	25.5					
Toronto Blue Jays	AL East	2001	80	82	0.494	3 of 5	16					
Toronto Blue Jays	AL East	2000	83	79	0.512	3 of 5	4.5					
Toronto Blue Jays	AL East	1999	84	78	0.519	3 of 5	14					
Toronto Blue Jays	AL East	1998	88	74	0.543	3 of 5	26					
Toronto Blue Jays	AL East	1997	76	86	0.469	5 of 5	22					
Toronto Blue Jays	AL East	1996	74	88	0.457	4 of 5	18					
Toronto Blue Jays	AL East	1995	56	88	0.389	5 of 5	30					
Toronto Blue Jays	AL East	1994	55	60	0.478	3 of 5	16					
Toronto Blue Jays	AL East	1993	95	67	0.586	1 of 7	+7	1	1		1	
Toronto Blue Jays	AL East	1992	96	66	0.593	1 of 7	+4	1	1		1	
Toronto Blue Jays	AL East	1991	91	71	0.562	1 of 7	+7				1	
Toronto Blue Jays	AL East	1990	86	76	0.531	2 of 7	2					
Toronto Blue Jays	AL East	1989	89	73	0.549	1 of 7	+2				1	
Toronto Blue Jays	AL East	1988	87	75	0.537	3t of 7	2					
Toronto Blue Jays	AL East	1987	96	66	0.593	2 of 7	2					
Toronto Blue Jays	AL East	1986	86	76	0.531	4 of 7	9.5					
Toronto Blue Jays	AL East	1985	99	62	0.615	1 of 7	+2				1	
Toronto Blue Jays	AL East	1984	89	73	0.549	2 of 7	15					
Toronto Blue Jays	AL East	1983	89	73	0.549	4 of 7	9					
Toronto Blue Jays	AL East	1982	78	84	0.481	6t of 7	17					
Toronto Blue Jays	AL East	1981	37	69	0.349	7, 7 of 7	19, 7.5					
Toronto Blue Jays	AL East	1980	67	95	0.414	7 of 7	36					
Toronto Blue Jays	AL East	1979	53	109	0.327	7 of 7	50.5					
Toronto Blue Jays	AL East	1978	59	102	0.366	7 of 7	40					
Toronto Blue Jays	AL East	1977	54	107	0.335	7 of 7	45.5					
			2674	2709	0.497			2	2	0	5	0

Washington Nationals

Stats

History

Year of Origin 1969   Years Played.. 42

Score & Rank

Total Points Score .... 1.5   Average Points Score.. 0.04
Total Points Rank 30   Average Points Rank.. 30

Postseason Results	No.	Years
World Series Won	0	
League Championship Series Won	0	
League Division Series Won	1	1981
World Series Lost	0	
League Championship Series Lost	1	1981
League Division Series Lost	0	

Postseason Won-Loss Records and Winning Percentages

	Postseason Games		Postseason Series	
All Postseason Series	5-5	.500	1-1	.500
World Series	0-0	.000	0-0	.000
League Championship Series	2-3	.400	0-1	.000
League Division Series	3-2	.600	1-0	1.000

Regular Season Results

All-Time Won-Loss Record 3167-3502
All-Time Winning Percentage .... .475

	No.	Years
League Titles before 1969	0	
Division Titles	1	1981
Wild Cards	0	

Regular Season High & Low Points

		Year(s)
Most Wins in a Season	95	1979
Most Losses in a Season	110	1969
Highest Winning Percentage	.649	1994
Lowest Winning Percentage	.321	1969
Longest Streak with Won-Loss Record .500 or Higher	5 years	1979-1983
Longest Streak with Won-Loss Record Below .500	10 years	1969-1978

Years with .500 record or Better

1960's	0 (out of 1)
1970's	1
1980's	8
1990's	5
2000's	3
2010's	0

17 out of 42 seasons played = 40%

Years Making Postseason

1960's	0
1970's	0
1980's	1
1990's	0
2000's	0
2010's	0

1 out of 42 seasons played = 2%

Streaks

- When the Washington franchise was the Montreal Expos, they were very good from 1979-1983. Over the five year period they won one Division Title and one League Division Series and they had the best overall record in the National League at 413-341 (.547), but only made the postseason once, in 1981. The Expos were in contention in the National League East Division into September in all five seasons.
- During the sixteen year period from 1979-1994 no team won more regular season games (1,317) than the Montreal Expos. The Yankees won 1,315 regular season games over that period.

Extra Bases

- Montreal probably would have won the National League East Division in 1994, but the season ended on August 12th because of a players strike. The Expos had the best record in all of baseball with a 74-40 won-loss record and .649 winning percentage when the season ended.
- At the final game in Montreal in 2004, before the franchise moved to Washington, a banner was hung saying "1994 Best Team in Baseball" to honor the team that had the best record in baseball when the season ended in August due to the players strike.

Scoring Opportunities

1970's
- The Expos contended for the National League East Division title in 1973 in one of the closest divisional races ever as all six teams in the division were in the race going into the final month of the season. On September 17th Montreal was in second place only one game behind Pittsburgh but the Expos lost their next seven games and lost nine out of ten and fell to fifth place 4.5 games behind the Mets on September 25th. Montreal won three of its last four games of the year but finished the season in fourth place 3.5 games behind New York who went 9-2 after the 17th and won the division. Pittsburgh went 5-10 and the Expos went 4-9 after the 17th.
- In 1979 Montreal had a half-game lead over the Pirates in the National League East Division on September 24th when the two teams met in Pittsburgh for a four game series. But the Expos lost three out of the four games and then lost two of their last three games to the Phillies. Montreal lost five of their last seven games of the season while the Pirates went 5-3 over the same period and the Expos finished in second place two games behind Pittsburgh.

1980's
- The Expos were tied for first place in the National League East Division with the Phillies on

October 3rd in 1980 with three games left to play against Philadelphia in Montreal. In the first game the Expos trailed by one run in the bottom of the sixth inning when they had runners on first and second with two outs, but their next batter up grounded out. In the bottom of the seventh they had runners on first and second with one out, but their next two batters flied out and popped out and they lost the game 2-1. In the second game Montreal had a 4-3 lead after eight innings. In the top of the ninth they walked the first Phillies batter and then got two ground outs, with the runner advancing to second base on the second out. The next Philadelphia hitter singled and drove in the tying run. The game went into extra innings and in the top of the eleventh the Expos gave up a two-run home run with one out. They were retired in order in the bottom of the inning and lost the game 6-4 and were eliminated from winning the division. Montreal won the last game of the year and finished the season in second place one game behind the Phillies.

• Montreal made the playoffs in 1981 by winning the second half of the season in the National League East Division in the strike split season. In the first round of the playoffs they beat the Phillies and they played the Dodgers in the LCS. The Expos lost Game 1 5-1 and won Games 2 & 3 to take a two games to one series lead in the best of five game series. They only needed one more win to advance to their first World Series and the last two games of the series were at home. Game 4 was tied at four after seven innings. Montreal gave up a two-run home run in the top of the eighth and gave up four runs in the top of the ninth and lost the game 7-1. Game 5 was tied at one after six innings and in the bottom of the seventh the Expos had runners on first and second with two outs, but their next batter fouled out to the catcher. In the top of the ninth Montreal got the first two Dodgers batters out but then gave up a solo home run. In the bottom of the inning the Expos first two batters got out, and their next two hitters both walked. They had runners on first and second with the tying run at second base, but their next batter grounded out and they lost 2-1 and lost the series in which they had a two game to one lead.

1990's

• In 1994 the Expos had a 74-40 record (.649) and were six games ahead of Atlanta in the National League East Division on August 12th. This was the best record in baseball at the time, but the season ended due to a players strike. Montreal was projected to win the NL East Division and they would have been favored to win in the playoffs.

• Montreal was in a close race for the National League Wild Card in 1996. On September 19th they were tied with San Diego for the wild card lead. But the Expos lost four games in a row to Atlanta and went 3-7 the rest of the season. The Padres went 5-3 after the 19th and the Dodgers went 3-6 and San Diego won the NL West Division and Los Angeles won the wild card. Montreal finished two games behind the Dodgers for the wild card.

2000's

- On August 18th of the 2003 season, the Expos were in a five-team tie for the National League Wild Card. On September 1st the team rosters could expand to forty players, but the League, who owned the Expos this season, decided that it could not afford the extra $50,000 to call up players from the minors to the pro team. Montreal went 12-12 the rest of the season and finished eight games back in the wild card race behind Florida.

Year-to-Year Figures

Team Name	League	Year	W	L	Win%	Fin	GB/GA	WS	Lge	LDS	Div	WC
Washington Nationals	NL East	2010	69	93	0.426	5 of 5	28					
Washington Nationals	NL East	2009	59	103	0.364	5 of 5	34					
Washington Nationals	NL East	2008	59	102	0.366	5 of 5	32.5					
Washington Nationals	NL East	2007	73	89	0.451	4 of 5	16					
Washington Nationals	NL East	2006	71	91	0.438	5 of 5	26					
Washington Nationals	NL East	2005	81	81	0.500	5 of 5	9					
Montreal Expos	NL East	2004	67	95	0.414	5 of 5	29					
Montreal Expos	NL East	2003	83	79	0.512	4 of 5	18					
Montreal Expos	NL East	2002	83	79	0.512	2 of 5	19					
Montreal Expos	NL East	2001	68	94	0.420	5 of 5	20					
Montreal Expos	NL East	2000	67	95	0.414	4 of 5	28					
Montreal Expos	NL East	1999	68	94	0.420	4 of 5	35					
Montreal Expos	NL East	1998	65	97	0.401	4 of 5	41					
Montreal Expos	NL East	1997	78	84	0.481	4 of 5	23					
Montreal Expos	NL East	1996	88	74	0.543	2 of 5	8					
Montreal Expos	NL East	1995	66	78	0.458	5 of 5	24					
Montreal Expos	NL East	1994	74	40	0.649	1 of 5	+6					
Montreal Expos	NL East	1993	94	68	0.580	2 of 7	3					
Montreal Expos	NL East	1992	87	75	0.537	2 of 6	9					
Montreal Expos	NL East	1991	71	90	0.441	6 of 6	26.5					
Montreal Expos	NL East	1990	85	77	0.525	3 of 6	10					
Montreal Expos	NL East	1989	81	81	0.500	4 of 6	12					
Montreal Expos	NL East	1988	81	81	0.500	3 of 6	20					
Montreal Expos	NL East	1987	91	71	0.562	3 of 6	4					
Montreal Expos	NL East	1986	78	83	0.484	4 of 6	29.5					
Montreal Expos	NL East	1985	84	77	0.522	3 of 6	16.5					
Montreal Expos	NL East	1984	78	83	0.484	5 of 6	18					
Montreal Expos	NL East	1983	82	80	0.506	3 of 6	8					
Montreal Expos	NL East	1982	86	76	0.531	3 of 6	6					
Montreal Expos	NL East	1981	60	48	0.556	3, 1 of 6	4, +0.5*			1	1	
Montreal Expos	NL East	1980	90	72	0.556	2 of 6	1					
Montreal Expos	NL East	1979	95	65	0.594	2 of 6	2					
Montreal Expos	NL East	1978	76	86	0.469	4 of 6	14					
Montreal Expos	NL East	1977	75	87	0.463	5 of 6	26					
Montreal Expos	NL East	1976	55	107	0.340	6 of 6	46					
Montreal Expos	NL East	1975	75	87	0.463	5t of 6	17.5					
Montreal Expos	NL East	1974	79	82	0.491	4 of 6	8.5					
Montreal Expos	NL East	1973	79	83	0.488	4 of 6	3.5					
Montreal Expos	NL East	1972	70	86	0.449	5 of 6	26.5					
Montreal Expos	NL East	1971	71	90	0.441	5 of 6	25.5					
Montreal Expos	NL East	1970	73	89	0.451	6 of 6	16					
Montreal Expos	NL East	1969	52	110	0.321	6 of 6	48					
			3167	3502	0.475			0	0	1	1	0

* The 1981 season was divided into two halves due to a players strike in the middle of the season. Both halves were played with teams playing an uneven amount of games. In the second half of the season the Montreal Expos played one more game than St. Louis and won the division by 0.5 games.

Reference Tables

Regular Season Games Won

Rank	Team	Wins	Year of Origin
1	San Francisco Giants	10436	1883
2	Chicago Cubs	10318	1871
3	Atlanta Braves	10170	1871
4	Los Angeles Dodgers	10135	1884
5	St. Louis Cardinals	10107	1882
6	Cincinnati Reds	9915	1882
7	Pittsburgh Pirates	9810	1882
8	New York Yankees	9670	1901
9	Philadelphia Phillies	9135	1883
10	Boston Red Sox	8819	1901
11	Cleveland Indians	8691	1901
12	Detroit Tigers	8645	1901
13	Chicago White Sox	8628	1901
14	Oakland Athletics	8270	1901
15	Minnesota Twins	8232	1901
16	Baltimore Orioles	8079	1901
17	Los Angeles Angels of Anaheim	3967	1961
18	Houston Astros	3888	1962
19	Texas Rangers	3747	1961
20	New York Mets	3734	1962
21	Kansas City Royals	3210	1969
22	Washington Nationals	3167	1969
23	Milwaukee Brewers	3166	1969
24	San Diego Padres	3098	1969
25	Toronto Blue Jays	2674	1977
26	Seattle Mariners	2522	1977
27	Colorado Rockies	1364	1993
28	Florida Marlins	1363	1993
29	Arizona Diamondbacks	1035	1998
30	Tampa Bay Rays	922	1998

Regular Season Games Lost

Rank	Team	Losses	Year of Origin
1	Philadelphia Phillies	10233	1883
2	Atlanta Braves	10014	1871
3	Chicago Cubs	9765	1871
4	Pittsburgh Pirates	9684	1882
5	Cincinnati Reds	9619	1882
6	St. Louis Cardinals	9419	1882
7	Los Angeles Dodgers	9199	1884
8	Baltimore Orioles	8959	1901
9	San Francisco Giants	8958	1883
10	Minnesota Twins	8816	1901
11	Oakland Athletics	8752	1901
12	Detroit Tigers	8437	1901
13	Chicago White Sox	8413	1901
14	Cleveland Indians	8367	1901
15	Boston Red Sox	8233	1901
16	New York Yankees	7361	1901
17	Texas Rangers	4206	1961
18	New York Mets	4064	1962
19	Los Angeles Angels of Anaheim	4003	1961
20	Houston Astros	3921	1962
21	San Diego Padres	3580	1969
22	Milwaukee Brewers	3505	1969
23	Washington Nationals	3502	1969
24	Kansas City Royals	3455	1969
25	Seattle Mariners	2861	1977
26	Toronto Blue Jays	2709	1977
27	Colorado Rockies	1490	1993
28	Florida Marlins	1485	1993
29	Tampa Bay Rays	1181	1998
30	Arizona Diamondbacks	1071	1998

Regular Season Winning Percentage

Rank	Team	Win %	Year of Origin
1	New York Yankees	0.568	1901
2	San Francisco Giants	0.538	1883
3	Los Angeles Dodgers	0.524	1884
4	St. Louis Cardinals	0.518	1882
5	Boston Red Sox	0.517	1901
6	Chicago Cubs	0.514	1871
7	Cleveland Indians	0.509	1901
8	Cincinnati Reds	0.508	1882
9	Chicago White Sox	0.506	1901
	Detroit Tigers	0.506	1901
11	Atlanta Braves	0.504	1871
12	Pittsburgh Pirates	0.503	1882
13	Houston Astros	0.498	1962
	Los Angeles Angels of Anaheim	0.498	1961
15	Toronto Blue Jays	0.497	1977
16	Arizona Diamondbacks	0.491	1998
17	Oakland Athletics	0.486	1901
18	Minnesota Twins	0.483	1901
19	Kansas City Royals	0.482	1969
20	Florida Marlins	0.479	1993
	New York Mets	0.479	1962
22	Colorado Rockies	0.478	1993
23	Washington Nationals	0.476	1969
24	Milwaukee Brewers	0.475	1969
25	Baltimore Orioles	0.474	1901
26	Philadelphia Phillies	0.472	1883
27	Texas Rangers	0.471	1961
28	Seattle Mariners	0.469	1977
29	San Diego Padres	0.464	1969
30	Tampa Bay Rays	0.438	1998

Through the 2010 season, the fourteen expansion teams that joined the league after 1960 all have regular season winning percentages under .500.

Postseason Games Winning Percentage

Rank	Team	Win %	Year of Origin
1	Florida Marlins	0.647	1993
2	New York Yankees	0.601	1901
3	New York Mets	0.581	1962
4	Baltimore Orioles	0.571	1901
5	Oakland Athletics	0.531	1901
6	Cincinnati Reds	0.528	1882
7	St. Louis Cardinals	0.527	1882
8	Boston Red Sox	0.523	1901
9	Cleveland Indians	0.518	1901
10	Toronto Blue Jays	0.512	1977
11	Chicago White Sox	0.509	1901
12	Washington Nationals	0.500	1969
13	Detroit Tigers	0.494	1901
14	San Francisco Giants	0.490	1883
15	Arizona Diamondbacks	0.484	1998
	Atlanta Braves	0.484	1871
17	Philadelphia Phillies	0.480	1883
18	Tampa Bay Rays	0.476	1998
19	Colorado Rockies	0.474	1993
20	Pittsburgh Pirates	0.449	1882
21	Los Angeles Angels of Anaheim	0.443	1961
22	Seattle Mariners	0.441	1977
23	Los Angeles Dodgers	0.439	1884
24	Milwaukee Brewers	0.429	1969
25	Kansas City Royals	0.419	1969
26	Minnesota Twins	0.398	1901
27	Houston Astros	0.375	1962
28	San Diego Padres	0.353	1969
29	Texas Rangers	0.346	1961
30	Chicago Cubs	0.337	1871

This is the team's winning percentage for all the postseason games it has played. It is not the winning percentage for postseason series. That is located on page 274.

Year of Origin & Years Played

Rank	Team	Year of Origin	Years Played
1	Atlanta Braves	1871	140
2	Chicago Cubs	1871	138
3	Cincinnati Reds	1882	129
	Pittsburgh Pirates	1882	129
	St. Louis Cardinals	1882	129
6	Philadelphia Phillies	1883	128
	San Francisco Giants	1883	128
8	Los Angeles Dodgers	1884	127
9	Baltimore Orioles	1901	110
	Boston Red Sox	1901	110
	Chicago White Sox	1901	110
	Cleveland Indians	1901	110
	Detroit Tigers	1901	110
	Minnesota Twins	1901	110
	New York Yankees	1901	110
	Oakland Athletics	1901	110
17	Los Angeles Angels of Anaheim	1961	50
	Texas Rangers	1961	50
19	Houston Astros	1962	49
	New York Mets	1962	49
21	Kansas City Royals	1969	42
	Milwaukee Brewers	1969	42
	San Diego Padres	1969	42
	Washington Nationals	1969	42
25	Seattle Mariners	1977	34
	Toronto Blue Jays	1977	34
27	Colorado Rockies	1993	18
	Florida Marlins	1993	18
29	Arizona Diamondbacks	1998	13
	Tampa Bay Rays	1998	13

World Series Appearances

Rank	Team	Appearances	Year of Origin
1	New York Yankees	40	1901
2	Los Angeles Dodgers	18	1884
	San Francisco Giants	18	1883
4	St. Louis Cardinals	17	1882
5	Oakland Athletics	14	1901
6	Boston Red Sox	11	1901
7	Detroit Tigers	10	1901
	Chicago Cubs	10	1871
9	Cincinnati Reds	9	1882
	Atlanta Braves	9	1871
11	Pittsburgh Pirates	7	1882
	Baltimore Orioles	7	1901
	Philadelphia Phillies	7	1883
14	Minnesota Twins	6	1901
15	Chicago White Sox	5	1901
	Cleveland Indians	5	1901
17	New York Mets	4	1962
18	Florida Marlins	2	1993
	Toronto Blue Jays	2	1977
	Kansas City Royals	2	1969
	San Diego Padres	2	1969
22	Arizona Diamondbacks	1	1998
	Los Angeles Angels of Anaheim	1	1961
	Colorado Rockies	1	1993
	Houston Astros	1	1962
	Milwaukee Brewers	1	1969
	Tampa Bay Rays	1	1998
	Texas Rangers	1	1961
29	Seattle Mariners	0	1977
	Washington Nationals	0	1969

World Series Won

Rank	Team	Wins	Year of Origin
1	New York Yankees	27	1901
2	St. Louis Cardinals	10	1882
3	Oakland Athletics	9	1901
4	Boston Red Sox	7	1901
5	Los Angeles Dodgers	6	1884
	San Francisco Giants	6	1883
7	Cincinnati Reds	5	1882
	Pittsburgh Pirates	5	1882
9	Detroit Tigers	4	1901
10	Atlanta Braves	3	1871
	Baltimore Orioles	3	1901
	Chicago White Sox	3	1901
	Minnesota Twins	3	1901
14	Chicago Cubs	2	1871
	Cleveland Indians	2	1901
	Florida Marlins	2	1993
	New York Mets	2	1962
	Philadelphia Phillies	2	1883
	Toronto Blue Jays	2	1977
20	Arizona Diamondbacks	1	1998
	Kansas City Royals	1	1969
	Los Angeles Angels of Anaheim	1	1961
23	Colorado Rockies	0	1993
	Houston Astros	0	1962
	Milwaukee Brewers	0	1969
	San Diego Padres	0	1969
	Seattle Mariners	0	1977
	Tampa Bay Rays	0	1998
	Texas Rangers	0	1961
	Washington Nationals	0	1969

World Series Lost

Rank	Team	Losses	Year of Origin
1	New York Yankees	13	1901
2	Los Angeles Dodgers	12	1884
	San Francisco Giants	12	1883
4	Chicago Cubs	8	1871
5	St. Louis Cardinals	7	1882
6	Atlanta Braves	6	1871
	Detroit Tigers	6	1901
8	Oakland Athletics	5	1901
	Philadelphia Phillies	5	1883
10	Baltimore Orioles	4	1901
	Boston Red Sox	4	1901
	Cincinnati Reds	4	1882
13	Cleveland Indians	3	1901
	Minnesota Twins	3	1901
15	Chicago White Sox	2	1901
	New York Mets	2	1962
	Pittsburgh Pirates	2	1882
	San Diego Padres	2	1969
19	Colorado Rockies	1	1993
	Houston Astros	1	1962
	Kansas City Royals	1	1969
	Milwaukee Brewers	1	1969
	Tampa Bay Rays	1	1998
	Texas Rangers	1	1961
25	Arizona Diamondbacks	0	1998
	Florida Marlins	0	1993
	Los Angeles Angels of Anaheim	0	1961
	Seattle Mariners	0	1977
	Toronto Blue Jays	0	1977
	Washington Nationals	0	1969

League Titles

Rank	Team	League Titles	Year of Origin
1	New York Yankees	40	1901
2	Los Angeles Dodgers	22	1884
3	Atlanta Braves	21	1871
	St. Louis Cardinals	21	1882
	San Francisco Giants	21	1883
6	Chicago Cubs	16	1871
7	Oakland Athletics	15	1901
8	Boston Red Sox	12	1901
9	Cincinnati Reds	10	1882
	Detroit Tigers	10	1901
11	Pittsburgh Pirates	9	1882
12	Baltimore Orioles	7	1901
	Philadelphia Phillies	7	1883
14	Chicago White Sox	6	1901
	Minnesota Twins	6	1901
16	Cleveland Indians	5	1901
17	New York Mets	4	1962
18	Florida Marlins	2	1993
	Kansas City Royals	2	1969
	San Diego Padres	2	1969
	Toronto Blue Jays	2	1977
22	Arizona Diamondbacks	1	1998
	Colorado Rockies	1	1993
	Houston Astros	1	1962
	Los Angeles Angels of Anaheim	1	1961
	Milwaukee Brewers	1	1969
	Tampa Bay Rays	1	1998
	Texas Rangers	1	1961
29	Seattle Mariners	0	1977
	Washington Nationals	0	1969

This includes League Titles Won before 1969 as well as League Championship Series Won.
To see the ranked list for just League Championship Series won go to page 278.

League Titles Before 1969

Rank	Team	League Titles	Year of Origin
1	New York Yankees	29	1901
2	San Francisco Giants	18	1883
3	Los Angeles Dodgers	17	1884
4	Atlanta Braves	16	1871
	Chicago Cubs	16	1871
	St. Louis Cardinals	16	1882
7	Oakland Athletics	9	1901
8	Boston Red Sox	8	1901
	Detroit Tigers	8	1901
10	Pittsburgh Pirates	7	1882
11	Chicago White Sox	5	1901
	Cincinnati Reds	5	1882
13	Minnesota Twins	4	1901
14	Cleveland Indians	3	1901
15	Baltimore Orioles	2	1901
	Philadelphia Phillies	2	1883
17	Arizona Diamondbacks*	0	1998
	Colorado Rockies*	0	1993
	Florida Marlins*	0	1993
	Houston Astros	0	1962
	Kansas City Royals*	0	1969
	Los Angeles Angels of Anaheim	0	1961
	Milwaukee Brewers*	0	1969
	New York Mets	0	1962
	San Diego Padres*	0	1969
	Seattle Mariners*	0	1977
	Tampa Bay Rays*	0	1998
	Texas Rangers	0	1961
	Toronto Blue Jays*	0	1977
	Washington Nationals*	0	1969

* Indicates that team did not exist before 1969

Division Titles

Rank	Team	Divisions	Year of Origin
1	Atlanta Braves	16	1871
	New York Yankees	16	1901
3	Oakland Athletics	14	1901
4	Los Angeles Dodgers	11	1884
	Philadelphia Phillies	11	1883
6	Minnesota Twins	10	1901
	St. Louis Cardinals	10	1882
8	Cincinnati Reds	9	1882
	Pittsburgh Pirates	9	1882
10	Baltimore Orioles	8	1901
	Los Angeles Angels of Anaheim	8	1961
12	Cleveland Indians	7	1901
	Houston Astros	7	1962
	Kansas City Royals	7	1969
	San Francisco Giants	7	1883
16	Boston Red Sox	6	1901
17	Chicago Cubs	5	1871
	Chicago White Sox	5	1901
	New York Mets	5	1962
	San Diego Padres	5	1969
	Toronto Blue Jays	5	1977
22	Arizona Diamondbacks	4	1998
	Texas Rangers	4	1961
24	Detroit Tigers	3	1901
	Seattle Mariners	3	1977
26	Milwaukee Brewers	2	1969
	Tampa Bay Rays	2	1998
28	Washington Nationals	1	1969
29	Florida Marlins	0	1993
	Colorado Rockies	0	1993

Divisions started in 1969.

Wild Card Playoff Appearances

Rank	Team	Wild Cards	Year of Origin
1	Boston Red Sox	7	1901
2	New York Yankees	4	1901
3	Colorado Rockies	3	1993
4	Florida Marlins	2	1993
	Houston Astros	2	1962
	Los Angeles Dodgers	2	1884
	New York Mets	2	1962
8	Atlanta Braves	1	1871
	Baltimore Orioles	1	1901
	Chicago Cubs	1	1871
	Detroit Tigers	1	1901
	Los Angeles Angels of Anaheim	1	1961
	Milwaukee Brewers	1	1969
	Oakland Athletics	1	1901
	San Francisco Giants	1	1883
	Seattle Mariners	1	1977
	St. Louis Cardinals	1	1882
18	Arizona Diamondbacks	0	1998
	Chicago White Sox	0	1901
	Cincinnati Reds	0	1882
	Cleveland Indians	0	1901
	Kansas City Royals	0	1969
	Minnesota Twins	0	1901
	Philadelphia Phillies	0	1883
	Pittsburgh Pirates	0	1882
	San Diego Padres	0	1969
	Tampa Bay Rays	0	1998
	Texas Rangers	0	1961
	Toronto Blue Jays	0	1977
	Washington Nationals	0	1969

Wild Cards started in 1995.

255

Postseason Games Won – All Rounds

Rank	Team	Wins	Year of Origin
1	New York Yankees	218	1901
2	St. Louis Cardinals	98	1882
3	Boston Red Sox	79	1901
4	Oakland Athletics	78	1901
5	Atlanta Braves	77	1871
6	Los Angeles Dodgers	76	1884
7	San Francisco Giants	74	1883
8	Baltimore Orioles	48	1901
9	Philadelphia Phillies	47	1883
	Cincinnati Reds	47	1882
11	Cleveland Indians	44	1901
12	New York Mets	43	1962
13	Pittsburgh Pirates	40	1882
	Detroit Tigers	40	1901
15	Minnesota Twins	33	1901
16	Chicago Cubs	28	1871
	Chicago White Sox	28	1901
18	Los Angeles Angels of Anaheim	27	1961
19	Florida Marlins	22	1993
20	Houston Astros	21	1962
	Toronto Blue Jays	21	1977
22	Kansas City Royals	18	1969
23	Arizona Diamondbacks	15	1998
	Seattle Mariners	15	1977
25	San Diego Padres	12	1969
26	Tampa Bay Rays	10	1998
27	Colorado Rockies	9	1993
	Milwaukee Brewers	9	1969
	Texas Rangers	9	1961
30	Washington Nationals	5	1969

Postseason Games Lost – All Rounds

Rank	Team	Losses	Year of Origin
1	New York Yankees	145	1901
2	Los Angeles Dodgers	97	1884
3	St. Louis Cardinals	88	1882
4	Atlanta Braves	82	1871
5	San Francisco Giants	77	1883
6	Boston Red Sox	72	1901
7	Oakland Athletics	69	1901
8	Chicago Cubs	55	1871
9	Philadelphia Phillies	51	1883
10	Minnesota Twins	50	1901
11	Pittsburgh Pirates	49	1882
12	Cincinnati Reds	42	1882
13	Cleveland Indians	41	1901
	Detroit Tigers	41	1901
15	Baltimore Orioles	36	1901
16	Houston Astros	35	1962
17	Los Angeles Angels of Anaheim	34	1961
18	New York Mets	31	1962
19	Chicago White Sox	27	1901
20	Kansas City Royals	25	1969
21	San Diego Padres	22	1969
22	Toronto Blue Jays	20	1977
23	Seattle Mariners	19	1977
24	Texas Rangers	17	1961
25	Arizona Diamondbacks	16	1998
26	Milwaukee Brewers	12	1969
	Florida Marlins	12	1993
28	Tampa Bay Rays	11	1998
29	Colorado Rockies	10	1993
30	Washington Nationals	5	1969

Postseason Games Winning Percentage – All Rounds

Rank	Team	Win %	Year of Origin
1	Florida Marlins	0.647	1993
2	New York Yankees	0.601	1901
3	New York Mets	0.581	1962
4	Baltimore Orioles	0.571	1901
5	Oakland Athletics	0.531	1901
6	Cincinnati Reds	0.528	1882
7	St. Louis Cardinals	0.527	1882
8	Boston Red Sox	0.523	1901
9	Cleveland Indians	0.518	1901
10	Toronto Blue Jays	0.512	1977
11	Chicago White Sox	0.509	1901
12	Washington Nationals	0.500	1969
13	Detroit Tigers	0.494	1901
14	San Francisco Giants	0.490	1883
15	Arizona Diamondbacks	0.484	1998
	Atlanta Braves	0.484	1871
17	Philadelphia Phillies	0.480	1883
18	Tampa Bay Rays	0.476	1998
19	Colorado Rockies	0.474	1993
20	Pittsburgh Pirates	0.449	1882
21	Los Angeles Angels of Anaheim	0.443	1961
22	Seattle Mariners	0.441	1977
23	Los Angeles Dodgers	0.439	1884
24	Milwaukee Brewers	0.429	1969
25	Kansas City Royals	0.419	1969
26	Minnesota Twins	0.398	1901
27	Houston Astros	0.375	1962
28	San Diego Padres	0.353	1969
29	Texas Rangers	0.346	1961
30	Chicago Cubs	0.337	1871

This is the same chart as on page 247. It is listed here to be included with the other Postseason Games themed tables. It is located on page 247 to be used as a comparison to the data in the table on page 246, the Regular Season Winning Percentage table.

Postseason Games Played – All Rounds

Rank	Team	Games	Year of Origin
1	New York Yankees	363	1901
2	St. Louis Cardinals	186	1882
3	Los Angeles Dodgers	173	1884
4	Atlanta Braves	159	1871
5	Boston Red Sox	151	1901
	San Francisco Giants	151	1883
7	Oakland Athletics	147	1901
8	Philadelphia Phillies	98	1883
9	Cincinnati Reds	89	1882
	Pittsburgh Pirates	89	1882
11	Cleveland Indians	85	1901
12	Baltimore Orioles	84	1901
13	Chicago Cubs	83	1871
	Minnesota Twins	83	1901
15	Detroit Tigers	81	1901
16	New York Mets	74	1962
17	Los Angeles Angels of Anaheim	61	1961
18	Houston Astros	56	1962
19	Chicago White Sox	55	1901
20	Kansas City Royals	43	1969
21	Toronto Blue Jays	41	1977
22	Florida Marlins	34	1993
	San Diego Padres	34	1969
	Seattle Mariners	34	1977
25	Arizona Diamondbacks	31	1998
26	Texas Rangers	26	1961
27	Milwaukee Brewers	21	1969
	Tampa Bay Rays	21	1998
29	Colorado Rockies	19	1993
30	Washington Nationals	10	1969

World Series Games Won

Rank	Team	Wins	Year of Origin
1	New York Yankees	134	1901
2	St. Louis Cardinals	52	1882
3	San Francisco Giants	49	1883
4	Los Angeles Dodgers	45	1884
5	Boston Red Sox	41	1901
	Oakland Athletics	41	1901
7	Detroit Tigers	27	1901
8	Cincinnati Reds	26	1882
9	Atlanta Braves	24	1871
10	Pittsburgh Pirates	23	1882
11	Baltimore Orioles	21	1901
12	Chicago Cubs	19	1871
	Minnesota Twins	19	1901
14	Chicago White Sox	17	1901
15	Cleveland Indians	14	1901
	Philadelphia Phillies	14	1883
17	New York Mets	12	1962
18	Florida Marlins	8	1993
	Toronto Blue Jays	8	1977
20	Kansas City Royals	6	1969
21	Arizona Diamondbacks	4	1998
	Los Angeles Angels of Anaheim	4	1961
23	Milwaukee Brewers	3	1969
24	San Diego Padres	1	1969
	Tampa Bay Rays	1	1998
	Texas Rangers	1	1961
27	Colorado Rockies	0	1993
	Houston Astros	0	1962
	Seattle Mariners	0	1977
	Washington Nationals	0	1969

World Series Games Lost

Rank	Team	Losses	Year of Origin
1	New York Yankees	90	1901
2	Los Angeles Dodgers	60	1884
3	San Francisco Giants	54	1883
4	St. Louis Cardinals	53	1882
5	Oakland Athletics	34	1901
6	Chicago Cubs	33	1871
	Detroit Tigers	33	1901
8	Atlanta Braves	29	1871
9	Boston Red Sox	26	1901
10	Cincinnati Reds	25	1882
11	Pittsburgh Pirates	24	1882
12	Philadelphia Phillies	23	1883
13	Minnesota Twins	21	1901
14	Baltimore Orioles	18	1901
15	Cleveland Indians	16	1901
16	Chicago White Sox	13	1901
17	New York Mets	12	1962
18	San Diego Padres	8	1969
19	Kansas City Royals	7	1969
20	Florida Marlins	5	1993
21	Colorado Rockies	4	1993
	Houston Astros	4	1962
	Milwaukee Brewers	4	1969
	Tampa Bay Rays	4	1998
	Texas Rangers	4	1961
	Toronto Blue Jays	4	1977
27	Arizona Diamondbacks	3	1998
	Los Angeles Angels of Anaheim	3	1961
29	Seattle Mariners	0	1977
	Washington Nationals	0	1969

World Series Games Winning Percentage

Rank	Team	Win %	Year of Origin
1	Toronto Blue Jays	0.667	1977
2	Florida Marlins	0.615	1993
3	Boston Red Sox	0.612	1901
4	New York Yankees	0.598	1901
5	Arizona Diamondbacks	0.571	1998
	Los Angeles Angels of Anaheim	0.571	1961
7	Chicago White Sox	0.567	1901
8	Oakland Athletics	0.547	1901
9	Baltimore Orioles	0.538	1901
10	Cincinnati Reds	0.510	1882
11	New York Mets	0.500	1962
12	St. Louis Cardinals	0.495	1882
13	Pittsburgh Pirates	0.489	1882
14	San Francisco Giants	0.476	1883
15	Minnesota Twins	0.475	1901
16	Cleveland Indians	0.467	1901
17	Kansas City Royals	0.462	1969
18	Atlanta Braves	0.453	1871
19	Detroit Tigers	0.450	1901
20	Los Angeles Dodgers	0.429	1884
	Milwaukee Brewers	0.429	1969
22	Philadelphia Phillies	0.378	1883
23	Chicago Cubs	0.365	1871
24	Tampa Bay Rays	0.200	1998
	Texas Rangers	0.200	1961
26	San Diego Padres	0.111	1969
27	Colorado Rockies	0.000	1993
	Houston Astros	0.000	1962
	Seattle Mariners	0.000	1977
	Washington Nationals	0.000	1969

World Series Games Played

Rank	Team	Games	Year of Origin
1	New York Yankees	224	1901
2	Los Angeles Dodgers	105	1884
	St. Louis Cardinals	105	1882
4	San Francisco Giants	103	1883
5	Oakland Athletics	75	1901
6	Boston Red Sox	67	1901
7	Detroit Tigers	60	1901
8	Atlanta Braves	53	1871
9	Chicago Cubs	52	1871
10	Cincinnati Reds	51	1882
11	Pittsburgh Pirates	47	1882
12	Minnesota Twins	40	1901
13	Baltimore Orioles	39	1901
14	Philadelphia Phillies	37	1883
15	Chicago White Sox	30	1901
	Cleveland Indians	30	1901
17	New York Mets	24	1962
18	Florida Marlins	13	1993
	Kansas City Royals	13	1969
20	Toronto Blue Jays	12	1977
21	San Diego Padres	9	1969
22	Arizona Diamondbacks	7	1998
	Los Angeles Angels of Anaheim	7	1961
	Milwaukee Brewers	7	1969
25	Tampa Bay Rays	5	1998
	Texas Rangers	5	1961
27	Colorado Rockies	4	1993
	Houston Astros	4	1962
29	Seattle Mariners	0	1977
	Washington Nationals	0	1969

League Championship Series Games Won

Rank	Team	Wins	Year of Origin
1	New York Yankees	45	1901
2	Atlanta Braves	27	1871
3	St. Louis Cardinals	26	1882
4	Oakland Athletics	23	1901
5	Boston Red Sox	22	1901
	New York Mets	22	1962
	Philadelphia Phillies	22	1883
8	Baltimore Orioles	21	1901
	Los Angeles Dodgers	21	1884
10	Cincinnati Reds	18	1882
11	Pittsburgh Pirates	17	1882
12	San Francisco Giants	16	1883
13	Cleveland Indians	13	1901
	Los Angeles Angels of Anaheim	13	1961
	Toronto Blue Jays	13	1977
16	Kansas City Royals	12	1969
17	Houston Astros	11	1962
18	Detroit Tigers	10	1901
19	Minnesota Twins	9	1901
20	Florida Marlins	8	1993
21	Chicago White Sox	7	1901
	San Diego Padres	7	1969
23	Chicago Cubs	6	1871
24	Seattle Mariners	5	1977
25	Arizona Diamondbacks	4	1998
	Colorado Rockies	4	1993
	Tampa Bay Rays	4	1998
	Texas Rangers	4	1961
29	Milwaukee Brewers	3	1969
30	Washington Nationals	2	1969

The LCS started in 1969.

League Championship Series Games Lost

Rank	Team	Losses	Year of Origin
1	Atlanta Braves	33	1871
2	Boston Red Sox	29	1901
3	New York Yankees	28	1901
4	St. Louis Cardinals	27	1882
5	Pittsburgh Pirates	25	1882
6	Los Angeles Dodgers	23	1884
	Oakland Athletics	23	1901
8	Philadelphia Phillies	20	1883
9	Los Angeles Angels of Anaheim	19	1961
10	New York Mets	17	1962
11	Baltimore Orioles	16	1901
	Toronto Blue Jays	16	1977
13	Kansas City Royals	15	1969
14	Cincinnati Reds	14	1882
15	Houston Astros	13	1962
16	Cleveland Indians	12	1901
	Minnesota Twins	12	1901
	Seattle Mariners	12	1977
19	Chicago Cubs	11	1871
	San Francisco Giants	11	1883
21	Chicago White Sox	8	1901
22	Detroit Tigers	7	1901
23	Arizona Diamondbacks	5	1998
	Florida Marlins	5	1993
25	San Diego Padres	4	1969
26	Tampa Bay Rays	3	1998
	Washington Nationals	3	1969
28	Milwaukee Brewers	2	1969
	Texas Rangers	2	1961
30	Colorado Rockies	0	1993

The LCS started in 1969.

League Championship Series Games Winning Percentage

Rank	Team	Win %	Year of Origin
1	Colorado Rockies	1.000	1993
2	Texas Rangers	0.667	1961
3	San Diego Padres	0.636	1969
4	New York Yankees	0.616	1901
5	Florida Marlins	0.615	1993
6	Milwaukee Brewers	0.600	1969
7	San Francisco Giants	0.593	1883
8	Detroit Tigers	0.588	1901
9	Tampa Bay Rays	0.571	1998
10	Baltimore Orioles	0.568	1901
11	New York Mets	0.564	1962
12	Cincinnati Reds	0.563	1882
13	Philadelphia Phillies	0.524	1883
14	Cleveland Indians	0.520	1901
15	Oakland Athletics	0.500	1901
16	St. Louis Cardinals	0.491	1882
17	Los Angeles Dodgers	0.477	1884
18	Chicago White Sox	0.467	1901
19	Houston Astros	0.458	1962
20	Atlanta Braves	0.450	1871
21	Toronto Blue Jays	0.448	1977
22	Arizona Diamondbacks	0.444	1998
	Kansas City Royals	0.444	1969
24	Boston Red Sox	0.431	1901
25	Minnesota Twins	0.429	1901
26	Los Angeles Angels of Anaheim	0.406	1961
27	Pittsburgh Pirates	0.405	1882
28	Washington Nationals	0.400	1969
29	Chicago Cubs	0.353	1871
30	Seattle Mariners	0.294	1977

The LCS started in 1969.

League Championship Series Games Played

Rank	Team	Games	Year of Origin
1	New York Yankees	73	1901
2	Atlanta Braves	60	1871
3	St. Louis Cardinals	53	1882
4	Boston Red Sox	51	1901
5	Oakland Athletics	46	1901
6	Los Angeles Dodgers	44	1884
7	Philadelphia Phillies	42	1883
	Pittsburgh Pirates	42	1882
9	New York Mets	39	1962
10	Baltimore Orioles	37	1901
11	Cincinnati Reds	32	1882
	Los Angeles Angels of Anaheim	32	1961
13	Toronto Blue Jays	29	1977
14	Kansas City Royals	27	1969
	San Francisco Giants	27	1883
16	Cleveland Indians	25	1901
17	Houston Astros	24	1962
18	Minnesota Twins	21	1901
19	Chicago Cubs	17	1871
	Detroit Tigers	17	1901
	Seattle Mariners	17	1977
22	Chicago White Sox	15	1901
23	Florida Marlins	13	1993
24	San Diego Padres	11	1969
25	Arizona Diamondbacks	9	1998
26	Tampa Bay Rays	7	1998
27	Texas Rangers	6	1961
28	Milwaukee Brewers	5	1969
	Washington Nationals	5	1969
30	Colorado Rockies	4	1993

The LCS started in 1969.

League Division Series Games Won

Rank	Team	Wins	Year of Origin
1	New York Yankees	39	1901
2	Atlanta Braves	26	1871
3	St. Louis Cardinals	20	1882
4	Cleveland Indians	17	1901
5	Boston Red Sox	16	1901
6	Oakland Athletics	14	1901
7	Philadelphia Phillies	11	1883
8	Houston Astros	10	1962
	Los Angeles Angels of Anaheim	10	1961
	Los Angeles Dodgers	10	1884
	Seattle Mariners	10	1977
12	New York Mets	9	1962
	San Francisco Giants	9	1883
14	Arizona Diamondbacks	7	1998
15	Baltimore Orioles	6	1901
	Florida Marlins	6	1993
17	Colorado Rockies	5	1993
	Minnesota Twins	5	1901
	Tampa Bay Rays	5	1998
20	Chicago White Sox	4	1901
	San Diego Padres	4	1969
	Texas Rangers	4	1961
23	Chicago Cubs	3	1871
	Cincinnati Reds	3	1882
	Detroit Tigers	3	1901
	Milwaukee Brewers	3	1969
	Washington Nationals	3	1969
28	Kansas City Royals	0	1969
	Pittsburgh Pirates	0	1882
	Toronto Blue Jays	0	1977

The LDS started in 1995, and was played in 1981 due to a split season caused by a players strike.

League Division Series Games Lost

Rank	Team	Losses	Year of Origin
1	New York Yankees	27	1901
2	Atlanta Braves	20	1871
3	Houston Astros	18	1962
4	Boston Red Sox	17	1901
	Minnesota Twins	17	1901
6	Los Angeles Dodgers	14	1884
7	Cleveland Indians	13	1901
8	Los Angeles Angles of Anaheim	12	1961
	Oakland Athletics	12	1901
	San Francisco Giants	12	1883
11	Chicago Cubs	11	1871
	Texas Rangers	11	1961
13	San Diego Padres	10	1969
14	Arizona Diamondbacks	8	1998
	Philadelphia Phillies	8	1883
	St. Louis Cardinals	8	1882
17	Seattle Mariners	7	1977
18	Chicago White Sox	6	1901
	Colorado Rockies	6	1993
	Milwaukee Brewers	6	1969
21	Tampa Bay Rays	4	1998
22	Cincinnati Reds	3	1882
	Kansas City Royals	3	1969
24	Baltimore Orioles	2	1901
	Florida Marlins	2	1993
	New York Mets	2	1962
	Washington Nationals	2	1969
28	Detroit Tigers	1	1901
29	Pittsburgh Pirates	0	1882
	Toronto Blue Jays	0	1977

The LDS started in 1995, and was played in 1981 due to a split season caused by a players strike.

League Division Series Games Winning Percentage

Rank	Team	Win %	Year of Origin
1	New York Mets	0.818	1962
2	Baltimore Orioles	0.750	1901
	Detroit Tigers	0.750	1901
	Florida Marlins	0.750	1993
5	St. Louis Cardinals	0.714	1882
6	Washington Nationals	0.600	1969
7	New York Yankees	0.591	1901
8	Seattle Mariners	0.588	1977
9	Philadelphia Phillies	0.579	1883
10	Cleveland Indians	0.567	1901
11	Atlanta Braves	0.565	1871
12	Tampa Bay Rays	0.556	1998
13	Oakland Athletics	0.538	1901
14	Cincinnati Reds	0.500	1882
15	Boston Red Sox	0.485	1901
16	Arizona Diamondbacks	0.467	1998
17	Colorado Rockies	0.455	1993
	Los Angeles Angels of Anaheim	0.455	1961
19	San Francisco Giants	0.429	1883
20	Los Angeles Dodgers	0.417	1884
21	Chicago White Sox	0.400	1901
22	Houston Astros	0.357	1962
23	Milwaukee Brewers	0.333	1969
24	San Diego Padres	0.286	1969
25	Texas Rangers	0.267	1961
26	Minnesota Twins	0.227	1901
27	Chicago Cubs	0.214	1871
28	Kansas City Royals	0.000	1969
	Pittsburgh Pirates	0.000	1882
	Toronto Blue Jays	0.000	1977

The LDS started in 1995, and was played in 1981 due to a split season
caused by a players strike.

League Division Series Games Played

Rank	Team	Games	Year of Origin
1	New York Yankees	66	1901
2	Atlanta Braves	46	1871
3	Boston Red Sox	33	1901
4	Cleveland Indians	30	1901
5	Houston Astros	28	1962
	St. Louis Cardinals	28	1882
7	Oakland Athletics	26	1901
8	Los Angeles Dodgers	24	1884
9	Los Angeles Angels of Anaheim	22	1961
	Minnesota Twins	22	1901
11	San Francisco Giants	21	1883
12	Philadelphia Phillies	19	1883
13	Seattle Mariners	17	1977
14	Arizona Diamondbacks	15	1998
	Texas Rangers	15	1961
16	Chicago Cubs	14	1871
	San Diego Padres	14	1969
18	Colorado Rockies	11	1993
	New York Mets	11	1962
20	Chicago White Sox	10	1901
21	Milwaukee Brewers	9	1969
	Tampa Bay Rays	9	1998
23	Baltimore Orioles	8	1901
	Florida Marlins	8	1993
25	Cincinnati Reds	6	1882
26	Washington Nationals	5	1969
27	Detroit Tigers	4	1901
28	Kansas City Royals	3	1969
29	Pittsburgh Pirates	0	1882
	Toronto Blue Jays	0	1977

The LDS started in 1995, and was played in 1981 due to a split season caused by a players strike.

Postseason Series Won – All Rounds

Rank	Team	Wins	Year of Origin
1	New York Yankees	48	1901
2	St. Louis Cardinals	21	1882
3	Oakland Athletics	17	1901
4	Boston Red Sox	16	1901
5	Atlanta Braves	14	1871
	Los Angeles Dodgers	14	1884
7	Cincinnati Reds	11	1882
	San Francisco Giants	11	1883
9	Baltimore Orioles	10	1901
	Philadelphia Phillies	10	1883
11	New York Mets	9	1962
12	Cleveland Indians	8	1901
13	Detroit Tigers	7	1901
	Pittsburgh Pirates	7	1882
15	Florida Marlins	6	1993
	Minnesota Twins	6	1901
17	Chicago White Sox	5	1901
	Los Angeles Angels of Anaheim	5	1961
19	Arizona Diamondbacks	4	1998
	Toronto Blue Jays	4	1977
21	Chicago Cubs	3	1871
	Houston Astros	3	1962
	Kansas City Royals	3	1969
	San Diego Padres	3	1969
	Seattle Mariners	3	1977
26	Colorado Rockies	2	1993
	Tampa Bay Rays	2	1998
	Texas Rangers	2	1961
29	Milwaukee Brewers	1	1969
	Washington Nationals	1	1969

Postseason Series Lost – All Rounds

Rank	Team	Losses	Year of Origin
1	New York Yankees	22	1901
2	Los Angeles Dodgers	20	1884
3	Atlanta Braves	18	1871
4	San Francisco Giants	17	1883
5	Chicago Cubs	14	1871
	Oakland Athletics	14	1901
7	Boston Red Sox	13	1901
	St. Louis Cardinals	13	1882
9	Minnesota Twins	11	1901
	Philadelphia Phillies	11	1883
11	Houston Astros	9	1962
	Pittsburgh Pirates	9	1882
13	Baltimore Orioles	8	1901
	Cincinnati Reds	8	1882
	Cleveland Indians	8	1901
	Detroit Tigers	8	1901
	Los Angeles Angels of Anaheim	8	1961
18	Chicago White Sox	6	1901
	Kansas City Royals	6	1969
20	New York Mets	5	1962
	San Diego Padres	5	1969
22	Seattle Mariners	4	1977
	Texas Rangers	4	1961
24	Arizona Diamondbacks	3	1998
	Colorado Rockies	3	1993
	Milwaukee Brewers	3	1969
	Toronto Blue Jays	3	1977
28	Tampa Bay Rays	2	1998
29	Washington Nationals	1	1969
30	Florida Marlins	0	1993

Postseason Series Winning Percentage – All Rounds

Rank	Team	Win %	Year of Origin
1	Florida Marlins	1.000	1993
2	New York Yankees	0.686	1901
3	New York Mets	0.643	1962
4	St. Louis Cardinals	0.618	1882
5	Cincinnati Reds	0.579	1882
6	Arizona Diamondbacks	0.571	1998
	Toronto Blue Jays	0.571	1977
8	Baltimore Orioles	0.556	1901
9	Boston Red Sox	0.552	1901
10	Oakland Athletics	0.548	1901
11	Cleveland Indians	0.500	1901
	Tampa Bay Rays	0.500	1998
	Washington Nationals	0.500	1969
14	Philadelphia Phillies	0.476	1883
15	Detroit Tigers	0.467	1901
16	Chicago White Sox	0.455	1901
17	Atlanta Braves	0.438	1871
	Pittsburgh Pirates	0.438	1882
19	Seattle Mariners	0.429	1977
20	San Francisco Giants	0.414	1883
21	Los Angeles Dodgers	0.412	1884
22	Colorado Rockies	0.400	1993
23	Los Angeles Angels of Anaheim	0.385	1961
24	San Diego Padres	0.375	1969
25	Minnesota Twins	0.353	1901
26	Kansas City Royals	0.333	1969
	Texas Rangers	0.333	1961
28	Houston Astros	0.250	1962
	Milwaukee Brewers	0.250	1969
30	Chicago Cubs	0.176	1871

Postseason Series Played – All Rounds

Rank	Team	Series Played	Year of Origin
1	New York Yankees	70	1901
2	Los Angeles Dodgers	34	1884
	St. Louis Cardinals	34	1882
4	Atlanta Braves	32	1871
5	Oakland Athletics	31	1901
6	Boston Red Sox	29	1901
7	San Francisco Giants	28	1883
8	Philadelphia Phillies	21	1883
9	Cincinnati Reds	19	1882
10	Baltimore Orioles	18	1901
11	Chicago Cubs	17	1871
	Minnesota Twins	17	1901
13	Cleveland Indians	16	1901
	Pittsburgh Pirates	16	1882
15	Detroit Tigers	15	1901
16	New York Mets	14	1962
17	Los Angeles Angels of Anaheim	13	1961
18	Houston Astros	12	1962
19	Chicago White Sox	11	1901
20	Kansas City Royals	9	1969
21	San Diego Padres	8	1969
22	Arizona Diamondbacks	7	1998
	Seattle Mariners	7	1977
	Toronto Blue Jays	7	1977
25	Florida Marlins	6	1993
	Texas Rangers	6	1961
27	Colorado Rockies	5	1993
28	Milwaukee Brewers	4	1969
	Tampa Bay Rays	4	1998
30	Washington Nationals	2	1969

World Series – Series Winning Percentage

Rank	Team	Win %	Year of Origin
1	Arizona Diamondbacks	1.000	1998
	Florida Marlins	1.000	1993
	Los Angeles Angels of Anaheim	1.000	1961
	Toronto Blue Jays	1.000	1977
5	Pittsburgh Pirates	0.714	1882
6	New York Yankees	0.675	1901
7	Oakland Athletics	0.643	1901
8	Boston Red Sox	0.636	1901
9	Chicago White Sox	0.600	1901
10	St. Louis Cardinals	0.588	1882
11	Cincinnati Reds	0.556	1882
12	Kansas City Royals	0.500	1969
	Minnesota Twins	0.500	1901
	New York Mets	0.500	1962
15	Baltimore Orioles	0.429	1901
16	Cleveland Indians	0.400	1901
	Detroit Tigers	0.400	1901
18	Atlanta Braves	0.333	1871
	Los Angeles Dodgers	0.333	1884
	San Francisco Giants	0.333	1883
21	Philadelphia Phillies	0.286	1883
22	Chicago Cubs	0.200	1871
23	Colorado Rockies	0.000	1993
	Houston Astros	0.000	1962
	Milwaukee Brewers	0.000	1969
	San Diego Padres	0.000	1969
	Seattle Mariners	0.000	1977
	Tampa Bay Rays	0.000	1998
	Texas Rangers	0.000	1961
	Washington Nationals	0.000	1969

Please note that World Series Won and World Series Lost tables are
located on pages 250 and 251, respectively.

World Series – Series Played

Rank	Team	Series Played	Year of Origin
1	New York Yankees	40	1901
2	Los Angeles Dodgers	18	1884
	San Francisco Giants	18	1883
4	St. Louis Cardinals	17	1882
5	Oakland Athletics	14	1901
6	Boston Red Sox	11	1901
7	Chicago Cubs	10	1871
	Detroit Tigers	10	1901
9	Atlanta Braves	9	1871
	Cincinnati Reds	9	1882
11	Baltimore Orioles	7	1901
	Philadelphia Phillies	7	1883
	Pittsburgh Pirates	7	1882
14	Minnesota Twins	6	1901
15	Chicago White Sox	5	1901
	Cleveland Indians	5	1901
17	New York Mets	4	1962
18	Florida Marlins	2	1993
	Kansas City Royals	2	1969
	San Diego Padres	2	1969
	Toronto Blue Jays	2	1977
22	Arizona Diamondbacks	1	1998
	Colorado Rockies	1	1993
	Houston Astros	1	1962
	Los Angeles Angels of Anaheim	1	1961
	Milwaukee Brewers	1	1969
	Tampa Bay Rays	1	1998
	Texas Rangers	1	1961
29	Seattle Mariners	0	1977
	Washington Nationals	0	1969

Please note that World Series Won and World Series Lost tables are
located on pages 250 and 251, respectively.

League Championship Series – Series Won

Rank	Team	Wins	Year of Origin
1	New York Yankees	11	1901
2	Oakland Athletics	6	1901
3	Atlanta Braves	5	1871
	Baltimore Orioles	5	1901
	Cincinnati Reds	5	1882
	Los Angeles Dodgers	5	1884
	Philadelphia Phillies	5	1883
	St. Louis Cardinals	5	1882
9	Boston Red Sox	4	1901
	New York Mets	4	1962
11	San Francisco Giants	3	1883
12	Cleveland Indians	2	1901
	Detroit Tigers	2	1901
	Florida Marlins	2	1993
	Kansas City Royals	2	1969
	Minnesota Twins	2	1901
	Pittsburgh Pirates	2	1882
	San Diego Padres	2	1969
	Toronto Blue Jays	2	1977
20	Arizona Diamondbacks	1	1998
	Chicago White Sox	1	1901
	Colorado Rockies	1	1993
	Houston Astros	1	1962
	Los Angeles Angels of Anaheim	1	1961
	Milwaukee Brewers	1	1969
	Tampa Bay Rays	1	1998
	Texas Rangers	1	1961
28	Chicago Cubs	0	1871
	Seattle Mariners	0	1977
	Washington Nationals	0	1969

The LCS started in 1969.

League Championship Series – Series Lost

Rank	Team	Losses	Year of Origin
1	Pittsburgh Pirates	7	1882
2	Atlanta Braves	6	1871
3	Boston Red Sox	5	1901
	Los Angeles Angels of Anaheim	5	1961
	Oakland Athletics	5	1901
6	Baltimore Orioles	4	1901
	Kansas City Royals	4	1969
	Los Angeles Dodgers	4	1884
	Philadelphia Phillies	4	1883
	St. Louis Cardinals	4	1882
11	Chicago Cubs	3	1871
	Cincinnati Reds	3	1882
	Houston Astros	3	1962
	Minnesota Twins	3	1901
	New York Mets	3	1962
	New York Yankees	3	1901
	Seattle Mariners	3	1977
	Toronto Blue Jays	3	1977
19	Chicago White Sox	2	1901
	Cleveland Indians	2	1901
	Detroit Tigers	2	1901
	San Francisco Giants	2	1883
23	Arizona Diamondbacks	1	1998
	Washington Nationals	1	1969
25	Colorado Rockies	0	1993
	Florida Marlins	0	1993
	Milwaukee Brewers	0	1969
	San Diego Padres	0	1969
	Tampa Bay Rays	0	1998
	Texas Rangers	0	1961

The LCS started in 1969.

League Championship Series – Series Winning Percentage

Rank	Team	Win %	Year of Origin
1	Colorado Rockies	1.000	1993
	Florida Marlins	1.000	1993
	Milwaukee Brewers	1.000	1969
	San Diego Padres	1.000	1969
	Tampa Bay Rays	1.000	1998
	Texas Rangers	1.000	1961
7	New York Yankees	0.786	1901
8	Cincinnati Reds	0.625	1882
9	San Francisco Giants	0.600	1883
10	New York Mets	0.571	1962
11	Baltimore Orioles	0.556	1901
	Los Angeles Dodgers	0.556	1884
	Philadelphia Phillies	0.556	1883
	St. Louis Cardinals	0.556	1882
15	Oakland Athletics	0.545	1901
16	Arizona Diamondbacks	0.500	1998
	Cleveland Indians	0.500	1901
	Detroit Tigers	0.500	1901
19	Atlanta Braves	0.455	1871
20	Boston Red Sox	0.444	1901
21	Minnesota Twins	0.400	1901
	Toronto Blue Jays	0.400	1977
23	Chicago White Sox	0.333	1901
	Kansas City Royals	0.333	1969
25	Houston Astros	0.250	1962
26	Pittsburgh Pirates	0.222	1882
27	Los Angeles Angels of Anaheim	0.167	1961
28	Chicago Cubs	0.000	1871
	Seattle Mariners	0.000	1977
	Washington Nationals	0.000	1969

The LCS started in 1969.

League Championship Series – Series Played

Rank	Team	Series Played	Year of Origin
1	New York Yankees	14	1901
2	Atlanta Braves	11	1871
	Oakland Athletics	11	1901
4	Baltimore Orioles	9	1901
	Boston Red Sox	9	1901
	Los Angeles Dodgers	9	1884
	Philadelphia Phillies	9	1883
	Pittsburgh Pirates	9	1882
	St. Louis Cardinals	9	1882
10	Cincinnati Reds	8	1882
11	New York Mets	7	1962
12	Kansas City Royals	6	1969
	Los Angeles Angels of Anaheim	6	1961
14	Minnesota Twins	5	1901
	San Francisco Giants	5	1883
	Toronto Blue Jays	5	1977
17	Cleveland Indians	4	1901
	Detroit Tigers	4	1901
	Houston Astros	4	1962
20	Chicago Cubs	3	1871
	Chicago White Sox	3	1901
	Seattle Mariners	3	1977
23	Arizona Diamondbacks	2	1998
	Florida Marlins	2	1993
	San Diego Padres	2	1969
26	Colorado Rockies	1	1993
	Milwaukee Brewers	1	1969
	Tampa Bay Rays	1	1998
	Texas Rangers	1	1961
	Washington Nationals	1	1969

The LCS started in 1969.

League Division Series – Series Won

Rank	Team	Wins	Year of Origin
1	New York Yankees	10	1901
2	Atlanta Braves	6	1871
	St. Louis Cardinals	6	1882
4	Boston Red Sox	5	1901
5	Cleveland Indians	4	1901
6	Los Angeles Angels of Anaheim	3	1961
	Los Angeles Dodgers	3	1884
	New York Mets	3	1962
	Philadelphia Phillies	3	1883
	Seattle Mariners	3	1977
11	Arizona Diamondbacks	2	1998
	Baltimore Orioles	2	1901
	Florida Marlins	2	1993
	Houston Astros	2	1962
	Oakland Athletics	2	1901
	San Francisco Giants	2	1883
17	Chicago Cubs	1	1871
	Chicago White Sox	1	1901
	Cincinnati Reds	1	1882
	Colorado Rockies	1	1993
	Detroit Tigers	1	1901
	Minnesota Twins	1	1901
	San Diego Padres	1	1969
	Tampa Bay Rays	1	1998
	Texas Rangers	1	1961
	Washington Nationals	1	1969
27	Kansas City Royals	0	1969
	Milwaukee Brewers	0	1969
	Pittsburgh Pirates	0	1882
	Toronto Blue Jays	0	1977

The LDS started in 1995, and was played in 1981 due to a split season caused by a players strike.

League Division Series – Series Lost

Rank	Team	Losses	Year of Origin
1	Atlanta Braves	6	1871
	New York Yankees	6	1901
3	Houston Astros	5	1962
	Minnesota Twins	5	1901
5	Boston Red Sox	4	1901
	Los Angeles Dodgers	4	1884
	Oakland Athletics	4	1901
8	Chicago Cubs	3	1871
	Cleveland Indians	3	1901
	Los Angeles Angels of Anaheim	3	1961
	San Diego Padres	3	1969
	San Francisco Giants	3	1883
	Texas Rangers	3	1961
14	Arizona Diamondbacks	2	1998
	Chicago White Sox	2	1901
	Colorado Rockies	2	1993
	Milwaukee Brewers	2	1969
	Philadelphia Phillies	2	1883
	St. Louis Cardinals	2	1882
20	Cincinnati Reds	1	1882
	Kansas City Royals	1	1969
	Seattle Mariners	1	1977
	Tampa Bay Rays	1	1998
24	Baltimore Orioles	0	1901
	Detroit Tigers	0	1901
	Florida Marlins	0	1993
	New York Mets	0	1962
	Pittsburgh Pirates	0	1882
	Toronto Blue Jays	0	1977
	Washington Nationals	0	1969

The LDS started in 1995, and was played in 1981 due to a split season caused by a players strike.

League Division Series – Series Winning Percentage

Rank	Team	Win %	Year of Origin
1	Baltimore Orioles	1.000	1901
	Detroit Tigers	1.000	1901
	Florida Marlins	1.000	1993
	New York Mets	1.000	1962
	Washington Nationals	1.000	1969
6	St. Louis Cardinals	0.750	1882
	Seattle Mariners	0.750	1977
8	New York Yankees	0.625	1901
9	Philadelphia Phillies	0.600	1883
10	Cleveland Indians	0.571	1901
11	Boston Red Sox	0.556	1901
12	Arizona Diamondbacks	0.500	1998
	Atlanta Braves	0.500	1871
	Cincinnati Reds	0.500	1882
	Los Angeles Angels of Anaheim	0.500	1961
	Tampa Bay Rays	0.500	1998
17	Los Angeles Dodgers	0.429	1884
18	San Francisco Giants	0.400	1883
19	Chicago White Sox	0.333	1901
	Colorado Rockies	0.333	1993
	Oakland Athletics	0.333	1901
22	Houston Astros	0.286	1962
23	Chicago Cubs	0.250	1871
	San Diego Padres	0.250	1969
	Texas Rangers	0.250	1961
26	Minnesota Twins	0.167	1901
27	Kansas City Royals	0.000	1969
	Milwaukee Brewers	0.000	1969
	Pittsburgh Pirates	0.000	1882
	Toronto Blue Jays	0.000	1977

The LDS started in 1995, and was played in 1981 due to a split season caused by a players strike.

League Division Series – Series Played

Rank	Team	Series Played	Year of Origin
1	New York Yankees	16	1901
2	Atlanta Braves	12	1871
3	Boston Red Sox	9	1901
4	St. Louis Cardinals	8	1882
5	Cleveland Indians	7	1901
	Houston Astros	7	1962
	Los Angeles Dodgers	7	1884
8	Los Angeles Angels of Anaheim	6	1961
	Minnesota Twins	6	1901
	Oakland Athletics	6	1901
11	Philadelphia Phillies	5	1883
	San Francisco Giants	5	1883
13	Arizona Diamondbacks	4	1998
	Chicago Cubs	4	1871
	San Diego Padres	4	1969
	Seattle Mariners	4	1977
	Texas Rangers	4	1961
18	Chicago White Sox	3	1901
	Colorado Rockies	3	1993
	New York Mets	3	1962
21	Baltimore Orioles	2	1901
	Cincinnati Reds	2	1882
	Florida Marlins	2	1993
	Milwaukee Brewers	2	1969
	Tampa Bay Rays	2	1998
26	Detroit Tigers	1	1901
	Kansas City Royals	1	1969
	Washington Nationals	1	1969
29	Pittsburgh Pirates	0	1882
	Toronto Blue Jays	0	1977

The LDS started in 1995, and was played in 1981 due to a split season caused by a players strike.

Most Wins In A Season

Team	Most Wins	Year
Arizona Diamondbacks	100	1999
Atlanta Braves	106	1998
Baltimore Orioles	109	1969
Boston Red Sox	105	1912
Chicago Cubs	116	1906
Chicago White Sox	100	1917
Cincinnati Reds	108	1975
Cleveland Indians	111	1954
Colorado Rockies	92	2009
Detroit Tigers	104	1984
Florida Marlins	92	1997
Houston Astros	102	1998
Kansas City Royals	102	1977
Los Angeles Angels of Anaheim	100	2008
Los Angeles Dodgers	105	1953
Milwaukee Brewers	95	1979, 1982
Minnesota Twins	102	1965
New York Mets	108	1986
New York Yankees	114	1998
Oakland Athletics	107	1931
Philadelphia Phillies	101	1976, 1977
Pittsburgh Pirates	110	1909
St. Louis Cardinals	106	1942
San Diego Padres	98	1998
San Francisco Giants	106	1904
Seattle Mariners	116	2001
Tampa Bay Rays	97	2008
Texas Rangers	95	1999
Toronto Blue Jays	99	1985
Washington Nationals	95	1979

Most Losses In A Season

Team	Most Losses	Year
Arizona Diamondbacks	111	2004
Atlanta Braves	115	1935
Baltimore Orioles	111	1939
Boston Red Sox	111	1932
Chicago Cubs	103	1962, 1966
Chicago White Sox	106	1970
Cincinnati Reds	101	1982
Cleveland Indians	105	1991
Colorado Rockies	95	1993, 2005
Detroit Tigers	119	2003
Florida Marlins	108	1998
Houston Astros	97	1965, 1975, 1991
Kansas City Royals	106	2005
Los Angeles Angels of Anaheim	95	1968, 1980
Los Angeles Dodgers	104	1905
Milwaukee Brewers	106	2002
Minnesota Twins	113	1904
New York Mets	120	1962
New York Yankees	103	1908
Oakland Athletics	117	1916
Philadelphia Phillies	111	1941
Pittsburgh Pirates	113	1890
St. Louis Cardinals	111	1898
San Diego Padres	111	1969
San Francisco Giants	100	1985
Seattle Mariners	104	1978
Tampa Bay Rays	106	2002
Texas Rangers	106	1963
Toronto Blue Jays	109	1979
Washington Nationals	110	1969

Highest Winning Percentage In A Season

Team	Highest Win %	Year
Arizona Diamondbacks	0.617	1999
Atlanta Braves	0.899	1875
Baltimore Orioles	0.673	1969
Boston Red Sox	0.691	1912
Chicago Cubs	0.798	1880
Chicago White Sox	0.649	1917
Cincinnati Reds	0.688	1882
Cleveland Indians	0.721	1954
Colorado Rockies	0.568	2009
Detroit Tigers	0.656	1934
Florida Marlins	0.568	1997
Houston Astros	0.630	1998
Kansas City Royals	0.630	1977
Los Angeles Angels of Anaheim	0.617	2008
Los Angeles Dodgers	0.682	1899, 1953
Milwaukee Brewers	0.590	1979
Minnesota Twins	0.651	1933
New York Mets	0.667	1986
New York Yankees	0.714	1927
Oakland Athletics	0.704	1931
Philadelphia Phillies	0.623	1886, 1976, 1977
Pittsburgh Pirates	0.741	1902
St. Louis Cardinals	0.705	1885
San Diego Padres	0.605	1998
San Francisco Giants	0.759	1885
Seattle Mariners	0.716	2001
Tampa Bay Rays	0.599	2008
Texas Rangers	0.586	1999
Toronto Blue Jays	0.615	1985
Washington Nationals	0.649	1994

Lowest Winning Percentage In A Season

Team	Lowest Win %	Year
Arizona Diamondbacks	0.315	2004
Atlanta Braves	0.248	1935
Baltimore Orioles	0.279	1939
Boston Red Sox	0.279	1932
Chicago Cubs	0.364	1962, 1966
Chicago White Sox	0.325	1932
Cincinnati Reds	0.344	1934
Cleveland Indians	0.333	1914
Colorado Rockies	0.414	1993, 2005
Detroit Tigers	0.265	2003
Florida Marlins	0.333	1998
Houston Astros	0.398	1975
Kansas City Royals	0.346	2005
Los Angeles Angels of Anaheim	0.406	1980
Los Angeles Dodgers	0.316	1905
Milwaukee Brewers	0.346	2002
Minnesota Twins	0.252	1904
New York Mets	0.250	1962
New York Yankees	0.329	1912
Oakland Athletics	0.235	1916
Philadelphia Phillies	0.173	1883
Pittsburgh Pirates	0.169	1890
St. Louis Cardinals	0.221	1897
San Diego Padres	0.321	1969
San Francisco Giants	0.353	1902
Seattle Mariners	0.350	1978
Tampa Bay Rays	0.342	2002
Texas Rangers	0.346	1963
Toronto Blue Jays	0.327	1979
Washington Nationals	0.321	1969

Regular Season Winning Percentage
of .500 or Higher Streak

Team	Number of Years	Duration
Arizona Diamondbacks	5	1999-2003
Atlanta Braves	15	1991-2005
Baltimore Orioles	18	1968-1985
Boston Red Sox	16	1967-1982
Chicago Cubs	14	1926-1939
Chicago White Sox	17	1951-1967
Cincinnati Reds	10	1972-1981
Cleveland Indians	10	1947-1956
Colorado Rockies	3	1995-1997
Detroit Tigers	11	1978-1988
Florida Marlins	3	2003-2005
Houston Astros	7	1993-1999
Kansas City Royals	6	1975-1980
Los Angeles Angels of Anaheim	6	2004-2009
Los Angeles Dodgers	13	1945-1957
Milwaukee Brewers	6	1978-1983
Minnesota Twins	6	2001-2006
New York Mets	7	1984-1990
New York Yankees	39	1926-1964
Oakland Athletics	9	1925-1933, 1968-1976
Philadelphia Phillies	10	1975-1984
Pittsburgh Pirates	15	1899-1913
St. Louis Cardinals	15	1939-1953
San Diego Padres	4	1982-1985, 2004-2007
San Francisco Giants	14	1958-1971
Seattle Mariners	4	2000-2003
Tampa Bay Rays	3*	2008-2010
Texas Rangers	3	1977-1979, 1989-1991
Toronto Blue Jays	11	1983-1993
Washington Nationals	5	1979-1983

* = Active

Regular Season Winning Percentage
Under .500 Streak

Team	Number of Years	Duration
Arizona Diamondbacks	3	2004-2006
Atlanta Braves	11	1903-1913
Baltimore Orioles	13*	1998-2010
Boston Red Sox	15	1919-1933
Chicago Cubs	10	1953-1962
Chicago White Sox	9	1927-1935
Cincinnati Reds	11	1945-1955
Cleveland Indians	7	1969-1975, 1987-1993
Colorado Rockies	6	2001-2006
Detroit Tigers	12	1994-2005
Florida Marlins	5	1998-2002
Houston Astros	7	1962-1968
Kansas City Royals	8	1995-2002
Los Angeles Angels of Anaheim	7	1971-1977
Los Angeles Dodgers	11	1904-1914
Milwaukee Brewers	12	1993-2004
Minnesota Twins	11	1901-1911
New York Mets	7	1962-1968, 1977-1983
New York Yankees	4	1912-1915, 1989-1992
Oakland Athletics	15	1953-1967
Philadelphia Phillies	16	1933-1948
Pittsburgh Pirates	18*	1993-2010
St. Louis Cardinals	9	1902-1910
San Diego Padres	9	1969-1977
San Francisco Giants	4	1899-1902, 1974-1977, 2005-2008
Seattle Mariners	14	1977-1990
Tampa Bay Rays	10	1998-2007
Texas Rangers	8	1961-1968
Toronto Blue Jays	6	1977-1982
Washington Nationals	10	1969-1978

* = Active

Percentage of Seasons with a Regular Season Won-Loss Record .500 or Higher

Rank	Team	Number of Seasons	Years Played	Percentage
1	New York Yankees	88	110	80.00%
2	San Francisco Giants	89	128	69.53%
3	Boston Red Sox	73	110	66.36%
4	Los Angeles Dodgers	80	127	62.99%
5	St. Louis Cardinals	80	129	62.02%
6	Detroit Tigers	66	110	60.00%
7	Chicago White Sox	64	110	58.18%
8	Houston Astros	28	49	57.14%
9	Atlanta Braves	79	140	56.43%
10	Toronto Blue Jays	19	34	55.88%
11	Pittsburgh Pirates	72	129	55.81%
12	Cleveland Indians	60	110	54.55%
13	Cincinnati Reds	70	129	54.26%
14	Arizona Diamondbacks	7	13	53.85%
15	Chicago Cubs	73	138	52.90%
16	Oakland Athletics	52	110	47.27%
17	New York Mets	23	49	46.94%
18	Los Angeles Angels of Anaheim	22	50	44.00%
19	Kansas City Royals	18	42	42.86%
20	Philadelphia Phillies	54	128	42.19%
21	Minnesota Twins	46	110	41.82%
22	Washington Nationals	17	42	40.48%
23	Baltimore Orioles	43	110	39.09%
24	Colorado Rockies	7	18	38.89%
25	San Diego Padres	16	42	38.10%
26	Texas Rangers	18	50	36.00%
27	Milwaukee Brewers	14	42	33.33%
	Florida Marlins	6	18	33.33%
29	Seattle Mariners	11	34	32.35%
30	Tampa Bay Rays	3	13	23.08%

Percentage of Seasons in Postseason

Rank	Team	Number of Seasons	Years Played	Percentage
1	New York Yankees	49	110	44.55%
2	Arizona Diamondbacks	4	13	30.77%
3	Oakland Athletics	23	110	20.91%
4	Los Angeles Dodgers	26	127	20.47%
5	Houston Astros	9	49	18.37%
6	Boston Red Sox	20	110	18.18%
7	Los Angeles Angels of Anaheim	9	50	18.00%
8	San Francisco Giants	23	128	17.97%
9	St. Louis Cardinals	23	129	17.83%
10	Colorado Rockies	3	18	16.67%
	Kansas City Royals	7	42	16.67%
12	Tampa Bay Rays	2	13	15.38%
13	Atlanta Braves	21	140	15.00%
14	Toronto Blue Jays	5	34	14.71%
15	New York Mets	7	49	14.29%
16	Minnesota Twins	14	110	12.73%
17	San Diego Padres	5	42	11.90%
18	Seattle Mariners	4	34	11.76%
19	Chicago Cubs	16	138	11.59%
20	Florida Marlins	2	18	11.11%
21	Detroit Tigers	12	110	10.91%
22	Pittsburgh Pirates	14	129	10.85%
23	Philadelphia Phillies	13	128	10.16%
24	Cincinnati Reds	13	129	10.08%
25	Baltimore Orioles	11	110	10.00%
26	Cleveland Indians	10	110	9.09%
27	Chicago White Sox	9	110	8.18%
28	Texas Rangers	4	50	8.00%
29	Milwaukee Brewers	3	42	7.14%
30	Washington Nationals	1	42	2.38%

Biggest Difference Between Regular Season and Postseason Winning Percentage for Games Played

Rank	Team	Regular Season	Postseason	Difference
1	Chicago Cubs	0.514	0.337	0.177
2	Florida Marlins	0.479	0.647	0.168
3	Texas Rangers	0.471	0.346	0.125
4	Houston Astros	0.498	0.375	0.123
5	San Diego Padres	0.464	0.353	0.111
6	New York Mets	0.479	0.581	0.102
7	Baltimore Orioles	0.474	0.571	0.097
8	Los Angeles Dodgers	0.524	0.439	0.085
	Minnesota Twins	0.483	0.398	0.085
10	Kansas City Royals	0.482	0.419	0.063
11	Los Angeles Angels of Anaheim	0.498	0.443	0.055
12	Pittsburgh Pirates	0.503	0.449	0.054
13	San Francisco Giants	0.538	0.49	0.048
14	Milwaukee Brewers	0.475	0.429	0.046
15	Oakland Athletics	0.486	0.531	0.045
16	Tampa Bay Rays	0.438	0.476	0.038
17	New York Yankees	0.568	0.601	0.033
18	Seattle Mariners	0.469	0.441	0.028
19	Washington Nationals	0.476	0.500	0.024
20	Atlanta Braves	0.504	0.484	0.020
	Cincinnati Reds	0.508	0.528	0.020
22	Toronto Blue Jays	0.497	0.512	0.015
23	Detroit Tigers	0.506	0.494	0.012
24	Cleveland Indians	0.509	0.518	0.009
	St. Louis Cardinals	0.518	0.527	0.009
26	Philadelphia Phillies	0.472	0.48	0.008
27	Arizona Diamondbacks	0.491	0.484	0.007
28	Boston Red Sox	0.517	0.523	0.006
29	Colorado Rockies	0.478	0.474	0.004
30	Chicago White Sox	0.506	0.509	0.003

The Postseason Winning Percentage is for Games Played. It is NOT the teams Postseason Series Winning Percentage.

World Series Champion & Runner Up By Year

( ) Indicates franchise location and team name today
1904: There was no postseason

Year	World Series Winner	World Series Runner Up
1903	Boston Americans (Boston Red Sox)	Pittsburgh Pirates
1904	None	None
1905	New York Giants (San Francisco Giants)	Philadelphia A's (Oakland A's)
1906	Chicago White Sox	Chicago Cubs
1907	Chicago Cubs	Detroit Tigers
1908	Chicago Cubs	Detroit Tigers
1909	Pittsburgh Pirates	Detroit Tigers
1910	Philadelphia A's (Oakland A's)	Chicago Cubs
1911	Philadelphia A's (Oakland A's)	New York Giants (San Francisco Giants)
1912	Boston Red Sox	New York Giants (San Francisco Giants)
1913	Philadelphia A's (Oakland A's)	New York Giants (San Francisco Giants)
1914	Boston Braves (Atlanta Braves)	Philadelphia A's (Oakland A's)
1915	Boston Red Sox	Philadelphia Phillies
1916	Boston Red Sox	Brooklyn Robins (Los Angeles Dodgers)
1917	Chicago White Sox	New York Giants (San Francisco Giants)
1918	Boston Red Sox	Chicago Cubs
1919	Cincinnati Reds	Chicago White Sox
1920	Cleveland Indians	Brooklyn Robins (Los Angeles Dodgers)
1921	New York Giants (San Francisco Giants)	New York Yankees
1922	New York Giants (San Francisco Giants)	New York Yankees
1923	New York Yankees	New York Giants (San Francisco Giants)
1924	Washington Senators (Minnesota Twins)	New York Giants (San Francisco Giants)
1925	Pittsburgh Pirates	Washington Senators (Minnesota Twins)
1926	St. Louis Cardinals	New York Yankees
1927	New York Yankees	Pittsburgh Pirates
1928	New York Yankees	St. Louis Cardinals
1929	Philadelphia A's (Oakland A's)	Chicago Cubs
1930	Philadelphia A's (Oakland A's)	St. Louis Cardinals
1931	St. Louis Cardinals	Philadelphia A's (Oakland A's)
1932	New York Yankees	Chicago Cubs
1933	New York Giants (San Francisco Giants)	Washington Senators (Minnesota Twins)
1934	St. Louis Cardinals	Detroit Tigers
1935	Detroit Tigers	Chicago Cubs
1936	New York Yankees	New York Giants (San Francisco Giants)
1937	New York Yankees	New York Giants (San Francisco Giants)
1938	New York Yankees	Chicago Cubs
1939	New York Yankees	Cincinnati Reds
1940	Cincinnati Reds	Detroit Tigers

World Series Champion & Runner Up By Year

( ) Indicates franchise location and team name today

Year	World Series Winner	World Series Runner Up
1941	New York Yankees	Brooklyn Dodgers (Los Angeles Dodgers)
1942	St. Louis Cardinals	New York Yankees
1943	New York Yankees	St. Louis Cardinals
1944	St. Louis Cardinals	St. Louis Browns (Baltimore Orioles)
1945	Detroit Tigers	Chicago Cubs
1946	St. Louis Cardinals	Boston Red Sox
1947	New York Yankees	Brooklyn Dodgers (Los Angeles Dodgers)
1948	Cleveland Indians	Boston Braves (Atlanta Braves)
1949	New York Yankees	Brooklyn Dodgers (Los Angeles Dodgers)
1950	New York Yankees	Philadelphia Phillies
1951	New York Yankees	New York Giants (San Francisco Giants)
1952	New York Yankees	Brooklyn Dodgers (Los Angeles Dodgers)
1953	New York Yankees	Brooklyn Dodgers (Los Angeles Dodgers)
1954	New York Giants (San Francisco Giants)	Cleveland Indians
1955	Brooklyn Dodgers (Los Angeles Dodgers)	New York Yankees
1956	New York Yankees	Brooklyn Dodgers (Los Angeles Dodgers)
1957	Milwaukee Braves (Atlanta Braves)	New York Yankees
1958	New York Yankees	Milwaukee Braves (Atlanta Braves)
1959	Los Angeles Dodgers	Chicago White Sox
1960	Pittsburgh Pirates	New York Yankees
1961	New York Yankees	Cincinnati Reds
1962	New York Yankees	San Francisco Giants
1963	Los Angeles Dodgers	New York Yankees
1964	St. Louis Cardinals	New York Yankees
1965	Los Angeles Dodgers	Minnesota Twins
1966	Baltimore Orioles	Los Angeles Dodgers
1967	St. Louis Cardinals	Boston Red Sox
1968	Detroit Tigers	St. Louis Cardinals
1969	New York Mets	Baltimore Orioles
1970	Baltimore Orioles	Cincinnati Reds
1971	Pittsburgh Pirates	Baltimore Orioles
1972	Oakland A's	Cincinnati Reds
1973	Oakland A's	New York Mets
1974	Oakland A's	Los Angeles Dodgers
1975	Cincinnati Reds	Boston Red Sox
1976	Cincinnati Reds	New York Yankees
1977	New York Yankees	Los Angeles Dodgers
1978	New York Yankees	Los Angeles Dodgers

World Series Champion & Runner Up By Year

( ) Indicates franchise location and team name today
1994: Postseason was cancelled due to Players Strike

Year	World Series Winner	World Series Runner Up
1979	Pittsburgh Pirates	Baltimore Orioles
1980	Philadelphia Phillies	Kansas City Royals
1981	Los Angeles Dodgers	New York Yankees
1982	St. Louis Cardinals	Milwaukee Brewers
1983	Baltimore Orioles	Philadelphia Phillies
1984	Detroit Tigers	San Diego Padres
1985	Kansas City Royals	St. Louis Cardinals
1986	New York Mets	Boston Red Sox
1987	Minnesota Twins	St. Louis Cardinals
1988	Los Angeles Dodgers	Oakland A's
1989	Oakland A's	San Francisco Giants
1990	Cincinnati Reds	Oakland A's
1991	Minnesota Twins	Atlanta Braves
1992	Toronto Blue Jays	Atlanta Braves
1993	Toronto Blue Jays	Philadelphia Phillies
1994	None	None
1995	Atlanta Braves	Cleveland Indians
1996	New York Yankees	Atlanta Braves
1997	Florida Marlins	Cleveland Indians
1998	New York Yankees	San Diego Padres
1999	New York Yankees	Atlanta Braves
2000	New York Yankees	New York Mets
2001	Arizona Diamondbacks	New York Yankees
2002	Anaheim Angels (Los Angeles Angels of Anaheim)	San Francisco Giants
2003	Florida Marlins	New York Yankees
2004	Boston Red Sox	St. Louis Cardinals
2005	Chicago White Sox	Houston Astros
2006	St. Louis Cardinals	Detroit Tigers
2007	Boston Red Sox	Colorado Rockies
2008	Philadelphia Phillies	Tampa Bay Rays
2009	New York Yankees	Philadelphia Phillies
2010	San Francisco Giants	Texas Rangers

League Titles By Year
American League & National League

This included the winners of the League Championship Series from 1969-2010
( ) Indicates franchise location and team name today
Italics indicates team ceased existence as a franchise

Year	American League	National League
1876		Chicago White Stockings (Chicago Cubs)
1877		Boston Red Caps (Atlanta Braves)
1878		Boston Red Caps (Atlanta Braves)
1879		*Providence Grays*
1880		Chicago White Stockings (Chicago Cubs)
1881		Chicago White Stockings (Chicago Cubs)
1882		Chicago White Stockings (Chicago Cubs)
1883		Boston Beaneaters (Atlanta Braves)
1884		*Providence Grays*
1885		Chicago White Stockings (Chicago Cubs)
1886		Chicago White Stockings (Chicago Cubs)
1887		*Detroit Wolverines*
1888		New York Giants (San Francisco Giants)
1889		New York Giants (San Francisco Giants)
1890		Brooklyn Bridegrooms (Los Angeles Dodgers)
1891		Boston Beaneaters (Atlanta Braves)
1892		Boston Beaneaters (Atlanta Braves)
1893		Boston Beaneaters (Atlanta Braves)
1894		*Baltimore Orioles*
1895		*Baltimore Orioles*
1896		*Baltimore Orioles*
1897		Boston Beaneaters (Atlanta Braves)
1898		Boston Beaneaters (Atlanta Braves)
1899		Brooklyn Superbas (Los Angeles Dodgers)
1900		Brooklyn Superbas (Los Angeles Dodgers)
1901	Chicago White Stockings (Chicago White Sox)	Pittsburgh Pirates
1902	Philadelphia A's (Oakland A's)	Pittsburgh Pirates
1903	Boston Americans (Boston Red Sox)	Pittsburgh Pirates
1904	Boston Americans (Boston Red Sox)	New York Giants (San Francisco Giants)
1905	Philadelphia A's (Oakland A's)	New York Giants (San Francisco Giants)
1906	Chicago White Sox	Chicago Cubs
1907	Detroit Tigers	Chicago Cubs
1908	Detroit Tigers	Chicago Cubs
1909	Detroit Tigers	Pittsburgh Pirates
1910	Philadelphia A's (Oakland A's)	Chicago Cubs
1911	Philadelphia A's (Oakland A's)	New York Giants (San Francisco Giants)
1912	Boston Red Sox	New York Giants (San Francisco Giants)

League Titles By Year
American League & National League

This included the winners of the League Championship Series from 1969-2010
( ) Indicates franchise location and team name today

Year	American League	National League
1913	Philadelphia A's (Oakland A's)	New York Giants (San Francisco Giants)
1914	Philadelphia A's (Oakland A's)	Boston Braves (Atlanta Braves)
1915	Boston Red Sox	Philadelphia Phillies
1916	Boston Red Sox	Brooklyn Robins (Los Angeles Dodgers)
1917	Chicago White Sox	New York Giants (San Francisco Giants)
1918	Boston Red Sox	Chicago Cubs
1919	Chicago White Sox	Cincinnati Reds
1920	Cleveland Indians	Brooklyn Robins (Los Angeles Dodgers)
1921	New York Yankees	New York Giants (San Francisco Giants)
1922	New York Yankees	New York Giants (San Francisco Giants)
1923	New York Yankees	New York Giants (San Francisco Giants)
1924	Washington Senators (Minnesota Twins)	New York Giants (San Francisco Giants)
1925	Washington Senators (Minnesota Twins)	Pittsburgh Pirates
1926	New York Yankees	St. Louis Cardinals
1927	New York Yankees	Pittsburgh Pirates
1928	New York Yankees	St. Louis Cardinals
1929	Philadelphia A's (Oakland A's)	Chicago Cubs
1930	Philadelphia A's (Oakland A's)	St. Louis Cardinals
1931	Philadelphia A's (Oakland A's)	St. Louis Cardinals
1932	New York Yankees	Chicago Cubs
1933	Washington Senators (Minnesota Twins)	New York Giants (San Francisco Giants)
1934	Detroit Tigers	St. Louis Cardinals
1935	Detroit Tigers	Chicago Cubs
1936	New York Yankees	New York Giants (San Francisco Giants)
1937	New York Yankees	New York Giants (San Francisco Giants)
1938	New York Yankees	Chicago Cubs
1939	New York Yankees	Cincinnati Reds
1940	Detroit Tigers	Cincinnati Reds
1941	New York Yankees	Brooklyn Dodgers (Los Angeles Dodgers)
1942	New York Yankees	St. Louis Cardinals
1943	New York Yankees	St. Louis Cardinals
1944	St. Louis Browns (Baltimore Orioles)	St. Louis Cardinals
1945	Detroit Tigers	Chicago Cubs
1946	Boston Red Sox	St. Louis Cardinals
1947	New York Yankees	Brooklyn Dodgers (Los Angeles Dodgers)
1948	Cleveland Indians	Boston Braves (Atlanta Braves)
1949	New York Yankees	Brooklyn Dodgers (Los Angeles Dodgers)

League Titles By Year
American League & National League

This included the winners of the League Championship Series from 1969-2010
( ) Indicates franchise location and team name today

Year	American League	National League
1950	New York Yankees	Philadelphia Phillies
1951	New York Yankees	New York Giants (San Francisco Giants)
1952	New York Yankees	Brooklyn Dodgers (Los Angeles Dodgers)
1953	New York Yankees	Brooklyn Dodgers (Los Angeles Dodgers)
1954	Cleveland Indians	New York Giants (San Francisco Giants)
1955	New York Yankees	Brooklyn Dodgers (Los Angeles Dodgers)
1956	New York Yankees	Brooklyn Dodgers (Los Angeles Dodgers)
1957	New York Yankees	Milwaukee Braves (Atlanta Braves)
1958	New York Yankees	Milwaukee Braves (Atlanta Braves)
1959	Chicago White Sox	Los Angeles Dodgers
1960	New York Yankees	Pittsburgh Pirates
1961	New York Yankees	Cincinnati Reds
1962	New York Yankees	San Francisco Giants
1963	New York Yankees	Los Angeles Dodgers
1964	New York Yankees	St. Louis Cardinals
1965	Minnesota Twins	Los Angeles Dodgers
1966	Baltimore Orioles	Los Angeles Dodgers
1967	Boston Red Sox	St. Louis Cardinals
1968	Detroit Tigers	St. Louis Cardinals
1969	Baltimore Orioles	New York Mets
1970	Baltimore Orioles	Cincinnati Reds
1971	Baltimore Orioles	Pittsburgh Pirates
1972	Oakland A's	Cincinnati Reds
1973	Oakland A's	New York Mets
1974	Oakland A's	Los Angeles Dodgers
1975	Boston Red Sox	Cincinnati Reds
1976	New York Yankees	Cincinnati Reds
1977	New York Yankees	Los Angeles Dodgers
1978	New York Yankees	Los Angeles Dodgers
1979	Baltimore Orioles	Pittsburgh Pirates
1980	Kansas City Royals	Philadelphia Phillies
1981	New York Yankees	Los Angeles Dodgers
1982	Milwaukee Brewers	St. Louis Cardinals
1983	Baltimore Orioles	Philadelphia Phillies
1984	Detroit Tigers	San Diego Padres
1985	Kansas City Royals	St. Louis Cardinals
1986	Boston Red Sox	New York Mets

League Titles By Year
American League & National League

This included the winners of the League Championship Series from 1969-2010
( ) Indicates franchise location and team name today
1994: No league titles as season was cancelled due to Players Strike

Year	American League	National League
1987	Minnesota Twins	St. Louis Cardinals
1988	Oakland A's	Los Angeles Dodgers
1989	Oakland A's	San Francisco Giants
1990	Oakland A's	Cincinnati Reds
1991	Minnesota Twins	Atlanta Braves
1992	Toronto Blue Jays	Atlanta Braves
1993	Toronto Blue Jays	Philadelphia Phillies
1994	None	None
1995	Cleveland Indians	Atlanta Braves
1996	New York Yankees	Atlanta Braves
1997	Cleveland Indians	Florida Marlins
1998	New York Yankees	San Diego Padres
1999	New York Yankees	Atlanta Braves
2000	New York Yankees	New York Mets
2001	New York Yankees	Arizona Diamondbacks
2002	Anaheim Angels (Los Angeles Angels of Anaheim)	San Francisco Giants
2003	New York Yankees	Florida Marlins
2004	Boston Red Sox	St. Louis Cardinals
2005	Chicago White Sox	Houston Astros
2006	Detroit Tigers	St. Louis Cardinals
2007	Boston Red Sox	Colorado Rockies
2008	Tampa Bay Rays	Philadelphia Phillies
2009	New York Yankees	Philadelphia Phillies
2010	Texas Rangers	San Francisco Giants

Division Titles By Year
American League

( ) Indicates franchise location and team name today

1981: Season was split into two halves. There were two winners for each division.

Year	American League East Division	American League West Division
1969	Baltimore Orioles	Minnesota Twins
1970	Baltimore Orioles	Minnesota Twins
1971	Baltimore Orioles	Oakland A's
1972	Detroit Tigers	Oakland A's
1973	Baltimore Orioles	Oakland A's
1974	Baltimore Orioles	Oakland A's
1975	Boston Red Sox	Oakland A's
1976	New York Yankees	Kansas City Royals
1977	New York Yankees	Kansas City Royals
1978	New York Yankees	Kansas City Royals
1979	Baltimore Orioles	California Angels (Los Angeles Angels of Anaheim)
1980	New York Yankees	Kansas City Royals
1981	New York Yankees, Milwaukee Brewers	Kansas City Royals, Oakland A's
1982	Milwaukee Brewers	California Angels (Los Angeles Angels of Anaheim)
1983	Baltimore Orioles	Chicago White Sox
1984	Detroit Tigers	Kansas City Royals
1985	Toronto Blue Jays	Kansas City Royals
1986	Boston Red Sox	California Angels (Los Angeles Angels of Anaheim)
1987	Detroit Tigers	Minnesota Twins
1988	Boston Red Sox	Oakland A's
1989	Toronto Blue Jays	Oakland A's
1990	Boston Red Sox	Oakland A's
1991	Toronto Blue Jays	Minnesota Twins
1992	Toronto Blue Jays	Oakland A's
1993	Toronto Blue Jays	Chicago White Sox

Division Titles By Year
American League

( ) Indicates franchise location and team name today

1994: No division winners as season was cancelled due to Players Strike

Year	American League East Division	American League Central Division	American League West Division
1994	None	None	None
1995	Boston Red Sox	Cleveland Indians	Seattle Mariners
1996	New York Yankees	Cleveland Indians	Texas Rangers
1997	Baltimore Orioles	Cleveland Indians	Seattle Mariners
1998	New York Yankees	Cleveland Indians	Texas Rangers
1999	New York Yankees	Cleveland Indians	Texas Rangers
2000	New York Yankees	Chicago White Sox	Oakland A's
2001	New York Yankees	Cleveland Indians	Seattle Mariners
2002	New York Yankees	Minnesota Twins	Oakland A's
2003	New York Yankees	Minnesota Twins	Oakland A's
2004	New York Yankees	Minnesota Twins	Anaheim Angels (Los Angeles Angels of Anaheim)
2005	New York Yankees	Chicago White Sox	Los Angeles Angels of Anaheim
2006	New York Yankees	Minnesota Twins	Oakland A's
2007	Boston Red Sox	Cleveland Indians	Los Angeles Angels of Anaheim
2008	Tampa Bay Rays	Chicago White Sox	Los Angeles Angels of Anaheim
2009	New York Yankees	Minnesota Twins	Los Angeles Angels of Anaheim
2010	Tampa Bay Rays	Minnesota Twins	Texas Rangers

Division Titles By Year
National League

( ) Indicates franchise location and team name today

1981: Season was split into two halves. There were two winners for each division.

Year	National League East Division	National League West Division
1969	New York Mets	Atlanta Braves
1970	Pittsburgh Pirates	Cincinnati Reds
1971	Pittsburgh Pirates	San Francisco Giants
1972	Pittsburgh Pirates	Cincinnati Reds
1973	New York Mets	Cincinnati Reds
1974	Pittsburgh Pirates	Los Angeles Dodgers
1975	Pittsburgh Pirates	Cincinnati Reds
1976	Philadelphia Phillies	Cincinnati Reds
1977	Philadelphia Phillies	Los Angeles Dodgers
1978	Philadelphia Phillies	Los Angeles Dodgers
1979	Pittsburgh Pirates	Cincinnati Reds
1980	Philadelphia Phillies	Houston Astros
1981	Montreal Expos (Washington Nationals), Philadelphia Phillies	Houston Astros, Los Angeles Dodgers
1982	St. Louis Cardinals	Atlanta Braves
1983	Philadelphia Phillies	Los Angeles Dodgers
1984	Chicago Cubs	San Diego Padres
1985	St. Louis Cardinals	Los Angeles Dodgers
1986	New York Mets	Houston Astros
1987	St. Louis Cardinals	San Francisco Giants
1988	New York Mets	Los Angeles Dodgers
1989	Chicago Cubs	San Francisco Giants
1990	Pittsburgh Pirates	Cincinnati Reds
1991	Pittsburgh Pirates	Atlanta Braves
1992	Pittsburgh Pirates	Atlanta Braves
1993	Philadelphia Phillies	Atlanta Braves

Division Titles By Year
National League

1994: No division winners as season was cancelled due to Players Strike

Year	National League East Division	National League Central Division	National League West Division
1994	None	None	None
1995	Atlanta Braves	Cincinnati Reds	Los Angeles Dodgers
1996	Atlanta Braves	St. Louis Cardinals	San Diego Padres
1997	Atlanta Braves	Houston Astros	San Francisco Giants
1998	Atlanta Braves	Houston Astros	San Diego Padres
1999	Atlanta Braves	Houston Astros	Arizona Diamondbacks
2000	Atlanta Braves	St. Louis Cardinals	San Francisco Giants
2001	Atlanta Braves	Houston Astros	Arizona Diamondbacks
2002	Atlanta Braves	St. Louis Cardinals	Arizona Diamondbacks
2003	Atlanta Braves	Chicago Cubs	San Francisco Giants
2004	Atlanta Braves	St. Louis Cardinals	Los Angeles Dodgers
2005	Atlanta Braves	St. Louis Cardinals	San Diego Padres
2006	New York Mets	St. Louis Cardinals	San Diego Padres
2007	Philadelphia Phillies	Chicago Cubs	Arizona Diamondbacks
2008	Philadelphia Phillies	Chicago Cubs	Los Angeles Dodgers
2009	Philadelphia Phillies	St. Louis Cardinals	Los Angeles Dodgers
2010	Philadelphia Phillies	Cincinnati Reds	San Francisco Giants
2010	Philadelphia	Cincinnati	San Francisco

League Division Series Winners By Year

( ) Indicates franchise location and team name today

Year	American League	National League
1981	New York Yankees, Oakland A's	Los Angeles Dodgers, Montreal Expos (Washington Nationals)
1995	Cleveland Indians, Seattle Mariners	Atlanta Braves, Cincinnati Reds
1996	Baltimore Orioles, New York Yankees	Atlanta Braves, St. Louis Cardinals
1997	Baltimore Orioles, Cleveland Indians	Atlanta Braves, Florida Marlins
1998	Cleveland Indians, New York Yankees	Atlanta Braves, San Diego Padres
1999	Boston Red Sox, New York Yankees	Atlanta Braves, New York Mets
2000	New York Yankees, Seattle Mariners	New York Mets, St. Louis Cardinals
2001	New York Yankees, Seattle Mariners	Arizona Diamondbacks, Atlanta Braves
2002	Anaheim Angels (Los Angeles Angels), Minnesota Twins	St. Louis Cardinals, San Francisco Giants
2003	Boston Red Sox, New York Yankees	Chicago Cubs, Florida Marlins
2004	Boston Red Sox, New York Yankees	Houston Astros, St. Louis Cardinals
2005	Chicago White Sox, Los Angeles Angels	Houston Astros, St. Louis Cardinals
2006	Detroit Tigers, Oakland A's	New York Mets, St. Louis Cardinals
2007	Boston Red Sox, Cleveland Indians	Arizona Diamondbacks, Colorado Rockies
2008	Boston Red Sox, Tampa Bay Rays	Los Angeles Dodgers, Philadelphia Phillies
2009	Los Angeles Angels, New York Yankees	Los Angeles Dodgers, Philadelphia Phillies
2010	New York Yankees, Texas Rangers	Philadelphia Phillies, San Francisco Giants

Wild Card Playoff Teams By Year

( ) Indicates franchise location and team name today

Year	American League	National League
1995	New York Yankees	Colorado Rockies
1996	Baltimore Orioles	Los Angeles Dodgers
1997	New York Yankees	Florida Marlins
1998	Boston Red Sox	Chicago Cubs
1999	Boston Red Sox	New York Mets
2000	Seattle Mariners	New York Mets
2001	Oakland Athletics	St. Louis Cardinals
2002	Anaheim Angels (Los Angeles Angels of Anaheim)	San Francisco Giants
2003	Boston Red Sox	Florida Marlins
2004	Boston Red Sox	Houston Astros
2005	Boston Red Sox	Houston Astros
2006	Detroit Tigers	Los Angeles Dodgers
2007	New York Yankees	Colorado Rockies
2008	Boston Red Sox	Milwaukee Brewers
2009	Boston Red Sox	Colorado Rockies
2010	New York Yankees	Atlanta Braves

League Titles By Year
National Association, American Association, Union Association, Players League, Federal League

( ) Indicates franchise location and team name today

Italics indicates team has ceased existence as a franchise

Year	National Association (1871-1875)		
1871	*Philadelphia Athletics*		
1872	Boston Red Stockings (Atlanta Braves)		
1873	Boston Red Stockings (Atlanta Braves)		
1874	Boston Red Stockings (Atlanta Braves)		
1875	Boston Red Stockings (Atlanta Braves)		

Year		American Association (1882-1891)	
1881			
1882		Cincinnati Red Stockings (Cincinnati Reds)	
1883		*Philadelphia Athletics*	Union Association (1884)
1884		*New York Metropolitans*	*St. Louis Maroons*
1885		St. Louis Browns (St. Louis Cardinals)	
1886		St. Louis Browns (St. Louis Cardinals)	
1887		St. Louis Browns (St. Louis Cardinals)	
1888		St. Louis Browns (St. Louis Cardinals)	
1889		Brooklyn Bridegrooms (Los Angeles Dodgers)	Players League (1890)
1890		*Louisville Colonels*	*Boston Reds*
1891		*Boston Reds*	

Year			Federal League (1914-1915)
1913			
1914			*Indianapolis Hoosiers*
1915			*Chicago Whales*

Score and Rank Comparison

Team	Total Points	Total Rank	Average Points	AVG Rank
Arizona Diamondbacks	23.1	23	1.78	2
Atlanta Braves	153.4	6	1.10	9
Baltimore Orioles	70.4	12	0.64	18
Boston Red Sox	134.7	7	1.22	7
Chicago Cubs	94.4	9	0.68	16
Chicago White Sox	60.6	15	0.55	20
Cincinnati Reds	100.8	8	0.78	12
Cleveland Indians	58.9	16	0.54	21 (tie)
Colorado Rockies	6.8	27	0.38	25
Detroit Tigers	81.6	11	0.74	13
Florida Marlins	27.9	21	1.55	3
Houston Astros	23.8	22	0.49	23
Kansas City Royals	28.2	20	0.67	17
Los Angeles Angels of Anaheim	34.8	18	0.70	15
Los Angeles Dodgers	168.4	3	1.33	6
Milwaukee Brewers	6.5	28	0.15	29
Minnesota Twins	68.3	14	0.62	19
New York Mets	47.9	17	0.98	11
New York Yankees	438.8	1	3.99	1
Oakland Athletics	163.6	4	1.49	5
Philadelphia Phillies	69.2	13	0.54	21 (tie)
Pittsburgh Pirates	94.3	10	0.73	14
St. Louis Cardinals	198.8	2	1.54	4
San Diego Padres	16.6	24	0.40	24
San Francisco Giants	154.8	5	1.21	8
Seattle Mariners	9.9	26	0.29	26 (tie)
Tampa Bay Rays	3.8	29	0.29	26 (tie)
Texas Rangers	11.1	25	0.22	28
Toronto Blue Jays	33.7	19	0.99	10
Washington Nationals	1.5	30	0.04	30

References

Acocella, Nicholas and Dewey, Donald. Total Ballclubs. Toronto: SPORT Media
Publishing, Inc., 2005.

Birnbaum, Phil, Deane, John, and Thorn, John. Total Baseball. Toronto: SPORT Media
Publishing, Inc., 2004.

Creamer, Robert W. Baseball in '41. New York: Penguin Books, 1991.

Gillette, Gary, and Palmer, Pete. The Baseball Encyclopedia. New York: Barnes & Noble
Books, 2004.

Gorman, Lou. One Pitch from Glory. Champaign, IL: Sports Publishing L.L.C., 2005.

Halberstam, David. Summer of '49. New York: William & Morrow Company, Inc., 1989.

Halberstam, David. October 1964. New York: Villard Books, 1994.

Johnson, Richard, and Stout, Glenn. Red Sox Century. Boston: Houghton Mifflin, 2000.

Prager, Joshua. The Echoing Green. New York: Pantheon Books, 2006.

Purdy, Dennis. The Team-by-Team Encyclopedia of Major League Baseball. New York:
Workman Publishing, 2006.

Schuerholz, John, with Guest, Larry. Built to Win. Boston: Warner Books, 2006.

Sports Reference LLC. Baseball-Refernce.com – Major League Statistics and information.
http://www.baseball-reference.com.

About the Author

Tim lives in Massachusetts with his wife Rhiannon and son Carter. He is an active member of the Society for American Baseball Research and the Baseball Bloggers Alliance. Tim earned his Bachelors degree in Marketing from Salem State University and is currently working on his Masters in Business Administration at Suffolk University. He works in the marketing & advertising industry and is a devoted follower of the Red Sox, Celtics, and Patriots.

For more information about Tim and this book go to the website www.baseballfranchiserankings.com

Made in the USA
Lexington, KY
07 April 2011